angkok

ti out.com/bangkok

WITHDRAWN FROM
SANDWELL
SANDWELL LIBRARIES
I 1838319

D1137421

SANDWELL LIBRARY & INFORMATION

I 1838319	
CO	27/10/2005
915.93	12.99

Published by Time Out Guides Ltd, a wholly owned subsidiary of Time Out Group Ltd.
Time Out and the Time Out logo are trademarks of Time Out Group Ltd.

© Time Out Group Ltd 2005
Previous edition 2003.

10 9 8 7 6 5 4 3 2 1

This edition first published in Great Britain in 2005 by Ebury Publishing
Ebury Publishing is a division of The Random House Group Ltd,
20 Vauxhall Bridge Road, London SW1V 2SA

Random House Australia Pty Limited, 20 Alfred Street, Milsons Point, Sydney, New South Wales 2061, Australia
Random House New Zealand Limited, 18 Poland Road, Glenfield, Auckland 10, New Zealand
Random House South Africa (Pty) Limited, Endulini, 5A Jubilee Road, Parktown 2193, South Africa

Random House UK Limited Reg. No. 954009

Distributed in USA by Publishers Group West
1700 Fourth Street, Berkeley, California 94710

Distributed in Canada by Penguin Canada Ltd
10 Alcorn Avenue, Toronto, Ontario, Canada M4V 3B2

For further distribution details, see www.timeout.com

ISBN 1-904978-44-4

A CIP catalogue record for this book is available from the British Library

Colour reprographics by Icon, Crowne House, 56-58 Southwark Street, London SE1 1UN

Printed and bound in Germany by Appl

Papers used by Ebury Publishing are natural, recyclable products made from wood grown in sustainable forests

All rights reserved. No part of this publication may be reproduced, stored in a retrieval system, or transmitted in any
form or by any means, electronic, mechanical, photocopying, recording or otherwise, without prior permission from the
copyright owners.

Time Out Guides Limited
Universal House
251 Tottenham Court Road
London W1T 7AB
Tel + 44 (0)20 7813 3000
Fax + 44 (0)20 7813 6001
Email guides@timeout.com
www.timeout.com

Editorial

Bangkok Editor Philip Cornwel-Smith
London Editor Ismay Atkins
Editorial assistance Edoardo Albert,
Sam Le Quesne
Listings Editor Manapiti Ramasoot
Proofreader Tamsin Shelton
Indexer Jonathan Cox

Editorial/Managing Director Peter Fiennes
Series Editor Ruth Jarvis
Deputy Series Editor Lesley McCave
Business Manager Gareth Garner
Guides Co-ordinator Holly Pick
Accountant Kemi Olufuwa

Design

Art Director Scott Moore
Art Editor Tracey Ridgewell
Designer Josephine Spencer
Freelance Designer Tessa Kar
Digital Imaging Dan Conway
Ad Make-up Pete Ward

Picture Desk

Picture Editor Jael Marschner
Deputy Picture Editor Tracey Kerrigan
Picture Researcher Helen McFarland

Advertising

Sales Director Mark Phillips
International Sales Manager Ross Canadé
International Sales Executive Simon Davies
Advertising Sales (Bangkok) Jane Bay for Asia City
Publishing Group
Advertising Assistant Lucy Butler

Marketing

Marketing Director Mandy Martinez
Marketing & Publicity Manager, US Rosella Albanese

Production

Production Director Mark Lamond
Production Controller Marie Howell

Time Out Group

Chairman Tony Elliott
Managing Director Mike Hardwick
Group Financial Director Richard Waterlow
Group Commercial Director Lesley Gill
Group General Manager Nichola Coulthard
Group Circulation Director Jim Heinemann
Group Art Director John Oakey
Online Managing Director David Pepper
Group Production Director Steve Proctor
Group IT Director Simon Chappell

Contributors

Introduction Philip Cornwel-Smith. **History** Anon Nakornthab (*Historical Flashbacks & Rama Reincarnate* Philip Cornwel-Smith). **Bangkok Today** Philip Cornwel-Smith. **Arts & Architecture** Alex Kerr (*Back to the Origin* Philip Cornwel-Smith). **Modern Faith** Mettanando Bhikku (Sacred Charms & High Spirits Philip Cornwel-Smith). **Where to Stay** Korakot Punlopruksa (*Hip hotels* Philip Cornwel-Smith). **Sightseeing Introduction** Kathareeya Jumroonsiri. **Phra Nakorn** Philip Cornwel-Smith, Steven Pettifor. **Banglamphu** Jim Algie. **Thonburi, River & Canals** Stirling Silliphant (*Pier groups* Philip Cornwel-Smith). **Dusit** Jim Algie. **Chinatown** Jennifer Gampell. **Downtown & Suburbs** Philip Cornwel-Smith, Steven Pettifor. **Further Afield** Philip Cornwel-Smith. **Restaurants** Howard Richardson. **Bars & Pubs** Juliana Ross. **Markets** Rob McKeown, Korakot Punlopruksa. **Shops & Services** Anon Nakornthab. **Festivals & Events** Philip Cornwel-Smith, Brian Mertens. **Children** Andrea Francis. **Film** Philip Cornwel-Smith. **Gay & Lesbian** Robin Newbold (*Dee light* Philip Cornwel-Smith). **Galleries** Philip Cornwel-Smith. **Mind & Body** Chamsai Jotisalikorn (*A spa too far? & The art of doing nothing* Philip Cornwel-Smith). **Music** Tim Carr (*Jazz* Howard Richardson). **Nightlife** Juliana Ross (*Adult nightlife* Thomas Schmid). **Performing Arts** Pichayanund Chindahporn (*Young masters* Philip Cornwel-Smith). **Sport & Fitness** Howard Richardson (*Fight clubs* Phil Cornwel-Smith). **Beach Escapes** Terry Blackburn, Philip Cornwel-Smith (*Ko Chang* Jo Smith). **Directory** Kathareeya Jumroonsiri, Philip Cornwel-Smith.

The Editor would like to thank Bon Bon, Alex Kerr, Rungsaeng Sripaoraya of TAT, Bangkok Tourist Bureau, Anucha Thirakanont, Nilobol Phanichkarn, Andrew Spooner, Chatchai Ngoenprakairat and all contributors to previous editions of *Time Out Bangkok*, whose work forms the basis for parts of this book.

Maps JS Graphics (john@jsgraphics.co.uk). Map data supplied by Bangkok Guide Co Part, 1276 Onnut Soi 34/1, Suan Luang, Bangkok 10250 (0 2311 1439/www.bangkokguide.homepage.com).

Photography Photography Mark Parren Taylor, except: page 10 Horace Bistol/ Corbis; pages 13, 15, Old Maps & Prints Co., Ltd; pages 16, 29, 30, 33, 34, 38, 41, 58, 59, 73 (top right), 75, 78, 80, 89, 93, 94, 103, 107, 205 Jonathan Perugia; page 18 Kantana Group PLC; page 158 Empics; page 165 Moviestore Collection; page 171 Getty Images; page 197 Philip Cornwel-Smith. The following images were provided by the featured establishments/artists: pages 168, 182, 183, 212, 220.

© Copyright Time Out Group Ltd
All rights reserved

Contents

Contents

Introduction

Film industry hub, spa capital of Asia, aviation hub, kitchen of the world, global rubber hub, Detroit of the east, health tourism hub... Bangkok had declared itself a world-class hub in no fewer than 30 bewilderingly diverse fields at the last count. Though it might not fulfil every one of its boasts, the Thai capital is certainly significantly more cosmopolitan, efficient and fashion-savvy than it used to be. Bangkok is also marginalising its notorious aspects, mitigating somewhat its sleazy reputation. These forward-moving trends have inflated not only egos but prices too, though Bangkok remains a bargain in global terms.

Though modern attractions and malls figure large, Thailand's cachet as a tourism hub still draws heavily on heritage. Temples, beaches, palaces, dancers, floating markets, monks collecting alms – these sights invariably dazzle and enchant, no matter how tawdry the concrete, pollution and touts that breakneck development has brought.

Bangkok has changed so much so quickly – and crucially with so little planning – that skyscrapers now rise next to gilded spires, and in its rural enclaves you'll still see cockfights and thatched roofs. Few visitors delve beyond the tourist-friendly surface into genuinely Thai environs, but in this guide we lead you to Isaan music clubs, youth cult shrines, temple fair sideshows and food pilgrims' favoured street stalls. Not all such places match the tidy image official Thailand prefers to project, nor the exotic image perceived from abroad. Popular culture tends to get glossed over, something that is countered by a non-conformist young generation that prides itself on being 'indie'.

Despite the uncontrived and unexplained events that beguile visitors, official Thainess couldn't be more self-conscious, as illustrated by its tag: 'Land of Smiles'. Visitors do receive a lot of smiles, and *sanuk* (fun) infuses every activity, but smiles come in many kinds, each named after its purpose, whether deference, defence, delight, sabotage or the supression of confrontation. Getting swept up in this finely tuned niceness leaves visitors charmed, if often nonplussed by the underlying textures and arresting contrasts.

A geographical crossroads for millennia, this uncolonised land has absorbed myriad influences, fusing them with ancient ways rather than displacing them. The resulting sense of otherness answers to a different kind of logic. The state's desire to brand Bangkok as a world-class hub goes beyond mere marketing; Thais have a long-standing cultural trait of giving auspicious names to gain face and fortune. Most Thai personal and place names are compounds of lucky, honorific words, often royally bestowed or divined by astrology.

While foreigners call the town Bangkok ('Village of Plum Olives'), Thais honour it with the title Krung Thep ('City of Angels'), which, in its full 64-syllable version, is the world's longest name. Translated it means 'great city of angels, the supreme repository of divine jewels, the great land unconquerable, the grand and foremost realm, the royal and delightful capital city of the nine noble gems, the highest regal dwelling and grand palace, the divine shelter and living place of the reincarnated spirits'. In other words 'hub of angels'.

ABOUT THE TIME OUT CITY GUIDES

This is the second edition of *Time Out Bangkok*, one of an expanding series of Time Out guides produced by the people behind the successful listings magazines in London, New York and Chicago. Our guides are all written by resident experts who have striven to provide you with all the most up-to-date information you'll need to explore the city or read up on its background, whether you're a local or a first-time visitor.

THE LIE OF THE LAND

To make the book (and the city) easier to navigate, we have divided Bangkok into areas, which are reflected in the chapters and headings in our Sightseeing section, starting on p54. Although these areas are a simplification of Bangkok's geography, they follow official districts and local terms where possible. These areas are used in addresses throughout the guide and in the series of fully indexed colour street maps at the back of the guide, starting on p248.

Though signs in English are a common sight in tourist areas, addresses nationwide can often be confusing, with imprecision, variable spellings and inconsistent numbering. In those cases, we've noted landmarks for orientation. All bus destination boards are in Thai, though airports, the BTS SkyTrain, subway, trains and taxis have wording in English. For more guidance on getting around, *see p224*.

ESSENTIAL INFORMATION

For all the practical information you might need for visiting the area – including visa and customs information, details of local transport, a listing of emergency numbers, information on local weather and a selection of useful websites – turn to the Directory at the back of this guide. It begins on page 224.

THE LOWDOWN ON THE LISTINGS

We have tried to make this book as easy to use as possible. Addresses, phone numbers, opening times and admission prices are all included in the listings. However, businesses can change their arrangements at any time. Before you go out of your way, we'd strongly advise you to phone ahead to check opening times and other particulars. While every effort and care has been made to ensure the accuracy of the information contained in this guide, the publishers cannot accept responsibility for any errors it may contain.

PRICES AND PAYMENT

We have listed prices in Thai baht (B) throughout. In cases where rates are in US dollars ($), payment is accepted in baht. We have noted whether venues such as shops, hotels and restaurants accept credit cards or not, but have only listed the major cards: American Express (AmEx), Diners Club (DC), MasterCard (MC) and Visa (V). Many businesses will also accept other cards, including Switch/Maestro or Delta, JCB, Discover and Carte Blanche. Beyond major hotels, banks and exchange booths, extremely few venues will accept travellers' cheques.

The prices we've listed in this guide should be treated as guidelines, not gospel. If prices vary wildly from those we've quoted, ask whether there's a good reason. If not, go elsewhere. Then please let us know. We aim to give the best and most up-to-date advice, so we want to know if you've been badly treated or overcharged. For advice on bargaining, tipping, touts, scams and higher charges for non-Thais, *see p54*.

TELEPHONE NUMBERS

All Thailand's phone numbers incorporate the former area code in a national system of eight digits plus an initial 0, even when you're phoning from within the same area. Mobile phones are common in Thailand, even as a formal business number, with numbers that start 01, 04, 05, 06, 07 or 09; they cost more than land lines, but are cheaper long-distance. Some mobile numbers look indistinguishable from upcountry landlines. Landlines are cheaper to call upcountry if 1234 is dialed before the 0 and eight-digit number.

To dial numbers as given in this book from abroad, use your country's exit code (00 in the UK, 01 in the US), followed by the country code for Thailand (66), then omit the initial 0 before dialing the eight-digit number.

For more details of phone codes and charges, *see p234*.

MAPS

We've provided map references for most places listed in central Bangkok, indicating the page and grid reference at which an address can be found on our street maps. These are located at the back of the book on pp246-252. There's also a street index, on pp253-5.

LET US KNOW WHAT YOU THINK

We hope you enjoy *Time Out Bangkok*, and we'd like to know what you think of it. We welcome tips for places that you consider we should include in future editions and take note of your criticism of our choices. You can email us your comments at guides@timeout.com.

Advertisers

We would like to stress that no establishment has been included in this guide because it has advertised in any of our publications and no payment of any kind has influenced any review. The opinions given in this book are those of Time Out writers and entirely independent.

There is an online version of this book, along with guides to over 45 other international cities, at **www.timeout.com**.

Introduction

JIM THOMPSON
LEGENDARY THAI SILK.

USA • JIM THOMPSON + 1 404 325 5004 / 800 262 0336
UK • JIM THOMPSON / FOX LINTON +44 20 7368 7700
FRANCE • PIERRE FREY +33 1 44 77 3600
FABRIC • MAI'S CORSAGE • AVAILABLE WORLDWIDE THROUGH ARCHITECTS AND DESIG

www.jimthompson.com

In Context

Features

History

The Thai past is a current affair.

History in Thailand is not just about the past; how that past is presented remains front-page news. Debate rages about how to portray events still within living memory, such as the school textbook treatment (or omission) of former enemies and popular uprisings. Historians also face the appropriation of Thai history by an official narrative. The Thai word for history derives from *prawat* (biography) and Thai history is substantially the biography of kings. However, revisionists are broadening 'Thai Studies' to encompass economic, social and geo-political factors.

While experts are split over the origins of Thai ethnicity, adequate records exist to document the Thai domain and the peoples who have occupied it. Royal manuscripts serve as the official record, while historical literature and theses by the indefatigable 'father of Thai history', Prince Damrong, have provided the framework. An old-school, Oxbridge-trained view – exemplified by Damrong's half-brother, King Vajiravudh, Prince Chula Chakrabongse and ML Manich Jumsai – then shaped a master narrative of the Thai nation.

The most authoritative book on the subject is *A History of South-east Asia* by the late DGE Hall, many of whose students have advanced alternatives to the nationalist approach. Chief among this generation are David Wyatt (*Thailand: A Short History*) and Thongchai Winichakul (*Siam Mapped*). Thongchai charts how (before the 19th-century unitary state) the borders, compositions and allegiances of empires, city states and ethnic enclaves in the broad Siamese 'geo-body' were incredibly fluid. So then, how did Siam start?

FROM PREHISTORY TO SUKHOTHAI

When present-day Bangkok was under the sea in the Cretaceous Age, *Siamotyrannus isanensis*, possibly the world's oldest tyrannosaur, roamed the Khorat Plateau to the north-east. Later in that area, early South-east Asians fashioned some of civilisation's earliest bronze axes and invented the outrigger canoe.

By the time that Prince Sitthatha Gotama (who became the Buddha) was wandering northern India six centuries before Christ, merchants from the subcontinent had established trading posts in Suwannaphum ('Golden Land'), a region close to present-day Bangkok. They traded and intermarried with indigenous inhabitants who over thousands of years had farmed around the Gulf of Siam. Suwannaphum (a name claimed by many countries and adopted by Bangkok's new airport) became important enough that in the third century BC it received two monks dispatched by Emperor Asoka of India, a Buddhist convert.

Meanwhile, over millennia, tattooed Tai clans (tribal ancestors of modern Thais) migrated through Yunnan in southern Han-dynasty China, into lowland South-east Asia. Living in stilt houses, they tended rice in water-filled fields using buffaloes, a status symbol until recent times. Subduing earlier settlers, they carved a pastoral society out of forest in what became upper-central Siam. Some spread as far as Assam in India and upper Vietnam, where Tai tribes are still found today.

From the sixth century, Suwannaphum was supplanted by Dvaravati, a little-known Mon civilisation of devout Therevada Buddhists with centres at Suphanburi, Nakhon Pathom and Nakhon Ratchasima (formerly Khorat). The sole evidence of Dvaravati's name is a clay inscription found near Bangkok. From the eighth- to 13th-centuries, Southern Thailand was part of the equally elusive Mahayana Buddhist empire of Srivijaya, centred in Sumatra.

Dvaravati eventually succumbed to ninth-century Khmers under King Jayavaraman II of Angkor. From the Khmer, the Tais adopted the Hindu concept of *devaraja* – divine kingship. Some Dvaravati fringes like Lavo (now Lopburi) defied Khmer overlords for two more centuries, sending diplomats to China and becoming heavily populated by Tais – whom the Khmer referred to as Syam (Sanskrit for 'swarthy'). Angkor Wat features an 1150 bas-relief of idiosyncratic Syamese troops from Lopburi, their commander atop a war elephant.

By Angkor's decline around 1220, a Tai-Mon-Khmer blend in the Chao Phraya basin gelled into a Siamese ethnicity. Power then shifted northwards when King Sri Indraditya (c1240-70) established a Tai kingdom at Sukhothai ('Dawn of Happiness'), which became a major force under King Ramkhamhaeng (c1279-98). From further north, King Mangrai of Lanna ('One Million Rice Fields') forged an alliance with Sukhothai and Phayao in 1287 that repelled Mongol China after the Mon empire of Bagan in Burma was sacked by the Mongol armies of Kublai Khan. Tai troops kept raiding China until a truce in 1312, with China accepting elephants in tribute.

During Ramkhamhaeng's 19-year reign, Sukhothai blossomed into a federation of Buddhist states, including Si Satchanalai and Kamphaengphet. Wielding influence more through *dhammaraja* (Buddhist kingship) than military might, Sukhothai reached west to the Indian Ocean, east to Lao Vieng Chan (Vientiane) and south to Nakhon Si Thamarat in the Malay peninsula, though skirting the Lopburi-run lower plains.

The court supported a stylised Buddhist aesthetic most celebrated in the world's first statues of the Buddha walking. In the first Thai script to distinguish the language's five tones, Sukhothai left royal engravings including a still-quoted line on self-sufficiency: 'fish are in the rivers, rice is in the fields'.

AYUTTHAYA RISES

While Sukhothai's moral authority disintegrated after Ramkhamhaeng's death, Suphanburi and Lopburi vied for supremacy in the central plains. During a cholera outbreak, the Lopburi aristocrat U Thong (conveniently wed to a noblewoman from each ruling house) fled south to a riverine island. There on 4 March 1351 he founded a new kingdom: Ayutthaya (named after the Indian city of Rama, hero of the *Ramayana* epic). As King Ramathibodi (1351-69), U Thong sent his relatives to rule Suphanburi and Lopburi, thus pitting the two dynasties to squabble over Ayutthaya's throne for generations.

> **'Ayutthaya prospered in the 17th century to become a great trading hub with a million-strong population, then larger than London's.'**

Already busy with Asian merchants, Ayutthaya quickly grew, while the rivermouth trading post of Bang Makok (aka Bangkok) became a strategic gateway. The first of several canals to bypass Bangkok's river meanders was cut in the long reign of King Baromtrailokanart (1448-88). On the west bank, Thonburi gained a fortress just before the Burmese sacked Ayutthaya in the reign of King Chakkrapat (1548-69).

After a spell under King Mahathamaracha (1569-90), Ayutthaya reasserted its independence through his son, King Naresuan (1590-1605), who'd grown up as a hostage at the Burmese court. At the Battle of Nong Sarai, waged on war elephants, Naresuan slew the crown prince of Burma, restoring Thai freedom.

In the 17th century Ayutthaya prospered into a trading hub with over a million people, then larger than London. As a duty port, Bangkok received European ships, while myriad nations were granted quarters around Ayutthaya. Visiting traders, explorers, writers and engravers attested to Ayutthaya's gilded opulence and magnificent rituals, such as presentations of white elephants and the royal barge processions that still grace the Chao Phraya river.

Under the diplomatic King Narai (1656-88) and his lead minister, the Greek adventurer Constantine Phaulkon, Ayutthaya became an international power. In 1687 Narai invited Louis XIV of France to establish a military mission in the southern port of Songkhla. Secretly hoping to control trade and to convert King Narai to Christianity, the French occupied a fort in Bangkok.

Siamese xenophobia at foreign influence swept the court as Narai lay dying. A conspiracy installed as regent his foster brother, Phra Phetracha, who eliminated Narai's heirs, had Phaulkon executed for treason and, on Narai's death, usurped the throne. Phetracha (1688-1703) then exchanged cannon fire with the French in Bangkok before negotiating the French exit.

Siam was effectively closed to *farang* (foreigners) for two centuries, though interaction with Asia flourished. Theravada Buddhism had been introduced from Sri Lanka in the 13th century via Nakhon Sri Thammarat. In 1751 the Sinhalese asked King Barommakot (1733-58) to help restore Buddhism to Sri Lanka, where it had waned during Portuguese and Dutch rule. Meanwhile, Ayutthaya's treasury had swelled through rice exports to China, and come under the administration of newly arrived Chinese and descendants of Persians and Indian Brahmins, who had entered service under Narai – notably, the still-influential Bunnag family.

During dynastic power struggles, the spectre of Burma reappeared. After subduing the Mon in Hongsawadi, then Lanna and the Lao kingdom of Luang Prabang, the Burmese besieged Ayutthaya in 1766. Famine, disease and fires ensued until the summer of 1767. King Ekatat (1758-67) offered to surrender, but the Burmese refused. After penetrating the walls, they systematically reduced the city to a smouldering wreck.

So long, Siam

People and publications often erroneously refer to Sukhothai, Ayutthaya, Thonburi and Bangkok as successive capitals of Thailand, when in reality the country's official name, Prathet Thai (Thailand), dates only from 1939. For eight centuries before that, the multi-ethnic land had been widely known as Siam, a Sanskrit term for 'swarthy', which the Khmers used to denote Thais.

During the ultra-nationalist trend of the mid 20th century, the dictator Plaek Phibunsongkhram made Thai ethnicity key to the identity of the nation he had renamed. Influenced by the ideologue Luang Wichit Wathakarn, he told Thais that they needed 'national traditions', such as standing for an anthem that opens with the line 'Thailand embodies the blood and flesh of the Thai race'. Yet, his 'cultural mandates' often favoured modern Western traits over bygone Thai ways as expressions of the new Thai nation concept. Phiphat music was suppressed in favour of big band jazz, while government offices wouldn't serve people in traditional clothing, to encourage adoption of Western suits, dresses, shoes and hats, irrespective of culture or climate.

But few Thais lament the disuse of the term Siam. After all, it was more favoured by foreigners and still casts an especially exotic spell over Western imaginations. Siam was formally adopted by King Rama IV's realm when the colonial menace made independence contingent on the defining and labelling of national borders, as well as flying a national flag. That flag depicted a royal white elephant upon a red standard, until King Rama VI switched to the current tricolour to emphasise nationalism, modernity and equivalence to Western powers.

Historically, however, most Thais have known their lands by the name of the *meuang* ('city state'), focusing on the power centre rather than the amorphous jungle frontiers. Hence the many contemporary references and maps to the Kingdom of Ayutthaya, rather than Siam. Still today, provinces are named after their principal town, and Thais talk of their country as 'Meuang Thai'. Though some feel Siam embraces more ethnic and regional diversity, the success of Phibun's Thailand concept pervades not just officialdom but every aspect of daily life, media and identity.

SIAM REBORN

In October 1767 a fleet commanded by Chaophraya Taksin landed at Thonburi as dawn light bathed Wat Makok (now Wat Arun, the 'Temple of Dawn'). Having escaped from Ayutthaya, Taksin's forces took Chantaburi on the Gulf then doubled back by sea up the Chao Phraya. With Ayutthaya reduced to anarchy, they started anew at Thonburi.

On being crowned, Taksin (1767-82) invited the old nobility to help restore order. Over the next three years, he subdued Phimai, where Prince Thepphiphit, King Ekatat's half-brother, had set up court, then to Fang and Phitsanulok, both run by red-robed renegade monks. By annexing Battambang and Siem Reap, Taksin eliminated any threat from Cambodia and reacquired all the territories of Ayutthaya. The campaign required the support of the Teochiu Chinese in strategic trading posts. After all, the new king of Siam was a son of China, a fact not lost on the court's public relations people, who advertised his ancestry in bids to improve trade with the Chinese.

'Spoils of war included the Emerald Buddha, which remains a symbol of Thai independence.'

Burma, by then at war with China, had largely withdrawn and Lanna joined Siam as a buffer against its former Burmese oppressors. With Taksin's authority, Chaophraya Chakri and his brother Chaophraya Surasi then moved on Lao. Surasi returned home with spoils of war from defeated Vientiane including the Emerald Buddha, which many cities claim to have possessed. Enshrined in Thonburi, and later at Wat Phra Kaew in Bangkok, the jadeite image remains a palladium of Thai independence.

Around 1779 Taksin's behaviour turned aberrant. His religious visions and arbitrary lashing out puzzled visitors and alienated the old nobility. In April 1782 rebels opposing a tax official were urged to march on Thonburi, and install Chaophraya Chakri. In keeping with a 15th-century edict that no royal blood should touch the ground, King Taksin the Great was bound in a cloth sack and struck above the neck with a sandalwood club, then secretly buried in the capital he had founded.

THE BANGKOK ERA

Chaophraya Chakri returned from quelling a Cambodian revolt to assume the throne as King Ramathibodi, aka Rama I (1782-1809), thereby founding the current Chakri dynasty. While keeping Thonburi as a stronghold, he relocated the capital to the river's more defensible east bank at Bangkok.

The Bangkok period often gets dubbed 'Rattanakosin', after the royal island formed by a girdle of canals on the model of Ayutthaya. Its walls reused bricks from the former capital, leaving little to be seen at Ayutthaya. Additional canals were dug and the so-called 'Venice of the East' soon swelled into a vibrant, cosmopolitan city. Princes and officials erected stately homes on the central canals. Displaced from Rattanakosin, Chinese merchants scrambled for sites along the river, forming Sampaeng (Chinatown). Indians, Muslims and Catholics, too, formed communities.

Rama I's Three Seals Laws underpinned justice for a century, and his Buddhist reforms included ecclesiastical laws and compilation of the *Tipitaka* scriptures. To ensure manpower and to prevent private armies, peasants had to serve *corvée* (forced labour) for four months per year, and be tattooed with the names of their masters and locality.

In the year of his full coronation, 1785, Rama I faced Burma's last major attack. He repulsed 100,000 men in nine armies, though skirmishes continued (indeed, until today).

Bangkok's water traffic in the 1880s.

Rama I further secured Siam's borders by cementing relationships with Lanna and Lao, and imposing authority over Malay states including Pattani, which remains a restive region of Thailand.

One of Rama I's 40-odd children succeeded him as Rama II (1809-24) and sired 73 offspring – a testament to the stability of his 15-year reign. The first two Chakri reigns entertained a literary revival, restoring the chronicles and dramatic works lost at Ayutthaya. Each country's adaptation of the Indian epic *Ramayana* reflects its culture. Rama I's translation, the *Ramakien*, has a Siamese resonance; its kings are named after the hero, Rama, while monkey general Hanuman brims with *sanuk* (fun). Scribes also translated foreign classics like the Indonesian *Inao* and the Chinese text on governance and warfare, *Sam Kok* ('Romance of Three Kingdoms'). A notable poet himself, Rama II sponsored the star of this renaissance, the UNESCO-recognised poet Sunthorn Phu.

'South-east Asian warfare has been as much about populations as territory, with Siam a particularly receptive crossroads of cultures and ethnicities.'

In the early 1820s Burma's constant will to attack was less of a concern than minor tussles with Vietnam over Cambodia, which they divided. Siam got Angkor and parts of Lao, which then turned aggressor. Feeling slighted by the new monarch Rama III (1824-51) on a visit to Bangkok, the Lao ruler of Vientiane, Chao Anuwong, pushed troops south in 1827 in a bid to take Bangkok. But Chaophraya Bodindecha soon sent the Lao scattering, occupied Vientiane, withdrew and then returned to raze Vientiane. So many Lao were brought over the Mekong river to Isaan (Siam's north-east) that today 17 million of the 21 million Lao live in Thailand.

South-east Asian warfare has been as much about populations as territory, resulting in a cultural cross-fertilisation, with Siam a receptive crossroads of cultures and ethnicities. For example, Siamese dance was influenced by performers captured from Angkor, Burma seized Ayutthayan troops to enrich its own court arts, and Siam reinfluenced Khmer dance and culture after further campaigns by Bodindecha reoccupied Cambodia. By Rama III's passing in 1851, Bangkok ran the biggest Siamese empire yet.

COLONIALISM AVOIDED

When Europeans intensified imperial intentions in South-east Asia after the Napoleonic Wars, Siam was the region's leading power. Britain and France had encroached upon Burma and Vietnam respectively, by the time King Mongkut (aka Rama IV, 1851-68) ascended the throne after 27 years as a Bhuddist monk. In 1855 former Hong Kong governor Sir John Bowring forced the king and his cabinet, led by the powerful Chao Phraya Si Suriyawong, into an unequal agreement that dismantled state monopolies, restricted duties and limited Siam's judicial power over British subjects. The following decade the French seized Siamese Cambodia and swept up the Mekong river.

'Western colonialists claimed to bring civilisation, a pretext undermined by the modernisation of Siam by Rama IV and his son.'

During the reign of King Chulalongkorn (aka Rama V, 1868-1910) a crisis erupted when French agents in Laos were expelled and one was killed. French gunboats invaded the Chao Phraya river, forcing Siam to concede Laos and western Cambodia to French Indochina. Britain later received four Malay states after relinquishing legal jurisdiction over its subjects and agreeing to provide a loan for building a railway. Siam lost territories it had annexed or reclaimed over the past century, but was the only South-east Asian country to remain independent.

Western colonialists trumpeted the rationale that they brought civilisation, a pretext that was deftly undermined by the modernisation of Siam by Rama IV and his son. Rama IV sponsored the publication of a government gazette, initiated educational reforms and issued laws easing the conditions of slavery and *corvée*. Foreign tutors hired to educate the king's children included Anna Leonowens, whose famous memoirs are as inaccurate and self-aggrandising as her job application. Hence Thai distaste for the subsequent musical *The King & I* and films that exaggerated her faulty depiction of Rama IV. Newly discovered letters by the king, however, reveal his discussion of state matters with Anna.

King Chulalongkorn continued his father's reforms, establishing the civil service, abolishing slavery and modernising the army. He became the first Thai monarch to travel abroad. After visits to British Singapore and Dutch Java in 1871, he conformed the court

Rama reincarnate

When the King's Anthem plays before every performance, including cinema screenings, all stand in awed silence. Thai Olympians donate their medals to their monarch. Money is handled respectfully because it bears at least one regal head. Royal portraits are a fixture in every home, business and organisation. Kingship in Thailand remains special.

The universal love and respect Thais have for **King Bhumibol Adulyadej** (1946-present) – the world's longest reigning monarch – reflect a deep cultural belief that each Thai monarch is a reincarnated god. But the respect he commands also stems from his grassroots development work and from his diverse talents – he's a sailor and boat-builder, writer and photographer, painter and jazz composer (see p182). He was also the world's first monarch to earn a patent (for a water aerator). These deeds are recorded in photographic museums at **Dusit Park** (see p82).

The king's constitutional powers may be similar to those of Britain's Queen Elizabeth II, but 'divine rule' remains a cultural reality. While European royal houses find their mystique eroded through relentless public exposure, Thais maintain taboos about commenting upon what is dubbed 'the highest institution', and lese-majesty is a serious crime.

In ancient Ayutthaya, Thai Buddhist and animist faith acquired a Hindu influence centred on the *devaraja* (god-king) concept. Indivisible from Thainess, this divine cosmology infuses royal decorations, festival rites and the traditional arts.

King Bhumibol is also known as Rama IX. Each king of the Chakri dynasty (like many earlier monarchs of Ayutthaya) is named after Rama, hero of the *Ramayana* epic and incarnation of the Hindu god Vishnu. That is why the mythical bird-man Garuda adorns symbols of national dominion like highway signs, power poles and government documents, as well as companies by royal appointment such as banks. Garuda is Vishnu's vehicle and thus acts as the royal insignia.

Since Thai social life remains governed by fine delineations of rank, the hierarchy requires a figure of utmost probity at the apex. Embodying gracious, righteous heroism, Rama is also the ideal of Thai

male behaviour: proud and dutiful, calm and beautiful, gentle and refined. Hence the rarity of crass, laddish aggression in Thailand, even among crowds.

Monarchy acts as role model in modern governance too. Under King Bhumibol's proactive guidance, dozens of Royal Projects play a leading role in development, regenerating land, preserving crafts, preventing floods and mentoring sustainable agriculture (see p79 **Chitrlada**). Time after time, the king's advice, gleaned from personal study and experiment, has proven more effective than institutional efforts. Viewing King Rama IX as their guiding light, Thais in turn bathe the country in candles and fairylights on his birthday (5 Dec).

Rama V in regalia.

Ancient arts survive in Thai dance.

dress and hairstyles to European trends. Several princes were sent to study in Europe. In 1897 Rama V's visits to Europe influenced Bangkok's layout and architecture, especially in the new royal district of Dusit.

NATION BUILDING

In November 1911 the 13-day coronation of King Vajiravudh (Rama VI, 1910-25) cost almost ten per cent of the state budget. Three months later, some military officers were arrested for conspiring to mount a coup. It was Siam's first test of absolute monarchy.

As Bangkok spread eastwards, Rama VI donated Lumphini Park, presided over by his statue, and expressed his love of theatre. He translated classics, acted in plays and installed theatres in his palaces. Meanwhile, nationalism was on the rise, encouraged by Western trade restrictions and Chinese dominance of the Thai economy. Rama VI's concept of the Thai nation called for a homogenous society rallying under a new flag. The red standard bearing a white elephant was replaced by the current tricolour: red (nation), white (religion) and blue (monarchy). Surnames were introduced and education was made compulsory.

The capital then became the stage for a succession of power struggles. On 4 June 1932 the self-dubbed 'People's Party' – principally, young officials and officers who had studied in

Europe – seized the city in a quiet, bloodless coup that installed a constitutional monarchy and parliament. King Prajadhipok (Rama VII, 1925-35) abdicated while in England three years later, and the cabinet invited his nephew Ananta Mahidol, who was at school in Switzerland, to assume the throne. As Rama VIII (1935-46), he did not return for another ten years, while the 1932 coup promoters squabbled over power.

A coup leader, Plaek Phibunsongkhram, twice assumed the prime ministership (1938-44 and 1948-57). Styling himself on fascist leaders of Europe, he propagated an ideal of the ethnically Thai nation, renamed the country Thailand (see p12 **So long, Siam**), established paramilitary troops, expanded the military and, during World War II, reclaimed disputed parts of Laos and Cambodia. (The debonair nationalist soldier also advocated Western-style hats and encouraged husbands to kiss their wives on the cheek when leaving home.) With Japan occupying Thailand in 1942, Phibulsongkram's regime declared war on the Allies. Regent Pridi Banomyong refused to endorse the declaration, and the Seri Thai ('Free Thai') covert network was formed to undermine Japanese occupation. Co-ordinated by Seni Pramoj, the Thai ambassador in Washington, Seri Thai saved the country from suffering post-war reparations.

As the new peacetime prime minister, Pridi was preparing Thailand for democracy when, in June 1946, King Ananta was found dead in his royal chamber with a gunshot wound to his head. The death, never since clarified, was used as a pretext for branding Pridi a communist. A military coup in 1947 then forced Pridi – who many call the 'father of Thai democracy' – into permanent exile. In a strange twist, Phibulsongkram, who had declared war on the Allies, returned in 1948 to head a regime that received economic and military aid from the US.

COUPS AND PROTESTS

For the next quarter-century, military strongmen staged coups and counter-coups while young King Bhumibol Adulyadej (Rama IX, 1946-present) was confined to ceremonial duties. For three days in February 1949 the capital shut down as the navy and marines unsuccessfully battled the army- and police-led government in a failed attempt to restore Pridi to power. But the army and police couldn't quell a two-day naval uprising two years later. The air force settled it by bombing the royal flagship *Sri Ayudhya* in the Chao Phraya river, allowing the captured Phibulsongkram to swim to safety. More than 1,000 soldiers and civilians were killed, and 2,000 wounded. Eight years later, Phibulsongkram's protégé, General Sarit Thanarat, staged a bloodless overnight coup that drove his mentor into a final exile.

A semblance of order at the expense of democracy buoyed economic fortunes, especially in the growing capital, while US aid poured in to prevent Thailand becoming the next communist domino. Demand for rice and other commodities saw Bangkok's port expand, while highways and airports eclipsed the railways, trams and increasingly paved-over canals. With increased electrification, consumer goods poured in through new commercial centres in Bangkok.

As the Vietnam War intensified, Thailand became the centre of US operations. With more than 40,000 US troops stationed here in the 1960s, parts of Bangkok, Pattaya and other cities turned into R&R playgrounds. Hostess bars opened along Patpong Road and sleepy Petchaburi Road reinvented itself as a neon-lit strip of massage parlours and hotels. The capital's population expanded even faster than the national average, as migrants left no-longer-bucolic rural life in search of service and construction jobs. New infrastructure also supported the crucial tourist industry – though the environment suffered alarming degradation.

Arbitrary abuse of power by the 'Three Tyrants' – Prime Minister Thanom Kittikachorn, his son Colonel Narong Kittikachorn, and Field Marshal Prapas Charusathien, Narong's son-in-law – finally proved too much for a new generation of educated Thais raised on Pridi's ideals. On 14 October 1973 more than half a million students, workers and merchants gathered at Thammasat University to demand a constitution. Protestors and troops were locked in a stand-off when an unidentified commando unit opened fire. Bloodshed ensued and the Three Tyrants' were forced into exile.

After an interval of turbulent democracy Thanom returned in September 1976, prompting another protest at Thammasat that snowballed into a mass demonstration. The right wing struck back, identifying the students with communist China. On 6 October the police opened fire on demonstrators, killing hundreds, while quasi-military units took special glee in lynching, beating and even burning some alive. Their hopes crushed, many of the students joined rural communist insurgents. This brutal suppression left a scar on the national psyche that has yet to heal.

In the 1980s the nation slowly eased into a new rhythm. Moderate military rule under General Prem Tinsulanond allowed a degree of stability, political participation and media comment, while insurgents were persuaded to rejoin society. The groundwork for democracy was laid and the economy boomed under Prime Minister Chatichai Choonhavan's elected government. His 'buffet cabinet' swelled with industry captains who scrambled for lucrative ministerial portfolios.

FOREVER BLOWING BUBBLES

Double-digit growth ushered in the 1990s. Farmers and orchard owners became instant millionaires as developers snapped up land for condominiums, luxury hotels, offices, factories and housing estates. Elevated expressways barely kept pace with Bangkok's notorious traffic, swelled by German cars and the world's second biggest market for pick-up trucks. The affluent new middle classes went shopping with a vengeance, showing off imported labels and mobile phones at grand malls and giant discotheques. The elite developed a taste for wine, though the tipple of choice remained Scotch whisky. Students clamoured for the high-tech trappings and *manga* taste of Japan – the bubble-era model of the next Asian 'tiger economy'. Risking fortunes on dubious stocks caught on in a town where gambling, although illegal, is endemic.

'In June 1997 the baht crashed, dragging the economy down with it. The bubble had vaporised.'

The party was briefly interrupted when Chatichai and his 'unusually rich' ministers were toppled in a bloodless military coup in February 1991 by the National Peace-Keeping Council (NPKC). Respected diplomat Anand Panyarachun was installed as interim prime minister to appease the public until the intended NPKC-backed premier was linked to alleged drug trading. NPKC leader General Suchinda Kraprayoon then took the top job.

This time, the middle classes rallied for his removal, led by the ascetic vegetarian General Chamlong Srimuang, an ex-governor of Bangkok. Protests climaxed in 'Black May' 1992, when the Democracy Monument again witnessed the killing of dozens of protestors (and of others still unaccounted for). Suchinda was forced to resign and Anand led for a second interregnum until September elections brought in a coalition under the modest, principled Chuan Leekpai.

Order was restored and serious urban planning and mass transit finally got under way, but influential figures continued to enrich themselves, and the buying of votes accelerated, prompting the new liberal constitution of 1997,

Historical flashbacks

With official records about ancient Siamese life thin on the ground, particularly given the loss of archives in the razing of Ayutthaya, literature serves a double purpose in Thailand: art and social history. Probably the richest insight into late Ayutthayan ways is the anonymous epic **Khun Chang Khun Paen**. The long tussle over the feisty heroine, Nang Pim, between Paen (a brave, handsome, self-indulgent lothario) and Chang (a fat, balding, but loyal Sino-Thai trader) adds spice to the archetypal love triangle, not least because Paen collects women on his adventures. Aside from its romance, the saga is also beloved of filmmakers because of the art direction potential of ancestral Thai lifestyles, from decor and dress to traditions and auspicious plants.

Recent remake *Khun Paen* spices up the supernatural sub-plot with special effects. Most notoriously, Paen cuts the baby from his pregnant mistress and roasts it in occult rites to create a *gumarn thong* (golden boy), a wrathful spirit assistant. The lad's effigy still features as a trade talisman in many home and shop altars, typically holding a money bag, wearing traditional garb and requiring offerings of red drink and sweets (he is an eternal kid after all).

For a more gentlemanly guide to conduct, Thais consult (and still read in school) **Sawasdee Raksa** by Sunthorn Phu (1787-1855). From this we glean a rich appreciation of hierarchical responsibility, ritual and traditions, such as the designated colours of each day, something seen today in royal colours and the scarves around sacred trees, shrines and fronts of vehicles, but reflected in dress in the past. Falling in and out of favour during the second and third Chakri reigns, this UNESCO-recognised poet also fell in and out of love affairs, prompting the verse-story **Phra Aphai Manee**, a more human text for dramas than the stylised **Ramakien**. There are monuments to the rollicking tale of a dashing prince who fell for a mermaid and was seduced by a giantess, both on Ko Samet (*see pp208-222*) and at the site of his father's home, some 20 kilometres (12.5 miles) east of Ko Samet's Baan Phe Pier at Bam Klam, near Klaeng. A festival held here on his birthday (26 June) features folk entertainment.

As Thailand modernised, though, Thais rediscovered – and also projected – a narrative of how things were in past golden ages. The much-filmed **Sii Phandin** (*Four Reigns*), by former prime minister Kukrit Pramoj, traces a role-model noble lady under Kings Rama V-VIII. Soap operas maintain rigid personality types for most leading characters. Historical costume movies came particularly into vogue after the 1997 economic crash, with the lavish biopic *Suriyothai* revelling in period detail. Queen Suriyothai was a model of sacrifice, dying on elephant back battling against the Burmese in 1548. King Bhumibol's daughter, Princess Ubonrat, played the title role in a TV drama about another Ayutthayan princess, *Kasatariya* (*pictured below*). *Suriyothai*'s blue-blooded director, MC Chatri Chalerm Yukol, is breaking budget records again in filming **Naresuan**, about the king who as a bold prince always wore black – because, as the *Sawasdee Raksa* explains, he was born on a Saturday.

drafted under Anand. Speculation and market manipulation peaked under the governments of Banharn Silpa-archa and Chavalit Yongchaiyudh until the baht crashed in June 1997, dragging the Asian economy down with it. The bubble had vaporised, leaving a Bangkok skyline scarred with half-built concrete eyesores.

In the aftermath came denial. Many were quick to blame foreigners, notably George Soros and the IMF. A second Chuan administration steadied the economy, but failed to invigorate it. Few conceded that the boom had been one big pyramid scheme. Fortunately, the response was practical subsistence not social upheaval. Rolex watches were sold by weight in plastic bags at the 'Market for the Former Rich' and traffic eased due to vehicles getting repossessed. Car boot sales became a short-lived phenomenon, but because selling belongings involves a loss of face, middlemen surreptitiously traded many luxury used goods abroad.

As in Japan, recovery was stifled by rich debtors not being held accountable. Saving face and the power of corrupt networks mean that 'influential' transgressors, the 'unusually rich' or the merely incompetent almost never get punished – they're typically transferred to an 'inactive post'. Finally, in 2003 an ex-minister was jailed, though major scandals continually get muffled as soon as they're revealed.

ONE PARTY RULE

The constitution envisaged both more stable governments and decentralisation, yet power has concentrated to an unparalleled degree in the hands of billionaire Thaksin Shinawatra. Under the Thai Rak Thai ('Thais Love Thais', TRT) Party he formed, this telecom tycoon swept to Thailand's first absolute parliamentary majority in 2000 and led the first government to complete a four-year term. Having narrowly escaped conviction in a constitutional court trial, Thaksin consolidated his self-styled CEO authority in most national institutions, appointing his cousin to head the army, treating non-governmental organisations as foreign-funded subversives, and subduing academics and constitutional watchdogs. Meanwhile, his family's and cabinet cohorts' businesses outpaced the wider economy in wealth generation, while refuting accusations of 'policy corruption' – the alleged biasing of laws and appointments for private gain.

After several clashes with Thaksin, the media – once one of Asia's most free – self-censors. Some critical journalists have been sacked, had programmes pulled off-air, or been investigated. Thaksin stresses that the media – and the parliamentary opposition – should be 'constructive'. All TV stations are run by either the state, the military or the

families of Thaksin or other ministers. Parallels with Italy's Silvio Berlusconi are legion.

A perceived deterioration in human rights has sparked local and international concern. Numerous activists and protestors have disappeared, and a crackdown on drugs claimed well over 2,500 lives, with many suspecting extrajudicial killings rather than the gangland retribution that the authorities allege. Bloodshed in the Muslim deep south hit crisis point in 2004 when dozens of insurgents died in clashes with the military in April and again in October. Bombings have continued in the South despite Thaksin's idea to drop 65 million paper cranes (one per Thai). This Japanese peace offering made Buddhist Thais feel good, but offended Muslim taboos against depicting living things. In 2005, a moderate new approach saw Anand appointed to lead a national reconciliation commission to rebuild trust.

> ## 'It remains to be seen whether Thaksin will emulate the disciplined statesmanship of Singapore or the temptations of the Marcos-era Philippines.'

In an echo of Phibun-style authoritarian social engineering, Thaksin pledges to transform Thailand drastically. His populist policies include universal healthcare, bureaucracy reform, a new moral order, cheap credit for entrepreneurs, and poverty alleviation through handouts and grassroots development. Despite these redistributive aims, TRT's earlier support among academics, progressives and the middle classes has dwindled due to infringements against civil society and fear of another bubble, this time of personal debt.

The tsunami that engulfed Thailand's Indian Ocean coast in December 2004 affected the country significantly, yet only mildly impacted the national economy. Thaksin deftly managed the aftermath, refusing international help and promising a planned rebuilding. Six weeks later, Thais elected their first single-party government. TRT vanquished all small parties it hadn't yet absorbed and largely limited the Democrats to the South, where TRT lost all but one seat. It remains to be seen whether Thaksin will emulate the disciplined statesmanship of Singapore or the temptations of the Marcos-era Philippines. Whatever the outcome, Thaksin seems set to define Thailand for a generation.

HUNGRY FOR NEW PLACES TO EAT?

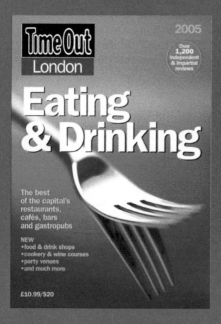

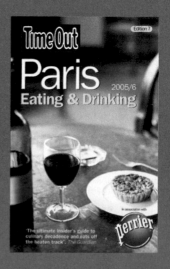

Available at all good bookshops
and at www.timeout.com/shop

Bangkok Today

Balancing tradition and transition, the Thai capital gets ever more cosmopolitan.

In October 2003 the Thai government launched its project to turn the capital into 'Bangkok Fashion City'. The same week it restricted nightlife hours to 1am with a further threat to impose midnight closure. Fashionistas wondered quite how you can get the money and prestige from creative industries while restricting one of the conditions for them to thrive, namely social liberty. This schizophrenic moment captures the dilemma of Bangkok as it hurtles towards the future while grappling for anchors from an often-imagined past.

Bangkok has some great designers, as well as high-achieving industries from cars and spas, to film and furnishings. But in claiming to be the next Milan, Detroit or Hollywood, it does overreach somewhat. The more immediate challenge is, in fact, to match regional rivals.

Prime Minister Thaksin Shinawatra cites the models of Singapore and Malaysia, both of which conveniently happen to be conservative societies dominated by one party under a strong father figure. The great irony is that Bangkok squandered the asset of its easy-going party past to formerly staid Singapore, which loosened up in order to get those same creative industries. These templates, however, require discipline. So far, though, Bangkok has been a byword for unplanned metropolitan sprawl.

PLANNING THROUGH CHAOS

Many of Bangkok's challenges can be summarised in one word: traffic. One reason for its notorious jams lies in its unusually small road area for a city its size, while also being riddled with dead ends, bottlenecks and zigzags. While the car is undoubtedly a status symbol and a reflection of prosperity, vehicles keep increasing in numbers, partly because so many *moo baan* (housing estates) are located down alleys with minimal access, or other amenities.

If mass transit had started in the 1970s, as intended, suburbs would have grown around it, as is happening now. After expanding horizontally into an endless plain, Bangkok now expands vertically through BTS SkyTrains, underground subways and hundreds of concrete towers. Mass transit has made downtown apartments hip, resulting in a real estate bubble that's pushing the poor to the fringes.

While technically superb, the separately run subway and BTS boast 'intersections' that don't properly intersect with each other, nor with the buses. So jealously is each fiefdom guarded that some official maps of the 361 kilometres (224 miles) of new or extended lines promised by 2012 omit the SkyTrain.

Planning failures often derive from new office holders scuppering integrated schemes

Boat trips on the **Chao Praya river** – a refreshing way to see the hottest city on earth.

in favour of their own pet projects, or repaying voter support. Nevertheless, many basics have been upgraded, such as water and sewer mains, construction standards, flood defences and limits on groundwater pumping.

After progressive, eco-aware Governor Bhichit Rattakul, the city stagnated for four years under hot-tempered Governor Samak Sundaravej. The public accountability of City Hall was restored in 2004 on the election of Governor Apirak Kosayothin. An earnest young executive, he advocates micro-reforms to improve the quality of life, from safety and recycling, to making selected canals swimmable and reviving the Art Museum that Samak had tried to turn into a mall. But Apirak faces huge challenges in carving out new parkland, eradicating mafia extortion of vendors, improving schools and easing traffic through Bus Rapid Transit (BRT) routes to supplement the rail lines.

One difficulty is that the governor has too little power, yet Bangkok tries to do too much. It's the focus for almost all national life: royalty, government, finance, commerce, tourism, nightlife, shopping, entertainment, industry, the military, universities, road, rail, port and air transport, and ceremony. Decentralisation is, however, the new mantra, and even the parliament may move out. The finance minister suggested building ten more Bangkoks, though that would require ten more countries' resources.

Built on sediment, Bangkok is gradually sinking and, alarmingly, its once expanding delta has started to erode. The erstwhile

'Venice of the East' may yet need to re-dig the canals it has paved over. The car's primacy results in many roads being raised above shop and house doorsteps so that residents, not drivers, suffer during floods. While Thai buildings no longer stand on stilts, the expressways invariably do.

BULLDOZING THE PAST

Thais still emulate the Japanese focus on state-subsidised mega-construction: of roads, dams and grand urban monuments. The results may or may not bring benefits, but frequently entail the destruction of something precious.

Conservation work tends to focus on particular buildings, yet it's often the overall streetscape that matters most in creating a sense of historic character. While much of the city's heritage has disappeared, some buildings are being converted into restaurants, spas, bars and so on. This tends to delight foreigners more than Thais, who often assume old houses will be haunted.

In addition, preservation initiatives constantly suffer from misperceptions about what constitutes 'modernisation', as when mature trees get replaced by seedlings and concrete in new parks. Meanwhile, attempts at scaling down back-jarring high signs, minimising pavement obstacles and burying wires are making minimal headway, hampered by the continuing irrational actions of councils and utility workers, such as butchering decades-old trees into rows of stumps as a quick solution.

Fortune tends to favour places that maintain their character, beauty and environment. Yet Bangkok continues to erase or standardise such subtle, fragile assets as markets, old communities, greenery, cultural diversity and the laid-back lifestyle. Highways now fragment Bangkok's last expanse of boat-accessed canal at Bang Kruay, ruining an irreplaceable asset for the coming post-industrial era.

'The market value of Thai goods shot into focus when foreigners tried to patent *tuk-tuks*.'

REBRANDING THAINESS
The market value of what Thais had long taken for granted came firmly into focus in 2002, when international companies tried to patent Thai jasmine rice and *tuk-tuks*. It wasn't long before potential indigenous brands were classified as 'Thai Wisdom' and marketed under the state's 'One Tambon [village], One Product' (OTOP) scheme. Herbal medicines earlier derided by the authorities now get encouraged as fuel for the spa boom that Thailand is currently leading. Rustic materials formerly viewed as too folkish lend distinction to the chic products of Thai designers.

Foreign store buyers routinely scour Chatuchak Weekend Market for new things to import, or even to counterfeit – an ironic reversal of the intellectual property infringements for which Bangkok is infamous. Local record labels now campaign against copying, though it persists so rampantly one marvels at the pirates' untouchability. Thai films have already won prizes at Cannes, and music might be the next thing to go *inter* (break out internationally).

Many of the creators and consumers of these new Thai products are a young, globalised generation who self-identify as *indie* (independent) within a conformist society. Raised under democracy, open to outside influences and often foreign-educated, these *dek naew* (trend kids) seek stimulation and self-discovery in underground music, avant-garde movies, art installations, extreme sports, provocative plays and radical fashion.

Indie Bangkok is like the Bauhaus, the 1960s sexual revolution, psychedelia, punk, postmodernism, the internet and mass consumerism all happening at once, with a strong dose of Japanese 'cute' thrown into the mix. They express these interests in a raft of inventive, often intellectual, fanzines and handmade books, sold

where like minds gather, such as 'art bars' and the Fat Festival (*see p157*).

An earlier generation – students who resisted dictatorship in the 1970s – had already radicalised the arts. Many of its veterans now influence government but, while encouraging people to think outside the box, the authorities can't seem to bring themselves to let people actually live outside the box.

NEW SOCIAL ORDER
In making Thailand more like Singapore, Thaksin has imposed a moralistic campaign. Unlike previous nightlife crackdowns, this time it has been unremitting. The intention is, in part, to purge Bangkok of its sleazy reputation, just as Singapore has sanitised Bugis Street. But while Singapore scrupulously upholds the rule of law, the social order campaign in Thailand has drawn international headlines for its violence, partiality and the detention of members of the public in indiscriminate raids. Nightlife venues have been an easy target in the war on drugs, since narcotics are far harder to extract from the wider society: taxi drivers, school crammers, untouchable rich kids and those who take *yaa baa* (the so-called 'crazy drug' amphetamine) to work harder.

'The nanny-state hectoring also reflects the application of industrious immigrant Chinese values upon an easygoing South-east Asian culture.'

Underlying the campaign is a rearguard action to keep the younger generation from discarding traditional values. The authorities went apoplectic about spaghetti straps revealing teenage shoulders, but as historians point out, until the influence of missionaries and Western education, it was authentically Thai to bare shoulders or even go topless.

The nanny-state hectoring also reflects the application, as in Singapore, of industrious immigrant Chinese values upon an easygoing South-east Asian culture. Tycoon ministers want happy-go-lucky street vendors to borrow against their carts in order to become capitalists like themselves. Historically, the conformist aspects of Thai life were balanced by liberating values like *sanuk* (fun), *mai pen rai* (never mind), *yaa kit maak* (don't think too much) and a tolerance of quirks. With those pressure valves increasingly blocked, it's unclear how Thais will take to the new wave of unyielding discipline.

In Context

HUB CAPITAL

Bangkok's ambitions to be the hub of myriad industries have location on their side. With its long history as a crossroads of both commerce and culture, Bangkok has the potential to be the fulcrum of a region bigger than the EU, a feat that the kingdom of Ayutthaya once managed.

With the opening up of formerly closed neighbours, a transcontinental transport network will resemble spokes extending from Bangkok. Aside from the many young budget airlines serving its huge new airport, the city will handle increasing road and rail traffic with India and China via Myanmar; with Vietnam via Laos and Cambodia; and with Singapore via Malaysia.

Plans for other mega-projects abound: a humungous causeway cutting across the Gulf seas from Bangkok to Hua Hin; a Kra Canal across the southern isthmus; or a 'land-bridge' to funnel oil between port refineries just north of Phuket to just south of Samui. The impacts on reefs, beaches, forests and mangroves worry many, yet Thailand also wants to double tourist numbers to 20 million per year – a target that hasn't been helped by the damage caused by the tsunami of December 2004 (*see pp208-222*).

The once pristine Mekong river, too, is being reduced by China into a shipping conduit and hydroelectric exhaust duct that overrides natural water levels, to the alarm of increasingly drought-prone downstream countries.

Much else in Bangkok's future depends on China. Thai commerce, diplomacy, tourism and even entertainment are all orienting northwards. Thais are appreciating Chinese fashions, making Sino-Thai fusions, celebrating Chinese festivals and generally sharing its wavelength – in the same deft way that Thailand has repeatedly, and impressively, kept its independence from overarching powers, while also interacting with them.

Look how Bangkok has dealt with its current encroaching force: tourism. Decades of relentless hospitality have taken their toll, but the city has also benefited, and not just financially. In making its amenities more comfortable, cultivating cosmopolitan tastes, rethinking how its culture can be presented and dispatching goodwill worldwide, Bangkok has compromised many things, but not its essence. By embracing every onslaught so warmly, Bangkok remains steadfastly Thai.

Tusk force

Elephants never forget – and nobody forgets an elephant – especially one plodding through the Bangkok traffic fumes, its swaying rear light flashing red. Startled tourists reach for their cameras – and buy sugar cane from the mahout to feed the poor pachyderm. Thais pay to swoop under its belly for luck, but also wince at their national animal being reduced to begging.

Formerly gracing the flag of Siam and carrying kings into battle, the elephant is lauded by all. Yet like so much traditional culture, it's exploited to gain face and money, without sufficient care and investment to sustain it long-term. From 20,000 in the mid 1980s, under 5,000 Thai elephants remain. No more than 1,500 survive in the wild, from which babies still get snatched (usually requiring the protective mother's death), as captive breeding is rare. Farmers even kill them for eating the crops that encroach on the animal's domain.

The 1988 logging ban left most domesticated elephants jobless, particularly in the north. A few get used in illegal logging, sometimes being fed amphetamines to labour longer. Meanwhile, the habitat of southern Isaan has been so denuded, and the 125-kilogram (276-pound) daily diet costs so much,

that the area's elephants must beg in Bangkok, where there's better foraging in empty suburban lots. A Dusit Zoo (*see p80*) vet estimated in 2000 that 30 elephants roam downtown, plus 20 in the suburbs. He treats injuries for free, since Thai roads can be hot, sharp and hazardous, with motorists fined only B500 for collisions that frequently result in the animal's death. Their use in post-tsunami clear-ups also exposed them to potential harm.

City authorities keep trying to ban elephants, threatening the mahouts with fines and dispossession, but no one has yet come up with a viable alternative. The only other options are tourist trekking, hazardous showbiz trips overseas, or their sometimes callous treatment as commodities by entertainment companies.

The species' future depends on samaritans with insufficient funding, like the **Thai Elephant Conservation Centre** (www.thaielephant.org) in Lampang in the north. A hospital and refuge for orphans, it boasts the world's first elephantine sperm bank and school for mahouts, whose skills and partnership are critical for the safe handling of domesticated elephants. That 4,000-year-old relationship seems in jeopardy; and most mahout students are now tourists.

Modern Faith

Thai monk **Mettanando Bhikkhu** examines Thai Buddhism against the backdrop of modern society.

How do the residents of this chaotic capital maintain such light-hearted serenity? The answer, 94 per cent of Thais will tell you, is Buddhism. Calming concepts such as *jai yen* (keep cool) and *mai pen rai* (never mind) derive from their tolerant, non-violent Buddhist philosophy. Now growing numbers of Westerners go to Thailand to study what to many seems a relevant way to handle modern life (*see p178* **The art of doing nothing**).

One of the 20th century's most influential monks, the late Buddhadasa Bhikku, got this message out to modern Thais via his writings on Buddhist economics, environmentalism and modern life, such as *A Handbook for Mankind*. He prescribed accessible meditation techniques to discover mindfulness through simply watching the breath.

This is the wisdom of Siddhartha Gautama, a sixth-century BC Indian prince who only became a Buddha ('awakened one') after rejecting first his privileged upbringing, then ascetic hermithood. Finally, through meditation he achieved enlightenment as the 'Middle Way' between luxury and austerity. Buddhism doesn't require a belief in Buddha as a god; it's a practical technique to liberate one's self from

conditioning, dealing more with the here and now than metaphysical meanderings or moralistic judgement.

Finding that path has become increasingly challenging as industrialisation has exposed Thais to new ideas, activities, possessions and temptations. Yet the past two decades have seen great spiritual energy, with temples being built, modern Buddhist communities organised, massive social projects undertaken and missions overseas growing. Headlines about Buddhism have, however, often dwelt on tabloid scandals about dubious fundraising, charismatic sects and monks dabbling in worldly pleasures. Calls for reform also spark controversy. Coupled with a perceptible slipping in Buddhist practice, particularly by urbanites, this has created what some call a crisis of faith. Still, the *Dharma* (teachings) reassuringly stresses that everything is subject to change.

BORN AGAIN (AND AGAIN)

Buddhist theory is big on numerical lists. The Three Marks of Existence (*anicca*, impermanence of everything; *dukkha*, unsatisfactoriness; and *anatta*, absence of self) describe how everything in mind, body and environment arises and passes away, moment to moment. The Four Noble Truths help us see that dissatisfaction is caused by craving (*tanha*); since nothing lasts, craving can never be permanently satisfied. The way to end craving (and hence suffering) is explained in the Noble Eightfold Path and elaborated upon by the Thirty-Seven Factors of Enlightenment. All these labels describe a simple progression in the mind when meditating. When you apply it to caffeine addiction or seeking the perfect beach, it's quite amazing how quickly the craving fades. Entrenched things like lust or anger are a bit tougher.

The ultimate aim is attaining *nirvana*, a final disengaging from the cycle of birth-death-rebirth. One's degree of suffering depends on *karma* (action) earlier in this life or a previous existence. In Buddhism, time is cyclic and endless, unlike the linear, finite human life of monotheistic Judaism, Christianity and Islam. The Buddhist cosmos is eternal and houses innumerable world systems, in which Gautama was the fourth Buddha, and Lord Maittreya the future fifth.

In pre-Siam times Buddhism in Thailand was of the Mahayana school prevalent in northern Asia, which embraces *bodhisattva* (enlightened beings delaying *nirvana* in order to help others). Some Mahayana customs remain, like statue worship, though almost all Thai Buddhists follow stricter Theravada doctrine – as in Myanmar, Laos, Cambodia and Sri Lanka, from where Theravadism entered Siam.

> ## 'Religion in Thailand still sits on a high social pedestal, alongside monarchy and nation.'

Reincarnation was part of Indian belief at the foundation of Buddhism, but direct Hindu influences are also visible everywhere. The **Erawan Shrine** (*see p95* **Gods of today**) is the most prominent of countless Thai shrines to Brahma, while ministry logos depict the elephant-headed Ganes, Garuda bird-men adorn banks, the City Pillar is partly a phallic Shiva lingam, and the *Ramayana* epic permeates all the arts. The Chakri kings (the current line) are considered emanations of Rama, an incarnation of Vishnu, while Brahmin priests conduct royal rites.

Religion sits on a high social pedestal alongside monarchy and nation, so visitors are obliged to show due respect to all three. Thailand's tricolour flag signifies royalty (blue), religion (white) and people (red). Therevada Buddhism has been the official religion since the time of Sukhothai, and is enshrined in the 1997 constitution, though it guarantees religious freedom.

Many consider being Thai synonymous with being Buddhist, and often refer to those of Muslim, South Asian or Middle Eastern origin as *khaek* (guests). This unsurprisingly grates with the four per cent of Thais who follow Islam. In 2004 sectarian (and seemingly separatist) violence in the mostly Muslim southernmost provinces escalated to include attacks on monks as symbols of central Thai hegemony, shocking the wider population.

MAKING MERIT

On a practical level, most Thais concern themselves with accruing positive karmic points through *tham boon* (making merit). This encompasses offerings (from standard lotus buds, candles and three incense sticks to elaborate assemblages), donations, charity, putting food in monks' alms bowls at daybreak, and acts of kindness like freeing caged birds. This may also be done on behalf of a deceased relative.

In organised Buddhism, making merit involves revering the *trirattana* (triple gems): Buddha, *Dharma* and *Sangha* (the monkhood). Essentially, the public subsidises Thailand's 270,000 *bhikkhu* (monks) and 90,000 *samaneras* (novices) to live a life of moral example at more than 30,000 *wat* (monasteries), by donating food, clothing and money for necessities like shelter. The core of traditional life, a *wat* is not just a symbolically designed place of worship, meditation and scripture, but may serve as a community centre, orphanage, hospital, hostel, school, market, monastery, playground, crematorium, meeting place, festival site, foundation, museum, theatre, garden, zoo and, after the tsunami, a mass morgue.

The high number of monks is due to the convention that young men (typically before marriage) ordain for a short period. Considered the most noble way to express gratitude to one's parents, and to generate them great merit, this must, like conscription, be accommodated by employers. Historically, this lasted one *phansaa* – the three-month rainy season retreat – or perhaps just for the day of an elder relative's cremation. Some enter on retirement. Generally, men can join and leave up to three times.

Aside from meditation and scholarship, monks perform rites at weddings, funerals, installations of spirit houses and anointings of new buildings, businesses or vehicles. Less orthodox monks may also read fortunes, inscribe protective tattoos or issue lottery numbers. Ideally, it's a life of peace and renunciation, free from harm to fellow beings. Through 227 restrictive precepts (which preclude sex, soft bedding, entertainment, possessions and female contact) a Theravadin monk learns to recognise and then relinquish his attachments in order to free his mind.

Modern distractions and compulsions mean that young single men increasingly can't – or won't – find the time. Many join for just a week, or maybe never. Hence the suggestion of mass ordination for school or university students during vacations. While some initiates stay on as monks, inspired by their faith, the shortage of those with long-term commitment has caused a sixth of all *wat* to be abandoned. By contrast, some disreputable types don saffron robes to gain lenience and have reoffended while ordained, leading to calls for tighter screening.

Nevertheless, the *Sangha* refuses to ordain devout *mae chi*: white robed women who follow fewer precepts. Buddha founded an order of yellow-robed *bhikkuni* (nuns), but the line faded out before Buddhism arrived in Siam. In February 2001 Chatsumarn Kablisingh – ex-professor and daughter of a Buddhist nun ordained in Taiwan – became a nun in Sri Lanka, intensifying an already heated debate.

CONTROVERSY AND CHANGE

Within the brotherhood of *bhikkhus*, successive scandals have tarnished public faith, which faltered most noticeably on disclosure that two monks with large followings had had affairs with female disciples and patronised prostitutes. One of them, Phra Yantra Amaro, was sentenced to three months in jail for second-degree murder, but escaped to lead a Buddhist community in San Diego. Meanwhile, the abbot of Wat Dhammakaya – a temple north of Bangkok with aggressive fundraising tactics, hundreds of thousands of followers and a B500 million *chedi* – was arrested and charged with embezzlement. The case lingers on in court and will haunt Thai Buddhists for years to come.

Both monks and lay people have called for stricter supervision of monks and reform of the *Sangha*, a largely self-governing body headed by the royally appointed Supreme Patriarch. Administered under semi-democratic structures in 1941, it was placed under a hierarchical bureaucracy by General Sarit Thanarat's dictatorship in 1962. Some factions suggest that it might have become overly preoccupied with ritual, purity and amulet mass production, rather than addressing social problems.

Sacred charms

Dangling in a gold case around the neck of most men and many women, covering the dials of cars, or tucked into a boxer's armband, amulets are the talisman of choice for the Thai. Most amulets are miniature images of the Buddha, Hindu gods, venerable monks or great kings like Rama V in bronze, wood, gold or clay.

Amulets come in other classes, too, from medicinal herb roots and natural oddities to cabalistic diagrams and inscriptions in archaic

Khmer upon cloth (*pha yan*), as tattoos (*sakyan*) or rolled foil (*ta-krut*) that can be tiny enough to embed under the skin. The tradition for boys to sling a carved phallus (*palad khik*) around their waist often continues into adulthood. *Palad khik* are one of many fetish objects that shopkeepers think bring custom, along with fish traps and dolls of a beckoning woman (*nang kwak*) or the golden ghost boy (*gumarn thong*).

Talismans all require a blessing to activate their powers to, say, heal the sick, bring fortune, boost sexuality or protect, hence their association with those in dangerous professions. The issuing shaman, medium or unorthodox monk would utter the mantra that the wearer might repeat at moments of peril. Wayward behaviour (and sometimes contact by women) may negate the spell.

Not considered property, holy items may only be 'rented', yet Thailand is the world's largest market for amulets (*see also p133*), with collectors catered to in papers and magazines. Prices, often in the millions of baht, depend on quality, popularity, rarity and antiquity. The most prolific amulet producer is Luang Phor Khoon, abbot of Wat Baanrai in Khorat, who donates proceeds to good causes.

State involvement in teaching and welfare has deprived *wat* of their social and educative role. A consequence, suggested by the respected monk and scholar Phra Dhammapitaka (PA Payutto), is that some of the *Sangha* have developed a 'habit of idleness', subsisting on the patronage system. However, certain monks are far from idle, such as the Buddhadasa disciple Phra Payom Kalyano, an outspoken social activist who has initiated large projects for the poor. In the early 1990s Phra Alongkot converted his *wat* in Saraburi into Thailand's first AIDS hospice, receiving support from the king, the princess mother, the WHO and the UN, and he also supports a grassroots youth network.

Female ordination is supported by a prominent group, Santi Asok, advocating strict vegetarianism, austerity and sharing of community property. Its founder, Phra Phothirak, a former TV announcer, declared himself independent of the *Sangha* and was arrested, tried and lightly punished in 1988,

though the community and its vegetarian restaurants continue. Its most famous adherent is Chamlong Srimuang, a general who was governor of Bangkok, founder of a political party and leader of the anti-dictatorship demonstrations of 1992.

Monks themselves demonstrated in late 2002, when a so-called 'saffron-robed mob' demanded, unsuccessfully, that the new Ministry of Religion and Culture be made specifically into a Ministry of Buddhism. So far, Thai monks do not have the right to vote or to have ID cards or passports like fellow Thai citizens.

Ultimately, though, Theravada Buddhism places responsibility on the individual to overcome conditioning, become enlightened and act with compassion. For lay practitioners, Sulak Sivaraksa – Thai Buddhism's sharpest-tongued commentator and a past Nobel Prize nominee for his human rights work – advocates 'engaged Buddhism': active and reflective practice for the benefit of individuals and society.

High spirits

The Buddhist canon rejects faith in rituals and the supernatural, yet animist heritage infuses each Buddhist country. With organised Buddhism resistant to change, modern Thais are increasingly drawn to alternative beliefs old and new, from the Chinese cult of Kuan Yin to luck propitiation. Most Thais believe in ghosts, omens, mediums, astrology and amulets, and pervasive numerology (the number nine is lucky) means that shrines are especially busy ahead of lottery draws.

Animism is most evident in the white wrist thread (*sai sin*) – tied by monks or elders to keep a person's 32 bodily spirits from wandering – and the spirit house. Installed at most building plots at an auspiciously divined location and time, spirit houses typically come as a pair. The higher one (*saan phra phum*) resembles a mini-temple on a pedestal for the Hinduised 'spirit of the land', sometimes sheltering a Hindu statue, especially of Brahma. The lower, simpler shrine (*phra phum chao thii*) resembles a stilt house for the indigenous 'spirit of the place', akin to spirits that guard domains like forests, fields, waterways, mountains and vehicles.

Spirits must be appeased with daily offerings and a staff of model servants and dancers, as a spirit's personality is apparently won over by offering its favourite food, drinks, habit or mantra. Delays at Bangkok's new airport were blamed on late installation of a spirit house.

Brahma in a spirit house.

Less benign are the restless spirits of the dead (*phii*), who suffer in our midst until dispatched by exorcism or karma to heaven or hell, before eventual rebirth. Thai ghosts tend to be generic: elongated *phii phraet* (hungry ghosts) suffer pin-hole mouths due to greed; elderly *phii bhop* witches scoff raw chicken entrails; and disembodied *phii kraseu* trail their innards while seeking rotten food. With *phii* so prevalent, Thais often shun big trees, old houses, antique furniture and developments built on cemeteries. Many drivers garland shrines at accident black spots. Unsurprisingly, ghost stories dominate movies, comics and soap operas, especially classics like **Nang Nak** (*see p99* **Wat Maha But**).

Art & Architecture

Divine design and foreign fusions.

Few world monuments match Bangkok's Grand Palace for surreal imagination and dazzle. Façades and pilasters shimmer with inset glass and mirrors. Slanting columns soar to overlapping gables, carved pediments and multi-layered gilded spires. Surfaces dance with multicoloured paintings and statues of gods, demons and heroes.

The dazzle is no accident, but an intended effect. It has deep religious and political significance (think reflection, transience, illumination, majesty) and has been refined over centuries. Thai art absorbed streams of influence from China, India, Sri Lanka, Cambodia, Java and the Malay peninsula. As in Japan, most of the culture can be traced to some outside source, yet the Thais have moulded all these imports into something utterly and distinctively Thai. Copying (and thus honouring) a master has long been the

ideal of anonymous Thai artisans, and the aesthetic therefore adapts incrementally.

Thai art's first trace is the patterned Baan Chiang pottery left by mysterious Neolithic peoples. By the fifth to eighth centuries, the Mon Dvaravati culture combined Theravada Buddhism with animism, giving rise to sacred *bai sema* (boundary stones) and stone sculptures so realistic their features resemble Thais today. Under Khmer sway from the ninth to the 13th centuries, Siam inherited massive temple complexes, stone satellites of Angkor evoking a Hindu cosmology by way of India and Java.

Khmer temples were microcosms of heaven. Surrounded by moats and sub-temples symbolising the seas and continents, they centred on a scripture vault beneath a *prang* (tower) representing sacred Mount Meru, axis of the universe, and the home of Shiva,

MR Kukrit Pramoj's
Heritage Home.
See p31.

represented by a *lingam* (phallus). Such manifestations of gods reinforced the powers of empire and divine kingship.

Although Thailand is devoutly Buddhist, an enduring faith in Hinduism means that spires are capped with Shiva's trident; pediments feature Vishnu (the creator) mounted on the man-bird Garuda, Indra (King of the Gods) riding the multi-headed elephant Erawan, and elephant-headed Ganesha, remover of obstacles, god of the arts (and, indeed, logo of the government's Fine Arts Department). Thailand, it's said, boasts far more shrines to Brahma than India. Also from the Khmers came an architectural vocabulary, including the *prang*, multi-stepped altars with redented corners, and relief carvings of intertwining vines and flame motifs.

SIAMESE STYLE

By the 13th century Tai tribes had founded the Lanna and Sukhothai kingdoms. Hailing from northern forests, the Tai came from a tradition of wood, not stone. They brought Chinese-influenced house and temple forms, distinguished by long sloping roofs.

> **'By the Bangkok period, every surface had become encrusted with gilding, filigree and a mosaic of glass and ceramic.'**

From India, Thais took the visual language of the Buddha image's features and postures, as well as *stupa* (towers holding relics of the Buddha or a revered person). *Stupa* evolved into Thai *chedi* by way of the bell-shaped Sri Lankan *dagoba*. The inhabitants of Sukhothai applied what could be called 'Thai grace', elongating

stupa into elegant bud-shaped *chedi* and being the first to portray the Buddha walking (descending from heaven). In contrast to solemn Khmer art, the walking Buddhas of Sukhothai are flowing, rounded and almost appear to float.

As power moved south to Ayutthaya from the 14th century, this elongation and 'etherealisation' stretched the *dagoba* into a soaring spire, its indentations reduced to ribs. The rounded Khmer *prang* lengthened into a lofty corn cob; walls and columns extended, lifting the multi-tiered roofs high into the heavens.

Statues acquired crowns and jewellery, while inset glass glowed from elaborately tiered palaces. By the 17th century, Ayutthayan art was heavily preoccupied with light: gleam and sparkle were exaggerated by enclosing open temple pavilions, allowing only slits to let in light. By the Bangkok period, every surface had become encrusted with gilding, filigree and a mosaic of glass and ceramic.

The trapezoid added the final touch. The walls of ancient Tai houses leaned slightly for stability, outward in the north, inward in the south. This tapering turned increasingly oblique to impart elegance. Doors and windows tilted too. Chests and boxes became trapezoids, and bases of temples and thrones swooped like boats. This merging of styles, eras and peoples continues today, resulting in art that is discerningly Thai.

ABSOLUTELY PREFAB

The archetypal Thai house comprises of hardwood modular components, raised on stilts, with high peaked roofs. It belongs to a domestic architectural theme originating in the Asian tropics and spanning from Indonesia to Japan. The stilts raised homes above flooding, and multiple eaves allowed ventilation while protecting from fierce rain and sun. Not every element, however, is utilitarian. Erected with elaborate rites, houses also embody ancient animist symbolism about earth and heaven, fire and water. Hence the fish, bird, *naga* and flame imagery upon gables, eaves and ridgelines.

A defining feature of Thai design, the elegant rooflines vary by region. The earlier ones swept low and wide, as visible up north, where they peak in the criss-cross *kalae* finial. Central Thai roofs pitch steeper, their end bargeboards curving down from sharp points until rising again with *ngao* (a flame-like flick). More elaborate home and temple roof ridges end in upward bird-like finials called *chofa*. Plainer houses are thatched with palm or teak leaves; grander roofs are tiled with teak shingles or glazed ceramic.

MR Kukrit Pramoj's Heritage Home, **Jim Thompson's House**, **Suan Pakkard Palace** and **Thai House** cooking school are prime examples. Interiors are sparsely furnished for multi-purpose living, *tang* (low seat/bed/table with hoof or claw legs) being a constant, along with triangular *maun khwan* (axe pillows).

Though now rare and expensive, Thai house building remains a living art. You can buy a new house in old style in **Ang Thong** province, or even **Chatuchak Market**. Craftsmen carve

modular units like stepped wall-panels to be reassembled with pegs to enable future moves.

WHAT MAKES A *WAT*?
Whatever its secular roles, even the most humble *wat* (Thai Buddhist temple) is sacred ground, removed from the mundane world by walls beyond an initial gate or fortified moat. To the Khmer cosmological plan, Thais added *chedi*, and their ancestral rooflines, the eaves chiming with brass bells.

The key building is the *bot* (or *ubosot*), the ordination hall rarely open to the public and demarcated by eight *bai sema* (now the Thai Airways logo). Often leaf-shaped, these flat standing monoliths may be sheltered in miniature shrines. Most temples have one or more *vihaan* (assembly halls). Lacking *bai sema*, but resembling *bot* in their decorative gables, crown-like window frames, raised terrace and roofs of green and orange tiles, *vihaan* usually host the principal Buddha images and public worship.

Thai trademarks also embellish other temple structures. The cubic *mondop*, with complex cruciform roof, houses a Buddha footprint or scriptures. *Hor trai* (libraries) sit upon a pedestal or stilts over water to

Back to the origin

Twentyfirst-century Thailand teeters on the edge of a cultural precipice. Centuries of accumulated artistic knowledge may die with the passing of the few remaining masters. Charged with cultivating new passion for and participation in traditional arts, many Thai art venues lack adequate explanation and the requisite attributes to spark much new interest – an especially difficult task among the passive consumers of modern media. Thus dance shows can seem like a chore, rituals pass in a mystifying blur and the meanings in design go unrecognised.

Fortunately, East Asian nations – having swapped native ways for high-tech development and fashion – seem to be relishing their cultural heritage anew. This renaissance is in its infancy in Thailand, but there is a growing interest in performance arts (*see p197* **Young masters**), folk sports (*see p203* **Fight club**) and *lai thai*, the traditional Thai design methods that infuse contemporary design (*see p33* **Creative flames**).

As ever in Thailand, significant interest also comes from outside. Fascinated by

native culture, foreign tourists and residents make up a major chunk of performance-goers, and students of traditional skills, from massage or boxing, to cooking or elephant mahoutship. Such arts are a potential tourist bonanza. But while tourism provides new jobs, income, venues and audiences, it also tends to produce a regurgitated 'greatest hits' of Thai arts with little cultural value.

A positive contribution to this renaissance is **Origin** (*see p55*), a programme in English exploring Central Plains culture at a teak compound in Bangkok, and its folkier Lanna equivalent in Chiang Mai. Through courses of one, two or more days, people in small groups try their hand at skills like dance gestures, floral offerings, costuming, *lai thai* and the *wai khru* (teacher honouring rite) of martial arts. Trying these activities can reveal profound insights into Thai culture, especially since the course leaders are experts in their fields and often have an engaging, informal manner. All the themes combine in a final event that is far more personal and rewarding than a tourist show.

protect against fire and insects. Sometimes Buddha images line a cloister. And as in secular spaces, *sala* (elevated open pavilions) can shelter any activity, from resting, eating or meeting, to music, dance or massage.

Chedi, however, are usually the dominant structures. Beside the massive *prang* at **Wat Arun** in Bangkok or record-breaking **Phra Pathom Chedi** in Nakhon Pathom, the surrounding buildings are merely grace notes.

'The focus of all this florid decoration is the serene image of Lord Buddha.'

Inside temple halls, complex symbolism infuses murals, lacquer work and carved wooden doors, lintels, walls, furniture and ceilings. Attending Hindu gods are lesser deities, like the half-woman, half-bird *kinnaree*, *apsara* (heavenly dancers), *thep* (angels) and the aquatic serpent *naga*. The supreme protector of Buddhism, who must be placated, *naga* shelters the Buddha under his multi-headed hood, curves round walls and through decorative panels and slithers along bridges to holy ground.

BUDDHA IMAGERY DECODED

The focus of all this florid decoration is the serene image of Lord Buddha. He sits exalted on a throne built up of complex angles like Khmer temples, or decorated with lotus petals. The ubiquitous lotus, rising from the mud to bloom in purity, is Buddhism's favoured symbol. Framing the Buddha is the *mandorla*, a flame-like vortex of light similar to the halo in Christian iconography.

Buddhist sculpture is very stylised. Initial prohibition of a human likeness left a legacy of abstract representations in Thai *wat* – the wheel of law, the footprint or the bodhi tree (under which Buddha was enlightened). It was the ancient Greek-influenced Gandhara sculpture in today's Afghanistan/Pakistan that first gave form to the Buddha attributes listed in scriptures, such as curly hair, broad shoulders, a clinging robe and the *ushnisa* (bulge atop the head). Over time, distinct styles emerged. The *ushnisa* rose to resemble a flame, then a spire. Dvaravati Buddhas feature thick lips, heavy lidded eyes and sweet smiles. Sukhothai statues have rounded, androgynous faces and bodies, with long pointy noses. In affluent Ayutthaya, Buddha images with crowns, jewels and elongated faces express the hauteur of a powerful court. Bangkok Buddhas verge on the baroque, with robes and pedestals profuse with minute detail.

The Buddha's various postures and *mudra* (gestures) convey philosophical principles and incidents in his life. Oft-seen sets of eight postures denote each weekday (Wednesday is halved), and are worshipped according to one's day of birth. In the most common *mudra* Bhumisparsa ('calling the earth to witness'), the Buddha sits in lotus position, right fingers pointing downward to resist the temptations of Mara, the devil. Standing with one or both hands held up, palm frontward, the Buddha reassures or calms; when the thumb and forefinger touch, he is teaching, or 'turning the wheel of law'. In culmination, the 'reclining Buddha' shows the moment of final release: nirvana.

2-D OR NOT 2-D

In Thailand painting is frozen dance. Whether flying or seated quietly, *thep* and heroes in murals typically appear in the posed attitudes of dance: fingers bent, elbows arched back, legs splayed. By the same token, classical dance is painting come to life. Dancers wear costumes and masks inspired by murals, and pose in ensemble tableaux.

'Thai dance is rooted in the ancient Indian concept that it was the gods who were doing the dancing.'

Thai dance is rooted in the ancient Indian concept that it was the gods who were doing the dancing. A performer's repertoire of poses and *mudra* evoke the divine. The courts of Java and Cambodia modified these, with an emphasis on outward curving fingers and heroic stances. Movements in *khon* and *lakhon* – traditional thai performing arts – are clearly recognisable from 12th-century bas reliefs at Cambodia's Angkor Wat.

Thais characteristically elongated and elaborated Angkorean dance, adding stylisation and sparkle. Fingernails (often with metal extensions) twist backwards at impossible angles; *chadaa* (headdresses) rise into sleek spires like those crowning temples; shoulder finials curve upwards. Costumes heavy with gold thread and beaded with reflective glass gleam like temple walls.

Pivotal to painting and dance is the *Ramakien*, the Thai version of India's *Ramayana* saga. Painting and dance part company, however, when it comes to foreign influence. Classical dance, centred on the court until very recently, remained conservative (though modern troupes now reinterpret it). But painting embraced China and the West with the same gusto as did architecture.

Creative flame

Contemporary Thai design products – from cushions to cutting-edge spas – manage to distil an essence of Thainess. One way that they achieve this is to apply elements of *lai thai*, a language of design derived from ancient patterns. These involve the geometric repetition of certain forms in countless variations; these patterns adorn traditional crafts in profusion, from wood carvings and mother-of-pearl inlay to *benjarong* (five-colour) ceramics. Hints, outlines and fractions of these patterns are now often used as postmodern motifs in architecture, decor and clothing.

The swirls and geometry on Neolithic pottery from Ban Chiang recur in crafts today, though more widespread are the natural shapes traced from Khmer lintels and 13th-century BC Chinese pottery, such as the distinctive *lai kranok* (a twirling flame). True to form, the Thais stretched and elaborated *kranok* until they became long, sinewy and pointy. *Kranok* merge with other forms into hybrids; leaves and flowers, even animals and gods flow into rhythms of flame that curl delicately like the fingers of classical dancers. The huge *lai Thai* lexicon also includes *lai bua* (lotus forms), *lai krajang* (pointed leaf forms), interlocking rectangles and diamonds, floral scrolls, vines, hexagons, octagons, roundels, trefoil and quatrefoil lozenges, and 'animal interlace' (snake tails, Naga heads, bird beaks, fishtails and lions). Also, figures of dancers, warriors, Garuda, *thep* (angels), *apsara* (heavenly dancers), cumbersome elephants and the masked pantheon of the Ramakien epic are all miraculously rendered fluid.

Architecture and crafts merge, with tapering spires, redented corners, incisions and trapezoid lines scaling up or down, so that, for example, lacquer boxes take the shape of altar bases, *hor trai* (libraries) or lotus buds. In garlands and offerings, flowers and leaves are folded and threaded into shapes themselves inspired by flowers and leaves. The effect is of art folded back upon itself, combining complex detail with seamless finishing.

More rustic than *lai thai*, which grew out of the courts, village handicrafts apply patterns for practical ends from basketry to textiles. Handwoven cloth replicates templates unique to each village, most ambitiously in *mudmee* images woven from pre-tie-dyed thread. Simple natural materials – bamboo slivers, weathered wood, interwoven reeds – give texture to much of the nation's new craftwork. Contemporary Thai design (*see p144* **High Thai designs**) is a continuing outgrowth of both classic and rustic traditions, while also drawing on a well of international influences.

A *naga*, with its multi-headed hood.

Painters place Thai temples within natural landscapes resembling Western paintings and among figures with dynamic movement, notably at **Wat Suwannaram**. These stand beside Chinese panels depicting fretwork, antiques and the surreal Thai bonsai: globular *mai dut* bushes. Masterpieces of this merger include the *Ramakien* murals at **Wat Phra** **Kaew**. Other attempts, as at **Wat Bowoniwet**, result in a bizarre, Dali-esque fusion. This coded religious heritage remains a vibrant force in contemporary Thai arts.

FOREIGN FUSIONS
All Asian cultures experimented with foreign modes, but none mixed styles with such breathtaking abandon as the Thais. In

17th-century Ayutthaya and Lopburi Persian windows, Chinese gardens and French mirrored wall panels were in vogue. Countless examples reflect the international outlooks of Kings Rama IV, V and VI, most notably the Gothic interior of **Wat Rachabophit** and the kaleidoscope of Thai, Chinese, Gothic and baroque at **Bang Pa-in Palace**.

Most prevalent is the gleeful appropriation of Greco-Roman classicism. The archetypal example, **Chakri Maha Prasat Throne Hall** in the Grand Palace, caps a Renaissance-style marble edifice with Thai roofs rising to three soaring spires. Its English architect, John Chinitz, had planned for a dome, but Chao Phraya Srisuriyawongse, the former regent, convinced King Rama V to inject a Thai accent. Dubbed 'a *farang* in a Thai hat', this odd hybrid solidified into a 20th-century institutional template visible in the **National Museum**, **National Library** and myriad ministries.

Urban architecture has otherwise been dominated by the Chinese shophouse. As in the Peranakan Sino-Malay culture, Sino-Thai *hong taew* (literally, 'row house') blend the crowded mercantile streets of old China – where people live above trading premises – and colonial Portuguese masonry terraces, with shutters and colonnades. Prime examples adorn old Bangkok, especially **Tha Chang**, while wooden shophouses survive in pockets in Bangkok and at **Nakorn Chaisri Market** and Chachoengsao's **Baan Talad Mai**. The part-timber mansions of nobility and Chinese merchants also borrowed tropical colonial devices such as porches, verandas and fretworked vents. Many are now restaurants, like **Café Siam**, **China House**, and **Starbucks** on Thanon Khao San.

Today's streetscapes still aspire to Western classicism, though often as clip-art appendages devoid of proportion, context or restraint. Countless shophouses, mansions and offices boast Roman columns, balustrades and sculptures – in whitewashed concrete. Even temples aren't immune. Extreme examples are the domed, porticoed skyscrapers **State Tower** and **Chatpetch Tower** along the river. Others co-opt Gothic windows and spires, or even pharaonic pilasters (**Grand Hyatt Erawan Hotel**).

Modernism and postmodernism also made inroads, especially in skyscrapers, with novelty excesses like the 'Robot Building' (**Bank of Asia**) and **Elephant Building**. For those with retro taste, Chinatown is a trove of art deco, the **Atlanta Hotel** a 1950s diorama, while modernist remnants from the 1960s and '70s include Silom's **Dusit Thani Hotel**, the multi-cylinder **Fifty-nine Condo** off Witthayu,

Buddha sculpture at the **National Gallery**.

and motel-esque Sukhumvit inns. 'Ranch-style' homes in leafy compounds also line many residential *soi*, some converted into bars or restaurants (**A Day**, **Le Lys**, **Pickle Factory**).

Among attempts at Thai modernism, the best example, the Siam InterContinental Hotel (styled after a royal hat), was demolished in 2002, though Thai accents continue in the gilded peaks of **SCB Park Plaza**, Ratchayothin and on Sathorn Road, with the cascading slopes of **Harindhorn Tower**, the reflecting pools of the **Sukhothai Hotel**, and the trapezoids of **Sathorn City Tower** and **Diamond Tower**.

This gleeful fusion is so sustained it could be considered inherently Thai. Whether you think it kitsch or innovative, globalised Thai architecture has produced some of the world's most surprising buildings.

▶ Many of the buildings mentioned here are covered in more detail in other sections, notably **Sightseeing** and **Beach Escapes**.

Where to Stay

ideal location apartments/
short or long-term

BOON's residence

langsuan   662 652 2255/2288
naratiwasrajanakarin10   662 676 3636
mobile   666 304 2288
email   boonresidence@gmail.com

OPENING END OF 2005

design
budget
hotel

tel
66
(O)1
912
5577

66
(O)1
643
9928

the
PINQUINO
Bangkok

www.thepinquino.com
6/11 De jo rd. Bangruk Bangkok 10500 Thailand

THAILAND YOUR WAY!

- **Competitive Airfares**
- **Excursions**
- **Diving Holidays**
- **Golfing Holidays**
- **Escorted Touring**
- **Hotel Accommodation**
- **Luxury Train Journeys**

AWARD WIINING TOUR OPERATOR

ABTA
W2488

IATA
ACCREDITED AGENT

eTours-Online
Emerald Global Ltd

THAILAND

Please call for your
FREE 44 page brochure

Email:	tours@emerald.co.uk
Tel:	020 7312 1708
Web:	www.etours-online.com

Where to Stay

From flophouses to penthouses, hotels in Bangkok offer a lot for your baht.

When the likes of Joseph Conrad and Somerset Maugham were visiting Bangkok a century ago the only place to stay was the **Oriental**. Some present-day literati may still drop the name with a certain hauteur, yet this institution has now been rivalled – and even overtaken – by a clutch of world-class hotels. It's not just plush properties on the river – the **Shangri-La**, **Peninsula** and **Marriott Bangkok Resort** – there are also devotees of the **Four Seasons** (**Regent**), **Grand Hyatt Erawan**, **Sheraton Grande Sukhumvit** and, especially, the suavely chic **Sukhothai**. Dated grandes dames like the **Dusit Thani** and **Nai Lert Park** (formerly the Hilton) recently had facelifts to match swish, youthful arrivals, like the **Conrad**, **Triple Two** and the city's minimalist benchmark, the **Metropolitan**, a sister to the London pioneer (see p41 **Hip hotels**).

The top-end is great for indulgent splurges, but there's been an upgrading at the budget end too. Today's travellers seem to be somewhat richer than the penny-pinching backpackers who turned Thanon Khao San into the world's most famous flophouse. Now gap-year lawyers-to-be wheel their backpacks into modish lodges and boutique guesthouses in the **Banglamphu**, **Phra Nakorn** and **Dusit** districts. Equally convenient for the old town are the charming, if faded, no frills hotels of **Chinatown**.

Handy for mass transit, **Downtown** offers the most rooms, with higher (but still often reasonable) prices and better services, plus shopping, dining and nightlife. Rooms in **Bangrak** are at a slight premium on account of their business and nightlife convenience. Those prioritising shopping and dining settle in **Patumwan** or **Sukhumvit**, which has plenty of mid-range rooms, thanks to the Indian-run inns around **Nana**.

ROOMS AND RATES

Single rooms can often sleep two, while doubles may have two double beds. Some beds could even sleep three. So ask to view rooms first. In guesthouses and cheap Chinese hotels, rates can vary widely according to the room's size, whether it has a fan or air-conditioning, and en suite or shared bathrooms. Thanks to Thai communal sleeping habits, resorts in particular often have a few huge rooms. Bangkok has a habit of snaring visitors, and monthly rates start as low as B10,000, with studios and

apartments from B13,000. At the other extreme discreet motels charge by the hour. Thailand's ban on smoking in air-conditioned buildings includes hotels, but allows smoking rooms.

We've divided areas by price category, according to the cost of a standard double room: **deluxe** (from B6,000), **expensive** (B3,000-B5,999), **moderate** (B1,000-B2,999), **budget** (under B1,000). Note: big hotels add service and VAT (known as 'plus plus' or '++'). Rates given are for high season (Nov-Mar), but off-season discounts can be huge. 'Family' means a multi-bed room. Some hotels list their rates in dollars, but you can pay in baht. All hotels listed below have air-conditioning, unless we mention fan-cooled rooms.

BOOKINGS AND BACKGROUND

Booking in advance avoids traipsing around suitcase-unfriendly Bangkok streets. The better hotels fill up at busy times, but you can always find a room. Rates at major hotels may be higher if booked within Thailand.

The **Thailand Hotels Association** (www.thaihotels.org) offers information and reservations, and has a stall at the airport. The best website by far for cheaper prices is **www.hotelsdirect.com**, while other good online booking sites are **www.asia-hotels. com/thailand**, **www.asiarooms.com**, **www.bookingthaihotel.com**, **www.hotel**

The best Hotels

For eccentricity
Reflections Rooms in Bangkok (see p48) and **Atlanta Hotel** (see p47).

For in-house spas
The **Oriental**, **Shangri-La** (for both, see p42) and the **Banyan Tree Bangkok** (see p48).

For rooms with a view
Peninsula (see p49), **Banyan Tree Bangkok** (see p48) and **Riverview Guesthouse** (see p42).

For style credibility
The **Metropolitan** and **Sukhothai** (for both, see p48).

The riverside pool deck at the **Peninsula**. *See p40.*

thailand.com, www.sawadee.com and
www.siam.net. For hostels run to IYHA
standards, contact the **Thai Youth Hostels
Association** (0 2628 7413-5, www.tyha.org,
bangkok@tyha.org) and check **www.hostel
world.com**, which also lists good guesthouses.

Phra Nakorn & Banglamphu

A backpacker enclave since the early 1980s,
Thanon Khao San has grown from rabbit-
hutch guesthouses (immortalised on page and
screen in *The Beach*) to embrace more modern
comfort. But as this 'Freak Street' is becoming
increasingly cacophonous, many travellers are
opting for the quieter confines of **Thanon
Rambuttri**, **Thanon Phra Arthit** and,
towards Dusit, the soi off **Thanon Samsen**.

Deluxe

Chakrabongse Villas
*396 Thanon Maharat, Phra Nakorn (0 2622
3356-8/fax 0 2622 1900/www.thaivillas.com).
Tha Ratchinee.* **Rooms** 3. **Rates** double $160-
$200. **Credit** MC, V. **Map** p248 A4.
A little-known jewel on the river, this 19th-century
mansion built by Prince Chakrabongse Bhuvanath
now has three Thai-style guest villas by his granddaughter MR Narisa Chakrabongse (a publisher and
mother of musician/actor Hugo Chakrabongse).
Exquisitely furnished with teak, silk and modern
amenities, the rooms offer seclusion, views of Wat
Arun across the river from the boardwalks and dining pavilions, plus a pool in the lush garden – all
with the grand mansion as a backdrop. Expect a
warm welcome, but book early if you want to stay
here. Just outside the gate you're straight into the
Bangkok of the imagination, with Wat Pho, the
flower market, the apothecaries of Tha Tien and
river boat services on your doorstep.
Services *Internet (wireless). Parking (free). Pool.
Restaurants (1). Smoking rooms. TV (music/
widescreen/DVD).*

Moderate

Buddy Lodge
*265 Thanon Khaosan, Banglamphu (0 2629 4477/
fax 0 2629 4744/www.buddylodge.com).* **Rooms** 76.
Rates double B1,800; deluxe double B2,200; superior
double B2,400. **Credit** MC, V. **Map** p248 B3.
Resembling a toy town hall, the red brick façade at
Buddy Lodge hides modern rooms with olde worlde
fittings, such as wooden floors, writing desks, old-
fashioned lamps and white timber walls. The balconies in the deluxe rooms are bigger than the
standard rooms, and are nice spots for a nightcap.
Rooms on the east have views of the Golden Mount.
Services *Bars (1). Concierge. Internet (high-speed).
Pool. Restaurants (1). Room service. Spa. TV.*

Budget

Barn Thai Guesthouse
*27 Trok Mayom, Thanon Chakkraphong,
Banglamphu (0 2281 9041).* **Rooms** 15. **Rates**
double B200-B300. **No credit cards. Map** p248 C4.
'Call me Grandma,' says the elderly owner at Barn
Thai Guesthouse, one of few traditional houses hereabouts that still accepts guests. Her hospitality, near-
flawless English and local knowledge are all part of
Barn Thai's allure. Apart from Grandma it's worth
knowing that the rooms are fan-only, spartan and
spotless, with Western-style toilets. It can, however,
get a bit noisy come the evening time.

Mango Lagoon Place
*30 Soi Rambuttri, Banglamphu (tel/fax
0 2281 4783 ext 200).* **Rooms** 40. **Rates** double
B700-B800. **No credit cards. Map** p248 B2.
Tucked behind Wat Chanasongkram, this pleasant
guesthouse – opened in 2004 – has a cute garden
overlooked by all the rooms, which are light, airy,
spacious and well appointed, with hot water. Worth
the price, despite the lack of a lift.
Services *Bars (1). Business centre. Concierge.
Smoking rooms. Restaurants (1). Room service.
TV room.*

My House
*37 Soi Chanasongkhram, Banglamphu (0 2282
9263-4).* **Rooms** 60. **Rates** double with fan B350;
double with air-con B500. **No credit cards.**
Map p248 B3.
The area behind Wat Chanasongkram seems to be
in danger of becoming a cheap drinking substitute
for Thanon Khao San, but its former tranquillity
remains intact as this tidy, five-storey guesthouse.
A traditional Thai-style entrance, with accompanying large lounge/restaurant, belies rooms that are a
touch generic, but perfectly clean and comfy.
Services *Internet (pay terminal). Restaurants (1).
TV room.*

Nakorn Pink Hotel
*9/1 Samsen Soi 6, Banglamphu (0 2281 6574/fax
0 2282 3727).* **Rooms** 81. **Rates** double with fan
B300; double with air-con B400. *Hot water* B60
supplement. **No credit cards. Map** p248 C2.
Of the many old Chinese-style hotels off Samsen
Road, this is the plum. In sharp contrast to the pas-
tel-coloured exterior, the rooms themselves are particularly well decked out with clunky old wooden
furniture and small fridges. And while the hotel
doesn't have a restaurant, you'll find at the mouth
of the *soi* a fine seafood eaterie.
Services *Internet (high-speed). Parking (free).
TV (pay movies).*

Peachy Guesthouse
*10 Thanon Phra Arthit, Banglamphu (0 2281
6471/6659).* **Rooms** 56. **Rates** double with fan
& shared bathroom B160; double with air-con &
en suite B400 (shared bathroom B200). **No credit
cards. Map** p248 B2.

While many nearby lodgings induce claustrophobia, this converted school offers large double beds, wardrobes and a beer garden/restaurant serving breakfasts, crêpes, real coffee and Spanish omelettes. If that should all seem too much like home, remember that it's rumoured to be haunted by the spirits of an old lady and a handyman.

Services *Internet (pay terminal). Restaurants (1). TV room.*

Thonburi

Deluxe

Marriott Bangkok Resort & Spa

257/1-3 Thanon Charoennakorn (0 2476 0022/ fax 0 2476 1120/www.marriotthotels.com/bkkth). Saphan Taksin BTS then shuttle boat. **Rooms** 413. **Rates** double $210-$240; suite $300-$1,800. **Credit** AmEx, DC, MC, V. **Map** p250 D7.

Situated downstream from the other luxury river hotels, this unpretentious establishment arcs attractively around a verdant pool area and canal. The Marriott has plentiful facilities and dining options, including the excellent Mandara Spa (with walled garden treatment suites), a mini-mall and Trader Vic's, which has a great Sunday jazz brunch. It may be a bit of a trek to shops and nightlife, but guests relish the shuttle boat trip to the Saphan Taksin BTS/Pier and River City. The hotel's teak barge, *Manohra*, hosts dinner and overnight cruises.

Services *Bars (1). Business centre. Concierge. Disabled-adapted rooms. Gym. Internet (high-speed, wireless, pay terminal). Parking (free). Pool. Restaurants (4). Room service. Smoking rooms. Spa. TV (suites: music/DVD).*

Peninsula

333 Thanon Charoennakorn (0 2861 2888/fax 0 2861 1112/www.peninsula.com). Saphan Taksin BTS then shuttle boat. **Rooms** 370. **Rates** double $260-$400; suite $980-$2,000. **Credit** AmEx, DC, MC, V. **Map** p250 D7.

Voted Best Asian Hotel by *Condé Nast Traveller* readers in 2004, this stylish modern hotel has become the hotel of choice for those seeking an alternative to the slightly ageing (and more expensive) Oriental across the Chao Praya river. As you would expect, the interior exudes elegant sophistication, with impressive collections of contemporary Thai art. The rooms are all large and well-equipped, each of them offering fantastic panoramas of the river and Downtown beyond. Restaurants Jester's (Pacific Rim fusion; *see p109*) and Mei Jiang (Cantonese) are the city's best practitioners of both styles of cuisines. Beyond a canal, a five-pool deck cascades to the riverbank. The hotel boats, with romantic fairylights at night, ferry you to the other side of the river, to the SkyTrain and to River City.

Services *Bars (1). Business centre. Concierge. Disabled-adapted rooms. Gym. Internet (high-speed). Smoking rooms. Parking (free). Pools (5). Restaurants (4). Room service. TV (music/DVD).*

Expensive

Ibrik Resort

256 Soi Wat Rakang, Thanon Arun-Amrin (0 2848 9220/fax 0 2411 1183/www.ibrikresort.com). Boat from Tha Chang or Tha Prachan Pier to Tha Wat Rakang. **Rooms** 3. **Rates** double B2,800-B4,000. **Credit** AmEx, MC, V. **Map** p248 A4.

This trio of unique balconied rooms – called River, Sunshine and Moonlight – features pared-back design and oriental touches. With boats the main transport, Ibrik is a retreat destination, boasting characterful riverscapes of the Grand Palace.

Services *Restaurants (1). TV (widescreen).*
Other locations: 235/16 Thanon Sathorn, South.

Budget

The Artist's Place

61-63 Soi Tiem Boon Yang, Thanon Krung (0 2862 0056/fax 0 2862 0074). **Rooms** 12. **Rates** double with fan B180-B280; double with air-con B350-B450. **No credit cards.**

Thai artist Charlee Sodprasert has run this slightly ramshackle guesthouse, gallery and art school for a decade. Rooms are little more than a mattress and pillow, with a shared bathroom, but it's a unique experience. There's a common room where you can consume your own food and drink. The Artist's Place can be tricky to find, so call for directions.

Services *Business centre. Internet (pay terminal). Parking (free). Restaurant. TV room.*

Dusit

Budget

Budget options line **Thanon Si Ayutthaya**, between the National Library and **Kaloang** riverside restaurant (*see p109*). Village shops, a temple and bar-restaurants frequented by young Thais add to the charm.

Baan Phiman Resort

123 Samsen Soi 5 (0 2282 5594). **Rooms** 19. **Rates** double with fan B200 (*in hut* B400); double with air-con B500; tent B100. **No credit cards.** **Map** p248 C2.

The slogan for this strange complex amid an old community is 'the Romance of River Life'. Choose between bungalows right on the river or small rooms in a traditional house. It has a garden, riverside sun deck and a very cheap restaurant, plus two tents, equipped with a mattress, small fan and light.

Services *Bars (1). Business centre. Internet (pay terminal). Restaurants (1). Room service. TV room.*

Sri-Ayutthaya Guesthouse

23/11 Sri Ayutthaya Soi 14 (0 2282 5942/ 0 2281 6829). **Rooms** 16. **Rates** double with fan B450 (shared bathroom B350); double with air-con B500. **No credit cards.** **Map** p248 C1.

Hip hotels

The emergence of design hotels in Bangkok came to the world's attention with the opening of the **Metropolitan** (*see p48*). For the über-chic Singaporean hotel group to choose Bangkok over front-rank Asian cities wasn't misplaced, but rather a shrewd move to help define a rapidly evolving destination. With its artistic sensibility and craft heritage, Thailand has a huge design potential. This process had begun long before Kathryn Ong brought the Met to the Big Mango (along with Club 21 fashion franchises to the swish Erawan mall; *see p138*). Over a decade ago, Ed Tuttle pioneered the honing of Thai lines into a modern aesthetic at **Sukhothai** (*see p48; pictured right*) and Phuket's **Amanpuri** (*see p220*).

Contemporary Thai style boomed after the 1997 crash and it has been adopted by countless hotels, bars and restaurants, starting with the **Peninsula** (*see p40*), which also brought Thai modern art into the frame; and the **Sofitel Silom** (*see p42*). Dowdy establishments like the **Dusit Thani** (*see p42*) had no option but to strip out fussy trimmings and thus reveal its astonishing 1970s geometric structure.

The first new boutique hotel, **Triple Two Silom** (*see p43*), draws heavily on the Christian Liaigre cream-and-dark-brown look that so suits Asian aesthetics. But it also brightens its uncluttered spaces with invigorating colour.

The use of vari-hued light to impart mood, so redolent of Shrager/Starck hotels, has often been slapdash, but worked wonderfully at the **Conrad** (*see p43*). Its 'design with attitude' concept, applied to the finest of details by creative agency InHouse, has succeeded so well that it's influencing the Conrad chain's brand.

Boutique hotels are, by definition, petite. But none come smaller than the three unique riverside rooms of **Ibrik Resort** (*see p40*). The **Bangkok Boutique Hotel** (*see p46*) is good but tries perhaps too hard, as its name hints. The **Davis** (*see p46*) varies the design for each room, but the most individualistic boutique option is **Reflections Rooms in Bangkok** (*see p48*). Owner Anusorn Ngernyuang, the king of kitsch for a decade, invited Borek Sipek (a Czech version of Philippe Starck) to create this playful pink landmark. Artists transformed each room down to bed and bath, walls and windows. Guests enter realms of imagination from romance to sexiness, running water to recycled materials, pop art to radical cartoons. Bangkok hasn't just gone boutique, it's given birth to something genuinely original.

With traditional Thai touches, like wooden angels set in the brick walls, and a downstairs restaurant full of handicrafts, Buddha images and photos of Bangkok in 1917, this three-floor guesthouse is one of the area's classiest acts. The small rooms have rustic decor and stone-walled bathrooms with saloon doors. For cheaper digs, the owner has another guesthouse down the *soi*.

Services *Internet (high-speed, pay terminal). Restaurants (1). Room service. TV room.*
Other locations: Tawee Guesthouse 83 Sri Ayutthaya Soi 14, Dusit (0 2280 1447).

Chinatown

Moderate

Grand China Princess
215 Thanon Yaowarat (0 2224 9977/fax 0 2224 7999/www.grandchina.com). **Rooms** 165. **Rates** double B2,200-B4,000; suite B4,500-B8,000. **Credit** AmEx, DC, MC, V. **Map** p248 C5.

A great base for exploring the old town and Chinatown, the Grand China Princess has large

Where to Stay

rooms, some sporting huge balconies overlooking the city and the river. The top floor has Bangkok's only revolving club lounge, open in the evenings. Facilities are a bit worn and the decor rather thrown together, but it rewards those after some chaos and character.
Services *Bars (2). Business centre. Concierge. Disabled-adapted rooms. Gym. Internet (high-speed, wireless, pay terminal). Parking (free). Pool. Restaurants (4). Room service. Smoking rooms. TV (pay movies).*

Budget

New Empire Hotel
57 Thanon Yaowarat (0 2234 6990-6/ fax 0 2234 6997/www.newempirehotel.com). **Rooms** 130. **Rates** double B650-B720. **No credit cards.** **Map** p248 C5.
At the very top of Chinatown's main drag, the Empire is clean, cheap and comfortable, with well-equipped rooms, carpets and wallpaper straight out of a Wong Kar Wai movie. The staff speak just enough English for essential exchanges.
Services *Concierge. Disabled-adapted rooms. Internet (high-speed). Parking (free). Restaurants (1). Room service. Smoking rooms. TV.*

Riverview Guesthouse
768 Thanon Songwad (0 2235 8501/fax 0 2237 5428). **Rooms** 40. **Rates** double with fan B200-B450; double with air-con B690. **Credit** AmEx. **Map** p250 D6.
This guesthouse is very basic, but great value, and quiet, clean and friendly. It offers the chance to experience 'old' Bangkok – not least as you try to find it deep in the atmospheric maze of Chinatown alleys. The higher rooms do indeed overlook the Chao Phraya, as does the top-floor restaurant. The largest air-conditioned room has a fridge and (Thai) TV.
Services *Internet (pay terminal). Restaurants (1). Room service. Smoking rooms. TV room.*

Bangrak

Deluxe

Dusit Thani
946 Thanon Rama IV (0 2236 9999/fax 0 2236 6400/www.dusit.com). Saladaeng BTS/Silom subway. **Rooms** 517. **Rates** double $210-$290; suite $500-$2,500. **Credit** AmEx, DC, MC, V. **Map** p251 G6.
Dignitaries and royalty favour this large, spired establishment, which soars imperiously above Lumphini Park, Patpong and both BTS and subway. Its geometric 1970s architecture provides some interesting angles. The interior decor has been stripped back and its dowdy penthouse restaurant transformed by über-chic D'Sens. In MyBar, located in the lower lobby, live jazz complements garden views. Ringing the waterfall courtyard, Deverana Spa is perhaps the most beautiful, meditative and accomplished of the city's hotel spas (*see p177*).

Services *Bars (3). Business centre. Concierge. Disabled-adapted rooms. Gym. Internet (high-speed). Parking (free). Pool. Restaurants (9). Room service. Smoking rooms. Spa. TV (pay movies/widescreen).*

The Oriental
48 Thanon Charoen Krung Soi 38 (0 2659 9000/ fax 0 2659 0000/www.mandarinoriental.com). Saphan Taksin BTS. **Rooms** 396. **Rates** double $235-$440; suite $720-$1,500. **Credit** AmEx, DC, MC, V. **Map** p250 D7.
One of the world's grand hotels, this riverside institution started as a lodge for European traders. The original building burnt down in 1865 and two Danish naval captains, Jarck and Salje, constructed the hotel in its current location 11 years later. The hotel soon attracted the cultured guests for which it's famed. In 1887 another Dane, HN Anderson, built a more luxurious addition, now known as the Authors' Wing, containing suites named after the writers who have stayed here, starting a year after its completion with an unknown Joseph Conrad, and followed by Somerset Maugham, Noel Coward, Graham Greene, John le Carré and, er, Barbara Cartland. If you want to experience a piece of living history, the Oriental is still *the* hotel in Bangkok.
Services *Bars (1). Business centre. Concierge. Disabled-adapted rooms. Gym. Internet (high-speed, wireless). Parking (free). Pool. Restaurants (7). Room service. Smoking rooms. Spa. TV (pay movies/music/ suites: widescreen /DVD/TV room).*

Shangri-La
89 Soi Wat Suan Plu, Thanon Charoen Krung (0 2236 7777/fax 0 2236 8579/www.shangri-la.com). Saphan Taksin BTS. **Rooms** 799. **Rates** double $240-$320; suite $400-$2,500. **Credit** AmEx, DC, MC, V. **Map** p250 D7.
The largest hotel on the river, with two wings, two pools and leafy grounds, this branch of the Singapore chain is also one of the best, as its many awards testify. Linked to the BTS and Expressboats, it has first-rate service, facilities and dining options, including Angelini's (*see p112*), a family Sunday brunch at refurbished NEXT2 and river cruises on its luxury yacht. The modern rooms, with oriental accents, overlook either city or river. The new Chi Spa specialises in Himalayan healing arts (*see p176*).
Services *Bars (3). Business centre. Concierge. Disabled-adapted rooms. Gym. Internet (high-speed, wireless). Parking (free). Pool (2). Restaurants (5). Room service. Smoking rooms. Spa. TV (pay movies/ suites: music/widescreen/DVD/TV room).*

Sofitel Silom
188 Thanon Silom (0 2238 1991/fax 0 2238 1999/ www.sofitel.com). Chong Nonsi BTS. **Rooms** 454. **Rates** double $119-$147; suite $205-$210. **Credit** AmEx, DC, MC, V. **Map** p250 F7.
The first hotel in town to decorate its rooms in contemporary Thai design, this high-rise in the business district also exudes an elegant, French 'art de vivre' feel. It is a stimulating place to stay, with beautifully harmonised hues, smart furnishings and

Where to Stay

flamboyant artwork. To go with the decor there are tasteful refreshment options available, such as a branch of Parisian patisserie Le Nôtre and the panoramic penthouse wine bar V9 (*see p129*). **Services** *Bars (2). Business centre. Concierge. Disabled-adapted rooms. Gym. Internet (high-speed, wireless). Parking (free). Pool. Restaurants (3). Room service. Smoking rooms. Spa. TV (pay movies/music/widescreen/suites: DVD/TV room).*

Expensive

The Siam Heritage

115/1 Thanon Surawong (0 2353 6101/fax 0 2353 6123/www.thesiamheritage.com). Saladaeng BTS/Silom subway. **Rooms** 69. **Rates** double B4,900-B5,700; suite B7,100-B9,600. **Credit** AmEx, MC, V. **Map** p250 E7.
On entering this new boutique hotel beside Patpong, you are greeted by some striking artwork and incredibly thick teak boards. Decorated conservatively in a medley of Lanna, Rattanakosin and repro-Thai furnishings, the well-equipped rooms divide bed and living areas with custom-crafted wooden panels. There's a 'Balinese' rooftop pool, jacuzzi, 24-hour fitness centre, the Hermitage Spa and a restaurant meant to resemble Vimanmek Palace.
Services *Bars (1). Business centre. Concierge. Gym. Smoking rooms. Internet (wireless). Parking (free). Pool. Restaurants (1). Room service. Spa. TV (pay movies/widescreen/suites: music/DVD).*

Triple Two Silom

222 Thanon Silom (0 2627 2222/fax 0 2627 2300/ www.tripletwosilom.com). Saladaeng BTS/Silom subway. **Rooms** 75. **Rates** double B4,900; suite B5,200. **Credit** AmEx, DC, MC, V. **Map** p250 E7.
Bangkok's first contemporary Thai boutique hotel, which opened in 2002, Triple Two Silom has just the right kind of attitude and service to appropriate the mantle. The colours are mixed vibrantly by the use of various unusual materials: ornate marble floors covered with dashing mosaics, strikingly woven rugs flung carefully upon wooden boards, collaged panels of old photographs. Some of the finely appointed rooms overlook a garden. The pool and fitness facilities are in the adjoining parent hotel, the Narai, which is as drab as Triple Two is refreshing.
Services *Bars (1). Business centre. Concierge. Disabled-adapted rooms. Gym. Internet (high-speed, wireless, dataport). Parking (free). Pool. Restaurants (1). Room service. Smoking rooms. TV (DVD).*

Tarntawan Place Hotel

119/5-10 Thanon Surawong (0 2238 2620/ fax 0 2238 3228/www.tarntawan.com). Saladaeng BTS/Silom subway. **Rooms** 75. **Rates** double B3,000; suite B4,000-B6,000. **Credit** AmEx, DC, MC, V. **Map** p250 F6.
Bang in the middle of Patpong, yet also relatively quiet, this small hotel forgoes chic for other qualities: cosiness, convenience and efficiency. The Tarntawan Place Hotel is unusually gay-friendly for Bangkok. Find Utopia Tours in the lobby.

Services *Bars (1). Business centre. Concierge. Internet (wireless). Parking (free). Restaurants (1). Room service. Smoking rooms. TV (pay movies/ music/suites: widescreen/DVD/TV room).*

Moderate

La Résidence

173/8-9 Thanon Surawong (0 2266 5400-2/ fax 0 2237 9322). Saladaeng BTS/Silom subway. **Rooms** 26. **Rates** double B1,000-B1,700; suite B3,000-B3,800. **Credit** AmEx, MC, V. **Map** p250 F6.
Gleaning much repeat business from regulars, this small modern hotel is out of earshot of Patpong. Each room has its own theme, with colour schemes, wallpaper and art conjuring up different moods, whether cosy living room, grand European salon or dramatic red-walled suite. It's clean and friendly, and fairly good value (breakfast is extra), but has no leisure facilities save for a small library.
Services *Business centre. Concierge. Internet (high-speed, pay terminal). Parking (free). Restaurants (1). Room service. TV (TV room/ suites: pay movies/music/DVD).*

Rose Hotel

118 Thanon Surawong (0 2266 8268-72/ fax 0 2266 8096). **Rooms** 70. **Rates** double B1,290-B1,520; suite B2,340. **Credit** AmEx, DC, MC, V. **Map** p250 E7.
A long-time favourite, this handy hotel has had a face-lift thanks to the new generation of family owners. An urban retro look has replaced the previous kitsch, while retaining the atmosphere and service from yesteryear's friendly staff. Each room feels and smells brand new, and comes with a generously sized bath. Just don't expect a view.
Services *Business centre. Concierge. Internet (high-speed). Parking (free). Restaurants (1). Room service. Smoking rooms. TV.*

Pathumwan

Deluxe

Conrad Bangkok

87 Thanon Witthayu (0 2690 9999/fax 0 2690 9980/www.conradbangkok.com). Ploenchit BTS. **Rooms** 392. **Rates** double $240-$305; suite $460-$1,900. **Credit** AmEx, DC, MC, V. **Map** p251 H5.
This elegant tower hotel has, in just two years, achieved its aim of being the chicest Downtown hotel and wears the fact on its sleeves, literally: the staff have designer uniforms. The warm, luxurious decor features creative touches like vibrant carpets, backlit silk and flower installations by Sakul Intakul, though the window-walled bathrooms may not appeal to all. The Diplomat Bar (*see p129*) sets a suave jazzy note, and Liu Chinese restaurant was designed by Zhang Jin Jie of Beijing's hottest eatery, Green T House. Wi-fi enables laptoppers to access Bangkok's fastest internet link and the spa/health

What Londoners take when they go out.

LONDON'S WEEKLY LISTINGS BIBLE

club has extensive roof gardens. The bar, Italianate restaurant, ballroom and adjoining All Seasons Retail Centre have additional entrances on Soi Ruam Rudee. A late check-out at 4pm is, where possible, on offer at no extra charge.
Services Bars (2). Business centre. Concierge. Disabled-adapted rooms. Gym. Internet (high-speed, wireless). Parking (free). Pool. Restaurants (4). Room service. Smoking rooms. Spa. TV (pay movies/music/widescreen/suites: DVD).

Four Seasons Hotel

155 Thanon Ratchadamri (0 2254 9999/0 2251 6127/fax 0 2254 5390/www.fourseasons.com). Ratchadamri BTS. **Rooms** 340. **Rates** double $250-$300; suite $380-$2,200. **Credit** AmEx, DC, MC, V. **Map** p251 G5.
The former Regent has neatly incorporated Thai handicrafts and design influences (murals, silk, teak) into its furnishings, while still retaining its contemporary style and functionality. An impressive place for a rendezvous, the lobby wows with its murals and backlit marble columns. The stylish rooms offer generous bathrooms and separate dressing areas, while exclusive villas crown the roof. The Tony Chi-designed restaurants are impeccable and among the city's best – notably, Biscotti (Italian; *see p115*), Madison (grill) and Shintaro (Japanese) – while the sophisticated Aqua bar shares the space in the top-end atrium shopping arcade with a great pâtisserie, an exhibition and much running water.
Services Bars (1). Business centre. Concierge. Disabled-adapted rooms. Gym. Internet (high-speed, wireless, shared terminal). Parking (free). Pool. Restaurants (8). Room service. Smoking rooms. Spa. TV (pay movies/music/widescreen/by request: DVD).

Grand Hyatt Erawan

494 Thanon Ratchadamri (0 2254 1234/fax 0 2253 5856/www.bangkok.hyatt.com). Chidlom BTS. **Rooms** 387. **Rates** double $280-$1,800. **Credit** AmEx, DC, MC, V. **Map** p251 G5.
A sleek, contemporary aesthetic permeates the rooms behind the Grand Hyatt Erawan's brash neo-Egyptian façade. Furnished with hardwood, silk and modern Thai, these welcoming, businesslike rooms have spacious, elaborate marble bathrooms. The hotel retains a strong local following for the Spasso music bar (*see p187*), You & Mee noodle shop and the Chinese Restaurant, which makes dramatic use of crackled glass. The hotel connects through to the new Erawan mall, which contains the sophisticated Erawan Tea Room.
Services Bars (3). Business centre. Concierge. Disabled-adapted rooms. Gym. Internet (high-speed, dataport, shared terminal). Parking (free). Pool. Restaurants (6). Room service. Smoking rooms. Spa. TV (pay movies/widescreen/suites: music/DVD).

InterContinental Bangkok

973 Thanon Ploenchit (0 2656 0444/fax 0 2656 0555/www.ichotelsgroup.com). Chidlom BTS. **Rooms** 381. **Rates** double $300-$350; suite $500-$2,000. **Credit** AmEx, DC, MC, V. **Map** p251 G4.

Located between Chidlom BTS and the glittering Gaysorn mall, this bulbous, glass-sheathed high-rise has morphed from Le Royal Meridien into the InterContinental Bangkok without too many obvious changes. Beautiful, luxurious, extravagant even, it offers expansive views from stylish, modern rooms, and serves one of Bangkok's best Sunday brunches at Espresso. There's a pleasant rooftop pool (37 floors up) with a swim-up bar and a small tropical garden. The old Le Meridien President sharing its forecourt has been completely remodelled as a Holiday Inn. Both boast location, location, location.
Services Bars (3). Business centre. Concierge. Disabled-adapted rooms. Gym. Internet (high-speed, wireless). Parking (free). Pool. Restaurants (2). Room service. Smoking rooms. Spa. TV (pay movies/music/widescreen/DVD/TV room).

Nai Lert Park Hotel

2 Thanon Witthayu (0 2253 0123/www.nailertpark. swissotel.com). Ploenchit BTS. **Rooms** 338. **Rates** double $200-$230; suite $350-$1,500. **Credit** AmEx, DC, MC, V. **Map** p251 H5.
One of the few Bangkok hotels with expansive grounds, the refurbished former Hilton is now managed as a Swissotel by Singapore's Raffles International. All rooms have private balconies overlooking the lush canalside garden, and the bathrooms are bright and airy. Among its assets are the free-form swimming pool, the artsy arcade Promenade Decor and a lobby bar, Cyn, with suspended globular seats. At one side of the hotel stands the phallic Chao Mae Tubtim Shrine.
Services Bars (2). Business centre. Concierge. Disabled-adapted rooms. Gym. Internet (high-speed). Parking (free). Pool. Restaurants (5). Room service. Smoking rooms. Spa. TV (pay movies/music/widescreen/suites: DVD).

Expensive

Pathumwan Princess

444 Thanon Phayathai (0 2216 3700-29/fax 0 2216 3730-3/www.pprincess.com). National Stadium BTS. **Rooms** 462. **Rates** double B5,000-B6,600; suite B7,600-B8,400. **Credit** AmEx, DC, MC, V. **Map** p249/p250 F5.
Connected to the frenetic MBK and several other Siam Square malls, the Pathumwan Princess can hardly be said to count as a retreat, but with all conceivable facilities, and excellent transport and shopping links, it's certainly convenient. It's a family-friendly hotel (judging by the chaos in the foyer), and even the cheaper rooms are generously proportioned and comfortable. The 25m saltwater pool and the Olympic Health Club are both among the city's best, and the Korean restaurant is good. Staff are numerous and extremely helpful.
Services Bars (1). Business centre. Concierge. Disabled-adapted rooms. Gym. Internet (high-speed, wireless). Parking (free). Pool. Restaurants (6). Room service. Smoking rooms. Spa. TV (pay movies/suites: music/DVD).

Suk11 Guesthouse. *See p47.*

Budget

Between Jim Thompson's House and Siam Square, Kasemsan Soi 1 has developed into a friendly spot to stay for budget travellers.

Golden House

1025/5-9 Thanon Phloenchit (0 2252 9535-7/ fax 0 2252 9538/www.goldenhouses.net). **Rooms** 27. **Rates** double B1,300. **Credit** AmEx, MC, V. **Map** p251 H5.

Hidden away in a quiet, yet very convenient *soi* right beside Chidlom BTS, this guesthouse offers bright and clean standard-sized rooms.
Services *Business centre. Concierge. Internet (high-speed). Parking (free). Restaurants (1). Room service. Smoking rooms. TV.*

Reno Hotel

40 Kasemsan Soi 1, Thanon Rama I (0 2215 0026-7). National Stadium BTS. **Rooms** 57. **Rates** double B870-B1,180; suite B1,290. **Credit** MC, V. **Map** p250 F4.

The makeover that transformed the crisply styled lobby and made adjoining Reno Café into a hip hang-out hasn't yet extended to the dowdy rooms. But no matter – they're still clean and great value.
Services *Bars (1). Business centre. Concierge. Internet (high-speed). Parking (free). Pool. Restaurants (1). Room service. TV.*

White Lodge

36/8 Kasemsan Soi 1, Thanon Rama I (0 2215 3102). National Stadium BTS. **Rooms** 30. **Rates** double B400-B500; triple B600. **No credit cards.** **Map** p250 F4.

Despite competition from its budget neighbours, the small rooms here are extremely good value. Clean and functional, all rooms have air-con and a shower/toilet; some have TVs. There's also a tour desk and a solid range of street food options outside in the *soi*.
Services *Restaurants (1). TV room.*

Deluxe

Davis

88 Sukhumvit Soi 24, Thanon Rama IV end (0 2260 8000/fax 0 2204 0680/www.davis bangkok.net). Phrom Phong BTS then taxi. **Rooms** 165. **Rates** double B6,000-B8,000; suites B9,000-B18,000; Baan Thai B25,000-B30,000. **Credit** AmEx, DC, MC, V. **Map** p252 K7.

One of Bangkok's first boutique hotels, Davis was devised by massage parlour magnate Chuwit Kamonwisit. The rooms have radically individual designs, while the opulent public areas include the Saint Davis shopping arcade. Most interestingly, it includes one of the few places in Bangkok where you can stay in a traditional Thai-style house, at the Baan Davis compound on the quieter rear side.
Services *Bars (1). Business centre. Concierge. Disabled-adapted rooms. Gym. Internet (high-speed, wireless). Parking (free). Pools (2). Restaurants (2). Room service. Smoking rooms. Spa (2). TV (pay movies/music/widescreen).*

Sheraton Grande Sukhumvit

250 Sukhumvit Soi 12 (0 2654 8888/fax 0 2649 8000/www.starwoodhotels.com/bangkok). Asok BTS/Sukhumvit subway. **Rooms** 429. **Rates** double $250-$290; suite $450-$1,400. **Credit** AmEx, DC, MC, V. **Map** p251 J5.

There's no point in even thinking about this one unless you're comfortable haemorrhaging money. Yet, despite the haughty 'e' on Grand, the service is charming and excellent and, as you'd expect at these prices, the rooms are luxuriously finished, with fruit, slippers and robes. The pool is pleasant but small, with a spa attached. Among the restaurants, Basil (contemporary Thai) and Rossini (Italian) impress with impeccable food and mood, the Living Room hosts quality jazz and all three offer an awesome Sunday brunch. Riva's is a classy, if lacklustre, cover band venue. Booking for the Sheraton is essential and, owing to its year-round popularity, it doesn't need to offer low season rates.
Services *Bars (1). Business centre. Concierge. Disabled-adapted rooms. Gym. Internet (high-speed, wireless). Parking (free). Pool. Restaurants (6). Room service. Smoking rooms. Spa. TV (pay movies/widescreen/TV room).*

Moderate

Bangkok Boutique Hotel

241 Sukhumvit Soi 21 (Asoke) (0 2261 2850-4/fax 0 2664 0995). Asoke BTS/Sukhumvit subway. **Rooms** 54. **Rates** double B2,200-B3,950; suite B4,950-B6,000. **Credit** AmEx, MC, V. **Map** p252 K5.

The management has positioned this hotel rather obviously in the boutique market. We like the colourful and lively lobby design but the bijou rooms are rather standard, and the service isn't

Where to Stay

always up to scratch. However, its location close to the subway is useful, though the daytime traffic jams could frustrate your travel plans.
Services *Bars (1). Business centre. Concierge. Internet (dataport, high-speed, wireless). Parking (free). Restaurants (1). Room service. Smoking rooms. TV (pay movies/music/DVD).*

Honey Hotel
31 Sukhumvit Soi 19 (0 2253 0646-9). Asoke BTS/Sukhumvit subway. **Rooms** 75. **Rates** double B800-B1,000; suite B1,300-B1,700. **Credit** MC, V. **Map** p252 K6.
Superbly kitsch, the Honey's long, low, black granite foyer and aqua pool will suit anyone who thinks crimplene and cocktail frankfurters are 'faaabulous'. Rooms are unglamorous and slightly musty, but good value. Honey has tons of atmosphere, plus a cast of generic middle-aged white men and Thai girls casually lounging around the pool.
Services *Parking (free). Pool. Restaurants (1). Room service. Smoking rooms. TV.*

Majestic Suites
110-110/1 Thanon Sukhumvit, between Soi 4 & 6 (0 2656 8220/fax 0 2656 8201/www.majesticsuites.com). Nana BTS. **Rooms** 55. **Rates** double B1,165-B1,865. **Credit** AmEx, DC, MC, V. **Map** p251 J5.
Located beside the post office, this small, friendly, Indian-run inn offers good, air-conditioned rooms that are excellent value, especially the comfy double deluxe room. There's no pool, but it does have a lobby bar and Majestic Tailors. Includes breakfast.
Services *Bars (1). Business centre. Concierge. Internet (dataport). Restaurants (1). Room service. Smoking rooms. TV.*

Regency Park Bangkok
12/3 Sukhumvit Soi 22 (0 2259 7420-39/fax 0 2258 2862/www.accorhotel.com). Phrom Phong BTS. **Rooms** 120. **Rates** double B1,990-B2,390; suite B3,800. **Credit** AmEx, DC, MC, V. **Map** p252 K6.
Run by hotel chain Accor, this unassuming hotel offers friendly, first-rate service and well-appointed rooms at a fraction of bigger luxury hotel brands. Surrounding a leafy courtyard, all rooms are modern, thickly carpeted and have a separate bathtub and shower. The *soi* on which it is located is vibrant come nightfall and it's only a short walk to the BTS, Emporium and Banjasiri Park.
Services *Bars (2). Business centre. Concierge. Disabled-adapted rooms. Gym. Internet (high-speed, dataport). Parking (free). Pool. Smoking rooms. Restaurants (2). Room service. TV (pay movies/ by request: DVD).*

Budget

The area around Sukhumvit Soi 11/1 is crammed with more or less indistinguishable inns. All offer cheap, but rather sparse, dingy rooms with phones, air-con, cable TV and clean en suite bathrooms. The Bangkok Inn (155/12-13 Sukhumvit Soi 11/1, 0 2254 4834, www.

bangkok-inn.com, B845-B952) and the Business Inn (155/4-5 Sukhumvit Soi 11, 0 2255 7155-8, www.awbusinn.com, B500-B600), with a travel agency, are among the better ones.

Atlanta Hotel
78 Sukhumvit Soi 2 (0 2252 1650/6069/ www.theatlantahotel.bizland.com). Nana BTS. **Rooms** 49. **Rates** double with fan B330-B480; double with air-con B450-B600; family B1,300; suite B550-B700. **No credit cards**. **Map** p251 J5.
Founded in 1952, this one-time beau monde haunt has hosted the likes of Thailand's princess mother, Jim Thompson and Scandinavian royalty. Despite flood damage in the 1960s, the efforts of Charles Henn, son of the late founder, mean that the Atlanta is enjoying a new golden age. With moralistic literary notices dotting the bookshelves, walls and even the menu at its superb, mainly vegetarian Thai restaurant, the Atlanta boasts a cult following among a new generation of writers, photographers, producers and Asia obsessives. Its concrete exterior may be crumbling and the bathrooms basic, but its charm lies in its characterful style that owes as much to British influences as it does to the vintage 1950s deco in the lobby. There's a 24-hour pool, writing desks in the garden and traditional Thai dancing on Saturdays, yet one night's stay costs the same as brunch at the nearby Marriott (*see p40*).
Services *Gym. Pool. Restaurants (1). Smoking rooms. TV room.*

Miami
2 Sukhumvit Soi 13 (0 2253 0369). Nana BTS. **Rooms** 19. **Rates** double B600-B750; family B1,000. **No credit cards**. **Map** p251 J5.
The Miami has seen better days, but it's worth going just for its retro motel feel (check out the pale blue pool in the courtyard). Rooms may be plain and rather old-looking, but they are also large and functional. Friendly *kathoey* staff will cut the rates for weekly or monthly stays, and there are quieter rooms on the side, away from the non-stop street bustle. The Miami has a booking desk at Bangkok Airport.
Services *Business centre. Concierge. Internet (high-speed). Parking (free). Pool. Restaurants (1). Room service. Smoking rooms. TV.*

Suk11 Guesthouse
1/33 Sukhumvit Soi 11 (0 2253 5927-8/ fax 0 2253 5929/www.suk11.com). Nana BTS. **Rooms** 67. **Rates** double B450-B700; family B800-1,200; dorm B250. **No credit cards**. **Map** p251 J5.
Guesthouses are rare in Sukhumvit, but in the budget accommodation stakes Suk11 is a winner. It spreads over four beautifully decorated, old Thai-style wooden buildings, crammed into a sub-*soi* near Cheap Charlie's (*see p131*), a wall-less institution famed for its bargain beers. Rooms are smallish, but pleasant, clean and new-looking, while dorm beds cater to the most frugal travellers. All rooms have air-conditioning and the price includes breakfast.
Services *Internet (high-speed, wireless). Restaurants (1). TV room.*

North

Deluxe

Amari Watergate

847 Thanon Petchaburi (0 2653 9000/fax
0 2653 9045/www.amari.com). Ratchathewi BTS.
Rooms 569. **Rates** double $195-$298; suites $295-
$395. **Credit** AmEx, DC, MC, V. **Map** p251 G4.
A towering hotel in Bangkok's commercial centre.
It can feel mall-like due to its size (the escalators
don't help), but the excellent facilities include a top-
notch gym, a large pool and a unique eighth-floor
lawn. Rooms are well equipped and very good value,
but the hotel is too large to evoke much atmosphere.
Thai on 4 (modern Thai) and Grappino (Italian) are
fine restaurants, while the restaurant bar Henry J
Bean's serves American favourites with live music.
Services *Bars (1). Business centre. Concierge.*
Disabled-adapted rooms. Gym. Internet (high-speed,
dataport). Parking (free). Pool. Restaurants (4).
Room service. Smoking rooms. TV (pay
movies/music/widescreen/suites: DVD).

Moderate

Reflections Rooms in Bangkok

81 Soi Phaholyothin 7 (Soi Aree) (0 2270 3343-4/
fax 0 2617 0484/www.reflections-thai.com). Ari
BTS. **Rooms** 28. **Rates** double B1,900-B2,400.
No credit cards.
Created by Thailand's guru of kitsch – Anusorn
'Nong' Ngernyuang, who runs a home decor business
called Reflections – this unquestionably unusual
boutique hotel dares to think differently. For a start,
it's raspberry pink. Co-ordinated by celebrated Czech
architect Borek Sipek, each room is based around a
different concept, and is designed by (mainly Thai)
artists. The Taj Mahal Room employs the intense
oranges and pinks of India and has a Moorish door-
way. Thaiwijit Puangkasemsomboon created the
oddly shaped 'Post Industrial' room using his trademark recycled props. Meanwhile, in the Crystal
Spectrum room, one wall is a fish tank. Fabulously
camp products from Nong's shop are also fittings in
the hotel's Japanese and Thai seafood restaurants.
Though not central, Reflections is connected by the
BTS and is close to expressways.
Services *Bars (1). Internet (high-speed). Parking*
(free). Pool. Restaurants (2). Room service. Spa.
TV (DVD).

South

Deluxe

Banyan Tree Bangkok

21/100 Thanon Sathorn Tai (0 2679 1200/fax
0 2679 1199/www.banyantree.com). **Rooms** 216.
Rates double $300-$2,000. **Credit** AmEx, DC,
MC, V. **Map** p251 G7.

Better known for its award-winning Phuket spa
resort, this growing Singaporean chain also offers its
signature spa treatments (*see p219*) at this all-suite
luxury hotel. Located in a distinctive, wafer-thin
tower with an enormous hole through the middle, the
Banyan Tree offers every form of relaxation the
spoilt international exec could desire, including six
levels of spa facilities, an outdoor 'sky deck' and two
pools. Saffron serves contemporary Thai food from
the penthouse, while rooftop alfresco grill Vertigo
and its Moon Bar (an idea later adopted by Sirocco;
see p112) offer astonishing views and menus with
equally lofty prices. The rooms are stylishly decorated and the service is faultless.
Services *Bars (1). Business centre. Concierge.*
Disabled-adapted rooms. Gym. Internet (high-speed,
wireless, dataport). Parking (free). Pool. Restaurants
(4). Room service. Smoking rooms. Spa. TV (pay
movies/music/by request: DVD).

The Metropolitan

27 Thanon South Sathorn, Bangrak (0 2625
3333/fax 0 2625 3300/www.themetropolitan.com).
Rooms 171. **Rates** double $120-$180; suite $240-
$2,000. **Credit** AmEx, DC, MC, V. **Map** p251 G7.
Since opening in late 2003, this sister hotel to
London's pioneering minimalist icon has set the
benchmark in Bangkok for design-led hospitality.
Owner and Singapore-based interior designer
Kathryn Ong forged a sleek, modern oriental look
from the former YMCA, while London lighting architects Isometrix enabled the concrete shell to glow
softly at night. Staff in casual uniforms by Yohji
Yamamoto whisk guests to a lofty reception where
iMacs offer free internet access. Also pared down in
style, though not in texture, the rooms have been so
well thought through as to include a full desk set
from highlighters to metal rulers. By far the biggest
in Bangkok, the standard rooms pale beside the two-
storey suites, complete with kitchenette and floor-to-
ceiling windows, while the terrace rooms have a
balcony shower (though, thankfully, no one can see
you wash). Top chef Amanda Gale directs thrilling
cuisine at the poolside Cy'an (*see p124*) and health-
oriented Glow café. Only guests and members – the
cream of the city's creative young movers and shakers – are allowed to enter the Met Bar.
Services *Bars (1). Business centre. Concierge.*
Disabled-adapted rooms. Gym. Internet (high-speed,
wireless, shared terminal). Parking (free). Pool.
Restaurants (2). Room service. Smoking rooms.
Spa. TV (pay movies/music/widescreen/DVD).

Sukhothai

13/3 Thanon Sathorn Tai (0 2287 0222/
www.sukhothai.com). **Rooms** 219. **Rates** double
$280-$370; suites $390-$2,000. **Credit** AmEx, DC,
MC, V. **Map** p251 G7.
Designed by Ed Tuttle in an influential Siamese
minimalist fashion, which showcases exquisite artefacts and floral installations by engineer-turned-
florist Sakul Intakul, Sukhothai is arguably
Bangkok's most beautiful hotel. Set in six acres of

The Metropolitan. *See p48.*

gardens modelled on Sukhothai with pools containing brick *chedi*, this is a classy retreat, with exquisite service. Most rooms look out on to the gardens, and its planned extension (with spa) would almost double its peaceful grounds. Locals love the food and design at Celadon (Thai; *see p125*), the infamously indulgent Champagne brunch at the Colonnade and Italian restaurant La Scala (*see p125*). The health club and sublime pool are included; tennis, squash and massages cost extra.

Services *Bars (1). Business centre. Concierge. Disabled-adapted rooms. Gym. Internet (high-speed, wireless, dataport). Parking (free). Pool. Restaurants (5). Room service. Smoking rooms. Spa. TV (pay movies/widescreen/suites: music/by request: DVD)*

Moderate

Pinnacle Hotel

17 Soi Ngam Duphli, Thanon Rama IV (0 2287 0111-31/www.pinnaclehotels.com). Lumphini subway. **Rooms** 154. **Rates** double B1,300-B1,700; suite B3,000-B4,500. **Credit** AmEx, DC, MC, V. **Map** p251 H7.

Part of a big chain, this small hotel offers well-appointed, comfortable rooms at affordable prices, especially during the low season. Located in a lively neighbourhood close to Lumphini subway station, the Pinnacle Hotel has charm, but the decor has seen better days.

Reflections Rooms in Bangkok – for something completely different. *See p48.*

Services *Bars (1). Business centre. Concierge. Disabled-adapted rooms. Gym. Internet (high-speed, dataport). Parking (free). Smoking rooms. Restaurants (1). Room service. Spa. TV (music/by request: DVD).*

Budget

Around the Malaysia Hotel, the Soi Ngam Duphlee/Soi Sri Bumphen area became a pre-Khao San backpacker scene. Now it's more a hub for long-stayers in the country, some working on local wages, who enjoy its frisson and evident tolerance. Many guesthouses let night visitors to the rooms; others don't.

Charlie House

1034/36-37 Soi Saphan Khu, Thanon Rama IV (0 2679 8330-1/www.charliehousethailand.com). Lumphini subway. **Rooms** 17. **Rates** double B450-B750. **No credit cards. Map** p251 H7.
A shophouse lodgings with hotel-level facilities, Charlie also has access to great streetfood and now to the subway. Staff are very helpful – the walls are covered with testimonials to prove it – which may be why return visitors have included a minister from Bhutan. The great-value rooms, built on funny angles, are small, but clean and well equipped (private bathrooms, air-con, phone and TV).
Services *Internet (high-speed). Restaurants (1). Room service. TV.*

Malaysia Hotel

54 Soi Ngam Duphli, Thanon Rama IV (0 2679 7127-36/fax 0 2287 1457/www.malaysia hotelbkk.com). **Rooms** 119. **Rates** double B598-B838. **Credit** AmEx, DC, MC, V. **Map** p251 H7.
An old GI R&R joint, this block became Bangkok's first backpacker hotel in the 1970s and gets much return business for its value for money and people-watching quotient. Though there's a 10% service charge you get a lot for your money: rooms have phones, air-con and private bathrooms with hot showers. Superior rooms also have a small fridge, TV and video. There's a basic pool and travel services, while the notorious coffeeshop is an early-morning clearing house for those who have been working or partying too hard in Patpong.
Services *Internet (high-speed). Parking (free). Pool. Restaurants (1). Room service. Smoking rooms. TV (by request: DVD).*

Sala Thai Daily Mansion

15 Soi Sri Bamphen, Thanon Rama IV (0 2287 1436). Lumphini subway. **Rooms** 16. **Rates** double with fan B200-B400. **No credit cards. Map** p251 H7.
Tucked away in the quiet, snail-shaped *soi* off Sri Bamphen, this guesthouse remains eternally popular with journalists and English teachers. The rooms are all clean, basic and small, with shared bathrooms, rooftop garden and communal TV/reading area. The staff are lovely and owner Khun Anong may even turn you into a local star (she scouts for *farang* to model in brochures and adverts). If you're

looking for somewhere quiet to stay in this sometimes rowdy neighbourhood, you'll be relieved to know that Sala Thai refuses entry to nightwalkers, unlike many of its neighbours.
Services *Smoking rooms. TV room.*

Serviced apartments

Many residential blocks, having empty apartments, started to let rooms on a short-term basis at very good rates. Not too surprisingly, the local hotels hated the competition and pushed for a ban on apartment stays shorter than one week. What was surprising was the fact that they got it. Despite this difficulty, apartment stays can still offer things beyond pools, gyms and room servicing, such as domestic ambience, kitchenettes and multi-room layouts. They tend to appeal to families, businessmen, self-caterers and long-stay visitors wanting to feel at home. Owing to the law, apartments are coy about mentioning daily rates, but many will quote them when asked. Or compare and book apartments online at **www.sabaai.com**.

The Ascott Sathorn

187 Thanon South Sathorn (0 2676 6868/fax 0 2676 6888/www.the-ascott.com). Chong Nonsi BTS. **Rooms** 177. **Rates** suite B28,000-B59,000. **Credit** AmEx, DC, MC, V. **Map** p251 G7.
Central to the CBD (central business district), this breathtakingly fabulous new block caters to expats and upmarket Thais who prefer – nay require – a certain cachet. Some of Bangkok's most stimulating interior design graces a variety of rooms flush with modern comforts. The awesome Cascade Club fitness centre boasts the latest gym equipment and a swish spa. Offering romantic views, Aldo's Café and Wine Bistro has served the likes of Michael Douglas and Jeremy Irons. Out front stands a branch of Singapore's sophisticated Hu'u Bar (*see p132*).
Services *Business centre. Concierge. Gym. Internet (wireless). Parking (free). Pool. Restaurants (1). Room service. Smoking rooms. Spa. TV (music/DVD).*

Chateau de Bangkok

29 Ruamrudee Soi 1, Thanon Ploenchit, Pathumwan (0 2651 4400). Ploenchit BTS. **Rooms** 137. **Rates** (per month) studios B46,200-B58,800; suite B67,200-B85,000. **Credit** AmEx, DC, MC, V. **Map** p251 H5.
Located on a pleasant residential *soi*, this decade-old block run by hotel group Accor gets much repeat business. The apartments have luxury furnishings, daily cleaning (including linen and towel changes), king-size beds and fully equipped kitchens. All but the smallest studios have jacuzzis. There is a deli/café off the lobby, an Italian restaurant and a small rooftop pool/gym with city panoramas.
Services *Business centre. Concierge. Gym. Internet (high-speed, wireless). Parking (free). Pool. Restaurants (1). Room service. Smoking rooms. TV.*

THE WORLD'S YOUR OYSTER

Available at all good bookshops
and at www.timeout.com/shop

Sightseeing

Introduction

Advice on exploring Bangkok's byways – boats, trains and braving the traffic.

Asked directions to the city centre, Bangkok residents could well reply: 'Which centre?' As the capital grew, the centre of gravity kept shifting. History is most palpable in the old town of **Phra Nakorn**, containing **Rattanakosin Island** and the backpacker enclave **Banglamphu**. The former capital, **Thonburi** (here taken as the entire west bank of the Chao Phraya river, including parts of Nonthaburi province), retains traces of the earlier canal-borne 'Venice of the East' lifestyle. Grandly planned **Dusit** houses state institutions, while chaotic **Chinatown** retains its business might.

West of the railway, the modern **Downtown** is defined by where the BTS and new subway reach, an area that includes most hotels. Downtown comprises **Bangrak**, the core of finance and nightlife; **Pathumwan**, the shopping nexus; **Sukhumvit**, an avenue of drinking, dining and entertainment; **North**, the trading area between Pratunam and Chatuchak Weekend Markets; and **South**, a developing zone fringed by river commerce.

Until mass transit expands, the suburbs are best reached by expressways. Much investment is heading **East**, around the new Suvarnabhumi Airport in Samut Prakarn

province, while **Outer North** encompasses old Don Muang Airport and metropolitan parts of Nonthaburi and Pathum Thani provinces. In between, the residential **North-east** is also a major nightlife zone.

While traffic still frustrates exploration – don't make too many appointments in one day – the opening of the BTS SkyTrain in 1999 felt like the end of a war. The BTS is a tour in itself, the elevated rails revealing a hidden garden city and lost mansions behind forbidding walls and shophouses. Even more fun, the **Expressboats** link the BTS to the old town along Bangkok's original highway, the river. The many skyscrapers mean that Bangkok's flat floodplain now bristles with reference points, though zigzagging *soi* (smaller roads leading off main road, and often numbered) and one-way systems can make journeys circuitous. For transport options, *see pp234-27*. For the **Bangkok Tourist Bureau** and **Tourism Authority of Thailand** (universally called **TAT**), *see p235*.

TIPS FOR TOURISTS

● Treat etiquette and dress codes seriously (*see p228* **Attitude & etiquette**).

● Non-Thais are often charged much more than locals. Argument is futile.

● Many establishments close over Thai and Chinese New Years.

● State museums open early, shut around 4pm and close on Mondays, Tuesdays and holidays. Private museums usually keep office hours daily (including holidays), but may close on Sundays. Many have compulsory tours. Non-TAT guides may get ejected.

● Temples are usually free, but normally locked *bot* (ordination halls) might be opened on request.

● Many signs are in English, which is spoken widely in tourist centres, but, given differing accents, writing things down may clarify confusions. Transliterations into English vary.

● Cameras are banned from inside museums, malls and official places, but not most temples. Some places charge a camera fee. Thais (but not Muslims and hill tribes) generally like being snapped, but prefer to compose themselves. Smile through any awkwardness. 'No photo' means just that, though hill tribes may pose for a fee.

● As most shops close late, shopping can be saved for the evenings (or rainy season afternoons).

If you only have 48 hours

Start with a stretch
Dawn tai chi in **Lumphini Park** (*see p93*).

Wake with a *joke*
Have a rice porridge (*joke*) breakfast at **Sam Yan** market (*see p135*).

Must-see sights
Marvel at the **Grand Palace** (*see p57*) and **Wat Pho** (*see p65*).

Multicultural fix
Tour **Chinatown**, grand **Dusit** or modern **Downtown**, depending on your taste; see **Sightseeing** chapters.

Relive the 'Venice of the East'
Visit **Wat Arun** (*see p76*) and explore the **canals by boat** (*see p56*), followed by seafood at **River Bar Café** (*see p109*).

The art of drinking
Share whisky with arty Thais at **Thanon Phra Arthit**. For bars, *see p126*.

Shop
Buy Thai at **Siam Square** and its malls (*see p151*) – or visit the huge **Chatuchak Weekend Market** (*see p136*).

Food for the soul
Recover at **Being Spa** (*see p176*) before Thai dinner at **Hazara** (*see p119*).

Go up then sideways
Have drinks atop a skyscraper at **Sirocco** (*see p112*) before bed... or alternatively find your bed at **Bed Supperclub** bar (*see p129*).

Midnight refresher
Wade through orchids at the **Pak Khlong Talad** flower market (*see p135*).

TOUTS AND SCAMS
Aside from the pushers of porn, sex shows and massage in Patpong, touts plague major sights and piers. Ignore touts or *tuk-tuk* drivers saying 'it's closed today', 'festival across town', 'craft demonstration' or 'one-day tax break', and prevent them 'guiding' you to the sight.

Touts are paid out of what you are charged at the bar or shop they take you to (tours may do this as well). They're not usually dangerous, but food and drink that's offered might be doped. Don't believe promises of sudden wealth through gem dealing (*see p150* **Gems without scams**), but since touts are just opportunists making a living, politely say *mai ow khrub/kha* (male/female) ('don't want') or *mee laew khrub/kha* (male/female) ('have already') and move on.

Specialist tours
The **Bangkok Tourist Bureau** (*see p235*) offers canal tours of Bangkok Noi (B400, every second and fourth Sat) and four good walking tours (8am-noon, 1-5pm Wed-Sun, B100) of Thonburi, Sam Praeng, Wang Lang or Banglamphu. Ten people only, so book ahead. Cycling tours (maximum 25) run to Rattanakosin (6.30-9pm Sat, B390, B290 with own bike) and from Thonburi to Phutthamonthon (7am-4.30pm Sun, B650, B550 with own bike). Bus tours of Rattanakosin from/to the south-west corner of Sanam Luang, depart every 30 minutes (9am-5pm daily, B30).

ETC (Educational Travel Centre)
Room 318, Royal Hotel, 2 Thanon Ratchadamnoen Avenue, Phra Nakorn (0 2224 0043/fax 0 2622 1420/www.etc.co.th). Tha Saphan Phan Fah. **Open** 8.30am-5pm Mon-Sat. **Credit** MC, V. **Map** p248 B3.
A variety of trips from waterway homestays to culture and cooking to upcountry eco-adventures. Its Thanatharee river barge/bicycling trips won a TAT award, though accommodation is quite simple.

Origin
(0 2663 0472/fax 0 2259 4896/origin@ usianet.co.th/www.origin-asia.com). **Credit** call for details.
Authentic cultural experiences of one to two days, or longer, with Thai experts offering a hands-on insight into Central Thai arts like dance gestures, floral offerings, *lai Thai* design, cooking and martial arts. Courses are held in English at a teak compound in Bangkok, and also on Lanna culture in Chiang Mai. Origin requires no skills, but will enrich your appreciation of everything Thai.

Real Asia
5th floor, Sukhumvit Soi 49/9, Sukhumvit (0 2712 930-1/2/www.realasia.net). Thonglor BTS. **Open** 8am-8pm daily. **No credit cards. Map** p252 L5.
Real Asia runs daily cycling tours (maximum 40 people) run from 10am-3.30pm and 1-5pm to Phra Pradaeng and Bang Kra Jao for rural riverside biking. The canal/walking tour (usually weekly, 9.30am-4.30pm) leaves from Saphan Taksin-Nonthaburi by Expressboat, incorporating a market and community walk and returning on longtail boat via Khlong Om and Khlong Bangkok Noi. Space is limited to six, so it's advisable to book

ahead. Another tour takes the train to Mahachai village and fish market (8.30am-4.30pm daily, B1,750).

Tamarind Tours

Tarntawan Place Hotel, 119/5-10 Thanon Surawong, Bangrak (0 2238 3227/www.tamarindtours.com). Saladaeng BTS/Silom subway. **Open** 10am-6pm daily. **Credit** AmEx, MC, V. **Map** p250 F6.

Highly professional, non-touristy tours by unique personal guides with TAT training and dozens of specialisations, from history, culture and botany to fashion, food and undervisited sights. Tours are run in the daytime or evening in Bangkok, as well as upcountry and to neighbouring countries.

River & canal tours

If you hire a longtail boat, go for at least two hours – short tours barely explore canal life and forfeit time at sights better (and more cheaply) seen separately, such as Wat Arun. Major piers, such as Oriental, Chang and Nonthaburi, are now better signposted, but boat tour routes and prices vary (B300-B500 per hr, B700-B750 for 90mins, B900 for 2hrs). For **Bang Sai**, **Bang Pa-In** and **Ayutthaya**, *see pp101-104*; for nearer river sights, *see p74* **Pier groups**.

Aggressive touts may try illegally to bar non-Thai adventurers from cramped longtail buses plying canal routes for B8-B30. Hiring a small, bumpy *rua song torn* speedboat taxi gets you into minor *khlongs* (canals) amid orchards, temples and stilt houses. They cost B300-B500 per hour, from piers at **Nonthaburi**, or the **Southern Bus Terminal**.

Among hotel cruises, the **Oriental** (*see p42*) holds dinner aboard the *Maeyanang* (7.30-10pm Tue-Sun, B1,600, B900 under-12s), while **Marriott Bangkok Resort & Spa** (*see p40*) runs the *Manohra* for evening cocktails or tours to Bang Pa-In, overnighting in teak-panelled berths (0 2476 0021-2, www.manohracruises.com, 3 days 2 nights B46,000 for 2 people, B10,000 under-12s; dinner cruise 7.30-10pm daily, B1,500 adults, B750 under-12s). **Asian Oasis** also runs two-day cruises to Bang Pa-In/Ayutthaya on the exquisite *Mekhala* teak barge (0 2651 9768-9, www.asian-oasis.com, B8,350-B12,000 adults, B4,180-B4,920 under-12s). For Chao Phraya **Expressboat** tours, *see p227*. Despite the polluted water, jet-ski tours of these areas may happen.

Magic Eyes Chao Phraya Barge Programme

1867/150, Tridhos City Marina Tower, Thanon Charoen Nakhon, Thonburi (0 2439 4746-8/www.magiceyes.or.th/barge). Tha Sathorn (Saphan Taksin). **Open** 8.30am-5pm Mon-Fri. **No credit cards. Map** p250 D7.

This converted teak barge has been offering interactive day and overnight trips since 1995. Learn about riparian lifestyles, history and ecology from experts on the five themed public trips per year. Private hire available.

Mit Chao Phraya Travel Service

Tha Chang, Thanon Na Phra Lan, Phra Nakhon (0 2225 6179). **Open** *Office* 8am-5pm daily. **Rates** B600 1hr; B800 90mins; B1,000 2hrs. **No credit cards. Map** p248 4B.

This company offers three daily river and Thonburi canal tours over 60 or 90 minutes, plus weekend trips to Koh Kred via Khlong Om (9am-4pm Sat, Sun, B200) and to Bang Pa-In (8am-6pm Sun, B390). All depart from Tha Chang.

Si Phraya Boat Trip & Travel

Soi Captain Bush, Charoen Krung Soi 30, Bangrak (0 2235 3108). Tha Si Phraya. **Open** *Office* 7am-8pm daily. **Rates** B600 1hr; B800 1.5hrs; B1,200 2hrs. **No credit cards. Map** p250 D7.

River and canal tours around Thonburi depart from River City (7am-6pm daily), often combining longtail, *tuk-tuk* and Expressboat. A two-hour dinner cruise (6pm, 7pm or 8pm daily) costs B1,200. Book a day ahead for the Bang Pa-In/Ayutthaya trip (7am-5pm, B1,600).

Yok Yor Marina & Restaurant

885 Somdet Chao Praya Soi 17, Thonburi (0 2863 0565-6/www.yokyor.co.th). **Open** *Restaurant* 11am-midnight daily. *Tours* 8am-10pm daily. **Credit** AmEx, DC, MC, V. **Map** p250 6D.

A dinner boat on the double-decker steel boat comes with a live band and a taped guide in Thai and English (B120 plus food). The pier restaurant has a dance stage, but there are bigger shows at its branch. **Other locations:** Chao Phraya Cultural Centre, 885 Thanon Somdetchaophraya, Thonburi (0 2863 0565/6).

Eco tours

Ecotourism has become a much-abused buzzword, labelling all kinds of intrusive activities. But there are responsible operators out there. **Lost Horizons** (02 860 3936, www.losthorizonsasia.com) offers rafting, diving, trekking and remote island life, as well as culture and turtle conservation volunteering. **Friends of Nature** (0 2642 4426-7, www.friendsofnature93.com) runs trips to natural, historical and cultural sites for various age or interest groups, including birdwatching, snorkelling, rafting, waterfalls, trekking and elephant rides. **Responsible Ecological Social Tours** (REST, 0 2938 7007, www.ecotour.in.th) runs sensitive village homestays to learn about life in communities in the north and south. **Nature Trails** (0 2735 0644, www.naturetrailsthailand.com) organises weekend birdwatching trips, hosted by bilingual ornithologists, including Kamol Komolphalin, illustrator of *A Guide to the Birds of Thailand*.

Phra Nakorn

A grand setting for Bangkok's greatest sights, the streets of the old town remain a vibrant living museum.

Map p248

Mooted changes over the next two decades are set to turn the historically rich 'old town' into a hub of tourism, though it already holds many top attractions. Even before the controversial development plan (*see p65* **Theming heritage**) materialises, you need at least a couple of days to visit the many well- and lesser-known gems within Phra Nakorn ('Holy City'), the moated, once walled area that contained the entire capital for the first of its two centuries of existence.

At its core is **Ko Rattanakosin**, an elliptical island bounded by the Chao Phraya river and **Khlong Lord** (the first of three concentric canals girdling it to the east). Phra Nakorn stretches east past **Democracy Monument** to Khlong Ong Ang, and effectively includes the **Golden Mount** just beyond. North of Thanon Ratchadamnoen Klang lies the district of **Banglamphu**, which gained notoriety as an international backpacker ghetto – and is now rediscovering its initial identity as a fount of Thai arts. The commercial areas of Phra Nakorn, south of Thanon Charoen Krung, have always been identified with Chinatown (*see pp83-88*). Although royalty has moved to Dusit, Phra Nakorn still hosts regular pageantry.

Th old town is also one of Bangkok's few pedestrian-friendly areas (*see p60* **Walk 1: Living history** *and p66* **Walk 2: Khlong Lord**). Height and design restrictions keep modern construction at bay, though these conservation plans in some ways threaten the communities that make this one of the most active historic centres of any world city. The quickest way to reach it from Downtown remains by water, either via river expressboat or canal boat (for both, *see p227*) to Golden Mount.

Rattanakosin Island

When King Rama I moved the capital to the more defensible east-bank settlement of Bangkok in 1782, he modelled this artificial island on the layout of lost Ayutthaya – both aesthetically and symbolically. The architectural glorification likewise announced that the reunified kingdom was growing strong and independent. At its centre stand the **Grand Palace** and its astonishing temple,

Wat Phra Kaew, home of the Emerald Buddha. It faces **Sanam Luang**, the royal field that dominates the island's north, while to the south is **Wat Pho** and the Reclining Buddha.

Grand Palace & Wat Phra Kaew

Thanon Na Phra Lan (0 2222 8181). Tha Chang. **Open** 8.30am-3.30pm daily. **Admission** (incl access to Dusit Park & either Ananta Samakhom Throne Hall or Sanam Chan Palace in Nakhon Pathom) B250. **No credit cards. Map** p248 B4.

There are no two ways about it: you must see this exquisite architectural and spiritual treasure (preferably early on a sunny morning, when it most dazzles). Ignore the gem touts claiming 'it's shut today', and immerse yourself in the palace's palpable dignity (while observing the stringent dress code that bans sandals, shorts and bare shoulders). Nearly 2km (1.5 miles) of walls with lotus-shaped crenellations enclose what was once a 161-hectare (65-acre) self-contained city, comprising ceremonial

The best Views

For dining under the stars
Sirocco offers alfresco food on the top of a 63-storey skyscraper. *See p112.*

For the highest panorama
You can see the sea (just) through the windows of the **Baiyoke II Tower**. *See p96.*

For old town landmarks
Supatra River House surveys the Rattanakosin riverscape. *See p198.*

For peering into private places
The **SkyTrain** cruises above wall height. *See p225.*

For spiritual highs
The **Golden Mount** chedi offers 360° views of old and new. *See p69.*

For swimming in the clouds
Banyan Tree Bangkok Hotel (*see p48*) has open-air pools as high as the 51st floor, and the roof boasts the aptly named **Vertigo** restaurant and **Moon Bar** (*see p132*).

Sightseeing

The **Grand Palace** and **Wat Phra Kaew**. See p57.

buildings, royal chambers, servants' quarters, ministerial offices and a small prison. Begun in 1782, the palace was modified by each Chakri king. Laid out similarly to Chinese imperial palaces, it has a reception zone, followed by a royal audience zone (the interiors of which are open on National Children's Day; see p159). But the public isn't permitted to view even the exteriors of the inner chambers that lie beyond, where the kings' wives used to live. Disused once Rama VI had only one wife, those

quarters now house a finishing school for upper-class girls. Since the royals moved to Dusit, the Grand Palace gets used only for ceremonies and state visits, but it remains Thailand's proudest and holiest landmark.

Visitors entering Wat Phra Sri Rattana Sasadaram – better known as Wat Phra Kaew, the temple of the Emerald Buddha (Thailand's most sacred image) – are greeted by a statue of Buddha's physician, Shivaka Kumar Baccha, before being swamped by

Wat Pho.
See p65.

a kaleidoscope of forms and colours. Modelled on royal chapels in Sukhothai and Ayutthaya, and embellished to an astonishing degree, the temple omits monastic living quarters, since there are no resident monks.

The circular, Sri Lankan-style Phra Si Rattana Chedi, tiled in gold, enshrines a piece of the Buddha's breastbone. It stands on the upper terrace beside the Phra Mondop (library of palm-leaf scriptures), a columned cube of green and blue glass mosaic under a tiered spire; and the cruciform, *prang*-roofed Royal Pantheon, where on Chakri Day (*see p159*) the king honours statues of his forebears. Monuments to each Chakri reign stud the terrace, along with gilded statues of creatures from the mythical Himaphan Forest like the *apsarasingha* (lion-woman) and *kinnorn* (bird-man), with multi-coloured guardians supporting a pair of small gold *chedi* to the east. To the north, Ho Phra Nak (the royal mausoleum) and Hor Phra Monthien Tham (a library) flank porcelain-clad Vihaan Yod and a sandstone model of Angkor Wat temple in Cambodia (a vassal state when King Rama IV commissioned this carving).

On the temple's eastern side loom eight porcelain-covered pastel *prang* (representing Buddhism's eightfold path). Two stand within a notch in the cloister, which stretches 2km (1.5 miles), its walls adorned with 178 murals painted in Thai-Western style of the entire *Ramakien* epic. In the south-east corner, the shrine of the Gandharara Buddha in rain-summoning posture is used in the Royal Ploughing Ceremony (*see p160*). Six pairs of towering stone *yaksha* (demons) guard the *bot*, which is mosaiced in gold and glass and ringed by 112 *garuda* holding *naga* snakes. From a public altar you enter the *bot*'s murralled interior on your knees, facing a lofty gilded altar topped by the Emerald Buddha. Carved from solid jade, this statue is 66cm (26in) tall and dressed by the king in one of three seasonal robes: cool, hot or rainy. Of mysterious origin, but in late Lanna style, this paladium of

Thai independence was discovered in Chiang Rai in 1434 and arrived here via Lampang, Chiang Mai, Vientiane in Laos and Wat Arun in Thonburi.

Visitors may rest at one of the *sala* (pavilions) before entering the palace precinct. The halls make for a curious medley of each Thai period, alongside European classicism, Chinese sculpture and globular *mai dut* topiary. Visible through railings on the left, the belle époque Borom Phiman Mansion was built in 1903 for the future King Rama VI. Now a state guest house, it has hosted Queen Elizabeth II and Bill Clinton. Its Sivalai Gardens contain the Phra Buddha Ratana Sathan (Rama IV Chapel).

Next, the Phra Maha Montien Buildings include Amarin Winitchai Hall, where esteemed guests like the 19th-century ambassador Sir John Bowring were received by the king upon the boat-like throne. The main focus, however, is Chakri Maha Prasat Hall, a celebrated architectural fusion built (1876-82) by the Englishman John Chinitz. He had planned for a dome, but Chao Phraya Srisuriyawongse, the former regent, convinced

Walk 1 Living history

Only a stone's throw from showpiece sights, the fringes of Rattanakosin teem with activity. This walk leads you through pockets of traditional craft workshops, canal life, intact communities and temples. It takes the best part of a day, including refresher stops.

To get your bearings, begin at the **Golden Mount** (*see p69*). If you don't relish climbing, start to the north-west of the mount at Maha Uthit Bridge, famous for its bas-reliefs, and head down **Thanon Boriphat**, a street lined by timber merchants. The first left beyond Thanon Bumrung Muang is **Soi Ban Baat** – known as the **Monk's Bowl Village** – where descendants of Ayutthayan refugees keep alive a Khmer method of beating out alms bowls from eight strips of metal, representing the eight spokes of the Dharma wheel. The community leader's workshop is at 71 Soi Ban Baat (0 2621 2635, open 10am-8pm daily, admission free). When decorated and lacquered, the bowls are prized by collectors – despite their other function of symbolising non-attachment.

Backtrack and head along **Thanon Bamrung Muang**, an elephant trail that became one of the city's first paved streets. Its shopfronts glow with Buddhist images, regalia and ritual accoutrements. Passing the **Giant Swing** and **Wat Suthat** (*see p69*), head along **Thanon Dinso**, past the imposing **City Hall**. Facing

the **Democracy Monument**, turn left past the **Rim Khob Fah** shop of books on Thailand (*see p140*) and left again at the **14 October Monument** into **Thanon Tanao**.

South along Tanao, **Wat Mahanopharam** (0 2221 8245, temple open 8am-5pm daily, bot open 7am-5pm daily) is a tranquil Rama III-era retreat, where merit-making offerings include *takraw* balls, their tightly woven rattan representing group unity and strength. Further down and across Tanao, the **Chao Poh Seua Shrine** (0 2224 2110, open 6am-5.30pm daily) is dedicated to the Chinese tiger

King Rama V to add a Thai roof. This odd combination was dubbed 'a *farang* in a Thai hat'. Beneath its chamber for banquets and state visits is a public Weapons Museum; the top floor houses the ashes of Chakri kings.

To its west stand two sublimely proportioned structures: Aphonphimok Pavilion and Dusit Throne Hall. The Pavilion was built by Rama IV for changing gowns en route via palanquin to the cruciform Throne Hall, which contains the throne of Rama I and is still used for coronations and lying-in-state. Beyond these, a restored building will house the new Queen's Textile Museum. A cafeteria stands near the exit.

Expect to stay at least two hours, perhaps renting an audio guide (in eight languages; B100 with a passport/credit card deposit) or a guide (B300).

Sanam Luang & around

A broad field used for anything from royal ceremonies to public recreation, Sanam Luang is ringed by institutions. Clockwise from the

(*seua*) god. It's guarded by two golden tigers, with vendors selling tiger-appeasing offerings like pork, rice and eggs – and the inevitable lottery tickets. Barren couples place sugar tigers here in hope of pregnancy. Looming ahead on the right is the **Phraeng Sanphasat Palace Gate**, a neo-classical remnant of Prince Sanphasart Supakit's 1901 residence, which was (like many old landmarks) lost in a fire. To the east is narrow **Trok Chang Thong**, a goldsmiths' quarter destroyed by fire (prompting gold diggers to scavenge for treasure) and the former home of wartime dictator Phibunsongkhram.

For a fascinating peek into authentic Thai life, nip into **Thanon Phraeng Nara**, the middle lane of **Samphraeng** (three Phraeng streets), where you'll find a (somewhat self-consciously) characterful community. The last remnant of the palace of Prince Narathip (Rama IV's son) is now a lawyer's office, but the quaintly shuttered shophouses and cottage industries here and around the square on **Thanon Phraeng Poothon**, parallel to the south, offer authentic produce and unadulterated local cuisine. Government workers from nearby offices relish the toothsome home-made ice-cream (topped with corn, nuts and red beans) and potions like pig's brain noodles (to improve the intellect).

Grand Palace are **Silpakorn University**; a Buddhist University at **Wat Mahathat**; **Thammasat University** (for all, *see p64*); the **National Museum** (*see p63*); and the **National Theatre** (*see p196*). North of Phra Pinklao Bridge lies the **National Gallery** (*see p62*), then east along Sanam Luang stand the Royal Hotel; the Mae Toranee Fountain; **Lak Muang** (the City Pillar) and the **Ministry of Defence** (*see p62* **National Discovery Museum Project**).

The Rattanakosin waterfront was once reserved for minor palaces, but the tone is now set by the charming Phra Chan community between Tha Phra Chan and Tha Chang piers. The shophouses here burgeon with cultural regalia, traditional massage and herbal preparations, alongside outlets for local students, selling indie music, concert tickets, art-house film rentals and artists' materials. Fortune-tellers gather on the pedestrianised forecourt of Tha Phra Chan, while trinket stalls spread out from **Amulet Alley** market (*see p133*).

Flanked by 33 classically stuccoed shophouses (dating from the fifth reign) on land that once belonged to the poet Sunthorn Phu, Tha Chang's forecourt has also been paved, and food vendors shelter under its frangipani trees and in shacks behind the pier where touts flog canal tours. It is named 'Elephant Pier' because the palace pachyderms once bathed here. The landscaped embankment beside the Grand Palace, housing Ratchaworadit Royal Pier and Ratchakitwinitchai Throne Pavilion, is reserved for royal occasions.

Lak Muang

Thanon Sanam Chai (0 2222 9876). Tha Chang.
Open 5.30am-7.30pm daily. **Map** p248 B3/4.
Thais believe the guardian spirits of a Thai town reside at its foundation pillar. Bangkok's birth (and horoscope) thus dates from the auspicious time on 22 April 1782 when Rama I installed this bud-tipped wooden pillar, now housed in a Khmer-revival cruciform tower. Some claim it's a Shiva lingam – the phallic form of the Indian god; others trace its origins to the Tai tribal adoption of an animistic southern Chinese tradition of placing a phallus on a town crossroads. And Bangkok's laburnum-wood Lak Muang – 274cm (108in) above ground, 201cm (79in) below – is an infinite crossroads since all metropolitan distances are measured from it. Shellacked and gilded, it is accompanied by the taller Lak Muang of Thonburi, moved here when the former capital joined greater Krung Thep. Spirits of the city and country are embodied in statues housed in a pavilion to the east of this landscaped compound. Those whose wishes have been granted by these spirits pay *lakhon chatri* dancers to perform at a *sala* (pavilion).

National Discovery Museum Project

Former Commerce Ministry, behind Ratchawong Police Station, Thanon Sanam Chai (0 2357 3999). Tha Ratchinee. **Open** call for details. **Map** p248 B4.

A B3.7-billion Siamese 'Smithsonian' is due to be created in former ministries down Sanam Luang's east side to educate Thais, demonstrate Thailand's modernity and bolster Rattanakosin's status as a museum centre. Old ministries will house the four stand-alone institutions: the Museum of Thai History; the Museum of Natural History of SE Asia; the Museum of History of the People and the Land of SE Asia; and the Museum of Science and Technology. The former will be in the ex-Commerce Ministry, the latter in the 1885 classical edifice of the Defence Ministry. Since the dictatorship era, the 40 historic cannons at the Ministry (all honorifically named) have been on public display, their barrels notoriously pointing at the Grand Palace. In 2004 they were reversed (some say to dispel separatism in the deep South). Uneasy facing the barrels of the guns, the generals then turned them sideways towards the City Pillar and Wat Pho, in other words at civilians and monks, until they get moved to the new defence HQ.

National Gallery

5 Thanon Chao Fa, near Sanam Luang (0 2282 2639). Tha Phra Arthit. **Open** 9am-4pm Wed-Sun. **Admission** B10 Thais; B30 foreigners. **No credit cards.** **Map** p248 B3.

Most Thai artists dream of exhibiting at this high-ceilinged institution, established in 1977 in the neoclassical former Royal Mint. The small permanent

Rights sights

Achieving Thai democracy has been a tortuous path, one littered with coups, crackdowns and umpteen constitutions. Memorialising the struggle has proved just as fraught. Textbooks and histories allude to massacres as 'incidents', though the defining moments are now recorded by several monuments.

Inlaid in Royal Plaza, east of the King Rama V statue (*see p79*), the small brass **People's Party Plaque** reads: 'At this spot, the People's Party has introduced a constitution for the advancement of the nation at dawn on June 24, BE 2475 (1932).' The end of absolute monarchy is a delicate matter often finessed by official phraseology. Yet the new **King Prajadhipok Museum** (*see p68*) explains all aspects with refreshing candour.

The museum's inspired location is pivotal. It looks north up Thanon Ratchadamnoen Nok to Royal Plaza's plaque, **Ananta Samakhom Throne Hall**, where the first assembly convened, and behind it the current **Parliament House**. West down Thanon Ratchadamnoen Klang, the museum faces the **Democracy Monument**.

Designed by Italian sculptor Corrado Feroci (founder of Silpakorn University; *see p64*), this icon to the 1932 transition pointedly sits in a traffic circle interrupting the royal processional avenue. The date infuses the design. Around a sculpted constitution upon a three-metre- (ten-foot-) tall tray (June was then the third Thai month) array 75 cannons (for 2475) and four vertical wings (24 metres high for June 24) symbolising soldiers, police, officials and civilians. Instead of royal or Buddhist imagery, bas-reliefs depict armed revolution, the People's Party and labourers,

all in the muscular, heroic style typical of mid 20th-century monuments worldwide.

Demonstrators against dictatorship rallied here on 14 October 1973, before being mown down by the military. It took until 2002 for the authorities to erect a **14 October Monument**. Its granite spire bears the names of 73 victims, though an accurate toll still awaits investigation. The surrounding spaces will become a museum to inform later generations, who take their hard-won rights for granted, of the cost of freedom. Survivors and relatives voluntarily maintain the site and are keen to talk about their traumatic experiences. Open 24 hours daily, it also hosts protests on other rights issues.

The state is even more reticent about remembering those demonstrators murdered by troops and paramilitaries when the generals retook power on 6 October 1973. Thus Thammasat University, from where many of the student protestors came, unveiled a **6 October Monument**. Images of the martyrs are inscribed in marble inside the gate on Thanon Deuan Tula (October Road).

The tenuousness of Thai democracy was illustrated again when middle-class protestors, rallying at the Democracy Monument, were shot by a military dictatorship in 'Black May' 1992. The foundation stone has been laid for a monument to this incident on the site at the Sanum Luang end of Thanon Ratchadamnoen Klang. Some hope that the presence of 'October Generation' activists in government will prevent future 'incidents'. The struggles entered popular culture, with *pleng puer cheewit* ('songs for life'; *see p186*) helping to preserve the principles through music.

Lak Muang.
See p61.

collection hasn't kept pace with contemporary art, but includes work by such modern notables as Impressionist painter Fua Haripitak, sculptor Misiem Yipintsoi, portraitist Chamrus Khietkong and watercolourist Sawasdi Tantisuk. Shows tend to be of international calibre.

National Museum

4 Thanon Na Phra That (0 2224 1333/www.thailand museum.com). Tha Chang/Tha Prachan. **Open** 9am-4pm Wed-Sun (last entry 3.30pm). **Admission** B20 Thais; B40 foreigners; free 9.30am-noon Wed, Thur. **No credit cards. Map** p248 B3.

Boasting the largest museum hoard in South-east Asia, the capital's first public museum originated in 1874 as King Rama IV's collection of regalia within the Grand Palace. It went on to become a refuge for antiquities from gangs of smugglers, and is only starting to address signage and display to fulfill its educative role. With branches in historic sites around the country, the main exhibits reside in part of the former Wang Na ('front palace') of the 'deputy king', a shortlived office held by Rama IV's brother Phra Pinklao. Most unmissable is the Buddhaisawan Chapel, whose exquisite murals focus attention on the revered Phra Buddha Sihing, an image that is seven centuries old.

Front, left and right are small royal pavilions, including Baan Daeng, an Ayutthayan house with Rattanakosin furnishings and a rare indoor toilet. It's behind the Gallery of Thai History, which keeps the Ramkhamhaeng Stone, claimed to be the earliest inscription of tonal Thai lettering. The central audience hall contains rooms of such varied treasures as a life-size model elephant in battle armour, *khon* masks, and the Viceregal Puppets, restored by artist Chakraphan Posyakrit. Temporary shows fill the front Throne Hall.

Contributing to its charm, shaded courtyards enable you to recharge before tackling the north and south wings. These hold a badly lit and placed bombardment of religious iconography, running chronologically from Rooms S1-9, spanning Dvaravati and Lopburi periods, and continuing (Rooms N1-10) with Sukhothai, Ayutthaya, Lanna and Bangkok styles. But persevere; masterpieces await. Languishing at the back on a peeling hessian mount, the world-renowned Sukhothai walking Buddha faces arrestingly stylised Hindu bronzes on a stair landing, with a Dvaravati figure and a striking Ayutthayan Buddha head hidden under the steps.

The gilded funerary chariots from the first Chakri reign receive much better display. Their sheer scale and the glass-inlaid wood carving leaves are breathtaking. Moving these teak structures requires 300 men – a feat last done in 1996 for King Bhumibol's mother. Although the labelling lacks context or flair, the museum still provides a good grounding in Thai artistic and cultural history (and its guidebook fills in many of the blanks). The National Museum Volunteers offer tours (9.30am-noon Wed, Thur only, or by appointment) in English, German, French and Japanese. Disabled access has improved.

Sanam Luang

Tha Chang. **Map** p248 B3.

Fringed by tamarind trees, this large oval lawn is one of the city's few truly open spaces. Here elaborate pyres are constructed for royal cremations to resemble sacred Mount Meru, giving rise to the park's alternative name, the *pramane* ground. Among its annual ceremonies are the bathing of the Phra Buddha Sihing statue at Songkran, the Royal Ploughing Ceremony and the King's and Queen's Birthday celebrations (for all, *see pp156-161*). In decades past Bangkok's elite came here for horse racing, bird hunting and golf. Until 1982 it hosted the Weekend Market (now at Chatuchak; *see p136* **A day in JJ**), with produce arriving via Khlong Lord. Current diverse uses include folk

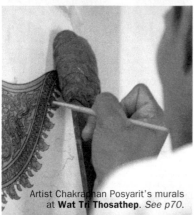

Artist Chakraphan Posyarit's murals at **Wat Tri Thosathep**. *See p70.*

entertainments, festivals, concerts and informal recreation, notably kite flying (Feb-Apr). Schemes to dig an underground car park and shopping arcade here have thus far been thwarted.

Silpakorn University & Gallery

31 Thanon Na Phra Lan (0 2623 6115-21/ www.su.ac.th/art centre 0 2221 3841/www.art-centre.su.ac.th). Tha Chang. **Open** 8.30am-4.30pm Mon-Fri. *Art Centre* 9am-7pm Mon-Fri; 9am-4pm Sat. Closed in holidays. **Map** p248 B3/4.

Thailand's oldest and most venerable fine art school, Silpakorn contains a small museum and a courtyard sculpture dedicated to its founder (Silpa Bhirasri, aka Corrado Feroci, an Italian commissioned in the 1920s to sculpt such landmarks as the Rama I stat-ue and the Democracy Monument). Hosting regular exhibitions by students, masters and foreign artists-in-residence, the serene Silpakorn Art Centre Gallery was once part of Tha Phra Palace. There are spe-cialist galleries in the faculties of architecture, dec-orative arts (products and textiles), and painting, sculpture and graphic arts.

Thammasat University

2 Thanon Phra Chan (0 2221 6111/www.tu.ac.th). Tha Chang/Tha Prachan. **Open** 8.30am-4.30pm Mon-Fri. **Map** p248 B3.

The country's second-most prestigious university after Chulalongkorn dates from 1932. A statue of its founder, statesman Pridi Bhanomyong, sits in front of its drill bit-shaped tower, near a Chinese stone lion bedecked with animalian offerings. Thammasat stu-dents are known for dissent and were the leading demonstrators (and victims) of the 14 October 1973 and 6 October 1976 incidents, recorded on two memorials inside the gate on Thanon Deuan Tula (October Road; *see p62* **Rights sights**). In 2002 all but postgraduates were shifted to the distant Rangsit campus, despite protests about the loss of the activist spirit of this political crucible. Some allege that was the motive.

Wat Mahathat

3/5 Thanon Maharat (0 2222 6011). Tha Chang. **Open** 7am-8pm daily. **Map** p248 B3.

Less handsome than its neighbours, this large monastic temple is nonetheless important. All Thai capitals have ritually required a royal temple of a holy relic (*maha that*), though the public cannot see the interior of this one. It's also the first of Thailand's two Buddhist universities, founded in the 18th cen-tury. This is where King Rama IV spent 24 years as a monk before assuming the throne in 1851. Later, Rama V donated a library for the monks.

This feels more like a working temple than many Rattanakosin *wats* and its International Buddhist Meditation Centre runs English-language medita-tion classes, Dhamma talks and retreats (*see pp175-179*). From Sanam Luang, you enter through the gates of the imposing Thawornwatthu Building, an East-meets-West architectural fusion designed by Prince Naris as a royal funerary hall.

Theming heritage

Cut by King Rama V in 1903, **Thanon Ratchadamnoen Klang** – or 'royal passage' – was remodelled in 1939 by the Phibunsongkram regime as a nationalistic boulevard based on the Parisian model. Though the avenue became dowdy, today's government aims to revive its status, envisaging it as the 'Champs-Elysées of Asia'. The buildings will be restored and zoned for (from west to east): art and culture, edutainment, import/export, Thai food and duty free. Hotel rooms will increase, with the Royal Hotel getting a boutique makeover. Already nightmarish, the consequent increase in traffic will be drained into underpasses, with subway lines running nearby. It has a projected cost of 13 billion baht and should be well under way by 2007, the king's 80th birthday and Bangkok's 225th anniversary. By then, Thailand's answer to the Smithsonian, the **National Discovery Museum**, will have started to occupy the old, former ministries.

This project will at least involve some public input, unlike the **Krung Rattanakosin Plan** of 1997, which seeks to turn the old town and Thonburi into a historical park through 20 projects over two decades. While glorifying landmarks and opening up vistas along a riverside promenade, the plan would halve the population, destroying old communities and their culture simply because they occupy younger buildings. Chinatown is to face a similar 'cleaning up'. Ironically, subordinating the city to tourism may ruin much of what draws tourists in the first place: the streetlife.

The apothecaries, shophouses, trades and decorated trucks of Tha Pra Chan and Tha Tien would disappear, while chainstores could stay, because they 'serve visitors'. The National Theatre (a prime example of later Thai design) would be demolished to reveal one side of Wat Bovornsathan Suttavat, which is noted more for its murals than its profile. The adjacent dance school and Thammasat undergraduates have already been banished to the suburbs. The loss of the dance school seems particularly counter-productive, since performances here would fill a tourism gap, while also boosting Thai heritage.

Residents and academics assail the plan, saying it would crush the city's soul for the sake of a 'nationalistic theme park'. In addition, Thai life favours ad hoc activity, so any bland new expanses that the plan succeeds in creating would simply be later eaten up, making the intervening loss all the more tragic. Some find hope in the fact that grand plans in Bangkok have a habit of fizzling out.

Wat Pho & around

Bangkok's oldest and largest temple, **Wat Pho**, spreads out behind the Grand Palace. To its east stand ministries, **Saranrom Park**, **Wat Ratchapradit** and, across Khlong Lord, the marvellous **Wat Ratchabophit**. Flanking the western side, Tha Tien has ferries to Wat Arun and offers a rare glimpse of early Bangkok market life. Dandied up with pilasters, pediments and stucco akin to Tha Chang's, its shophouses still function authentically. Aromas emanate from herbal apothecaries, dried fish stalls, cafés and warehouses. Shockingly, this atmospheric gem is under threat from 'conservation' (*see above* **Theming heritage**). From 9pm until 11pm daily, Thanon Maharat becomes the city's largest wholesale market for Thai *khanom* (sweets). At Rattanakosin's southern tip, the future Thailand History Museum and the 1914 Phra Ratchawong police station face across the Charoenrat 31 Bridge over Khlong Lord to **Pak Khlong Talad** flower market (*see p135*).

Saranrom Park

Thanon Charoen Krung, at Thanon Rachini (0 2221 0195). Tha Tien. **Open** 5am-9pm daily. **Map** p248 B4.
This picturesque former garden of Saranrom Palace has been public since the 1960s and, like all Thai parks, is liveliest around dawn and dusk. Expect loud music as mass aerobics classes step to the beat and joggers thud by the ponds, cherub fountain, Chinese pagoda (at the rear) and central memorial from King Rama V to his wife Queen Sunanda (who drowned in a boating accident in 1880).

Wat Pho

2 Thanon Sanam Chai (0 2221 2974/3686). Tha Tien. **Open** 8am-5pm daily. **Admission** B20. **No credit cards. Map** p248 B4.
Formally called Wat Phra Chetuphon, this mellow place rewards wandering, despite some touristy aspects. Its popular name derives from the 16th-century Wat Photharam, which was rebuilt as part of Rama I's grand Rattanakosin scheme. In one of several restorations, Rama III added its monumental Reclining Buddha in 1832. Rama III also turned Wat Pho into Thailand's 'first university', ordering the walls to be inscribed with lessons in astrology, history and literature. It remains a core repository

of traditional medicine, meditation and traditional massage (*see p178*) – perfect for weary sightseers.

Made from brick and gilded plaster, the Reclining Buddha is an awesome 46m (151ft) long and 15m (49ft) high. With pillars of the *vihaan* built around it obscuring a full view, the head and feet capture the photographer's focus. A picture of serenity, this recumbent position illustrates the Buddha passing into Nirvana. Visitors linger over its large, flat-footed soles, where mother-of-pearl inlay (an early Rattanakosin speciality) depicts 108 auspicious

signs. The mystical number 108 recurs in the quantity of bowls spanning the chapel wall, with a coin dropped in each bringing luck and longevity.

Wat Pho is also a refuge for antique Buddha images rescued by Rama I's brother from Ayutthaya and Sukhothai, with a major Ayutthayan image in the *bot*. (The ashes of Rama I were interred in its pedestal base by Rama IV.) Protecting the inner sanctuary are large pairs of stone guards with Western features. Wat Pho houses a staggering 99 *chedi* (nine is another lucky number to Thais), the

Walk 2 Khlong Lord

Dug as a defence for Rattanakosin Island, this tree-shaded canal carried produce from the river to the Weekend Market when it was at Sanam Luang, and now offers a tranquil setting for a stroll lasting an hour or so.

Its western side, **Thanon Ratchinee**, starts at Thailand's fanciest drinking fountain. Erected in 1872, it encloses a beautiful sculpture of Mae Phra Thorani, the Earth Goddess, who wrung water from her hair to wash away the demons trying to corrupt the Buddha. Heading south, you pass the Civil Court, the Department of Public Prosecutions and the **Ministry of Defence**. These look across the canal to Thanon Atsadang, where fifth-reign shophouses with crumbling European detailing peddle musical instruments, clocks and military uniforms. One of the canal's many interesting bridges is **Charoensri 34 Bridge**, which was named in honour of Rama VI's 34th birthday. Decorated with Thai number fours indicating the year of his reign, the structure was built to withstand an elephant's bulk.

Lining the canal route are timber lamp-posts shaped like the original wooden Thonburi city wall pillars. Just beyond, floral garlands hang from the snout of a gilded **Pig Memorial**, erected in 1913 to honour Rama VI's mother, who was born in the Year of the Pig. Donations for this monument also paid for **Saphan Pee Goon** ('pig year bridge'), which you can cross to reach the Euro-classical Ministry of the Interior on Atsadang and **Wat Ratchabophit**. On the opposite bank is **Wat Ratchapradit** (for both, *see p67*), which you can dart back over to on **Saphan Hok**, an amalgam of four similar footbridges that used to traverse the canal (it was reconstructed in 1982).

Also on the Ratchanee bank is **Saranrom Park**, a gay cruising area by night, offering walkers a verdant breather and fruit juice

vendors the chance to hawk their wares. A few metres south from here, you can cross back again to Atsadang for some even finer, even more crumbling shophouses, and **Baan Mor Market** (*see p134*), named after its hidden, still used private palace. Finally, grab dinner and a drink at **Café Today**, which faces Saranrom Park – by which time, Thanon Chakphet (running east from the end of Khlong Lord) will be knee-deep in **Pak Khlong Talad** flower market (*see p135*).

main four being the colour-themed Phra Maha Chedi, signifying the first four Chakri reigns. In Rattanakosin style, they resemble a square bell, with indented corners and floral ceramic cladding. Two hold the remains of Ramas II and III, while another enables slim sightseers to climb inside and enjoy a unique viewpoint. The *kuti* (monks' quarters) lie south of Thanon Chetuphon, where the main entrance is less tout-ridden than the gate by the Reclining Buddha.

Wat Ratchabophit

2 Thanon Fuang Nakhon (0 2221 1888). **Open** *Temple* 5am-8pm daily. *Bot* 9-9.30am, 5.30-6pm daily; 8.45am-3.30pm religious holidays. **Map** p248 B4.
With a fruit market at the side and schoolchildren playing in its grounds, this seldom-visited but fabulously ornate temple is most lively in late afternoon. Begun in 1869, its structure encloses the main *chedi* with a unique circular cloister encased in pastel Chinese porcelain, from which other buildings protrude. The small inner chapel feels European thanks to its Gothic columns, with intricate mother-of-pearl doors. The doors bear toy-like carvings of soldiers. The *wat* also has a cemetery for Rama V's family.

Wat Ratchapradit

2 Thanon Saran Rom (0 2223 8215). **Open** *Temple* 9am-5pm daily. *Bot* 9-9.30am, noon-5pm daily; 8am-5pm religious holidays. **Map** p248 B4.
Less grandiose than its neighbours, this pretty little grey marble temple has an inviting, contemplative atmosphere. Another amalgam of East and West, it was begun in 1864 on what was then a coffee plantation bought for the Thammayut Nikai sect by Rama IV (who is depicted observing a lunar eclipse in the murals focusing on Thai festivals). His ashes are contained under a replica of the Phra Buddha Sihing in a *vihaan* flanked by two *prang*.

Ratchadamnoen Klang

Once the city limit, this fascinating area was formally planned around **Thanon Ratchadamnoen Klang**, the 'royal passage' linking the Grand Palace and the regal residences of Dusit Park. Lit by lamps in the shape of mythical *kinnaree/kinnon* (half-bird, half-woman/man), this broad, tree-lined middle (*klang*) section has become a traffic artery flanked by identical rows of sleek buildings designed by Jitsen Aphaiwong under the Phibunsongkhram regime in 1939. After drifting into a commercial backwater the boulevard will soon be upgraded (*see p65* **Theming heritage**). Elaborate decorations bathe the road in fairylights at royal birthdays.

The avenue features two political landmarks: the **14 October Monument** at the corner of Thanon Tanao, and the **Democracy Monument** (for both, *see p62*

Rights sights). The latter's ringed by **Café Democ** dance bar (*see p190*), **Rim Khob Fah** specialist Bangkok bookshop (*see p140*) and a branch of McDonald's that won an award for architectural sensitivity.

To the south, a pleasantly walkable network of streets (*see p60* **Walk 1: living history**) surrounds the City Hall and the **Sao Ching Cha** (Giant Swing) of **Wat Suthat** (*see p69*), one of the country's six principal temples. East of the *wat* is the Brahmin temple of **Devasathan** and **Rommaninat Park** (for both, *see p68*). Another smaller Vishnu shrine stands west of Wat Suthat.

A cluster of sights rings Phanfa Bridge, which crosses Khlong Ong Ang at the point where Ratchadamnoen bends north towards Dusit. A park affords a view of **Wat Ratchannadda** and its unique **Loha Prasat** (*see p69*), the 'metal palace'. Beside it, another park will be created behind a remnant of the city wall at **Mahakan Fort**. Happily, the canalside community here will, after a long fight, now be accommodated in the landscaping, not evicted. The fort's cannons were disarmed in 2002, amid concern they might be fired in a terrorist plot. Out of 14 original watchtowers, the only other survivor is Phra Sumen Fort. Further anti-clockwise are **King Prajadhipok Museum** and the **Queen's Gallery**. Looming over the scene

Phra Sumen Fort. *See p70.*

The new face of the **Thanon Khao San**: Starbucks in an old mansion. *See p70.*

beyond Mahakan Fort, the peaceful **Golden Mount** of **Wat Saket** (*see p69*) offers a fine panorama.

Devasathan

268 Thanon Dinso (0 2222 6951). **Open** 8am-6pm daily. *Chapel* 10am-4pm Thur, Sun. **Map** p248 C4.
This refurbished row of three shrines (to Shiva, Ganesha and Vishnu) was built in 1784 at the same time as the Giant Swing – their interwoven history highlighting the integration of Brahminism with Buddhism in royal ritual.

King Prajadhipok Museum

2 Thanon Lanluang (0 2280 3413-4). Tha Saphan Phan Fah. **Open** 9am-4pm Tue-Sun. **Admission** B20 Thais (free Sat, Sun, hols); B40 foreigners. **No credit cards. Map** p248 C2.
Relocated from beneath King Rama VII's statue in front of Parliament, a collection of memorabilia and photographs pertaining to the seventh Chakri reign (1925-35) now enjoys state-of-the-art audio-visual displays at the graceful former Public Works Building. The candid, non-propagandistic narrative handles the delicate issue of democracy replacing absolutism with aplomb. Coverage of his youth, Eton schooling, marriage to Queen Rambai Barni,

unanticipated crowning, constitutional challenges, abdication and last years in England provide accessible insights into early 20th-century Siamese life.

Queen's Gallery

101 Thanon Ratchadamnoen Klang (0 2281 5360-1/ www.queengallery.org). Tha Saphan Phan Fah. **Open** 10am-7pm Mon, Tue, Thur-Sun. **Admission** free. **No credit cards. Map** p248 C2.
Remodelled from Bangkok Bank's Musical Arts Centre and dedicated to Queen Sirikit, this major multi-floor space offers world-class exhibitions by leading Thai and foreign artists. Selections by top-line alumni from the bank's prestigious art prize are usually on show. The café's gift shop has a rare stock of monographs and retrospective tomes, though catalogues soon sell out.

Rommaninat Park & Corrections Museum

Thanon Maha Chai (0 2226 1704). **Open** *Park* 5am-9pm daily. *Museum* 8am-4pm Mon-Fri. **Admission** free. **No credit cards. Map** p248 C4.
Once the site of a jail, this young park boasts ponds, fountains and a large bronze of a conch shell among its attractions. In the remaining prison buildings a small penal museum displays instruments of

punishment. Outside in the cool hours, locals discipline themselves through jogging, aerobics and weightlifting in an alfresco gym.

Sao Ching Cha & Wat Suthat

146 Thanon Bamrung Muang (0 2224 9845/ www.watsuthat.org). **Open** *Temple* 8.30am-9pm daily. *Swing* 24hrs daily. **Admission** *Temple* B20. **No credit cards. Map** p248 C4.
Sao Ching Cha (the Giant Swing) stands in front of Wat Suthat. In a Brahmin New Year event, symbolising an exploit of the god Shiva, four brave men swung from this lofty red structure to grab pouches of coins with their mouths. But the swing (first located at the Devasathan) caused such casualties that the rite was banned in the 1930s. The present timber poles were erected in 1919 by the Louis T Leonowens Company in honour of their namesake, the son of Anna Leonowens (the contentious governess of *The King and I*).
Looming in the *wat* behind, Bangkok's tallest *vihaan* houses the 8m (26ft) Phra Sri Sakyamuni Buddha. One of the largest surviving bronzes from Sukhothai, it was ferried south by boat, and its base contains the ashes of King Rama VIII. Begun by Rama I in 1807, the temple took three reigns to complete, though its mesmerising murals are now decaying despite restoration. Rama II himself started the carving of its elaborate teak doors. Numerous Chinese stone statues (found in several Rattanakosin temples) served as both tributes to the king, and as valuable ballast for Chinese junks collecting rice.

Wat Ratchanadda & Loha Prasat

2 Maha Chai Road (0 2224 8807). Tha Saphan Phan Fah. **Open** *Temple* 9am-5pm daily. *Bot* 8-9am, 4-5pm daily; 8.30-10am religious days. **Map** p248 C4.
The only version of this style of spiritual architecture still standing, the step-pyramidal Loha Prasat ('Metal Palace') is modelled on a Sri Lankan metal temple from the third century BC, which was in turn based on an Indian original of 2,500 years ago. Built by Rama III in 1846, it has 37 spires, each symbolising the virtues needed to attain enlightenment. On every level a labyrinth of passages leads to meditation cells (to which entry is forbidden), with a spiral staircase ascending to interesting rooftop views. In order to reveal the Prasat, the art deco Chalerm Thai Theatre was demolished in the early 1990s amid much public debate. In its place, a park surrounds the Rama III statue and the Mahachesdabodin Royal Pavilion used for receptions of dignitaries. Behind the *wat* is an amulet market.

Wat Saket & Golden Mount

344 Chakkraphatdiphong (0 2223 4561). Tha Saphan Phan Fah. **Open** *Temple* 8am-5pm daily. *Golden Mount* 7.30am-5.30pm daily. **Admission** *Temple* free. *Golden Mount* free Thais; B10 foreigners. **No credit cards. Map** p248 C3.
Assembled from canal diggings, the Golden Mount (Phu Khao Thong) was intended by Rama III to be clad as a giant *chedi*. Proving unstable, the rubble was instead reinforced with trees and plants to prevent erosion. Shrines dot the two spiral paths to the summit, where a gilded *chedi* contains Buddha relics from India and Nepal. Its breezy, bell-chiming concrete terrace offers a 360° panorama of both old and modern Bangkok. Phu Khao Thong belongs to Wat Saket, which spreads eastward with handsome *kuti* (monks' quarters), fine murals and a peaceful atmosphere. This *wat* was where fatalities from epidemics were once brought for cremation.

Banglamphu

Until the late 1990s the Thai press referred to Bangkok's backpacker central, **Thanon Khao San** ('street of uncooked rice'; *see p70*), as a slum. Meanwhile, *farang banglamphu* (a variant of *farang kii nok* – 'birdshit foreigner') became shorthand for the cliché of the decadent, hygienically challenged travellers who stayed here, demanding discounts then splurging the savings on Beer Chang. Even before the book and film *The Beach* made this road a pop icon, the TAT promoted Khao San as a sight, and tourists duly flock here to snap its dreadlocked, batik-trousered habitués.

With travellers themselves morphing from professional hippies to hip professionals, the area has been revamped through boutique hotels, designer bars and the first attempt at pedestrianisation in Thailand. It used to be a semi-scary adventure for moneyed young Thais to venture here, but once that exotic frisson became trendy, a parallel Thai nightlife culture sprung up amid (but largely separate from) the backpacker hangouts. The monthly magazine for travellers called *Farang* both records and symbolises the upgrade. Yet Banglamphu has clung to its roots. Descendants of palace dancers and artisans still live here and **Banglamphu Market** (*see p136*) remains a labyrinthine local bazaar.

Beyond **Wat Chana Songkhram** (*see p70*), **Thanon Phra Arthit** adds to the area's colour, with art bars and contemporary cultural events by the indie generation in the riverside **Santichaiprakarn Park**. Named after British independent music labels, indie in Thailand stands for contrarian thinking in a deeply conformist society. Unusually, the park caters for the blind with Braille-marked paths and maps of attractions, such as the district's last *lamphu* trees, after which it's named. Between the park and the Bangkok Tourist Bureau under Phra Pinklao Bridge, a walkway on stilts in the river offers front views of mansions built along Phra Arthit. From the south end, these include the UNICEF offices in a former home of the queen consort to Rama IV; a home of the late prime minister, novelist and cultural pundit, Kukrit

Pramoj; and the UN-FAO building at Baan Maliwan, where Pridi Bhanomyong lived as regent for Rama VIII and directed the anti-fascist wartime Seri Thai Movement. On Phra Arthit Road, the classical ex-palace Baan Chao Phraya faces art nouveauish Baan Phra Arthit. Built by a finance minister in 1926, it housed the Goethe Institut from 1962 to 1986, then the publishers Manager Group, and features a swish café.

The park's other focus is the octagonal **Phra Sumen Fort**, a rare surviving watchtower from the city walls. Demolished by King Rama V, the wall ran inland between Thanon Phra Sumen and Khlong Banglamphu, a once commercially and defensively important canal dug two centuries ago by Lao prisoners of war. Cutting across Thanon Phra Sumen, Samsen leads to Dusit and the elevated approach above Thanon Visut Kasat to the **Rama VIII Bridge**.

Continuing eastwards along Phra Sumen past Banglamphu Market, another slab of city wall, **Wat Bowoniwet** (*see below*) and shops stocking royal and religious imagery, you reach the **Queen's Gallery** (*see p68*). Though a slog to reach by road, Banglamphu is easily accessed by Expressboat to Tha Phra Arthit or by canal boat to Tha Saphan Phan Fah.

Thanon Khao San

www.khaosanroad.com. Tha Phra Arthit.
Map p248 B3.
Even before 1997, when Alex Garland's novel *The Beach* was published (the opening scene unravels in a Khao San guesthouse), this road was the world's most famous haunt for budget travellers. Now Khao San has some of Bangkok's priciest real estate. Hence flophouses are making way for chainstores, restaurants, bars and the rebuilding of Buddy Lodge

One of **Wat Pho** many chedis. See p65.

as a boutique hotel (*see p39*). It's a radical transformation. The first guesthouses only opened in 1982 to soak up the human flotsam spilling over from the city's bicentennial celebrations. Glimpses of the road's past can still be seen in the wooden shophouses just past Khao San Center, and in the restored mansions that now house the Sidewalk Café and the Sunset Street branch of Starbucks.

For many young travellers the road is just one long bucket shop, where they can purchase bus and ferry tickets to the islands, or plane tickets to Indochina, not to mention fake student ID cards. It also plays bargain basement for discounted clothes, beachwear and sandals – and services to 'buy anything'. The many second-hand bookshops have the best selection of contemporary fiction in Thailand. The night-time influx of young Thai artists means a wider selection of original paintings, clothing and jewellery on sale. Meanwhile, costumed Akha tribesfolk pester everyone to buy silverware.

Since closing times got earlier, Khao San is less of a party madhouse, though 'packers still pack out Gulliver's Traveller's Tavern (facing the police station) and Khao San Center (mid-way up the street). Young Thais prefer Suzy Pub, Austin Pub and the Club, in the side *soi* or quieter Thanon Rambuttri. There's still much diversity, though, from alfresco hair-braiding and Thai vegetarian cooking classes at May Kaidee (*see p109*) to receiving or studying massage at Pian (*see p179*), cheaper than at Wat Pho.

Wat Bowoniwet

248 Thanon Phra Sumen (0 2281 6411).
Open 8am-5pm daily. **Map** p248 C3.
Home to both the city's second Buddhist university and the Supreme Patriarch (leader) of Thai Buddhism, this temple is a major focus on Buddhist holidays. Founded in 1826, it melds Thai and Chinese designs, with gilded *naga* balustrades and windows adorning the main chapel. Kings Rama IV and Rama IX were both ordained here, the former becoming its abbot before his reign.

Wat Chana Songkhram

77 Thanon Chakrabong (0 2280 4415). Tha Phra Arthit. **Open** 6am-6pm daily. **Map** p248 B3.
Originally built in Mon style – because Rama I got many Burmese to lay the groundwork for the fledgling city – this great monastery was renovated and proudly renamed the 'winning the war temple' after the sovereign's brother won an important battle against the Burmese. Most of the 300 monks here study Pali (the ancient Sanskrit derivative in which the Buddhist scriptures were first written down) at the temple school.

Wat Tri Thosathep

Thanon Prachatipathai (0 2281 9906). **Open** 6am-9pm daily. *Murals* 8am-5pm Mon-Sat. **Map** p248 B3.
National Artist Chakraphan Posyakrit has undertaken one of the most ambitious murals of our times. Still five years from completion, his romantic, painterly images adorn this relatively recent temple.

Thonburi, River & Canals

The Chao Phraya's west bank evokes 'Venice of the East' clichés.

Maps p248 & p250

The Mae Nam Chao Phraya ('River of Kings'), with its attendant canals and watercourses, once united all Bangkok in its aquatic embrace. But auto-obsession has led to many *khlong* (canals) being paved over in service to the god of four wheels. However, the river still bisects Bangkok and its sister city of Thonburi, and there are signs that the city is slowly rediscovering its watery soul.

If you look at old maps and journals, you'll see Chao Phraya called River Menam, a tautology (it means 'River River'), but an indicative error nonetheless since *mae nam* literally translates as 'mother of waters'. Thai culture centres on water's maternal power and benevolence, whether for fish or *padi* (rice fields), transport or trade, ritual or play. Mythically, it's home to *naga* – wrathful serpents seen in temple decor, tattoos and other iconography. *Kwetiao reua* (boat noodles) still get served in boat-shaped containers today.

But rivers, even motherly ones, have dark aspects too. Draining a basin the size of Britain into a narrow funnel through Bangkok, the Chao Phraya instinctively wants to flood, despite embankments and canals. But with the flood comes fertility. The nourishing inundation of the central plains (though a nuisance to the concrete conurbation of today) was precious to pre-modern Siamese. Some stilt houses survive – though dam releases, motorboats and sanitation laws make raft-living untenable. Currently 30 kilometres (18 miles) to the south, the sea once lapped north of Bangkok, with silt expanding the delta five metres (16 feet) a year. But in an ominous sign, higher seas have started eroding the coastline.

The force of tide and current is apparent when you're aboard cross-river *kham fahk*. These tubby ferries chug strenuously in looped arcs, wallowing uneasily between the diverse traffic ploughing the ochre eddies, black *khlong* outflows and carpets of water hyacinths (a Brazilian plague that clogs waterways, but can be woven into furniture). The vessels range from commuter expressboats, pleasure cruisers and longtails with car engines, to canoe vendors, floating banks and dainty tugs pulling barges of commodities like rice or cement. Whether of teak or steel, the hulking beetle-shaped barges still support the floating lifestyle evocatively painted by Vorasan Suparp.

The *khlong* goodbye?

Bangkok's fabled 'Venice of the East' status survives – but only just – in the canal-laced orchard districts of Bang Phlad, Bang Kruay and Nonthaburi province. Looping through Khlong Om and Khlong Bangkok Noi by longtail or tour boat, you pass wooden stilt house communities, served by ancient *wats*, pierside stores and boat vendors selling hot noodles and produce to residents lounging on their flower-decked verandas. At dawn monks paddle for alms through the mist; come late afternoon, families bathe and boys dive-bomb off humpback bridges.

Increasingly, though, this lifestyle is threatened by new highways that criss-cross this idyll, opening it to concrete development that blocks canals, pollutes the water and paves the fertile soil. During the 1995 floods, the area was submerged longer in order to spare Bangkok (and, some suspect, to kill the orchards, thus facilitating land speculation). Embankments, however, damage the ecology and cause treacherous waves for small boats.

Bangkok's canalscape could be salvageable through gentrification by lifestyle-oriented commuters, though pioneer arrivistes seem to prefer classical edifices to the old Siamese style. You can also visit (and stay in) more intact canal areas south-west of Bangkok (*see pp101-104*).

Walk 3 Old Thonburi

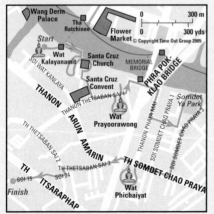

Sightseeing

Winding through riverside alleys, this pleasant walk reveals a virbant, 200-year-old Thonburi community; the Bangkok Tourist Bureau (see p235) also covers this route in a tour. Start at **Wat Kalayanamit**, near the mouth of Khlong Bangkok Yai. Founded in 1825 by a Chinese nobleman, the temple's huge *vihaan* boasts multi-superlatives: Thailand's highest *chofa* (roof finial), biggest bell and largest indoor sitting Buddha (15 metres/49 feet high).

A new river walkway leads round via the joss-hazed Chinese shrine of **Kiang An Keng** to the maze of wooden houses in the Sino-Portuguese Kudee Jeen community around **Santa Cruz Church and Convent**. Often rebuilt since King Taksin's time, the current cream-and-pink edifice topped by an octagonal dome dates from 1916. Known as 'Wat Kudee Jeen', it is elegantly simple inside, with light dappling through circles of stained glass depicting Jesus' life on to a stately marble pulpit under a coffered ceiling in blue and gold. A ferry from Tha Rachini serves the church's dainty pier.

A culinary legacy survives at **Khanom Farang Kudi Jeen**, a shophouse where pastries of apple and *jujube* are baked to the recipes of Portuguese mercenaries

who defended Ayutthaya from Burma. The powerful Persian-descended Bunnag clan, who helped administer Ayutthaya, built **Wat Prayurawongsawat** along Thanon Thetsaban Sai 1. Fenced in English cast iron, it features Bangkok's first Singh Hon (Sri Lankan-style) *chedi*, while across the road its verdant *Khao Mor* (artificial mountain) features Bunnag gravestones, and a pond teeming with turtles.

Turn left and curve round a riverside garden under Memorial Bridge on Thanon Phaya Mai to Thanon Somdet Chaophraya. Take two lefts into Somdet Chaophraya Soi 3 to reach **Somdet Phra Srinagarinda Boromarajajonani Memorial Park**. The king's late mother, known as Somdet Ya, was born a commoner to goldsmiths and practised nursing. This memorial recreates her girlhood home on land donated by Daeng and Lek Nana, landlords of Sukhumvit's Soi Nana, in 1993. Mature trees and plants frame a bas-relief depicting Somdet Ya's altruism. A museum documents Thonburi and royal family history (open 9am-4pm daily, admission B30), while a gallery holds quarterly exhibitions.

Cross Thanon Somdet Chaophraya and to your right is another Bunnag temple donated to Rama III, **Wat Pichayayatikaram Worawihan**, housing a Sukhothai-era Buddha image from Phitsanulok.

To extend the walk, cross thunderous Thanon Prachatipok into Thanon Thetsaban Sai 3, turn right then left into Itsaraphap Soi 24, then cross Thanon Itsaraphap into Soi 15 and **Baan Silpa Thai**, where the *khon* masks sold at Chatuchak Weekend Market have been made for two decades. The artisans may let you try crafting the gilded *Ramayana* characters (on sale for B1,000-B5,000; papier-mâché ones are B100). Nearby in **Baan Laos** (No.343; open 8-11am Mon-Fri) Jarin Klinbuppha now makes his *khlui* (bamboo flutes) in plastic.

Since the city was originally built to face the water, travelling by boat (see p74 **Pier groups** and p227) is not only quicker, but reveals the capital's oldest face, which neglect has helped preserve.

FANG THON

Despite its size and significance as the previous capital, *fang thon* ('Thonburi side') gets dismissed as the 'other' bank of the river. One official map appropriates its oldest districts

Bangkok's waterways are a hive of activity.

as 'West Rattanakosin'. Many sights lie between **Bangkok Noi** and **Khlong San**, but even Thonburi's prime tourist fetcher, **Wat Arun**, is usually visited on tour diversions from Bangkok itineraries. Heading west, many see just malls and a dense mass of low-income housing from the expressway heading west above thunderous Thanon Phra Pinklao and the Southern Bus Terminal. Yet the canals of Thonburi, Bang Khunthien, Bang Kruay and Nonthaburi still harbour a residual canal life (*see p71* **The** *khlong* **goodbye?**).

Around Khlong San

Facing the Bangrak finance hub, Khlong San has spawned three top hotels. Best reached by ferry, the **Marriott Bangkok Resort** is like

staying upcountry, while the equally luxurious **Peninsula** (for both, *see p40*) soars beside the **Oriental Spa** (*see p177*). Nearby, the white saucer-topped edifice built as a Sofitel was abandoned in 1996 amid whispers of subsidence, but is being restored as the Hilton. It faces River City and flanks the lively, commuter-jammed Khlong San Market and **Yok Yor Marina & Restaurant** (*see p56*), one of many dinner cruise operators, with a restaurant on the marina.

The SkyTrain will soon extend to Thailand's main southbound artery, Phetkasem Highway, which heads for Malaysia from just east of the equestrian statue of **King Taksin the Great** at the Wong Wien Yai intersection. The statue

– brandishing a sword and wearing a stetson-esque hat – directs a vehicular armada through Thonburi's daunting gridlock. From adjacent **Wong Wien Yai railway station** – unbeknown to many Bangkokians – you can catch a train heading south-west to Mahachai seafood market, where Yaowarat restaurants buy their catch. This may get upgraded into a commuter line.

A cluster of low-key sights near the mouth of **Khlong Bangkok Yai** makes for a fetching three-hour walking tour – for which you can use signs from the Bangkok Tourist Bureau (*see p235*) tour for B100. Tours down Khlong Bangkok Yai often branch off south-west at Wat Paknam where *khlong* lifestyles may still be glimpsed along **Khlong Daokhanong**, **Khlong Bangkhuntien** and **Khlong Lart**. Sadly, **Wat Sai Floating Market** is a concrete-and-souvenir shadow of its former role as an agricultural exchange. The Ayutthayan-era **Wat Sai** (Thanon Thavorn-wattana, 0 2415 7173) is noted for its circular belfry and *kanok* (flame) lacquer work on the Tamnak Thong monks' quarters.

Around Khlong Bangkok Yai

Its profile familiar from the TAT logo and B10 coin, the five-towered temple of **Wat Arun** is an icon of Bangkok. King Taksin appended it to his new palace, **Wang Derm** (inside the Royal Thai Navy headquarters). Walking distance north, **Wat Rakhang** (on Soi Wat Rakhang; open daily 6am-6pm) was restored by King Taksin and is famed for its red *hor trai*, comprising three teak scripture halls where Rama I stayed before his reign (his ashes are interred here). King Taksin replaced the melodious *rakhang* (bell) that he took to Wat Phra Kaew with the five bells that now hang in the belfry beside a perfectly proportioned *prang*.

Wat Rakhang can be combined with a weekend show at **Patravadi Theatre** (*see p196*) and/or the riverfront **Supatra River House** restaurant (*see p198*); they're run by daughters of the woman who founded the Expressboats. From there, an alley leads through **Prannok Market** to **Siriraj Hospital**, the world's fourth largest, which treats royalty and houses several museums

Pier groups

The Chao Phraya River offers some of Thonburi's – and Bangkok's – most evocative sights, whether you hire a longtail boat taxi, take a tour or ride the Expressboats to Nonthaburi, a suburban provincial capital 33 kilometres (20.5 miles) inland. For boat tours, *see p56*. For the sights noted, check the **Sightseeing** chapters.

Pak Nam to Saphan Taksin

Piers S3-S1 & Central; South and Thonburi.
Few tours visit Pak Nam (the river mouth). The furthest downstream most boat tours go is **Rama IX Bridge**, the suspension span beside the **Thai Farmer's Bank** headquarters. But a hired longtail can zip around the battleships and container behemoths between the vast green forest of trees at **Bang Kra Jao** and the vast grey forest of cranes at **Khlong Toey** port. Or you can view the harbour traffic from the wooden decks of **Baan Klang Nam** seafood restaurant (3792/160 Rama III Soi 14).

Expressboats U-turn at **Wat Ratchasinghkorn**, but it's classier to start the upstream journey from the **Marriott Bangkok Resort** (*see p40*), between **Krung Thep Bridge** and the white portico and campanile of the **First Presbyterian Church**, opposite early *godowns* (warehouses). The Marriott's free

teak shuttleboats and luxury converted barge *Manohra* pass a 19th-century **Protestant Cemetery**, replete with Gothic tombs, beside the **Menam Hotel**. On the western bank, the pointy **Tridhos Marina** condo was designed by Mom Tri Devakul. Thonburi's **Chao Phraya River Cultural Centre** faces the **Fisheries Organisation**'s market, the **Royal Thai Naval Dockyard** and the ship-shaped *chedi* of **Wat Yannawa**, for which you alight at Central Pier under Saphan Taksin BTS station.

Oriental Hotel to River City

Piers N1-N3. Bangrak and Thonburi.
The **Shangri-La** hotel (*see p42*) stands on the east bank beside the classical edifices of **Assumption College**, **EAC** (Eastern Asiatic Company) and the **Oriental** hotel (*see p42*) – which runs the **Oriental Spa** (*see p177*) and **Sala Rim Nam** restaurant (*see p198*) on the western bank beside the soaring tower of the **Peninsula** hotel (*see p40*). Historic edifices continue on the east side with the restored **French Embassy** and mouldering Italianate **Customs House**, soon to be an Aman Resort hotel; the green-glass slab of the **Communications Authority Tower** is typical of developments snubbing their location. Beyond the leaf-shaded

(*see below*). Skirting its historic buildings and **Wat Amarin Market** you reach **Bangkok Noi train station**, a Western-style, Rama V-era brick building. It was used by the Japanese in World War II, hence the heavy Allied bombing of Bangkok Noi. It acts as a tourist centre, from where some trains depart for Nakhon Pathom and Kanchanaburi.

Siriraj Hospital Museums

Thanon Phrannok (0 2419 7000 ext 6363). Tha Siriraj. **Open** *Parasitology & Thai Medicine museums* 9am-4pm Mon-Fri. *Other museums* 8.30am-4.30pm Mon-Fri. **Admission** free. **Map** p248 A3.

The six small museums within Siriraj Hospital are a bizarre testament to medical advancement. Dowdily displayed and aimed more at students, they're definitely not for the squeamish, though some of their prize exhibits were briefly stolen by a demented thief. The Si Ouey Forensic Medicine Museum (department of forensic medicine, second floor, 0 2419 7000 ext 6547) contains skulls, pickled organs, stillborn babies, crime scene photos and the preserved body of murderer Si Ouey, the subject of a recent movie. The Congdon Anatomical Museum (anatomy department, third floor, 0 2419 7035) displays human organs and bones from embryo to maturity, plus anomalies such as Siamese twins (named after Thai-Chinese conjoined brothers Chang and Eng, born in 1811). Two floors down, the Sood Sangvichien Prehistoric Museum & Laboratory (0 2419 7029) looks at human and animal evolution.

The Ellis Pathological Museum (department of pathology, second floor; 0 2411 2005) features diseases at macroscopic and microscopic scale. On the second floor of the parasitology department, the Parasitology Museum (0 2419 7000 ext 6488) contains home-lovin' hookworms, whipworms and tapeworms preserved with the organs they've adopted. The Ouay Ketusingh Museum of History of Thai Medicine (department of pharmacology, first floor, 0 2411 5026) examines indigenous healing knowledge, and includes mannequins of birth, ageing, sickness and death.

Wang Derm

Royal Thai Navy Headquarters, 2 Phra Ratcha Wang Derm, Thanon Arun Amarin (0 2475 4117/fax 0 2466 9355/www.wangdermpalace. com). **Open** 8.30am-4pm by written appointment. **Admission** B60. **No credit cards**. **Map** p248 A5.

Meaning 'original palace', King Taksin's compound of Chinese-influenced buildings orginally included

Santa Cruz Church.

Portuguese Embassy more concrete 'improvement' blights the mouth of Khlong Phadung Krung Kasem, between the overscaled **Royal Orchid Sheraton Hotel** and bland **River City** antiques mall (*see p139*), which serves all river hotel ferries. The saucer-topped tower opposite has finally been finished as a Hilton hotel.

River City to Bangkok Noi

Piers N4-N11; Chinatown, Phra Nakorn and Thonburi.

The dainty **Holy Rosary Church**, the classical **Siam Commercial Bank** (Thailand's first bank building) and an ancient Chinese temple precede a shambles of encroachment from Chinatown. So face west to admire the mural-rich temples **Wat Thong Noppakhun** and **Wat Thong Thammachat**. **Phra Pokklao Bridge** forms a double span with the river's first crossing, the obelisked **Rama I Memorial Bridge** (built in 1932). **Pak Khlong Market**'s emptied *godowns* are named after the mouth of Khlong Lord, beyond which, on Ko Rattanakosin, the exclusive **Ratchinee Girls School** sits in pert Palladian proportion near lantern-towered **Wang Chakrabongse**, a graceful palace where Prince Chakraphong's descendant now publishes 'River Books'

Sightseeing

Wat Arun, until Rama I reduced the palace grounds. Royals continued to live in Wang Derm, and three kings were born here. Rama V gave the palace to the Thai navy with instructions to preserve the throne hall and the oldest buildings. A shrine to Taksin features a sword-wielding statue of the king in a century-old *sala* that fuses Thai and Western forms. Both the palace and Wichaiprasit Fort, which guards Khlong Bangkok Yai, display antique ceramics, paintings, old Thai currency and weaponry. You must phone ahead, then fax/write two weeks before your appointment, and visit soberly dressed.

Wat Arun

34 Thanon Arun Amarin (0 2891 1149/0 2466 6752/www.watarun.org). Ferry from Tha Tien. **Open** 7am-6pm daily. **Admission** free Thais; B20 foreigners. **No credit cards**. **Map** p248 A5.
This landmark has been known as the 'Temple of Dawn' ever since Chaopraya Taksin landed by the then Wat Magog at sunrise in October 1767. Renamed Wat Jaeng when part of Taksin's palace, it became Wat Arunratchawararamat under Rama II, before being remodelled by Rama IV, who bestowed its present title, Wat Arunratchatharam Rajaworaramahavihara. The sundry Chinese-style structures pale before the iconic, 81m-high (266ft) Khmer-style *prang*, with four satellite *prang* at each cardinal corner. These slender 'corncob' spires are inlaid with an eye-popping array of polychromatic ceramic shards. Climbing the vertiginous *prang* is forbidden since a tourist fatally fell off in 1998. Briefly home to the Emerald Buddha, Wat Arun features a stunning statue pair of mythical *yaksa* (giants), ceramic gables on its *vihaan* and *bot*, and some 120 Buddha images.

Visiting Wat Arun as part of a tour takes much of the tour time at inflated expense, yet it's just a short B2 ferry ride from Tha Tien, where the pier becomes the studenty bar Boh (*see p126*) just as the *wat* is thrown into sunset silhouette. Intermittently, it hosts a so-so son et lumière.

Khlong Bangkok Noi

A former meander of the Chao Phraya river before a 17th-century shortcut, **Khlong Bangkok Noi** is the capital's most active canal. Now hemmed in by flood barriers, its wooden stilt houses have personal piers where residents hang out. Concrete walkways and

▶ Pier groups (continued)

in a compound that also houses tourists, **Chakrabongse Villas** (*see p39*).

South of Thonburi's Khlong Bangkok Yai, **Santa Cruz Church** and its filigree jetty are flanked by the triple *chedis* of **Wat Prayoonwong** and outsized **Wat Kalayanimit**. The canal's north-bank fortress, **Vichai Prasit**, defends King Taksin's palace, **Wang Derm**, and **Wat Arun's** crockery-covered *prang*.

To the east, **Wat Pho's** spires peek above gabled shophouses at **Tha Tien**, where *wai roon* (trendies) frequent **Boh** bar (*see p126*) on the pier, after sunset. The landscaped esplanade affording clear views of the **Grand Palace** may be extended under the Rattanakosin Plan by demolishing much of the ancient riverside communities, **Thammasat University** (but not its dome) and the **National Theatre** (*see p196*), which rim the river towards **Phra Pinklao Bridge**.

On the Thonburi side, heads of state at the 2003 APEC summit viewed a royal barge procession at night from the Royal Navy's new pavilions. Just to the north, you pass **Wat Rakhang**, restaurants-with-a-view at **Supatra River House** (*see p198*) and **Prannok Market** and **Siriraj Hospital** before reaching **Bangkok Noi railway station** at the mouth of Khlong Bangkok Noi.

Wat Prayoonwong.

North of Phra Pinklao Bridge

Piers *N12-N29; Thonburi, Dusit and Downtown: Outer North.*
Under the Bangkok foot of Phra Pinklao Bridge, a stilted walkway from the **Bangkok**

humpback bridges allow for localised walks, but roads are scarce and boating is the norm here. Tours typically take in the **Royal Barge Museum**, **Wat Suwannaram** (for both, *see below*), **Bang Bu Village**, and fish feeding at **Wat Sisudaram** and **Taling Chan Floating Market**. The market (open 8am-5pm Sat & Sun) is mostly on land rather than on boats, but the food and souvenir vendors occupy picturesque rural environs.

Royal Barge Museum

80/1 Rimkhlong Bangkok Noi, Thanon Arun Amarin (0 2424 0004). **Open** 9am-5pm daily. **Admission** B30; camera B100; video camera B200. **No credit cards. Map** p248 A2.

It's a rare, unforgettable sight when dozens of slim, ornate boats in ancient formation carry the royal family from Vasukri Pier to Wat Arun, to present monks' robes in a *kathin* ceremony; the last one marked King Bhumibol's sixth cycle (72nd) birthday in 1999. You can see the astonishing craftsmanship of the eight most prominent barges at dry berths in this canalside hangar. User-friendly, bilingual displays of regalia, dioramas and barge lore add to the impact. Most impressive is the king's barge,

Suphannahongse ('Golden Swan'), seen on the TAT logo. Carved from a single log and powered by 50 costumed, chanting oarsmen, the original of this 45.15m- (148ft-) long, 3.17m- (10.5ft-) wide vessel was destroyed at Ayutthaya. Rebuilt by Rama I and again by Rama V, its ageing woodwork is no longer risked much afloat. Second in importance is the 54-oar, Rama IV-era *Anantanakaraj*, its bow splayed with a seven-headed *naga*. The newest, *Narai Song Suban*, with Vishnu riding Garuda at its prow, was built for the king's golden jubilee in 1996. The barges will probably next process on the king's diamond jubilee in 2006. It's easiest to get to the museum by boat, given the long slog from the road via jumbled alleys with scant signposts.

Wat Suwannaram

33 Charan Sanit Wong Soi 32 (0 2433 8045). **Open** 8am-4.30 daily. **Admission** free.

Art students flock to the *wat*'s sublimely proportioned Ayutthaya-era *bot* to sketch the Rama III-era murals by Thai artist Thongyu (primarily *jataka* tales of the Buddha's life). Chinese artist Kong Pae used slim brushes and shadows to accentuate motion. Look out for apocalyptic images of Buddha subduing Mara, and some racy erotic poses.

Tourist Bureau HQ passes mansions on **Thanon Phra Arthit** on its way to **Santichaiprakarn Park**'s *lamphu* trees and **Phra Sumane Fort**. The classical masterpiece across the river languishes unrestored as **Intara School**. North of Khlong Banglamphu lie numerous Dusit mansions, including the art nouveau **Wang Bangkhunprom**, which influenced the design of **Rama VIII Bridge**. Fussily garnished with gilded trimmings, this harp-like 2.1-kilometre long (1.3-mile) span ingeniously suspends from one 300-metre-(984-foot-) high inverted-Y pillar beside the **Bangyikhan Distillery** for Mekhong whisky. The park at its foot hosts many festivities.

On the Dusit bank, **Thewes Flower Market** frames the mouth of Khlong Phadeung Krung Kasem, ahead of the **Royal Barge Dock**; just visible behind the dock is the childhood home of Queen Sirikit and **Kaloang Home Kitchen** seafood restaurant (*see p109*).

Beyond the green-shuttered royal pier Tha Vasukri, and **Wat Ratchathiwas**'s wooden *vihaan*, **St Francis Xavier Church** is the focus of a Vietnamese community. Most cruises turn back at the box-girder **Sang Hee (Krung Thon) Bridge**, the illuminated backdrop for **Khanab Nam** restaurant/boat, **River Bar Café** (*see p109*) and the **Royal River Hotel**.

Boats chugging further north encounter traditional and commercial activity interspersed with landmarks such as the **Singha** and **Amarit** breweries, **Rama VI Bridge** (carrying the southern railway), the curious-looking **Wat Khien** and **Rama V Bridge**, which opened in 2002.

Nonthaburi to Kred

Pier *N30; Outer North.*

At the Nonthaburi expressboat terminus, stroll to **Rim Fang** restaurant (235/2 Thanon Pracharat, 0 2525 1742) along the promenade (and impromptu skate park), passing the sublime wooden fretwork of **Nonthaburi Provincial Office**. Hired longtails loop back to Khlong Bangkok Noi via **Khlong Om**, which starts just after **Wat Chaloem Prakiat**, a lush, Chinese-style temple founded by Rama III in memory of his mother. Next door is the culturally themed **Chalerm Kanchanaphisek Park**. The endpoint for many river tours is **Ko Kred**, a rural, car-free islet renowned for the carved Mon ceramics at its north-eastern settlement. Facing the mainland's Pakkred ferry pier, **Wat Poramai** has a stunning Buddha image, a museum and two Mon-style *chedi*, one slipping into the river. For further excursions to **Bang Sai**, **Bang Pa-In** and **Ayutthaya**, *see pp101-104*.

Dusit

Monuments and leafy boulevards grace the royal and government quarter.

East meets West at **Wat Benchamabophit**. *See p80.*

Map p248 & p249

The attractions of this beautiful district are mainly royal, architectural and historic. Flanked by the river and the railway, its main thoroughfare, Thanon Ratchadamnoen Nok, is like a tree trunk, with branches to institutions and temples, and a crown that encompasses the grand headquarters of monarchy, military and government. The leafy enclave of Dusit Park, with its royal villas, harks back to the area's origins as Rama V's country retreat. Today it's still an escape from the hurly-burly of Downtown. A crash course in how Thai design meshed with the West, the environs of Thanon Ratchadamnoen Nok, Royal Plaza and **Chitrlada Palace** are gorgeously illuminated by fairylights for the king's and queen's birthdays (*see p157 and p161*). The ceremonial area is devoid of vendors and restaurants, but get sustenance in the Samsen district.

Ratchadamnoen Nok

In the first instance of modern Thai urban planning, Ratchadamnoen's three processional sections, from the Grand Palace to Dusit Park, were modelled on the Champs-Elysées (seen by Rama V during a trip to Paris). A row of streamlined 1940s blocks, the middle section (Thanon Ratchadamnoen Klang; *see p67*) will soon get refurbished with Champs-Elysées-style boutiques, while the more institutional outer arm (Thanon Ratchadamnoen Nok) focuses not on an arch, but on the Italianate marble and copper-domed **Ananta Samakhom Throne Hall** (Thanon Uthong Nai). The first Thai parliament convened here and it is still used for state occasions. Behind it lies the modern **Parliament** (Thanon Uthong Nai) in democratically horizontal concrete, with a brutalist-yet-breezy Brasilia aesthetic. It is open to the public only on Children's Day (*see p159*). In Parliament's forecourt stands a statue of King Rama VII, who granted the first constitution, though the collection of related artefacts has moved from here to the **King Prajadhipok Museum** (*see p68*). The National Assembly itself will move to a new, bigger parliament in the suburbs or even in Lopburi province. Also behind the Throne Hall, the wooden villas in **Dusit Park** (*see p82*) show the fretwork verandas and shutters of 'tropical European' taste – a more accurate term than 'colonial style' since Siam wasn't colonised.

The **Royal Plaza** in front of the Throne Hall contains the equestrian statue of King Rama V (*see right* **The god king**) and hosts ceremonies like the **Trooping of the Colour** (*see p157*). The plaza is flanked by the British-style former Supreme Command building and to the west, Amporn Gardens, whose art deco pavilions host occasional events, ranging from royal social events to a fair selling goods handmade by Thailand's prison population.

Bangkok is the United Nations' regional HQ, and the **UN ESCAP** (United Nations Economic and Social Commission for Asia and the Pacific, Thanon Ratchadamnoen Nok, 0 2288 1234, www.unescap.org, open by appointment) occupies an eye-catching Thai modernist building that curves around one corner of the double bridge over Khlong Phadung Krung Kasem. Bisecting Ratchadamnoen Nok and lined with flame trees, this majestic canal arcs west to **Thewet** flower market (*see p135*) and south-east to **Bo Bae** cloth market (*see p133*).

Further south down Ratchadamnoen Nok are a TAT office and the art deco **Ratchadamnoen Boxing Stadium** (*see p203*). The Royal Thai Army headquarters opposite houses the **Royal Thai Army Museum** and exemplifies the work of Italian classical architects at the early 20th-century court.

Ananta Samakhom Throne Hall

Thanon Uthong Nai (0 2628 6300-9 ext 5119-5121). **Open** 10am-4pm daily. **Admission** B20 Thais; B10 concessions; B50 foreigners; free with Grand Palace ticket stub. **Map** p249 D1.
Though ostensibly built in marble, this national symbol was the first Thai building constructed (1908-16) on ferro-concrete pilings, a technique that Rama V saw in Europe. Its awesome cruciform interior – heavily gilded, with mosaic scenes of Chakri reigns I-IV lining the dome – held the first Thai parliament, and still hosts state occasions.

Royal Thai Army Museum

113 Thanon Ratchadamnoen Nok (0 2297 8121-2/ www.rta.mi.th). **Open** by appointment. **Admission** free. **Map** p249 D2.

The god king

Thais refer to their kings as *pra jao paan din* ('god of the earth') and regard them as reincarnations of Vishnu, so they continue to be revered even after their deaths. **King Chulalongkorn** (aka Rama V), who reigned from 1868 to 1910, is particularly highly thought of. As well as abolishing slavery, developing institutions and staving off Western colonialism, he learned about his subjects' concerns by disguising himself as a commoner. In gratitude, his portrait is widely venerated in homes, restaurants and workplaces, as well as on amulets, banknotes and busts used as talismans. On Chulalongkorn Day, 23 October (the anniversary of his death), devotees gather in **Royal Plaza** (*see p79*) at his equestrian statue (a six-metre/20-foot bronze he had cast during a 1907 visit to France). Offerings are also made here on Tuesday and Thursday evenings, asking for luck in business, advice on marital matters or good exam results. The press reported that a gaggle of college girls even brought 999 pink roses to pray for new boyfriends. More common offerings tend to include two of the monarch's favourite things: cognac and cigars.

For more on Thai monarchy and the present king, *see p15* **Rama reincarnate**.

Models, weapons, flags, uniforms and insignia dominate this collection housed in the classical-style army headquarters and armoury of the Chulachomklao Royal Military Academy.

Chitrlada

King Bhumibol and Queen Sirikit reside at **Chitrlada Palace** amid tree-shaded gardens, protected by a wall and moat around which people stroll and jog. Although the royal quarters are private and concealed, the facilities of the **Royal Projects** (royally sponsored development schemes for sustainable agriculture and industry) may be toured and are just visible along the side facing the horse-racing track of the **Royal Turf Club** (*see p202*). This most royal of sports was introduced to Siam after Rama V's European tour in 1897, and the club was founded in his son's reign. As well as holding biweekly races and four annual derbies, it also tests and registers the country's thoroughbreds.

Between Chitrlada and Dusit Park is the remodelled **Dusit Zoo**. Flanking the zoo, Khlong Prem Prachakorn canal leads south past the touristy royal temple of **Wat Benchamabophit** to **Government House**, which was built in the sixth reign as a noble's villa. Housing the Prime Minister's Office, **Government House** (Thanon Phitsanulok, 0 2280 3000, www.thaigov. go.th) has appropriately Byzantine detailing, with a filigree stone frontage flanked by square and domed circular turrets, and frescoed ceilings. Refurbished to host the APEC (Asia-Pacific Economic Corporation) summit in 2003, it is open only on National Children's Day (*see p159*). Some years in the hot season rural demonstrators from the Forum of the Poor camp by the adjacent canal to voice grievances. Further down Thanon Phitsanulok stands **Baan Phitsanulok**, the prime minister's residence since 1982. Legend has it that this 1925 Venetian Gothic confection is haunted.

Chitrlada Palace

Thanon Ratchavithi (0 2283 9145/booking 0 2282 8200). **Open** by written appointment only 8.30am-3.30pm Mon-Fri. **Map** p249 E1.

Once a pastoral retreat where King Rama VI wrote theatrical works and books on military history, Chitrlada Villa was expanded into a palace by Rama VII. As it is now the king's permanent residence, public access is restricted to tours (by written appointment, seven days ahead) of the Royal Projects. Project and Support Foundation products are also sold in Chitrlada Shops here and at the Grand Palace (*see p57*), Dusit Park (*see p82*) and Thai airports. It's particularly worth taking a stroll around the palace's moated perimeter during royal birthdays, when it is beautifully illuminated.

Dusit Zoo

71 Thanon Rama V (0 2281 2000/www.zoothailand. org). **Open** 9am-6pm daily. **Admission** B30; B5 concessions. **No credit cards. Map** p249 E1.

Plans to move this state zoological park from its 19ha (47-acre) site in Rama V's former botanical garden to a spacious suburban spread lie in limbo. Meanwhile, a theme park facelift added amusement rides to cater to the Thai families who dress up on weekends for a visit to its mature gardens, open-air restaurants and lake, where pedalos dodge the fountain. Though it is one of Asia's better zoos, boasting rare fauna from home and abroad, grim concrete enclosures keep the creatures subdued. Activity is most animated among the hippos, aviaries and lofty monkey pens. Elephants also offer rides.

Wat Benchamabophit

69 Thanon Rama V (0 2282 7413). **Open** 8am-5.30pm daily. **Admission** B20. **No credit cards. Map** p249 D2.

Clad in Italian cararra stone (left over from Ananta Samakhom Throne Hall), the 'marble temple' is a well-proportioned melding of East and West by Italian architect Hercules Manfredi. Both the *bot* (which has stained-glass windows of Thai mythology) and cloister were commissioned in 1899 by Rama V, who was a monk in the original Ayutthaya-era temple. Another room contains his ashes. No major temple has been built in Bangkok since.

It houses a replica of Thailand's most venerated Buddha image after Phra Kaew (the Emerald Buddha): the Phra Phutta Chinirat (the haloed Sukhothai-era original is in Pitsanulok province). Lining the cloister, 53 Buddha images cover every era, style, *mudra* (gesture) and provenance. The temple is also a good spot to see Buddhist festivals and morning alms collection, since the monks don't perambulate, but stand outside.

Samsen

Dusit's northern hinterland is a grid of tree-lined avenues containing the **Ratchabhat Institute** college and the exclusive **Vachirawut School**. Thanon Sukhothai, between Thanons Rama V and Nakhon Ratchasima, has a small northern Thai community selling the favourite Lanna lunch dish *khao soi* (noodle curry). Branching off Sukhothai towards filthy Khlong Samsen, Thanon Suphan is a lovely, leaf-dappled street with some open-air food stalls and a sacred *bodhi* tree swathed in protective sashes and offerings.

More hectic Thanon Samsen follows the river north past Samsen railway station, co-op housing and fine art at **Numthong Gallery** (*see p170*), and heads south towards Banglamphu. Down Samsen Soi 13 a riverside Vietnamese community surrounds **St Francis Xavier Church**, with **Wat Ratchathiwat** nearby. Further south at the **National Library**, an extension of Thanon Sri Ayutthaya leads past guesthouses and a temple to **Kaloang** seafood restaurant. Take a breather in the little park on the corner of Uthong Nok Road or in **Thewet Flower Market** (*see p135*).

Finally, tucked behind shophouses on the east of Samsen, is **Wat Indrawihan**. Opposite stand the pleasingly modernist **Bank of Thailand** and its museum housed in **Wang Bangkhunprom** (*see p81*), a former palace best viewed from the dramatic new **Rama VIII Bridge**.

National Library

Tha Wasukri, Thanon Samsen (0 2281 5212/ www.natlib.moe.go.th). **Open** 9am-7.30pm daily. **Admission** free. **Map** p248 C1.

Though reading is often regarded in Thailand as a chore rather than a pleasure, this mid 20th-century, Thai-style structure gets quite crowded. This may, however, have something to do with the fashion and soap opera magazines, not to mention amulets, stored on the ground floor. The impressive lobby leads to upper floors with limited volumes in English. The compound also contains the King Bhumibol Commemorative Library and the Princess Sirindhorn Music Library, devoted to Thai instrumentation.

St Francis Xavier Church

94 Samsen Soi 13 (0 2243 0060-2). **Services** 6am, 7pm Mon-Sat; 6.30am, 8.30am, 10am, 4pm Sun. **Map** p248 C1.

Evidenced by cafés of Saigon fare, a Vietnamese community surrounds this mid 19th-century church where masses are held in Thai. Beyond the ornate gates it has a cheery Mediterranean feel, with a dainty shrine of its patron saint on the portico. In the basketball court behind, a statue of Christ healing a man attracts Thai-style garlands. The adjacent Soi 13 is quite picturesque, and on the north side is the strange Pou Pee House, its beautiful façade rendered in pink with cherubs, gold fittings and a Greek goddess brandishing a torch.

Wang Bangkhunprom & Bank of Thailand Museum

273 Thanon Samsen (0 2283 5286/www.bot.or.th). **Open** by appointment 9am-4pm Mon-Fri. **Admission** free. **Map** p248 C2.

The palace of Prince Baripatra until the end of absolutism in 1932, this baroque-cum-art nouveau edifice contains the Bank of Thailand's museum. It charts Thai monetary evolution from glass beads to notes, via *pot duang*, the 'bullet coins' that were in currency for six centuries from Sukhothai to Rattanakosin. But you can't just stroll in – seven days' written notice is required. The compound also contains the newly restored Wang Devavesm mansion.

Wat Indrawihan

144 Thanon Visut Kasat (0 2281 1406). **Open** 6am-6pm daily. **Admission** free. **Map** p248 C2.

Down an alley between shophouses, 'Wat In' is notable only for its standing Buddha. Eschewing normal proportions, this figure is a lofty 32m (105ft) tall – you can climb to its head for a so-so panorama – but unfeasibly thin and anchored by outsize feet. The adjacent *vihaan* (chapel) poignantly features jars of human ashes in its terrace walls.

Wat Ratchathiwat

3 Thanon Samsen Soi 9 (0 2243 2125). **Open** 5am-9pm daily. **Admission** free. **Map** p248 C1.

Restored by Rama IV, this monastery contains two remarkable buildings. The *ubosot* contains a mural by Italian professor C Rigoli behind a stone façade with Khmer accents by Prince Naris. Naris also restyled the Ayutthayan Sala Karnparian, a sublime wooden pavilion with intricate relief panels and complex eaves.

Ananta Samakhom Throne Hall. *See p79.*

Dusit Park

The lush royal estate of Dusit Park is best known for **Wang Vimanmek**, the world's largest golden teak building. But there are plenty of other museums in this canal-laced compound offering rare insights into royalty and court life, as outlined in the continuous audio-visual displays at the **Slide Multivision Hall**.

Completed in 1901, **Vimanmek** – 'abode of the angels in the clouds' – was home to Rama V for five years. The free, compulsory guided tour (every 30-40mins 9.45am-3.15pm daily) provides a chance to peek at regal domesticity; a winding staircase leads to the royal apartment (atop an octagonal tower), where such obscure personal items as a crystal chamber pot and Rama V's wooden wheelchair survive. Downstairs is the Throne Hall, with its four ornate thrones, while sublime panelled corridors connect yet more rooms bristling with antiques. In the lakeside *sala*, dance and martial arts are performed at 10.30am and 2pm (free).

Other mansions contain carriages, clocks and ritual paraphernalia, such as palanquins, plus treasures from the prehistoric World Heritage Site of Baan Chiang in Udon Thani province. An **Ancient Cloth Museum** illustrates the diversity, meanings and status indicators of the patterns in Thai textiles, while upstairs are scenes from Rama V's trips to Europe. **King Bhumibol Photographic Museums I and II** show pictures by Rama IX, while images of his youth appear in **Suan Hong Royal Ceremonies Photography Museum**, a gorgeous green wooden mansion. Another fretwork fantasia, **Suan Si Reudu Hall**, has been reconstructed on its original site and displays Golden Jubilee gifts to Rama IX. The filigree **Hor Pavilion** was also moved here in 1998.

For her part, Queen Sirikit has been pivotal in preserving the exquisite court arts and other Thai crafts through the SUPPORT Foundation at **Bang Sai** (*see p101*); you can find some of these masterpieces in the **SUPPORT Museum**, which is housed within the **Abhisek Dusit Throne Hall** (a gem of wooden tracery), whose shop is better than the souvenir-lined entrance to Vimanmek. The SUPPORT Museum faces **Ananta Samakhom Throne Hall** (*see p79*) and **Parliament** (*see p78*).

Often missed, the **Chang Ton National Museum** displays artefacts of the sacred white elephants housed in one of their former

Wang Vimanmek.

ห้ามแตะต้อง
DO NOT TOUCH

stables. The centrepiece is a model of the Brahmin ceremony that is held when a rare *chang ton* (white elephant) is discovered and automatically belongs to the king. Chang ton must display distinguishing marks, such as pinkish-white skin and features, including its hair, tail hair, eyes, nails, palate and genitals. Since *chang ton* must not labour, the obligation of caring for one could drain a noble's finances (hence the English phrase 'white elephant', denoting something prestigious yet impractical). Tusks, ivory regalia and *mahout* charms are displayed alongside details of catching and corralling the beast, and statues of Ganesh, the revered, elephant-headed Hindu god of art, knowledge and much else.

Dusit Park

16 Thanon Ratchawithi (0 2628 6300-9 ext 5119-5121). Bus 12, 18, 28, 70, 108, 510, 516. **Open** *9.30am-4pm daily.* **Admission** *B75 Thais; B20 concessions; B100 foreigners; free with Grand Palace ticket stub.* **Map** *p249 D1.*

Chinatown

Bangkok's roots can be traced to this maze of markets, shrines and alleys.

Map p248 & p249

Bangkok may be the capital, but it has never been a quintessentially Thai city. It was shaped by the Chinese, both economically and physically, from the earliest shophouses to modern skyscrapers. Many of the city's businesses and most banks (until post-1997 foreign mergers) owe their success to the industrious offspring of Chinese labourers who arrived en masse in the 18th century. Their political and social influence has never been higher: the cabinet boasts many wealthy Thai-Chinese businessmen – including the prime minister.

Thailand's savvy approach to the rise of China echoes its successful policy toward European colonialism: remain independent through embracing some of its attributes. Things Chinese have become fashionable, cultural exchanges are frequent, Chinese tourists are a huge and growing sector, and an ASEAN-China free trade zone is proposed. Sino-Thai firms are even investing in Shanghai malls. Renewed confidence in Chinese cultural expression is focused on historical Chinatown, with the formerly quiet, family-and-temple-oriented **Chinese New Year** (*see p159*) becoming a state-sponsored street festival, led by the finance minister in Chinese costume. That's the only time the area's merchants shut, when Chinatown – indeed, Bangkok – suddenly empties.

Chinese were living in Bangkok before the city even existed. Originally invited by King Taksin (himself half Teochew) to augment the workforce, they came by ship from southern China and settled on the opposite bank of the river from the then capital, Thonburi. When King Rama I relocated to Bangkok, the Chinese were shifted south of the new city wall in 1782 to a dirt alley called Sampheng. From that nucleus grew today's Chinatown

The Thai expression 'to travel with a mat and a pot' sums up how little the immigrants brought. Mainly Teochew, with some Hainanese, Cantonese and Hokkien, they worked hard and saved even harder. Soon they were among the wealthiest commoners and were generally looked upon favourably by the Thai authorities, despite nationalistic discrimination in the mid 20th century. King Mongkut (Rama IV, 1851-68) apparently promoted immigration and intermarriage with a view to imbuing his subjects with some of that famous Chinese work ethic.

Chinatown's arch. *See p85.*

Sightseeing

Until polygamy was abolished in the court, wealthy Chinese families offered daughters as consorts, thus entering the blue bloodline.

The original settlers maintained close ties with China, though they had little option but to assimilate after World War II, due to controls on teaching Chinese languages and on immigration because of fear of communist infiltration. Given the scarcity of ethnic Chinese women, many took Thai wives and surnames (usually long compounds of auspicious words). The Chinese have integrated so well that today it's hard to gauge their magnitude. Some estimate that more than ten per cent of the population and more than half of all Bangkokians have Chinese genes.

Fewer Sino-Thais live in Chinatown nowadays: the wealthier families have moved to suburban mansions, and the ubiquitous shophouses have become offices, warehouses or wholesale shops selling products now rarely made within the community. Yet many commute daily back to an air-conditioned cubicle in the back of their shop to have the final say and issue change on all transactions, overseeing a new migrant staff – from Thailand's north-east.

Until Bangkok sprawled, Chinatown sold goods unavailable elsewhere in the city, and it had Bangkok's first department stores, then convenient for the international traders down Charoen Krung near the Oriental hotel. The diverse markets here are Bangkok's oldest; for further details on markets, *see pp133-137*. While some streets are diverse, others specialise. One-street wonders include herbalists (Thanon Rama IV west of Hualamphong station); stationery (Thanon Chakrawat between Sampeng and Yaowarat); metal cables (Thanon Songwat near Phanu Rangsi); and plastic and jute rice sacks (Thanon Songsawat near Songwat). More culturally interesting, Thanon Phlubphlachai proffers paper funeral offerings and Thanon Plangnam stocks ritual paraphernalia, such as masks, swords and tea sets.

GET LOST

Officially bordered by Khlong Phadung Krung Kasem, the river, Khlong Ong Ang and Thanon Charoen Krung, Chinatown spreads west to Khlong Lord and north towards Khlong Mahanak. It can be divided into three swathes parallel to the river: **Thanon Yaowarat** and **Thanon Charoen Krung** are thoroughfares, while the lanes of **Sampeng Lane** and **Thanon Songwat** are better for strolling (*see p86* **Walk 4: *Godown* town**).

Explore Chinatown logically and you'll miss half the fun and many of the sights. It's better to follow your nose (both scents and stenches) down microscopic *trok* (paths) and risk getting lost until a landmark pops up. Confusingly, Chinese street names on rickety signs are giving way to Thai appellations on blue placards, hence fascinating **Soi Issaranuphap** is officially **Soi 16**, and **Wanit Soi 1** is actually **Sampeng**, Chinatown's first and foremost market (*see p134*). Once notorious for opium dens, brothels, pawnshops and gambling dens, today it teems with nothing more dangerous than roving snack merchants and motorbikes overloaded with bolts of fabric.

Depending on time – and energy – there are many ways to 'do' Chinatown. You could focus on temples (Buddhist, Taoist, Chinese and Sikh). Or markets. Or food (from stalls to fancy restaurants). Or weird juxtapositions: casket makers near chicken hatcheries; mosquito coils beside cock rings. Or crane your neck up at the architecture, notably along Charoen Krung, Songwat and Ratchawong, though there are details to relish on wooden shophouses in offshoots such as Charoen Krung Sois 20 and 23. The classical columns, Sino-Portuguese detailing, sculpted shutters, tiered balconies and bursts of art deco are often partially obscured, but are amazingly free of high-rises. Presumably, no one can afford enough land to build them.

All of the above can be found in any given area, so there's no need to rush around. Still,

Goldfingers

Stand on Thanon Yaowarat, at the intersection with Phadung Dao, and you can see why it is dubbed Thailand's gold street. You'll be dazzled by the garish red and gold frontages resembling art deco-era cinemas. Ubiquitous dragons adorn awnings over counters of jewellery, while guards lounge on stools outside, holding shotguns on their laps. The most famous gold merchant is **Tang Toh Kang** (345 Wanit Soi 1, 0 2225 2898). Others noted for high gold content include **Hua Seng Heng** (332-334 Thanon Yaowarat, 0 2225 0202) and **Chin Hua Heng** (295-7 Thanon Yaowarat, 0 2224 0077).

Yaowarat gold is soft and yellow thanks to its 97.5 per cent purity. It's sold not in ounces, but in baht (different from the currency, one baht is 15.2 grammes, equalling four *saleung* of 25 *satang*). Gold is viewed as portable (and visible) wealth, and banks and pawnshops post buy/sell rates for those needing cash in a hurry.

Street scenes in Chinatown.

you need a spirit of adventure, a tolerance for heat and crowds, light clothing, comfy shoes, plenty of fluids and the invaluably annotated *Nancy Chandler's Map of Bangkok*. Alternatively, follow two signposted walks from a booth dispensing maps at River City (*see p139*).

Thanon Yaowarat

To locals, Yaowarat *is* Chinatown – an orientation word for taxi drivers. Synonymous with gold (*see p84* **Goldfingers**), this long road is also famed for its restaurants and food stalls, both relatively expensive; for reviews *see p106-125*. Between dusk and 9pm it becomes one huge night market, with vendors spreading into Soi Plaeng

Nam and Soi Phadung Dao (aka Soi Texas Suki, after an exalted sukiyaki outlet). For respite, take Soi Issaranuphap south to **Talaat Kao** (Old Market) and **Sampeng Lane**, which have traded daily for two centuries, or north through **Talaat Mai** (New Market, a mere century old) to **Leng Noi Yee** temple (*see p88*).

Today's PR message is that Yaowarat has all along been shaped like a dragon – a lucky one, of course. This revelation accompanied the visit of Chinese President Jiang Zemin, who blessed the **Soom Pratu Chalerm Prakiat** – Chinatown's ceremonial arch, which commemorated King Rama IX's 72nd birthday in 1999, the illustrious sixth cycle of both Thai and Chinese 12-year calendars – at Odeon Circle, the creature's eye. One of the

Walk 4 *Godown* town

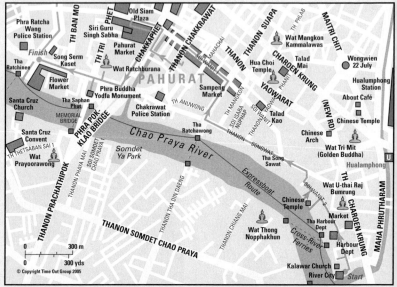

Chinatown's riverside is still cluttered with the *godowns* (warehouses) that were pivotal to Bangkok's aquatic trade. Weaving through the warehouses on the city's first inland roads, Thanon Songwat and Sampeng Lane, this half-day walk encapsulates the multicultural, multifaceted nature of the district perfectly.

Starting as an alley north from River City antiques mall, Wanit Soi 2 passes **Wat Kalawar** (Holy Rosary Church; 0 2266 4849) on the left, a Gothic riverside edifice built in 1787 on land given to the Portuguese for helping to fight the Burmese. On the path joining Soi Charoen Phanit, an ATM marks the gate of Thailand's first bank building (1904), a classical edifice that is still part of **Siam Commercial Bank**. The **Harbour Department** pier faces a famous duck-on-rice restaurant (*see p116* **One-dish wonders**) before you enter a maze of lanes coated in oil from engine parts, the trade of this precinct named

Talad Noi after a 'little market' on the right, between Charoen Krung Sois 22 and 20.

Down the left turn, follow signs to the **Riverview Guesthouse** (*see p42*), for a rooftop restaurant panorama. Secreted beyond is the 200-year-old **San Jao Sien Khong** (open 6am-6pm daily). Reputedly the oldest Chinese shrine in Chinatown, it's the only one facing the Chao Phraya river from this bank (a couple of Chinese pagodas loom on the Thonburi side). During the **Vegetarian Festival** (*see p161*) in mid October, palm oil replaces engine grease as the lubricant of choice at stalls selling meat-free and spice-free dishes to white-clad devotees of Kuan Yin, while the temple hosts non-stop Chinese opera, fairground games and giant incense.

Return via narrow, barely signed Wanit Soi 2 to its end at Soi Phanu Rangsi. Turn right and immediately left on to **Thanon Songwat**, which runs close to the river. Some time-warp alleys lead down to the river between *godowns* with

dragon's 'horns', tree-lined Thanon Traimit, boasts the solid gold Buddha at **Wat Traimit** (*see p87*), beyond which there are old bamboo stores, where brooms, baskets and utensils are still crafted by hand.

Traffic flows one way east up the dragon's mane (Charoen Krung) and west down its back (Yaowarat), with its forelegs supposedly Thanon Songwat. Another arch, **Pratu Sun Yat Sen** stands near the top of Thanon

deceptively modern frontages, where spice
and rice merchants store gunny sacks or
display huge grandfather clocks and heavy
mother-of-pearl inlaid furniture. When the
soi becomes one way, gaze up at several
beautiful but woefully unrestored Sino-
European buildings on the right.

Where Songwat ends at **Thanon
Ratchawong**, a famous vendor peddles
khanom jeeb (Chinese minced pork
dumplings) from a huge antique brass
steamer in front of the 7-11 shop. Cross
Ratchawong and head right (north), then go
left at the people-packed crosswalk marking
Sampeng Lane. Off this chaotic market alley
narrow walkways (often obscured by racks
of polyester clothes) lead left (south) to
unexpected adventures. Sampeng emerges
on to busy **Thanon Chakrawat**. Bear left to
a large metal grille (with a 100-year-old
Chinese herbalist on one side). This is the
entrance to **Wat Chakrawat**, a peaceful
temple with two tall prang, an artificial
hillside housing burial urns and a grotto with
a supposed Buddha shadow on one wall and
two ponds of large and languid crocodiles.

Back on Chakrawat, cross the footbridge,
then turn left a few steps north on to **Soi
Bhopit Phimuk**, an alley of shophouses
redolent of spices. After crossing tree-lined
Khlong Ong Ang, turn right back up to
Sampeng Lane, where a left puts you on
Thanon Chakraphet. Suddenly you're not
in Chinatown any more, Dorothy. You're
facing Little India (aka **Pahurat**, see p88).

Heading left toward the river, **Thanon
Chakkaphet** leads on to Phra Pok Klao
bridge, beside the elegant stone Saphan
Phut, the 'Memorial Bridge' to King Rama
I, whose statue commands its approaches
in a small riverside park. Behind him,
the royal temple of **Wat Ratchaburana**
(119 Thanon Chakkaphet, 0 2221 9544),
restored after bombing in World War II, was
built as Wat Liab Jeen in Ayutthayan times
by Liab, a Chinese trader. Come nightfall,
stalls flood **Saphan Phut Market** and **Pak
Khlong Talad** flower market (for both, see
p135) west along Thanon Chakkaphet.

Ratchawong, the purported hind legs. A
century after China's nationalist revolutionary
Sun Yat Sen fundraised in Bangkok (and was
twice deported for anti-monarchical conduct),
descendants of his supporters helped erect

the memorial gate in 2004. Then dubbed Trok
Sun (Sun Alley), the soi is today nicknamed
Trok Prasai (Speechgiving Alley). Yaowarat's
tail (lined with hardware shops) ends at **Merry
King Department Store**.

Wat Traimit
661 Thanon Charoen Krung (0 2225 9775).
Open 8am-5pm daily. **Admission** Temple free.
Golden Buddha free Thais; B20 foreigners.
No credit cards. Map p249 & p250 D8.
In drab surroundings, the world's biggest solid gold
Buddha statue has an almost liquid lustre that
is arguably less flattering than the gold leaf patina
on brass ones. The Sukothai-era image – 3m (10ft)
high and 5.5 tonnes (4.9 tons) in weight – had been
covered by stucco to hide it from marauding
Burmese and remained unrecognised until 1955,
when its shell cracked on being dropped from a crane
during its move here.

Thanon Charoen Krung

Occasionally still called 'New Road' because
it was Bangkok's first paved street (1861),
Thanon Charoen Krung begins around **Baan
Mor** market (see p134) and runs one way
south-east, detours at Mitraphan/Songsawat,
and re-emerges to skirt the river south through
Bangrak to Thanon Rama III.

Its first landmark is **Sala Chalermkrung**
theatre (see p166), the last remnant of an art
deco chain. With its well-restored wrought-
iron detailing and sweeping red-carpeted
staircase, it hosts everything from film
premières and festivals to Thai classical
dance and Bollywood screenings for the
Indian community of Pahurat. Completing this
block is **Old Siam Plaza**, a quaint mall of
sympathetic design stocking much that you'd
find in Chinatown, only in air-conditioned
comfort. Don't miss the ground-floor Thai
snacks and desserts. Using original recipes
and equipment, women in traditional dress
create ever-rarer delicacies, such as khanom
krok (coconut milk batter steamed in tiny
cast-iron moulds).

Beyond a block called Wang Burapha after
a long-gone palace, stalls line both sides of
Khlong Ong Ang at **Saphan Lek Market**,
and **Woeng Nakhon Kasem** retains its nom
de plume of 'Thieves' Market', though it's no
longer fencing stolen goods (for both, see p134).
Before **Khlong Thom Market** (see p134),
change pace south down Thanon Chakrawat
to enter **Wat Chai Channa Songkhram**
(0 2221 4317), notable both for its Khmer
prang and its proximity to a night-time dessert
vendor on Nakhon Kasem Soi 4 (create your
own confection from sweet ingredients in
antique copper bowls).

Passing **Leng Noi Yee** temple (*see below*)
are other entrances to Soi Issaranuphap and
Talad Mai, before a left turn leads to **Thanon
Phlubphlachai**, where dealers in funerary
paraphernalia congregate around **Li Thi
Miew Temple** (494 Thanon Phlubphlachai,
0 2221 6985), a small Daoist shrine with a
local feel. You can see satin banners and
paper accoutrements – fake money, clothes,
houses, cars – being made for burning with the
deceased to provide for the soul. Some corpses
were doubtless handled by the **Poh Teck
Tung** foundation nearby.

At the bewildering Charoen Krung/
Mitraphap/Rama IV junction, head north
up Thanon Mitraphap to the 22 July Circle
(the date Thailand dispatched forces to help
the Allies in World War I). Back southwards,
toward Rama IV, Thanon Maitreechit passes
San Chao Mae Tubtim, a joss house where
Chinese opera is performed in the **Vegetarian
Festival** (*see p161*) in October. North from
the circle lies Pomprab, a less congested
extension of Chinatown known for its **Talad
Fai Chai** (Flashlight Market) running from
5pm on Saturdays until 6pm Sunday around
Thanons Luang, Chakrawat, Charoen Krung
and Suapa. You need a torch to sift treasures
from all the drek.

Pomprab is bordered by Khlong Mahanak
and Khlong Phadung Krung Kasem, a canal
lined with flame trees, shophouses and the
railway line from Hualumphong station. From
here the subway will by 2011 pass beneath
Charoen Krung and the river to Thonburi.

About Café/About Studio

*402-408 Thanon Maitri Chit, Pomprab Sattruphai,
Chinatown (0 2639 8057/www.yipintsoi.com/
~aara). Hualumphong subway.* **Open** *periodically;
call for details.* **Map** p249 & p250 D4.

Just when the subway finally made it convenient,
this avant-garde space (host to legendary installations, performances, indie gigs, art-marts, bohemian parties and Bangkok's best library of art
criticism) goes into hibernation until 2007. By then
it will be neighbour to another gallery by AARA
(About Art Related Activities), the curatorial vehicle of alternative art darling Klaomard Yipintsoi. In
the meantime it will hold occasional events, but
maintain its international collaborations online, as
with AboutTV.

Leng Noi Yee

*Thanon Charoen Krung, between Thanon
Mangkorn & Soi Issaranuphap (0 2222 3975).
Bus 1, 16, 35, 36, 75, 93, 162.* **Open** 6am-6pm
daily. **Map** p249 & p250 D8.

Set behind an imposing multi-tiered entrance, the
'Dragon Flower Temple', also known as Wat
Mangkorn Kamalawat, is Chinatown's biggest.
Its courtyard is ringed by several sermon halls
filled with statues of Mahayana Buddhist and Taoist
deities. Dating from 1871, it takes on a livelier and
folksier ambience during the Vegetarian Festival
(*see p161*) in October.

Pahurat & Little India

From its inception, Chinatown was divided
into ethnic trading areas. The block framed
by Thanon Chakkaphet, Thanon Triphet and
Thanon Pahurat remains Little India. The
east side of Chakkaphet is known for its travel
agents, seedy cafés blasting Punjabi rock and
for the **Royal India** restaurant (*see p111*)
on a side alley. Outside its ornately carved
door, Indian sweet makers stir huge woks
of confectionery. Cross Chakkaphet and turn
right at a Chinese temple, passing the burnt-out
ATM Department Store before darting
left into 'ATM Alley'. With its open-air
shops selling incense, Indian CDs and DVDs,
Ganesh statues, saris, bangles, bindis and
spiced *chai* (tea), this funky passageway
feels more like Mumbai.

The maze-like **Pahurat** cloth market
(*see p134*) is similar to Sampeng, except it's
in rows under one large roof. Inside (directions
are hopeless) looms the yellow onion-domed
Sri Guru Singh Sabha, a four-storey Sikh
temple (0 2221 1011). The northern perimeter
on Thanon Pahurat stocks Thai classical
dancers' costumes.

Little India.

Downtown

Bangkok's diffuse commercial centre offers the city's best shopping,
dining and nightlife, studded with gems of heritage and modernity.

Sightseeing

Trunk road: **Thanon Silom.**

Ask a local where Bangkok's Downtown is
and the directions will depend on their age
and interests. Senior citizens point to the old
town, whereas youngsters would say Siam
Square. Business types proffer Thanons Silom
and Sathorn, but bus-riders would indicate the
nexus around Victory Monument. Shoppers,
meanwhile, advocate the retail crossroads of
Ratchaprasong, site of the Erawan Shrine.

Reinventing itself at speed, the capital keeps
shifting its centre of gravity, driven by whim,
rivalry, real estate and a legendary resistance
to urban planning. Fifteen years ago Thanon
Ratchadaphisek (in the North) was going to
be the new central business district (CBD);
five years later it was to be Thanon Rama III
(South), then the vaunted 'Bangkok plan',
drafted by the Massachusetts Institute of
Technology in 1996, posited the theory that
the rail junction at Makkasan's swamp (North)
represented the last chance to plan a central
business district. As we went to press,
construction was to start around Makkasan's
airport rail terminus (due in 2008) but the
plan still lacked clarity. The demarcation of
Downtown did, however, become clear with
the construction of the BTS SkyTrain in 1999.

And as mass transit expands, development
will increasingly cluster around stations.
The two BTS SkyTrain lines intersect at
Siam in **Pathumwan**, the hub of shopping,

fashion and youth culture. The Silom line
heads south to **Bangrak** via the financial
and nightlife district of Silom and Sathorn
and on to the river (*see p92* **Walk 5: Oriental
quarter**). The Sukhumvit line gives access
to the hotels, restaurants, bars and shops of
affluent **Sukhumvit**. The **North** occupies
a loop defined by Khlong Saen Saeb and the
BTS and subway, the latter two joining –
conveniently – at Chatuchak Weekend Market
(*see p136*). Attractions in Downtown's **South**,
a semi-industrial port zone, are served by both
the BTS and subway.

It's also possible to tour Downtown the
original way – by canal boat. Bisecting
Downtown, Khlong Saen Saep heads west to
Phra Nakorn and out to the suburban **East**
(*see pp98-104* **Suburbs**).

Downtown is the most convenient place to
stay, eat, shop and get things done, but since
its skyline and streetscapes continually mutate,
this makes for some fascinating juxtapositions:
spiritualism versus materialism, tastefulness
fending off vulgarity, extravagance skirting
destitution. Amid the gleaming malls and
mouldering slums, you will find traditional
houses, Asian antiquities, tranquil parks
and spiritual homes to Buddhism, Hinduism,
animism and Christianity – plus the chance
to cuddle some snakes.

Admission is free unless otherwise stated.

Bangrak

Map p250

In the mid 19th century a new grid of canals defined the triangular Bangrak district – namely, Rama IV, Si Phraya, Surawong, Silom and Sathorn, all later paved as roads, apart from Khlong Sathorn, now reduced to a polluted gutter. Bisecting them, Thanon Narathiwat Ratchanakharin follows Khlong Chong Nonsi, and features a modern sculpture of a windmill at Thanon Silom ('Windmill Road', once a site of irrigation turbines).

Bangrak's riverside is hugged by Thanon Charoen Krung, Thailand's oldest paved road (still sometimes dubbed 'New Road'). The international trading quarter once occupied this stretch between River City antiques mall and Sathorn Bridge. The lanes around the Oriental Hotel, the Assumption Cathedral and the Central Post Office retain human-scale appeal (*see p92* **Walk 5: Oriental quarter**) amid antique and craft shops, tailors, restaurants and the animated **Bangrak Market**, around the toy-like Robinson's Bangrak department store. Dwarfing a parade of classical shophouses is the pastiche classical State Tower, at the corner of Thanon Silom.

East up Silom, heritage gets packaged at **Silom Village**, a theatre, restaurant and shopping arcade in extended wooden houses.

Chao Mae Tubtim Shrine. *See p93.*

A hoard of gem stores and the towering Jewellery Trade Centre testify to Bangkok's status in the global gem trade (*see p150* **Gems without scams**). Beneath it, **Silom Galleria** is yet another art and antiques mall, containing the **Panorama Museum** (*see below*) and **Tang Gallery** (*see p170*).

Beyond the elaborate Hindu **Maha Uma Devi** temple (*see below*) and a half-demolished Chinese cemetery is Silom's busier northern end, where BTS and subway again meet. Siberian swallows flock here from October to March, but copping a dropping is, rationalise the Thais, good luck. That could explain the good fortunes of the corporate headquarters and the surrounding restaurants, shops, seafood stalls, **Silom Complex** mall, and hotels, including the spired, triangular **Dusit Thani** (*see p42*), which overlooks Lumphini Park. Off Silom toward Sathorn lie **Soi Convent** – a parade of eating places passing the Catholic St Joseph's Convent and School and the Gothic Anglican Christ Church – and **Soi Saladaeng**, a forked lane of restaurants ending in **Surapon Gallery** (*see p170*).

Bangrak means 'Village of Love' but another kind of love is pursued nightly in the go-go land of **Patpong Sois 1** and **2**, from which a tourist night market spreads past the bar strips of **Silom Soi 4** (beautiful people), **Silom Soi 2** (gay) and **Soi Thaniya** (a Little Tokyo).

Patpong and Thaniya link to slightly dingy Thanon Surawong, once Bangkok's tourist hub. Halfway back to the river down Surawong, the neighbouring **British Club** and **Neilson Hays Library** both date from the early 20th century and remain social and cultural centres for expats.

Maha Uma Devi

2 Thanon Pan (0 2238 4007). **Open** 6am-8pm Mon-Thur, Sat, Sun; 6am-9pm Fri. **Map** p250 E7.
Founded in the 1860s by the still-resident Tamil community, this Hindu temple is dubbed Wat Khaek ('guest temple') by Thais. It buzzes with Thais and Chinese making offerings to a small bronze statue of Uma Devi (Shiva's consort), and other images of Vishnu, Buddha and Uma's son, Ganesh. The multi-coloured walls, dome and tower bristle with sculptures. Rites of self-mortification happen here during the Vegetarian Festival (Sept/Oct, *see p161*) and the temple observes Diwali (Oct/Nov).

Panorama Museum

4th floor, Silom Galleria, 919/1 Thanon Silom (0 2235 4311/http://webmuseumofbangkok. pantown.com). Surasak BTS. **Open** 10am-5pm Mon-Fri; 11am-3pm Sat. **Admission** free. **No credit cards. Map** p250 E7.
A collection (with prints for purchase) of early photographic panoramas of Rama IV-era Bangkok, shot in incredible detail.

Patpong

The late Thai-Chinese millionaire Khun
Patpongpanit turned a marshy banana
plantation into this world-renowned fleshpot.
Initially a recreation ground for wealthy locals
and airline crews, it went go-go in the late
1960s as American GIs flocked here on R&R
from the Vietnam War. While outdoor bars on
Patpong Soi 2 tank up lonely booze-hounds,
the main *sois* blanded out into a Disneyfied
coach party stop, flogging tit and tat to
tourists. Guys gawp through doors at
lacklustre pole-dancing and oft-raided sex
shows, while their wives, kids and many
Thais shop for copy watches, fake Levi's or
pirate CDs of music, movies, porn and games.
Trendier clubwear and decor items spread
along Silom between **Sois 2** and **8**.

Pathumwan

Map p251

Dug during the early 19th century for
commerce and defence, Khlong Saen Saeb has
got filthy, but still offers glimpses of a bygone
canalside life at **Jim Thompson's House
Museum** (*see p93*). East of Thanon Phayathai,
the canal passes **Saprathum Palace**; this
private ochre edifice was home to the king's
late mother, whose funerary tower is kept next
door at **Wat Pathumwanaram** (*see p94*).
Past the Pratunam canal boat interchange, the
khlong skirts the phallic **Chao Mae Tubtim
Shrine** (*see p93*) in the grounds of **Nai Lert
Park Hotel** (*see p45*).

Parallel with the canal to the south, the
contiguous avenues of Thanon Rama I and
Thanon Ploenchit is Bangkok's main shopping
street. East of the **National Stadium
Pathumwan** (*see p201*) is the epicentre of
Thai youth culture: an amalgam of things cute,
cheap, loud, colourful, slogan-clad and clued
into international trends. Along with Thai
designs, fads come from the West, Japan or
South Korea. Ground zero for teens is the
tumultuous maze of shoplets, fast food and
karaoke boxes at **MBK** (Mahboonkrong Centre;
for all malls mentioned, *see p152*) and **Siam
Square** next door, which runs its own radio
station and magazine. This bohemian refuge
is getting increasingly gentrified, and rents are
soaring. Though a timid scene by Western
standards, it prompts shrill denunciations by
moralists. Get your T-shirt here at the **Hard
Rock Café** (*see p187*).

Across the road, chic rules at the malls of
Siam Discovery, **Siam Centre** and, due by
late 2005, **Siam Paragon**. The latter alone will
offer more shops and entertainment facilities

Jim Thompson's
House Museum.
See p93.

Sightseeing

Walk 5 Oriental quarter

The Bangrak riverside was Bangkok's original trading centre and its tranquil lanes still host foreign banks, businesses and embassies, godowns (warehouses), cottage industries, mansions and the city's earliest hotels.

Start at **River City** antiques mall. Just beyond the **Royal Orchid Sheraton** hotel is the capital's oldest embassy, the 1820s Portuguese Residence. Take **Thanon Charoen Krung**, past the formidable art deco **Central Post Office**. Right, down Soi 34, you reach **Wat Muang Khae** and **Harmonique**, a shophouse converted into a restaurant. Back on Charoen Krung, head past the **Rare Stone Museum** and into Soi 34. Perusing exquisite timber mansions to the right, you reach the restored **French Embassy** (seen best from the river). Beside it, the crumbling classical **Old Customs House** (the set for old Hong Kong in Wong Kar Wai's *In the Mood for Love*) will become the jet-set, 33-room Aman Resort Bangkok by 2007. Behind it, a path leads north then west past wooden houses to **Haroon Mosque**, before circling back south across Soi 36 to the French Embassy again.

Soi 38 leads to **OP Place**, a department store from 1905 now housing antiques shops. One block south, Soi 40 features crafts workshops with temple-style roofs and twin timber villas: the former **Commercial Company of Siam** and the **China House** restaurant. Soi 40 is dubbed 'Oriental Lane', after the historic hotel. Its original river entrance (now the Author's Wing) is visible from **Oriental Pier**, as is the neglected classical edifice of the **East Asiatic Company** (EAC, built in 1901) and **Chartered Bank**,

now part of Assumption School. Through an arch behind the EAC building an elegant tree-lined piazza links a Catholic mission with **Assumption Cathedral**. Built in 1910, the red brick cathedral has twin towers and a fine marble altar. Soi 42 leads past wooden homes to where Thanons Charoen Krung and Silom meet. Looming above are the **State Tower**'s restaurant (Sirocco; *see p112*) and bar (Distil; *see p128*).

than possibly all of Thailand's second city, Chiang Mai, including **Siam Ocean World** (*see p93*). These malls all join aerial walkways linking National Stadium, Siam and Chidlom BTS stations, passing the impressive **Wat Pathumwanaram** (*see p94*) and the Royal Thai Police Headquarters before branching off to the vast **Central World Plaza** (formerly the World Trade Centre). Each cool season at its forecourt, rival beer gardens drown each other out in lager and live bands under the glow of South-east Asia's largest LCD screen. Across Thanon Ratchadamri stand the crafts mall of **Naranyaphand**, and the label havens of **Gaysorn Plaza** and the new **Erawan** centre. The latter looms behind the revered **Erawan Shrine** (*see p95* Gods of today). Further east

lie Amarin Plaza (soon to become a Thai design centre) and the city's best department store, **Central Chidlom** (*see p141*), which faces the restaurant avenue of Soi Lang Suan.

Two entire blocks between Thanons Rama I and IV belong to Chulalongkorn University, Thailand's most prestigious. West of Thanon Phayathai is Chulalongkorn Art Centre, east of the road are Chulalongkorn Auditorium and the Museum of Imaging Technology with park-like grounds, a Khmer-revival style auditorium and a pond used for Loy Krathong rituals. There's a **Snake Farm** (*see p93*) to the south. East of Thanon Henri Dunant, the **Royal Bangkok Sports Club** (RBSC; *see p202*) has remained *the* recreational spot for old-money Thais.

Sightseeing

East of the greenery of **Lumphini Park** (*see below*), redevelopment is displacing both the *Muay Thai* mecca of Lumphini Stadium (which has moved; *see p203*) and **Suan Lum Night Bazaar** (*see p137*), from where the **Joe Louis Puppet Theater** (*see p196*) will migrate to Phuket. Further up Thanon Witthayu, the British, American and Dutch embassies occupy several historic houses.

British Council

254 Chulalongkorn Soi 64, Pathumwan (0 2652 5480-5/www.britishcouncil.or.th). **Open** 10am-8pm daily. **Map** p250 F6.
This language school and library brings touring promotions of 'cool Britannia' culture to Thailand, with the likes of artist Damien Hirst, designer Tom Dixon and London-based Thai designer Ou Baholyodhin. It also hosts talks and shows by Thais studying in the UK, and runs July's British Film Festival.

Chao Mae Tubtim Shrine

Soi Nai Lert, at service entrance of Nai Lert Park Hotel. Chidlom BTS. **Open** 24hrs daily. **Map** p251 H5.
Hoping for fertility or prosperity, worshippers at this canalside shrine to the female deity Jao Mae Thapthim offer countless phallic offerings in every shape, size and material. They range from stylised Shiva lingams to realistic, red-tipped *palad khik* (animist phallic totems) and gargantuan shafts swathed in sacred scarves. Some are planted like a picket fence, while others have legs (to make luck mobile).

Jim Thompson's House Museum

6 Soi Kasemsan 2, Thanon Rama I (0 2216 7368/ www.jimthompsonhouse.com). National Stadium BTS. **Open** 9am-5pm daily. **Admission** B100; B50 under-25s; free under-10s. **Credit** AmEx, DC, JCB, MC, V. **Map** p250 F4.
The revival and global fame of Thai silk owes much to this American architect who came to Thailand at

Snake Farm.

the end of World War II with the OSS (now the CIA) and later settled. Thompson soon spotted the marketing potential of the disappearing craft of silk weaving, then still practised in the Muslim Baan Khrua community facing his home across Khlong Saen Saeb. The silks' brilliant hues and shimmering textures soon became a sartorial trademark of the society figures he entertained at his remarkable house. In 1959 he reassembled six teak houses, some two centuries old, from Ayutthaya and Baan Khrua. Influencing all later adaptations of Thai houses to modern living, he turned the original multi-use rooms into a dining room, bedroom, bathroom, air-conditioned study and open-sided lounge. Now a museum, it looks much like it was when he disappeared in Malaysia's Cameron Highlands in 1967. Conspiracy theories abound.
The guided tour starts in the lush tropical gardens, where pavilions display Thompson's catholic and discerning collection of Asian arts and antiquities. Two similarly styled annexes contain a bar-cum-hall above a canalside bar-restaurant, facing a shop topped by a textiles gallery for both traditional cloth and silk installations by artists such as Pinnaree Sanpitak and Montri Toemsombat.

Lumphini Park

192 Thanon Rama IV (0 2252 7006). Ratchadamri or Saladaeng BTS/Silom or Lumphini subway. **Open** 4.30am-9pm daily. **Map** p251 G/H6.
Named after Buddha's birthplace in Nepal, the capital's best green enclave was donated by King Vajiravudh (Rama VI), whose statue dominates the main (south-western) entrance. It's most interesting around dawn and dusk, when its pagoda and lakes (pedalos can be hired) are circled by joggers, its paths become t'ai chi classes and others perform mass aerobics or play acrobatic *takraw*. There are even open-air gyms. Its shaded grounds also refresh lazier souls: there's a restaurant to the north-west, and free concerts bring even more picknickers than usual on Sunday afternoons in the cool season. By night, the perimeter becomes a soliciting ground: women on the east, men on the west.

Siam Ocean World

Siam Paragon, Thanon Rama I, Pathumwan (0 2658 3000/www.siamparagon.co.th). Siam BTS. **Open** 10am-8pm (call to confirm). **Admission** call for details. **Credit** AmEx, DC, MC, V. **Map** p251 G4.
From late 2005 over two million visitors a year are expected to gaze at the 30,000 fish, sharks and penguins from 400 species living in this Australian-built high-tech aquarium. One of the world's biggest, it includes 10.5m-deep (34.5ft) -deep tanks, an 'Amazon Rainforest', educational areas and an amphitheatre.

Snake Farm

Queen Saovabha Memorial Institute, 1871 Thanon Rama IV (0 2252 0161-4/www.redcross.or.th). Saladaeng BTS. **Open** 8.30am-4.30pm Mon-Fri; 8.30am-noon Sat, Sun. *Demonstrations* 11am, 2.30pm

Sightseeing

Mon-Fri; 11am Sat, Sun. **Admission** B20 Thais; B70 foreigners. **No credit cards**. Map p250 F6.

Run by the Thai Red Cross, the Queen Saovabha Memorial Institute was opened in 1922 as the Pasteur Institute. It does research and treatment involving vaccinations, animal bites and antivenins extracted from its snake farm (the second in the world). It's only worth visiting when the venom is milked. Thailand has six venomous snake species; note the deadly banded krait's black and yellow stripes, the huge king cobra, whose poison could kill 1,000 rabbits, and the python with a belly bulging from chicken dinners. Visitors can handle or pose for photos with the larger constrictors. The commentary is in Thai, but there's a booklet in English.

Wat Pathumwanaram
969 Thanon Rama I (0 2254 2545). Siam BTS. **Open** 8.30am-6pm daily. **Map** p251 G4.
This important *wat* is undervisited considering the verdant respite it offers. Fronted by a terrapin pond, it houses superlative murals and the ashes of Prince Mahidol, father of Kings Rama XIII and IX. In 1996 the ashes and elaborate crematorium of the king's mother were both brought here from Sanam Luang.

Sukhumvit

Map p251 & p252
Sukhumvit illustrates just how far and fast the metropolis has spread east. The **Siam Society** (*see below*) was built on Soi Asoke in 1933 amid fields. Today it's suffocated by high-rises and packed with luxury condominiums, hotels, shops and fashionable spots to dine, drink and dance. Much of Sukhumvit between Sois 3-11 is owned by Thai-Indian Sikhs, whose tailor shops, inns and restaurants proliferate. Other

Baiyoke II Tower.
See p96.

expatriate quarters include Arabs and Africans (Sois 3 and 3/1), Koreans (around Sukhumvit Plaza on Soi 12) and Japanese (Sois 31-53), with Westerners spread throughout.

The Nana area churns with souvenir stalls, travel agents, massage parlours (either healing or entrepreneurial) and hostess bars. The salacious nightstrips include **Soi Zero** (under the expressway), **Nana Entertainment Plaza** on Soi 4 and **Soi Cowboy** (Soi 23). To the east, **Benjasiri Park** and the new **Benjakitti Park** (for both, *see below*) offer much-needed green space.

The area between **Emporium** shopping centre (*see p151*) and Soi Ekamai (Soi 63) – where you can study traditional arts at **Baan Chang Thai** (*see p201*) or catch a coach to the coast from the **Eastern Bus Terminal** – shifts upmarket. Branching off the 'green route' (a shortcut through back *sois*), expensive compounds and condos intersperse spas, boutiques, furniture showrooms, bars, restaurants and complexes like **H1** and **J Avenue** catering to young *hi-so* (high society ingenues). The swishest avenues of Ekamai and Soi Thonglor (Soi 55) double as aisles of chintzy wedding plazas.

Benjakiti Park
Thanon Ratchadaphisek (0 2262 0810). Queen Sirikit Centre subway. **Open** 5am-8pm daily. **Map** p252 K6.
It has taken years to turn the leafy Thailand Tobacco Monopoly into a park. The first stage around Lake Ratchada was landscaped to mark Queen Sirikit's sixth cycle (72nd) birthday in 2004. With circuits for jogging and cycling (with bike hire), it boasts water features, a playground, boat hire, an outdoor gym and a meditation zone, though its attractive, shadeless saplings replaced many mature trees during construction. A road may cut through the top linking Ratchada with Soi Sarasin. You can explore this green zone with a Segway human transporter. Thailand Segway Tours (Woraburi Hotel, end of Sukhumvit Soi 4, 0 2253 6379, www.thailandsegwaytours.com) runs glides at 9am and 5pm daily (B1,800, 90mins), including training. Gliders must be ten years or older.

Benjasiri Park
Thanon Sukhumvit, between Sois 22 & 24 (0 2262 0810). Phrom Phong BTS. **Open** 5am-9pm daily. **Map** p252 K6.
Amid Benjasiri's fountains, ponds and pavilions are sculptures by Thai artists, notably Misiem Yipintsoi (*see p99* **Star cast**). It hosts festivals and exercisers relish the skate park, tiny swimming pool and courts for basketball and *takraw*.

Siam Society & Baan Kamthieng
131 Sukhumvit Soi 21 (0 2661 6470-77/ www.siam-society.org). Asoke BTS/Sukhumvit subway. **Open** 9am-5pm Tue-Sat. **Admission** B100. **No credit cards**. **Map** p252 K5.

Offering insight into northern Lanna culture in a 150-year-old wooden house, Baan Kamthieng ethnological museum now has multimedia displays on topics from courtship music and spirit dancing to spoken family histories and animated instructions on building a Lanna house. Set in a well-tended garden, it is said to be haunted by the spirits of three female ex-residents. The Siam Society Under Royal Patronage has a library with many rare books on Thailand, palm-leaf manuscripts and old maps. It holds regular lectures, exhibitions and study trips (consult the website or call for details of how you can get involved).

Thailand Creative & Design Centre
7th floor, Emporium, 622 Thanon Sukhumvit (0 2664 7667). **Open** 10am-10pm daily. **Admission** free, some activities may charge. **No credit cards.** **Map** p252 K6.

Opening in late 2005, this state enterprise both presents global design to Thais and showcases innovative Thai creativity. Home-grown exhibitions will alternate with shows from museums abroad. Accessed via this mall's cinema lobby, its stylish environs include a shop, an auditorium, seminar rooms and a library of film, digital information and 15,000 publications.

North

All of Downtown (and beyond) may be viewed from the city's tallest structure, **Baiyoke II Tower** (*see p96*), which soars out of congested **Pratunam Market** (*see p136*), with high-tech mall **Pantip Plaza** nearby (*see p143*). More cultured sights in northern downtown include the **Bangkok Dolls**

Gods of today

Far from declining with modern lifestyles, animism (the belief that everything contains a living soul) takes on fresh guises, offering refuges amid new uncertainties. Two modern shrines show the constant evolution of spirit beliefs. The **Erawan Shrine** receives near-universal worship from shoppers at surrounding malls or passing SkyTrain passengers and drivers. Pilgrims whose wishes get fulfilled return with offerings and may pay for dancers kept on costumed standby to perform.

This projection of fix-all faith far exceeds the shrine's origins as a spirit house. Erected in 1956, it finally appeased the tree spirits left homeless by the Erawan Hotel and blamed for misfortunes during construction. Tiled in mirror and decked in carnation garlands and wooden elephant offerings, the super-lucky shrine isn't to a spirit, nor even to Erawan (Airavata, elephant mount of Indra), but to another Hindu god, Brahma, the four-faced god of creation.

Trend-conscious worshippers now also visit different gods in the spirit house of another mall on the opposite corner, the **Trimurthi Shrine** (*pictured right*) at Central World Plaza. Again the original meaning has morphed. Combining the trinity of Brahma-Vishnu-Shiva (creator-preserver-destroyer), the five-faced Trimurthi has recently been interpreted as the 'god of love' by young Thais. They come at night, especially on Thursdays, to wish for a partner (many hoping for a *farang* mate). Since gods have colour themes, the incense, candles and flowers (in this case roses) must be red,

as should an item of clothing. Witnessing a new cult created by the globalised generation reinforces the endurance, depth and sheer fluidity of Thai belief.

Erawan Shrine
At Erawan mall, Thanon Ratchadamri (0 2252 8754). Chidlom BTS. **Open** 6am-10pm daily. **Map** p251 G5.

Trimurthi Shrine
At Central World Plaza, Thanon Ratchadamri. Chidlom BTS. **Open** 24hrs daily. **Map** p251 G5.

Sightseeing

museum (*see p162*), charming **Suan Pakkard Palace** (*see below*), and stately **Phyathai Palace**, which lies a ten-minute walk west of **Victory Monument**. Erected in 1941, this bayonet-like obelisk honours those slain in a brief dispute with France over Laos.

The BTS meets the subway at the immense **Chatuchak Weekend Market** (*see p136* **A day in JJ**). This essential stop stands between the quirky bars along Thanon Kamphaengphet and **Chatuchak Park**, which hosts the **Children's Discovery Museum** (*see p162*).

Following the subway clockwise, you skirt **Central Plaza Lad Prao** mall and arc down Ratchadaphisek Road, passing **Tadu Contemporary Art** (*see p97*), the **Thailand Cultural Centre** (*see p197*) and a nightlife zone of barn-like discos (known as *theques*), beer halls and gaudy massage parlours. Theme bars also proliferate at **Ratchada Soi** and nearby **Royal City Avenue (RCA)**.

Baiyoke II Tower

84th floor, 22 Thanon Ratchaprarop, in sub-soi north of Indra Regent Hotel (0 2656 3000). **Open** 10.30am-10pm daily. **Admission** B120. **Credit** AmEx, MC, V. **Map** p251 G3/4.
This gaudy unfinished tower has a high-speed elevator to an observation deck on the 84th floor for vertiginous panoramas of the megalopolis and even (on a clear day) the sea. The views are as great by night. There are also telescopic viewfinders, some drab displays and a bland restaurant.

Chatuchak Park, Rail Hall of Fame & Butterfly Garden

Thanon Phahon Yothin (0 2272 4575/01615 5776). Morchit BTS/Chatuchak Park subway. **Open** *Park* 4.30am-9pm daily. *Rail Hall of Fame* 7am-3pm Sat, Sun. *Butterfly Garden* 8.30am-4.30pm Tue-Sun. **No credit cards**.
This respite from market mayhem is branded a 'Learning Park' and displays sculptures by Southeast Asian artists. A small Rail Hall of Fame houses old locomotives and various vehicles, including London taxis and World War II Japanese patrol cars. Adjacent Suan Rotfai (Railway Park), the old railway golf course, offers bike hire, a good pool, a new Butterfly Garden and Insectorium (0 2272 4359) and, in 2007, a Bird Park. In more contiguous green space, Queen Sirikit Park hosts the Children's Discovery Museum (*see p162*) and a Botanical Garden with themes like herbs and flowers in literature.

Phyathai Palace

King Mongkutklao Hospital, 315 Thanon Ratchawithi (0 2354 7732/www.phyathaipalace.org). Victory Monument BTS. **Open** *Interiors* 9am-4pm Sat, by appointment Mon-Fri. **Map** p252 M4.
The European-style royal getaway of King Rama V – which has since been a luxury hotel, Thailand's first radio station and part of a hospital – is slowly

becoming a museum. Some audience halls have been restored, but the fading frescoed corridors lend poignancy to the place where King Rama VI experimented with democracy at a miniature town called Dusit Thani, which had its own economy and newspaper. The palace also houses the Army Medical Corps Museum. Guided tours in English available.

Siam Niramit

Ratchada Grand Theatre, 19 Thanon Tiam Ruammitr, North (0 2533 1152/www.siamniramit. com). Thai Cultural Centre subway. **Shows** 7.30pm daily. **Admission** B1,500. **Credit** call for details.
On the pseudo-historical model of Phuket FantaSea (*see p218*), this B1.5-billion, 2,000-seat theatre is one of the world's biggest, with a 65m by 40m (213ft by 131ft) stage and sets 10m (32ft) tall. It is designed to present *Siam Niramit* (Magical Siam), an 80-minute Thai cultural spectacular with special effects, 150 performers, 500 costumes and a phenomenal stage lift.

Suan Pakkard Palace & Marsi Gallery

352 Thanon Si Ayutthaya (0 2245 4934/www. suanpakkad.com). Phaya Thai BTS. **Open** 9am-4pm daily. **Admission** B50 Thais; B100 foreigners. **No credit cards**. **Map** p251 G3.
Named the 'cabbage patch palace' after the site where these five teak houses were assembled in 1952, this delightful museum was preserved after the death of its owners, Prince and Princess Chumbhot. Among their art and antiquities are Khmer Buddha statues, monks' fans, betel nut sets, shells and prehistoric Baan Chiang pottery. Most exquisite is the pond-side Lacquer Pavilion. A birthday gift from the prince to his wife, this 17th- to 18th-century Ayutthayan library features astonishing gold and black lacquer scenes from the life of Buddha, the *Ramakien* and Thai life. The grounds also contain the Marsi Gallery for art shows, and a multimedia Khon Museum on classical Thai drama.

Tadu Contemporary Art

7th floor, Barcelona Motors (Yontrakit) Building, Thanon Thiem Ruam Mitr (0 2645 2473/ www.tadu.net). Thailand Cultural Centre subway. **Open** 9am-6pm Mon-Sat. **Map** p252 M4.
Founded in 1996 by artists and collectors under director Luckana Kunavichyanont, Tadu ('a way to see') presents visual arts, films and innovative theatre. Now relocated, it promotes young Thai artists and educational projects, often in collaborations.

South

Bordering Bangrak, Thanon Sathorn flanks a canal dug by Chinese labourers in the late 19th century. It soon sprouted swanky, European-style wooden mansions for locals and foreigners. A few have survived through conversion to other uses. The splendid century-old Thai-Chinese Chamber of Commerce (built as the Bombay Department Store) is now the

Phyathai Palace. *See p96.*

Blue Elephant Thai restaurant (*see p111*), and **MR Kukrit Pramoj's Heritage Home** stands nearby (*see below*). Due to redevelopment, the **Lumphini Stadium** (*see p203*) has been moved to a location beyond Soi Suan Plu's Immigration Bureau.

Among the area's modern edifices, the precariously narrow **Thai Wah II Tower** has a hole 50 storeys up, the level at which you'll find the spa of the **Banyan Tree Hotel** (*see p48*), plus the building houses the open-air rooftop Vertigo restaurant (*see p124*) and the ultra-trendy Moon Bar (*see p132*). It overlooks the suave **Sukhothai** and **Metropolitan** hotels (for both, *see p48*). To the south stand two oddities: the robot-themed **Bank of Asia**, designed by Sumet Jumsai, and the boat-shaped chedi at **Wat Yannawa** (*see below*).

Later superseded by Thanon Khao San, Soi Ngam Duphlee was the original backpackers' flop zone, but it has since got a tad sleazy. Near here, the **Goethe Institut** and **Alliance Française** (for both, *see p166*) continue a tradition of foreign promotion of Thai arts. East along Thanon Rama IV to Khlong Toei, you pass **Plainern Palace**, which is open only on **Naris Day** (*see p159*). Khlong Toei's port here is famous for markets and slums. The loop in the Chao Phraya river, bounded by Thanon Rama III, is industrialised, with only **Central Rama III Shopping Centre** and **Tawandaeng German Brewhouse** (*see p186*) to divert visitors.

Bangkok University Art Gallery

3rd floor, Building 9, Kluaynam Thai campus, Thanon Rama IV, Sukhumvit (0 2350 3500). Bus 22, 46, 149, 507. **Open** *9.30am-7pm daily.*
A small but important space run by the faculty, this gallery's shows tend to be given by lecturers, students and foreign artists in residence. Its Brand New exhibition (annually Jan-Mar) has launched many a star.

MR Kukrit Pramoj's Heritage Home

19 Soi Phra Phinij, Thanon Sathorn Tai (0 2286 8185). Bus 22, 62, 67, 76, 116, 149, 530. **Open** *10am-5pm daily.* **Admission** B50; B20 students. **No credit cards. Map** p251 G7.
This assemblage of five houses on stilts from the Central Plains was the seat of Mom Ratchawong Kukrit, a late aristocratic prime minister in the turbulent mid 1970s. Something of a cultural colossus, he's best known for his writing (*see p18* **Historical flashbacks**), promotion of *khun* drama and role as an Asian prime minister in *The Ugly American*, acting with Marlon Brando. Set by a pond in a garden of indigenous species, the house contains the antiquities, photographs and memorabilia of a remarkable man. A charming museum.

Wat Yannawa

1648 Thanon Charoen Krung (0 2211 9317). Saphan Taksin BTS. **Open** *Temple 5am-9pm daily. Bot 8-9am, 5-6pm daily.* **Map** p250 D7.
This unique temple dates from Ayutthayan times, and was restored by Rama I. Rama III later constructed a *chedi* platform in the form of a Chinese junk, complete with eyes on the prow, four cannons and a shrine on an upper deck.

Suburbs

Suburban sprawl finds space for art, shrines and elephants.

The SkyTrain was planned in the 1970s to reach the capital's outskirts, but it took so long to build that its termini now delineate downtown. Instead of development following stations, transport infrastructure has played catch-up as fertile farmland gets eaten up by underplanned housing estates, golf courses, universities and some of the world's biggest shopping centres. The growing middle classes – plus workers migrating from downtown slums and upcountry farms – are adopting a suburban lifestyle but endure traumatic commutes. Though expressways have eased traffic, planned expansion of mass transit can't come soon enough, so you'll need a taxi or hired car to explore these areas. Canal life may persist on the peripheries (*see p71* **The khlong goodbye?**), but it barely survives in Bangkok's suburbs.

East

The BTS currently ends at Onnut (Sukhumvit Soi 77), which features the ghost-story location **Wat Maha But** and is also one of three routes east to the new **Suvarnabhumi Airport** (*see p224*), another being Thanon Bangna-Trad (and the Chonburi expressway overhead). It branches off Sukhumvit after Soi 103 and thunders through golf-strewn, semi-industrial Bangna to the Eastern Seaboard, passing the high-tech **Bangkok International Exhibition Centre** (BITEC), **Central City Bangna** mall, the **Nation Multimedia** tower (a cubist homage to Braque by Sumet Jumsai) and the bombastic campus of **ABAC University**. Sukhumvit continues, hugging the estuary, into suburban Samut Prakarn province, skirting the **Erawan Museum**, **Samut Prakarn Crocodile Farm** and **Muang Boran**.

North from Bangna, Thanon Srinakharin gives access to **Rama IX Park**, the mega malls of **Seri Centre** and **Seacon Square**, and the **Prasart Museum**. It ends at Thanon Ramkhamhaeng, an artery packed with malls, shops, bars (including a large gay scene) and 1.5-kilometre- (one-mile-) long **Na Ram Market** (between Sois 43-53, 4pm-midnight daily) – all frequented by students of the massive **Ramkhamhaeng University**. Beside it looms the **National Stadium Hua Mark** (*see p199*).

Erawan Museum

99/9 Moo 1, Bang Muang Mai, Samut Prakan (0 2371 3135-6/www.ancientcity.com). **Open** 8am-6pm daily. **Admission** B150; B50 under-12s. **No credit cards**.
A monument to religious harmony by the founder of Muang Boran (*see below*), this humungous 150-tonne metal statue depicts Erawan, the three-headed elephant mount of Hindu god Indra. From a kitschy museum in the base, steps and a lift up the rear legs take you to a multi-faith chapel in its body. Oddly deep and deeply odd.

Muang Boran (Ancient City)

Sukhumvit Sai Kao km33, Bangpu Mai, Samut Prakarn (0 2323 9253/www.ancientcity.com). **Open** 8am-5pm daily. **Admission** *Thais* B100; B50 under-12s. *Foreigners* B300; B200 under-12s. **No credit cards**.
One visionary created this undervisited, open-air architectural museum, reconstructing salvaged masterpieces and scaled-down versions of landmarks in a park shaped like Thailand. It's a sublime, relaxing half-day jaunt, but vast and without public transport, so it is best to go by car or tour. Suited to bicycle or Segway.

Prasart Museum

9 Krung Thep Kreetha Soi 4A (0 2379 3601). **Open** by appointment 9am-3pm (3pm last entry) Tue-Sun. **Admission** B1,000; B500 per person groups of 2 or more. **No credit cards**.
It's worth the hassle but perhaps not the price to luxuriate in this private collection. The replica historic buildings include a European-style mansion, Khmer shrine and Northern and Central Thai teak houses, plus Thai and Chinese temples. Collector Prasart Vongsakul's shop in the Peninsula Plaza (*see p152*) sells antiques and reproductions of the exhibits.

Rama IX Royal Park

Sukhumvit Soi 103 (Soi Udomsuk) (0 2328 1385/ www.suanluangrama9.or.th). **Open** 5.30am-7pm daily. **Admission** B10; free under-12s.
Bangkok may have about the least green space per head than any world city, but parkland is at least increasing. This 81ha (200-acre) addition in 1987 was a 60th birthday tribute to the king, to whom the small museum is also dedicated. It has botanical gardens, water lily pond, water garden and canal bridge.

Samut Prakarn Crocodile Farm

555 Thai Baan, Samut Prakarn (0 2703 5144-8/ www.crocodilefarm.com). **Open** 7am-5pm daily. **Admission** *Thais* B60; B30 under-12s. *Foreigners* B300; B200 under-12s. **Credit** MC, V.

Star cast

Public collections of modern Thai art are rare, but there are four significant private collections located on Bangkok's fringes that offer glimpses. **Bangkok Sculpture Centre**, near Ramindra expressway exit, houses 120 major works on lawns, ledges, warehouse gantries and the fountain terrace of this airy, dramatic edifice. Owner Sermkhun Khunawong aims to complete a 300-exhibit timeline of modern Thai sculpture, from Silpa Bhirasri and Khien Yimsiri, whose fluid figurative bronzes (*pictured right*) form the centrepiece, to the surrealist hinged bodies by Manop Suwanpinta and phantasmagorical wood carvings by Kham-ai Dejdoungtae.

Jean-Michel Beurdeley shows his pieces (by appointment, 0 2314 6645) at his home near Thanon Ramkhamhaeng, including works by luminaries such as Montien Boonma, Chatchai Pui-pia, Niti Wattuya, Natee Utarit, Wasan Sitthiket and Pinnaree Sanpitak. More accessibly, Boonchai Bencharongkul's 300-strong hoard at **UCOM** includes many primal pieces by Tawan Duchanee, as well as Chalermchai Kositphipat, Prateung Emjaroen and Kamol Tassananchalee.

To the west, **Misiem's Sculpture Garden** offers a rest from the monuments of Phuttha Monthon. Balletic modernist bronzes by the late self-taught National Artist Misiem Yipintsoi appear like sprites amid rustic landscaping by her granddaughter, Klaomard, who founded progressive **About Café**. Guest installations include Surojana Settabutr's ceramics (until 30 December 2007). Misiem's work also stars at Benjasiri Park (*see p95*).

Admission is free to the following collections.

Bangkok Sculpture Centre

4/18-19 Nuanchan Soi 56, Thanon Ramindra, North-east (0 2559 0505 ext 119, 232/ www.thaiartproject.org). **Open** 10am-4pm every 2nd & 4th Sat & by appointment 10am-4pm Mon-Fri.

Misiem's Sculpture Garden

38/9 Thanon Phuttha Monthon Sai 7, Nakhon Pathom (AARA office 0 2639 8057/www.yip intsoi.com/~aara). **Open** 9am-5pm Fri-Sun.

UCOM

Benchachinda Building, 499 Thanon Wiphawadee-Rangsit, facing Kasetsart University, Outer North (0 2953 1111 ext 23567). **Open** 9am-5pm Mon-Fri.

The world's biggest croc farm, with 100,000 occupants, including the near-extinct Siamese species and the longest living crocodile at six metres (20 ft). Hourly shows feature wrestling, head-in-jaws and similar touristy stunts, plus elephant shows and rides.

Wat Maha But

749 Onnut Soi 7, Sukhumvit Soi 77 (0 2311 2183). Onnut BTS. **Open** 7am-6.30pm daily. **Admission** free.

This nondescript temple by Khlong Prakhanong holds a shrine to Mae Nak, who died in childbirth while her conscripted husband was at war over 150 years ago. In a much-filmed legend, he returned to live with his wife and child, unaware they were both ghosts. Conscripts and mothers come to Wat Maha But to donate offerings such as dresses, wigs, make-up and toys to appease the vengeful spirits of mother and babe.

North-east

Outside Thanon Ratchadaphisek ringroad, diminishing marshland still offers foraging for the elephants that wander Bangkok's streets (*see p24* **Tusk force**). Dramatic architecture rings Ratchayothin junction, with the pachyderm-shaped **Elephant Building**, the world's largest **IMAX** cinema (*see p165*) and the gold-pointed towers of **SCB Park Plaza**, where Siam Commercial Bank runs the **Museum of Thai Banking** (9 Thanon Ratchadaphisek, 0 2544 4504, 10am-5pm Mon-Fri).

Ramindra offers the **Bangkok Sculpture Centre** (*see p99* **Star cast**), while further north are **Safari World**, **Siam Park**, **Dream World** and the museums at **Technopolis** (*see p163*). The latter two lie off Thanon Rangsit-Nakorn Nayok, beside which **Khlong Rangsit** offers beef noodles on floating restaurants, of which **Reua Sawasdee** serves the best.

Dream World

62 Moo 1, Thanon Rangsit-Ongkarak, Pathum Thani (0 2533 1152/www.dreamworld.com). **Open** 10am-5pm Mon-Fri; 10am-7pm Sat, Sun. **Admission** B120; B95 children under 145cm/57in (excl rides); B295 (for 25 rides); rides pass B330. **No credit cards**.

All the usual theme-park rides are here, including rollercoasters, the Big Splash, Snow Land, a petting zoo and Disneyesque characters. It concedes a few Thai touches like elephant rides and massage.

Kwan Im Shrine

Chokchai Soi 39, Lad Phrao Soi 53 (Chokchai 4) (0 2514 0715). **Open** 7am-9pm daily. **Admission** free.

The middle-class cult of Kuan Im (aka Kuan Yin, the Chinese bodhisattva of mercy) prompted this massive, gaudy sculpture garden, embellished with wagonwheels, barrels and a modern pagoda. Eye-popping offerings crowd the basement museum.

Safari World

99 Thanon Ramindra km9, Klong Samwa (0 2518 1000-5/2914 4100-5/www.safariworld. com). **Open** 9am-4.30pm Mon-Fri; 9am-5pm Sat, Sun. *Marine park* 10.40am-3.30pm daily. **Admission** *Safari park* B280; B120 children under 140cm/55in; free under 100cm/39in. *Marine park* B580; B400 children under 140cm/55in; free under 100cm/39in. *Both zones* B700; B450 children under 140cm/55in; free under 100cm/39in. **Credit** AmEx, MC, V.

This animal park is a 150-acre (61-hectare) enclosure containing mainly African beasts. You'll need a car (or tour bus) and be sure to arrive by 10am for the big cats' rip-roaring 'breakfast show'. Other shows include Marine Park acrobatics with sea lions and dolphins, parrot displays and human stunts.

Siam Park

99 Thanon Seri Thai, Kanna Yaow (0 2919 7200-5/ www.siamparkcity.com). **Open** 10am-6pm daily. **Admission** B200; B100 children under 140cm/55in; free under 90cm. **Credit** AmEx, MC, V, DC.

Fun-packed park, with a fun park, a water zone with slides and waves lapping a faux beach, and more.

Outer North

A century ago, expatriate hunters stalked birds around **Don Muang** (literally 'city heights'). Today the birds are mostly of the metallic variety jetting in and out of **Bangkok International Airport**, Thailand's flying hub from the 1930s until Suvarnabhumi Airport opens (*see p224*). Plane spotters will also relish the nearby **Royal Thai Air Force Museum** and art fans the **UCOM** collection futher south (*see p99* **Star cast**). East on Chaengwattana Road towards **Nonthaburi** (*see p73*), the **IMPACT Exhibition Centre** hosts trade shows, sports and concerts. North of the airport at Rangsit, a monorail rings the massive **Future Park** mall abutting Khlong Rangsit.

Royal Thai Air Force Museum

Royal Thai Air Force Base, Thanon Phahon Yothin, behind airport (0 2534 1575/1764). **Open** 8am-4pm daily. **Admission** free.

Rare exhibits include the only extant Model I Corsaire, one of only two Japanese Tachikawas, a Spitfire and Thailand's first completely home-grown aircraft, the Model II Bomber Boripatr.

Outer West

This area is the gateway to the western provinces and the Gulf (*see pp208-222*), with many tour buses stopping off here before heading further afield. Some tours visit **Phuttha Monthon**, a vast Buddhist-themed park centering on a 40-metre (131-foot) standing Buddha. The park's Utthayan Avenue shimmers with ornate bridges, fountains, flora and lamp-posts topped by a gilded phoenix. Just into Nakhon Pathom province, and under an hour from downtown, it can make a day trip combined with the diverse **Lord Buddha Images Museum** (5/9 Thanon Phuttha Monthon Sai 2, 0 2887 1265, admission B100), the wistful **House of Museums** and the serene **Misiem's Sculpture Garden** (*see p99* **Star cast**).

The House of Museums

Baan Phipitaphan, Khlong Pho Soi 2, Sala Thammasop Road (0 1257 4508/www.house ofmuseums.org). **Open** 10am-5pm Sat, Sun. **Admission** B30; under-12s B10. **No credit cards**.

Historian Anake Nawigamune's popular culture collection has three floors of interactive reconstructions, including a barbers, schoolroom and pharmacy.

Further Afield

Venture out of town to ancient cities, canalscape idylls and virgin jungle.

The Chao Phraya delta, one of the world's grain baskets, offers diverse sights within just a two-hour drive of the city. Beyond the river stops nearer central Bangkok (*see p74* **Pier groups**), boat tours head north to **Bang Sai**, the 19th-century **Bang Pa-In** summer palace and the ruined Siamese capital of **Ayutthaya**. Westwards, around ancient sacred **Nakhon Pathom** are intact canal tracts, while rainforest is accessible both in **Kanchanaburi**, where the 'Death Railway' was carved along the River Kwai, and north-east at **Khao Yai National Park**. Day or overnight trips from Bangkok are easiest with a tour or hired van and driver.

Bang Pa-In & Ayutthaya

Under Queen Sirikit's patronage, resuscitated crafts now help diversify the incomes of farmers trained at **Bang Sai Folk Arts & Crafts Centre** (0 35366 252-4, www.bang saiarts.com), located 55 kilometres (34 miles) north of Bangkok in tranquil riverbank worshops. Some 17 kilometres (11 miles) upstream, the island of **Bang Pa-In** (0 3526 1673-82, www.palaces.thai.net) has since 1632 been a summer royal retreat. In 1872 Rama V turned it into an eclectic palace named after a drowned princess. Set amid animal topiary, baroque pavilions contrast with dazzling Chinese **Wehat Chamrun Palace** and Gothic **Wat Nivet Dhammaparvat**. It is busiest in the morning.

From Bang Pa-In, longtail boats ply the scenic 45-minute trip to **Ayutthaya**, 21 kilometres (11 miles) to the north. Focused on an artificial island, this World Heritage Site is an essential visit. Not only is the ruined former capital impressive, but its fall is a cataclysm that still reverberates, as in recent anti-Myanmar movies. With its 400 temples razed and 90 per cent of its people gone, it was abandoned (and much looted) until the dictator Phibunsongkhram tidied it into a showpiece in the 1950s. During excavations, royal regalia was stolen from the frescoed crypt of **Wat Ratchaburana** and the old ritual centre, **Wat Mahathat**. Remnants of the gilded cache – plus marvellous statuary – fill **Chao Sam Phraya Museum** (108/16 Thanon Rotchana, 0 3524 1587, closed Mon & Tue). Other treasures occupy the fretworked **Chandra Kasem Palace Museum** (Thanon U-Thong, 0 3525 1586, closed Mon, Tue).

The Japanese-funded dioramas of the **Historical Study Centre** (Thanon Rotchana, 0 3524 5123-4, B100) offer more perspective than the **TAT** tourist office (108/22 Thanon Si Sanphet, 0 3524 6076-7, 8.30am-4.30pm daily). Visiting the ruins requires entry to **Phra Nakhon Si Ayutthaya Historical Park** (0 3524 2284, B30 per site). By staying overnight, you can enjoy quiet, cool sightseeing before the hordes descend after 11am.

Only foundations – and the **Trimuk Pavilion**, built by Rama V for ceremonies – indicate the presence of the old Grand Palace, though the iconic triple *chedi* (built in 1492) of its temple, **Wat Si Sanphet**, remain. Thais flock next door to the heavily restored Buddha image of **Vihaan Phra Mongkhon Bophit**. Beyond a market and the exquisite teak 1894 **Khun Phaen's House**, you can get elephant rides (B400 10mins, B500 30mins). Opposite is **Beung Phra Ram**, a park of lily ponds and a lone *prang*. Behind it, **Wat Mahathat** draws photographers to its root-encased Buddha head.

Outer-bank remains, seen clockwise, include **Wat Yai Chaimongkhon** to the south-east. Built by a Ceylonese sect, it boasts a 60-metre (197-foot) bell *chedi*, a reclining Buddha and a shrine to toys. East on Highway 3058, **Wat Maheyong** retains stucco elephants around a Sri Lankan-style *chedi*. To the north, the restored **Kraal** was where elephants were trained, and stunning **Wat Phramane** (Thanon U-Thong, 0 3525 1992, admission B10) is the only surviving original temple. Dominating the west is the immaculate five-*prang* **Wat Chaiwattanaram**.

To the south, King U-Thong stayed at the cloistered **Wat Phuttaisawan** before developing Ayutthaya. En route you pass **St Joseph's Church** in the old French settlement, one of many foreign quarters then housing, among others, Portuguese, Japanese, Dutch and Malays. Crafts fans can visit *khon* (*see p194*) mask-maker **ML Punsawat Sooksawasdi** (5/1 Thanon U-thong, 0 3524 1574) and the teak house carpenters at **Baan Pahan**, 13 kilometres (eight miles) north on Highway 32.

Where to stay & eat

Baan Khun Phra (48 Thanon U-Thong, 0 3524 1978, double B150-B350) is a wooden garden enclave near Chao Phrom Market's food stalls, while **PS Guest House** (23/1 Thanon Chakrapat, 0 3524 2394, double B120-B300) has the bonus of tasty home cooking. Riverside dining at **Ruen Rub Rong** (13/1-2 Thanon U-Thong, 0 3524 3090, main courses B150-B200) includes a dinner cruise option. Just to the north, the wooden **Ayothaya Riverside Inn** (0 2585 6001, rates B300-B1,200) also has rooms on a boat. Beyond it, via Wat Kasatrathirat, are two good Thai riverview restaurants: **Baan Watcharachai** (0 3532 1333, main courses B50-B140) has plush, Thai-style buildings set in a garden, and a dining boat; next door is the subtly rustic **Baan Mae Choi Nang Kam** (0 1823 9334, main courses B80-B250).

Getting there & around

Most tours of Ayutthaya combine 90min minibus rides with train or boat (*see p56* **Boat trips**) and call at Bang Pa-In. Otherwise, buses leave Bangkok's Northern Bus Terminal every 20mins 5.20am-8pm daily (B34), taking 90mins. Trains leave 4.20am-11.10pm daily from Bangkok's Hualumphong station (B12-B20, 90mins), calling at Bang Pa-In.

In Bang Pa-In, pedal rickshaws and tuk-tuks ply the short walk between station and palace. In Ayutthaya, tuk-tuks can be hired by the day (B200 per hour), as can boats at piers by Chandra Kasem Museum or Wat Phanan Choeng (B300-B500 per day), and bicycles from the tourist police (B50 per day) or near the train station (B30 per day). Or commission the Benjarong rice barge (0 3521 1036). For special-interest itineraries, try **Classic Tour** (0 3524 4978).

Canals near Nakhon Pathom

The canal communities of provinces to the west of the city retain some bygone lifestyles and markets, all best viewed in the early morning. Deluged by coachloads from 9pm, the extensive orchards, stilt houses and paddling traders of **Damnoen Saduak Floating Market** in the Ratchaburi province (0 3224 1204, 6am-noon daily) provide a full experience of old riverine Thai lifestyle, but the market suffers from souvenir touting and pricy boat tours (B200-B500 per hour). Fewer tourists reach Samut Songkhram province, with its scenic **Tha Kha Floating Market** (0 3476 6208, 7am-11am Sat, Sun and 2nd, 7th & 12th days of waxing and waning moons), part of itineraries from **Baan Tai Had Resort** (1 Moo 2, Thanon Wat Phuang Malai-Wat Tai Had,

0 3476 7220-4), which also runs dinner cruises to view fireflies and hires out kayaks.

Longtails (from B250 per hr) from **Samut Songkram** charming riverside market serve Tha Kha and the floating market at **Amphawa** (Wat Amphawan, 6am-6pm daily), a watery orchard district with stilt-house homestays at **Baan Song Thai Plai Pong Pang** (0 3473 2428, double B500), **Baan Tha Kha** (0 3476 6170, double B350) or **Baan Hua Had** (0 3473 5073, double B350).

Closer to Bangkok in Nakhon Pathom province, there's still charm at **Lam Phya Floating Market** (Wat Lam Phya, Bang Lane, 0 3439 1985, Sat & Sun only) and busy, notably untacky **Don Wai Floating Market** (near Wat Rai King, Tha Nakhon Chaisri, 0 3439 3637, 6am-6pm daily). Don Wai is best reached via a one-hour cruise on the Tha Chin from **Rose Garden Aprime Resort** (km32 Thanon Phetkasem, 0 3432 2544-7, www.rose-garden.com, double B3,000-B26,000), which also boasts elephant rides, golf, restaurants, a cultural show and other tours. Nearby, **Samphran Elephant Ground & Crocodile Farm** (km30 Thanon Phetkasem, Samphran, 0 2429 0361-2, www.elephantshow.com, admission B400) offers elephant rides, croc wrestling, costumed battle re-enactments and, on 1 May, the **Jumbo Queen** contest to find the most elephantine women.

Jaya Sri Lodge (Ngew Rai, Nakhon Chaisri) is a pleasant retreat in old teak houses offering ceramics, mask-making, dance and agrotourism, plus trips to Lam Phya, **Wat Suwan Floating Market** and **Nakhon Chaisri**'s two large markets, one thriving at the town's riverside, one decaying on the nearby canal dug for pilgrims to **Nakhon Pathom** town.

Siam's oldest city and entry point of Buddhism, Nakhon Pathom was a Mon centre two millennia ago. You can't miss **Phra Pathom Chedi** (0 3424 2143), reputedly the world's tallest *stupa* at 120 metres (414 feet). Since 1853 its bell shape has clad a Khmer *prang* that encased a Mon *stupa*. There's also a reclining Buddha, a circular cloister, and Dvaravati treasures in **Phra Pathom Chedi National Museum** (0 3427 0300, closed Mon, Tue, admission B30). Artefacts in the free **Phra Pathom Museum** (closed Mon & Tue) are less organised. Across town, the leafy grounds of **Sanam Chan Palace** (6 Thanon Rajamankha Nai, 0 3424 4236-7, 9am-4pm daily, admission B50) contain museums in divine timber residences of King Rama VI of Thai, tropical European and château style, plus a *wat*-like theatre. For sights en route from Bangkok, *see pp71-77*.

Elephant rides at **Ayutthaya**. *See p101.*

Getting there

Buses leave daily from the Southern Bus Terminal to Samut Songkram (every 30mins, 5am-9pm, B42) and Nakhon Pathom (every 10mins, 5.30am-11.15pm, B34). To Nakhon Pathom, nine trains leave 7.45am-10.50pm daily from Hualumphong station (B20-B40), while four 3rd-class trains run daily from Thonburi station (B22). To Samut Songkram, 3rd-class trains leave hourly 5.30am-8.10pm daily from Wongwian Yai station (B10).

Kanchanaburi

The base for exploring jungled 'Kan'buri', Thailand's fourth-largest province, is pleasant **Kanchanaburi** town, 129 kilometres (81 miles) west of Bangkok. Its infamous **Bridge on the River Kwai** (4 kilometres/2.5 miles north of today's bridge) was part of the World War II 'Death Railway' built by the Japanese to supply its army in Burma. An estimated 18,000 POWs and 90,000 Asian slave labourers perished in its construction and many of them are buried at the cemetery in town and at nearby **Chung Kai Cemetery**.

The Kwae Yai (larger tributary) joins the Kwae Noi (smaller tributary) to form the Maeklong river near the **JEATH War Museum** (Wat Chai Chumpon, Thanon Pak Praek, 0 3451 5203, admission B30), which tells the POWs' tale better than the kitsch **War Museum** beside the rail bridge over the Khwae Yai. Each November, the ten-day **River Kwai Bridge Week** has a sound and light show.

The tourist office (TAT, 310/2 Thanon Saeng Chuto, 0 3451 1200, open 8.30am-4.30pm daily) has information on sights in town and in the nearby national parks and fertile valleys dotted with Mon, Karen and ethnic Burmese villages. Some 65 kilometres (35 miles) up Route 3199, the nine-tier waterfalls in **Erawan National Park** (0 3457 4234) get crowded at weekends, while nearby **Srinagarind National Park** contains a reservoir. Both charge B200 entry.

Though mostly dismantled after the war, the 'Death Railway' still runs from Kanchanaburi over rickety viaducts along the Kwae Noi to Nam Tok (90mins, every 20mins, 6am-10am, 4-6pm daily, B100 one way), where *songtaews* (B100-B200) shuttle to **Sai Yok Noi** falls (km46 Highway 323). It's busy with picnickers, but inferior to the distant cascade at **Sai Yok Yai National Park** (km82, 0 3451 6163-4, admission B200). Australia has funded the impressive **Hellfire Pass Memorial & Museum** (km75, 0 1754 2098, www.hellfire pass.com) on the 4.5-kilometre (three-mile) jungle trail to the hand-chiselled rail cutting of **Hellfire Pass**. At km105-6, **Hin Dat Hot Springs** feature Japanese-built sulphurous hot baths next to a cooling stream. From here, a poor dirt road leads to the marvellous, multi-tiered **Phra That Waterfall**.

Highway 323 winds 260 kilometres (150 miles) to the Myanmar border, passing karst mountains and floating guesthouses along Khao Laem reservoir near **Thong Pha Phum**. Heading the flooded valley, the quaint Mon town of **Sangkhlaburi** boasts an awesomely tall wooden bridge. At the frontier, **Three Pagodas Pass** marks an old Burmese invasion route with a trio of tiny *chedi* and lots of Myanmese teak furniture.

Where to stay & eat

In Kanchanaburi Town, many of the hotels and guesthouses on Thanons Song Kwae and Maenam Kwae have bamboo raft rooms, such as **Sam's Place** (7/3 Thanon Song Kwae, 0 3451 3971, www.samsguesthouse.com, double B150-B350) and its two branches. Near the wire-operated ferry here, disco rafts moor before night-time party trips. Bars and floating restaurants moored along Thanon Song Kwae usually boast good food and sunset views. Upstream and considerably upmarket is the **Felix River Kwai** (Tha Makham, 0 3451 5061, www.felixriver kwai.co.th, double B2,200-B40,000).

Most remote and enchanting is **Jungle Rafts** (0 2642 5497, www.junglerafts.com, full-board double B1,600), an eco pioneer in a gorge below Sai Yok Yai, where unelectrified, oil-lamp-lit rafts offer great food, massages, elephants, a cave temple and dancers from the adjacent Mon village. It can be reached by boat from its sister **River Kwai Resotel** (0 2642 5497, www.riverkwaifloatel.com, double B2,000), with garden cottages and a pool.

Getting there

Buses to Kanchanaburi leave from Bangkok's Southern Bus Terminal every 20mins (5am-10.30pm daily, B79). Provincial buses are scarce. Trains leave daily to Kanchanaburi from Thonburi and Hualumphong stations. Rail tours (0 2225 6964 ext 5217, 6.30am Sat, Sun) include side trips by bus.

Khao Yai National Park

Thailand's first national park (1962) and, after Kaeng Krachan, its second largest (2,168 square kilometres/837 square miles), is also the most visited, marking the Khorat Plateau just 200 kilometres (124 miles) north-east of Bangkok. Waterfalls (fullest and busiest in winter, when warm clothing is essential) feature on most of the 12 trails from **Khao Yai Visitor Centre** (Thanon Thanarat km37, Nakorn Nayok province, 0 3731 9002, admission B200). You can get hiking permits here or at park gates. Though still poached, wildlife is abundant in this old-growth forest and gathers more at water sources in the hot season. Rangers run truck-borne **Night Safaris** (B330), with variable results, and join all tours, the most reputable being **Wildlife Safari** (0 4431 2922, B1,150 per day and a half).

Where to stay & eat

The Visitor Centre has basic lodging and food, but Khao Yai is ringed by golf courses and resorts offering restaurants and tours. **Kirimaya by ALiLa** (1/3 Moo 6, Thanon Thanarat, Pak Chong, 0 4442 6000, www.kirimaya.com, main courses B80-B500, double B4,200-B23,200) is a serene designer resort, with mountain views, Maya Spa and a Jack Nicklaus golf course. **Khao Yai Garden Lodge** (135/1 Thanon Thanarat km7, Pakchong, 0 4436 5178, www.khaoyai-garden-lodge.com, main courses B80, double B500-B1,500) has diverse rooms and tours. The not-for-profit **Cabbages & Condoms Resort** (98 Moo 6, Phaya Yen, Pak Chong, 0 3622 7065, www.pda.or.th/saptai, main courses B150, double B2,000-B5,000) has more eco-aware trips. Cheaper is the **Jungle House** (21/5 Thanon Thanarat km19.5, Pakchong, 0 4429 7307, www.jungle househotel.com, double B400-B1,000).

Thai wine is vastly improving and Khao Yai's charming vineyards offer Siamese *Sideways*-style tastings, especially while they're fruiting (Aug-Feb) and producing (Feb-Mar). Small, picturesque **GranMonte** (52 Thanon Phausak-Kudla, 0 3622 7334, www.granmonte.com, main courses B280) has a restaurant and sells other Thai wineries' output as well. Nearby **PB Valley Khao Yai Winery** (102 Thanon Mitrphap, Payayen, 0 3622 6393, www.khao yaiwinery.com, B2,500 sleeps 4) ships 500,000 bottles a year. Its substantial tour includes lunch (11am & 4pm Sat & Sun & by appointment, B350). Meander further to **Village Farm** (Tambon Thasamakee, Wan Nam Khieo, Khorat, 0 4422 8407-9, www.villagefarm.co.th double B2,000-B6,400, main courses B450), a boutique winery growing Thailand's top vintage in bucolic environs, offering chalet rooms and gourmet food.

Chachoengsao

Pilgrims progress an hour east of Bangkok by train or road to the revered Buddha image at **Wat Sothorn** (0 3851 1048). It's now housed under the soaring modern spire of the royal temple's multi-billion-baht new marble *vihaan*. On weekends, boats from Wat Sothorn's pier take 30 placid minutes to chug past **Chachoengsao** town's quaint Bangpakong River frontage (which faces lush plantations) to **Talad Ban Mai** (Thanon Supakit, near rail bridge, 0 3881 7336). The enchanting ancient teak shops and stalls of this much-filmed 'New Village Market' sell food worthy of culinary pilgrims. Two Chinese shrines nearby complete this memorable day trip. Contact **Bangpakong River Tour** (0 3851 4333, www.bpkcharter.com).

Eat, Drink, Shop

Features

Restaurants

Thais eat at any hour, in myriad ways, but always with discernment. So can you.

Food is both the staff of life and life itself in Thailand. It plays leading and supporting roles in events religious, familial, municipal and royal. This may be one of the only cities in the world where you can sit in front of a randomly chosen wok-slinger on a corner and eat something to be remembered forever.

There are four main variants of Thai food – Central, Southern, Northern and Isaan (North-eastern). Yet this much-exported cuisine is the original fusion fare, being influenced by merchants, migrants, soldiers and missionaries across historically elastic borders. Chinese, Khmers, Burmese, Indians, Indonesians, Mons, Malays and countless tribes have all stirred the pot. Meanwhile, Thais adopted the habits and ingredients of distant lands, from Portuguese bread to staple ingredients like chilli, papaya, tomato, corn and aubergine.

If there is one danger to dining in Bangkok, it is that it can be too easy. Don't just settle for English-language menus and air-conditioning; better Thai food is typically found in out-of-the-way shophouses and street stalls. Neither has Thai food translated well to hotels, aside from noble exceptions like **Celadon** (see *p125*) at the Sukhothai, **Basil** at the Sheraton Grande (see *p46*) or **Thai on 4** at the Amari Watergate (see *p48*). Avoid the bland touristy eateries and look out for where crowds of Thais choose to dine. Even if all you can do is point at what's on other tables, you'll eat well.

WHERE?
The answer: everywhere. There is no hour, alley, market, *soi* or hotel in which a restaurant of some sort can't be found. That's not to say there aren't any hot zones and connoisseurs will travel across town for a legendary speciality (see *p116* One-dish wonders).

Little India (see *p88*) is peppered with pots of masala and cases of Punjabi sweets. Ditto Chinatown for dim sum and Cantonese. Expat enclaves include the Korea Town of Sukhumvit Plaza on Soi 12, the Arab quarter of Sukhumvit Soi 3/1, African trader fuelstops in Pratunam, and Anglo-Irish pub grub clogs the arteries of Silom and Sukhumvit. Bangkok is one of the world's best cities to eat Japanese, and sushi bars and saké dens abound in Soi Thaniya and Sukhumvit between Sois 23 and 55, while quality chains

like **Zen** and **Fuji** prompt queues in malls. Or take to the river for a **dinner cruise**; see *p56*.

WHEN?
While Thais eat pretty much everywhere and at any time, the types of foods available change according to the time of day – *ahaan chao* (morning), *ahaan thiang* (daytime), *ahaan yen* (evening and beyond). Snacks in between are *ahaan waang* (empty food). Opening early and closing after lunch or early evening are *raan ahaan* (food shops), specialising in one dish, such as *khao man kai* (chicken rice), and *raan khao kaeng* (curry and rice shops), signposted by a table of silver trays or pots. At *raan ahaan tam sang* (food-to-order shops), you choose from hundreds of dishes cooked in the style of the particular shop, while *raan khao thom* serves food with boiled rice soup. *Rot khen* (vendor carts) ply the streets and *talaat* (markets), selling food appropriate to the time

The best Restaurants

For DIY Thai
The **Blue Elephant** and **Thai House** cooking schools (for both, see *p111*).

For meat treats
New York Steakhouse (see *p119*).

For old-style Siam
Ruen Mallika (see *p121*).

For open Italian kitchens
Biscotti (see *p115*) and La Scala (see *p125*).

For Parisian chic
D'Sens (see *p112*) and Café Le Notre (see *p115*).

For river views
Kaloang Home Kitchen (see *p109*) and River City BBQ (see *p114*).

For sky-high dining
Sirocco (see *p112*).

For vegetarian art
Tamarind Café (see *p122*).

of day. More formal restaurants in *baan* (houses) and *suan* (gardens) open for lunch (noon sharp in Thailand) and dinner (6pm to 9pm for local kitchens, but later at more international places). Some restaurants close on Sunday or Monday.

Nearly all drinking and music venues serve (usually Thai) food until midnight (*see pp126-32* **Bars** *and pp180-87* **Music**), plus *klub klaem* (drinking nibbles). Turfed out at 1am, clubbers head for street stalls or grab a hangover-clearing *khao tom* (boiled rice soup) at dawn markets.

Reservations are wise, sometimes a must, at hotspots from Thursdays to Saturdays and at hotels for Sunday brunch.

SERVICE AND TIPPING

The Western culture of tipping is spreading slowly to Thailand, along with Starbucks and David Beckham. Modern and hotel restaurants usually add ten per cent service plus tax to your bill; local places will not. Tips are customarily limited to small change from paying the bill up to a typical 20-30 baht. This is less of a tip than a polite gesture that you're not price haggling.

Thai service tends to excel in helpfulness, rather than speed. Dishes may arrive together

or trickle in three or 30 minutes apart. Be patient, in Thailand dishes come when they're ready.

For each restaurant we've given the average cost of a main course, or equivalent, since many don't follow the starter/main concept. For more on Thai food culture and key dishes, *see p122* **Menu and etiquette**. Note that all air-conditioned restaurants are non-smoking.

Phra Nakorn & Banglamphu

Late-night **Pak Khlong Talad** flower market (*see p135*) has stalls serving the traders, which offer fine midnight nibbling.

International

Chabad

96 Soi Rambuttri, Thanon Chakkraphong, Banglamphu (0 2282 6388/www.jewishthailand.com). **Open** 10am-10pm Sun-Thur; 10am-3pm Fri. **Main courses** B130. **No credit cards**. **Map** p248 B2.
There are a few Israeli cafés around Banglamphu and a good falafel stall opposite Gulliver's bar, but Rabbi Nechemya Wilhelm's Chabad offers comfy, upmarket surroundings without charging much extra for the usual chips and dips and occasional North African specials, such as Morrocan-style fish.

Cy'an: minimalist decor, maximum flavour. *See p124.*

Thai

Thai food is mostly horrible around **Thanon Khao San**, but authentic on **Thanon Phra Arthit**. For **Roti Mataba** and pad Thai at **Thip Samai**, *see 116* **One-dish wonders**.

Ming Lee

29-30 Thanon Na Phralan, next to Silpakorn University, Phra Nakorn (no phone). **Open** noon-8pm daily. **Main courses** B75. **No credit cards.** **Map** p248 B4.
Ming Lee represents the Bangkok of old serving classical Thai-Chinese food that's now a rarity. There's a secret-handshake quality to the place, reflected in the hushed response to recipe enquiries and the round table at the centre reserved for older customers. Mainstays include the *mee krob, tom kha kai* and the Hainan-influenced dishes.

Sky High

14 Thanon Ratchadamnoen Klang (0 2224 1947). Phra Nakorn. **Open** 8am-2am daily. **Main courses** B150. **Credit** MC, V. **Map** p248 C3.
Sky High's hushed tones could be coming from politicians, journalists, poets or gossiping friends. This is a seriously Thai place, with lasting popularity and spot-on cooking of Thai-Chinese staples. The steamed Chinese carp fish head is memorable.

Vegetarian

Many guesthouse cafés on **Thanon Khao San** also cater to vegetarians.

May Kaidee

111 Thanon Tanao, down soi beside Burger King, then take first left (0 2281 7137/www.may kaidee.com). **Open** 8am-11pm daily. **Main courses** B50. **No credit cards.** **Map** p248 C3.
Khun May cooks up veggie versions of Thai and Chinese standards. We recommend the spring rolls. She also gives cooking classes (B1,000 for 10 dishes). **Other locations**: 111/1-3 Thai Cozy House, Thanon Tanee, Phra Nakorn (0 2629 5870).

Thonburi

International

Few Sunday hotel brunches beat **Trader Vic's** at the Marriott (*see p40*), given the jazz, river views and boat transfer (from B1,000 per person).

Jester's

1st & 3rd floors, Peninsula Hotel, 333 Thanon Charoen Nakorn (0 2861 2888/www.peninsula.com). Saphan Taksin BTS then shuttle boat. **Open** 6pm-1am (dinner until 10.30pm) daily. **Main courses** B500. **Credit** AmEx, DC, MC, V. **Map** p250 D7.
With the best five-star river view through a wall of glass, Jester's offers a very inventive and restrained Pacific Rim fusion menu, which includes such delicacies as kaffir lime with lobster, and pork loin with chilli crab and black bean broth. Under the curving steel ceiling, giant bamboo canes and coloured ball lighting are signature touches, along with metal, breast-shaped goblets held in stands beside brushed metal placemats. One of Bangkok's best, and most individual, restaurants.

Other Asian

Mei Jiang

1st floor, Peninsula Hotel, 333 Thanon Charoen Nakorn (0 2861 2888/www.peninsula.com). Saphan Taksin BTS then shuttle boat. **Open** 11.30am-2.30pm, 6-10pm daily. **Main courses** B800. **Credit** AmEx, DC, MC, V. **Map** p250 D7.
Mei Jiang combines the dual traditions of haute Cantonese cooking and the striking modernity of the Peninsula Hotel in which it is housed. Tableside service, jewel-like presentation, blockbuster wines and pan-global accents are the result. Like the clean-lined decor, done up with local silks and smoked glass, the results can be astonishing.

Thai

Also try **Supatra River House** or **Sala Rim Nam** and (for both, and other dinner theatres, *see p198*). For **Yok Yor Marina & Restaurant**, *see p56*.

River Bar Café

405/1 Soi Chao Phraya Siam, Thanon Ratchawithi (0 2879 1748-9). Tha Saphan Krung Thon (Sang Hee). **Open** 5pm-2am daily. **Main courses** B200. **Credit** AmEx, DC, MC, V.
The glass-encased River Bar Café, tucked away near the Sang Hee Bridge, is one of the few places in the city where you can eat sea-fresh fish in style. The simple preparations (steamed, deep-fried, spicy salads, flamed prawns) are pleasingly unfussy and delicious. Riverbank terraces and a lofty glazed interior, done up with modish industrial touches, provide the party setting for an attractive crowd of foreigners and locals, though the live music can be loud.

Dusit

There are ethnic eats in the Vietnamese enclave around **St Francis Xavier Church**, and Northern Thai cafés on **Thanon Sukhothai**.

Thai

Kaloang Home Kitchen

2 Thanon Sri Ayutthaya, at end of soi beside National Library (0 2281 9228/0 2282 7581). **Open** 11am-10pm daily. **Main courses** B140. **Credit** AmEx, MC, V. **Map** p249 D1.

**YOU KNOW
WHO YOU ARE.**

BANGKOK
424/3-6 SIAM SQUARE SOI 11
PATHUMWAN
662-251-0797

©2005 Hard Rock Cafe International, Inc. All rights reserved.

This is the kind of rough-and-tumble fish house that can be found dotting the coasts. Wooden planking, Formica, wind-beaten chairs – every cliché is in place. But the food transcends the setting with sure-handed spicing, and faultless freshness informs *tom yum*, steamed, fried and grilled. Don't forget to order a *yum*, and take your time on the way down the temple-lined *soi* from Thanon Samsen.

Chinatown

Other Asian

Showy Chinese restaurants proliferate along **Thanon Yaowarat**, amid pricey yet unpretentious stalls serving top food, notably in **Soi Texas**; note that Chinatown shuts down around 9pm. Hindi eateries are scattered like bindis around **Pahurat Market**.

Hua Seng Hong

371-373 Thanon Yaowarat (0 2222 0635).
Open 8.30am-1am daily. **Main courses** B160.
No credit cards. Map p249 & p250 D5.
Obscured by glass cases of sharks' fins, steamed buns and hanging roast ducks, Hua Seng Hong sits in the heartland of Yaowarat's early evening madness. *Ba mee* noodles stir-fried with crab, plates of greens with salted fish, roast duck and oyster omelettes can be procured elsewhere – but they won't be handmade on site and served by no-nonsense yet grinning staff in baby blue shirts like they are here. The interior, all brownish tones and flickering light from the TV, is evocative.
Other locations: Charoen Krung Soi 14, Chinatown (0 2627 5030); Hong Min MBK, Pathumwan (1st floor 0 2620 9492; 3rd floor 0 2611 5643).

Royal India

392/1 Thanon Chakraphet (0 2221 6565).
Open 10am-10pm daily. **Main courses** B60.
No credit cards. Map p248 C5.
Pahurat is Little India and it teems with small curry operations, most famously Royal India. Photos of Thai politicians adorn the walls, though as Thais tend to dislike Indian food, they may not have sampled the dishes. A pity, as they're good and cheap.

Shangri-La Restaurant

306 Thanon Yaowarat (0 2224 5807/0 2622 7870).
Open 10am-10pm daily. **Main courses** B300.
Credit MC, V. **Map** p249 & p250 D5.
Shangri-La, a Yaowarat institution, is the kind of full-throttle Chinese place that belongs in the movies. It's big, always busy with families, has round tables and serves dependable (and fun) dim sum daily, as well as all the sweet and sour this and that in existence.
Other locations: 58/4-9 Soi Thaniya, Bangrak (0 2234 0861-4); 154/4-7 Silom Soi 12, Bangrak (0 2234 9147-9. **Shangri-La Kitchen** 2nd floor, Silom Complex, Bangrak (0 2632 1238-9); 188-188/1 Phiphat Soi 2, Bangrak (0 2636 6840-1).

Cooking classes

Many hotels and restaurants offer courses in Thai cuisine but before you sign up ensure you'll get utensils and some time on the range, not just a talking head. The **Oriental Thai Cooking School**, in wooden buildings across the river from the Oriental hotel (*see p43*), has top-notch demonstrations of each style (9am-noon Mon-Sat, $120 per class). **Cuisine of the Sun** (0 2714 0539/0 1894 3551/ cuisinebkk@hotmail.com) holds frequent classes in Thai and foreign cooking. **Pai Kin Khao** (www.pai-kin-khao.com), the chic publisher of cookbook/CD-Rom *Spice of Life*, runs periodic hands-on workshops with leading chefs exploring various themes and cuisines, such as fusion, healthy eating and entertaining. **May Kaidee** teaches vegetarian Thai cookery (*see p109*) and **Kuppa** (*see p117*) also has a cooking school.

Blue Elephant

233 Thanon Sathorn Tai, Bangrak (0 2673 9353-4/www.blueelephant.com). Surasak BTS. **Open** 11.30am-2.30pm, 6.30-10pm daily. **Main courses** B300. **Credit** AmEx, DC, MC, V. **Map** p250 E8.
This Belgium-based chain of contemporary Thai restaurants has converted the century-old Thai-Chinese Chamber of Commerce building into a restaurant. Innovation infuses the menu, but with moderate spiciness. Upstairs, a well-equipped school for its chefs worldwide offers public courses teaching four dishes per day (8.30am-1.30pm, 1.30-5pm daily, B2,800; 7-day course B14,000).

Thai House

32/4 Moo 8, Bangmuang, Bangyai, Nonthaburi province (0 2903 9611/ fax 0 2903 9354/www.thaihouse. co.th). **Open** 9.30am-4.30pm Mon-Sat. **Rates** single B1,200; double B1,400.
No credit cards.
A canalside cooking school in a beautiful compound with day or residential courses in classic dishes (9.30am-4.30pm Mon-Sat). Choose from one-day (B3,500), two-day (B8,950 shared room, B9,550 single) or three-day (B16,650 shared, B18,450 single). A rare chance to stay in a teak stilt house, it's remote, but not far from the expressway.

Eat, Drink, Shop

Thai

For **Pet Tun Jao Tha**'s delicious duck noodles, *see p116* **One-dish wonders**.

Bangrak

International

For the best baked goods and French snack meals, try **La Boulange** (*see p148*). For Anglo-Irish food, try the **Barbican** (*see p127*) and **Irish X-change** bars (*see p129*).

Angelini's

2nd floor, Shangri-La Hotel, 89 Soi Wat Suan Plu, Thanon Charoen Krung (0 2236 7777). Saphan Taksin BTS. **Open** 11.30am-2.30pm, 2.30-6pm, 6-11pm daily. *Bar* last orders 1.15am Mon-Sat; 12.30am Sun. **Main courses** B500. **Credit** AmEx, DC, MC, V. **Map** p250 D7.
Reminiscent of a cathedral with its floor-to-ceiling windows and sweeping balconies, this was the first high-class modern restaurant to open in Bangkok. The food is exceedingly good classic Italian, with the added benefit of romantic river views. There's an open kitchen and a bar on the mezzanine, which hosts a typically safe hotel band (8.15pm-midnight Mon to Sat) – perhaps the only blemish on the experience.

Le Bouchon

37/17 Patpong Soi 2 (0 2234 9109). Saladaeng BTS/Silom subway. **Open** noon-3pm, 7-11pm Mon-Sat; 7-11pm Sun. **Main courses** B440. **Credit** AmEx, MC, V. **Map** p250 F6.
Perhaps the most authentic French bistro in town, and consequently the top regular dining spot for local Gauls. The very small bar is abuzz with *joie de vivre* as diners wait to be seated at one of only seven tables. Expect simple but good country cooking.

D'Sens

Dusit Thani Hotel, 946 Thanon Rama IV (0 2236 9999). Saladaeng BTS/Silom subway. **Open** 11.30am-2.30pm, 6.30-10pm Mon-Sat. **Main courses** lunch B900; dinner B2,000. **Credit** AmEx, DC, MC, V. **Map** p251 G6.
The angular 1960s architecture of the Dusit Thani hotel (*see p42*) penthouse makes a distinctive setting for this branch of Le Jardin des Sens from Montpellier, France. Owners Jacques and Laurent Pourcel only come over for menu changes, but the chef came direct from their three Michelin-starred mother restaurant. Masterful dishes like roasted turbot fillet on a bed of parsley-stuffed pig's trotter with citrus flavoured meat jus, and wonderful desserts, justify the Michelin-star prices.

Eat Me!

1/6 Phiphat Soi 2, Thanon Convent (0 2238 0931). Saladaeng BTS/Silom subway. **Open** 3pm-1am daily. **Main courses** B300. **Credit** AmEx, DC, MC, V. **Map** p250 F7.

Always popular for its interesting East-West fusion menu that includes dishes like tuna tartar with soba noodles and cabbage salad, a now-expanded Eat Me! has evolved into the city's premier art restaurant. The usually quirky, sometimes confrontational canvases provide great conversation pieces and attract a cool clientele, making this as much a hangout as a restaurant. People tend to linger for postprandial drinks over the well-selected music.

Le Normandie

5th floor, Oriental Hotel, Charoen Krung Soi 38 (0 2236 0400/www.mandarinoriental.com). Saphan Taksin BTS. **Open** noon-2pm, 7-10.30pm daily. **Main courses** B1,800. **Set menus** lunch B850 (3 courses); dinner B3,900 (7 courses). **Credit** AmEx, DC, MC, V. **Map** p250 D7.
Bangkok's most famous restaurant offers the chance to eat high-class French cuisine at a fraction of what it would cost in Paris. The marmalade interior, dazzling under crystal chandeliers, offers European luxury overlooking the river through a full wall of windows. The food offers wonderful combinations of flavours, and is gorgeously presented, while the wine list is monumental in its range, but also has drinkable possibilities at around B1,700. Feast like a film star on the five-course tasting menu (with different wines for each course), for around $150 a head. A jacket and tie are compulsory for men, and are available at the door if you don't have them with you. The set menus can be incredible value.

Sirocco & Sky Bar

63rd floor, State Tower, 1055 Thanon Silom (0 2624 9555). Saphan Taksin BTS. **Open** 6pm-1am daily. **Main courses** B1,000. **Credit** AmEx, DC, MC, V. **Map** p250 D7.
An astonishing 200m-high (656-feet) rooftop restaurant with unrestrained Greco-Roman architecture and giddying views of Bangkok and the river. Sweep down the large stone staircase past the jazz quartet to the garden terrace tables and you'll find yourself not caring about the erratic food – this is still one of Asia's best dining experiences. The more specifically Italian food is now in Mezzaluna, a half-moon-shaped fine-dining restaurant inside the dome. Sirocco's Sky Bar (seemingly on the edge of space) mixes the stiff drinks needed to look down, as does the Distil bar indoors (for both, *see p128*). Booking is essential.

Zanotti

1st floor, Saladaeng Colonnade, 21/2 Soi Saladaeng (0 2636 0002). Saladaeng BTS/Silom subway. **Open** 11.30am-2pm, 6-10.30pm daily. **Main courses** lunch B370; dinner B800. **Credit** AmEx, DC, MC, V. **Map** p250 F6.
'Exuberance' sums up this restaurant – the jazz music is cranked up high, as is the conversation (the tables are so close you could spoon-feed your high-flying neighbours) – and it took Bangkok by storm on opening in 1998. The pace is frenetic – waiters become a blur in front of the metaphysical paintings by Rincicotti. The menu is good, and varied (orange

Chic eats

Bangkok's barely 30-year-old restaurant
scene is at last emerging from its youthful
flirtations with crapulent fusion, car-mechanic
cooks and maverick Mexicans. Its brave new
culinary world now has razor-sharp chefs,
an A-list of imported products and design by
mavens of swank. Sitting above them all –
literally – is **Sirocco** (*see p112*), an alfresco,
200-metre-high rooftop restaurant that
would, for its views alone, be premier league
dining in any city in the world. Its sister bar-
restaurant **Distil** (*see p128*) is all translucent
onyx, champagne and Iranian caviar.

The futuristic **Bed Supperclub** (*see p117*)
didn't just blow millions on its fabulous
tubular structure. So keen were the owners
to have the ovens manned by an expert, they
enlisted virtuoso chef Dan Ivarie. **Cy'an** (*see
p124*) also put cooking first in appointing
Amanda Gale, once of Neil Perry's Rockpool
restaurant in Sydney. And, in 2004, the
Big Mango got its first brush with Michelin
stardom when the Pourcel brothers opened
D'Sens (*see p112*), a branch of their award-
winning restaurant in France.

But it's not only international restaurants
that are raising the bar. The boutique mall
H1 (*see pp138-54*) introduced high-design
restaurants, such as **Extase** (*see p121*)
Kalapapreuk on First) and bar-eaterie **Chi** (*see
p131*) in a lifestyle-statement environment of
Euro furniture, collectibles and glossy art.

More Thais are leaving behind the recent
obsession with Westernisation. The growing
appreciation of Asian art and a worldwide
spa revolution that draws heavily on Asian
philosophies and ancient healing coincides
with a growing Thai confidence in its own
culture. Consequently, a new aesthetic

of traditional Asian references with
global sensibilities marks beautiful new
restaurants like **Maha Naga**, **Hazara** (for
both, *see p119*) and even the Italian **La
Scala** (*see p125*).

Haute cuisine at **Sirocco**.

wood charcoaling is a speciality), but the frantic
intensity of the operation means that the usually
high quality occasionally suffers. Ebullient chef-
patron Gian-Maria Zanotti – who suggests you tread
on the testicles of the brass bull in the lobby floor
(as they do at the Turin original) – also serves wood-
fired pizzas at Limoncello and by delivery.
Other locations: Pizzeria Limoncello 17
Sukhumvit Soi 11, Sukhumvit (0 2651 0707).
Pizzanotti delivery hotline (0 2800 8089).

Other Asian

The Little Tokyo of **Soi Thaniya** (including
the malls of **Thaniya Plaza** and **Charn**

Issara Tower) acts as one huge bento box
of Japanese restaurants, many at bargain prices.
Indian and Muslim restaurants are concentrated
around Silom's Hindu temple (*see p90*) and
along **Thanon Charoen Krung**.

Aoi

*132/10-11 Silom Soi 6 (0 2235 2321-2). Saladaeng
BTS/Silom subway*. **Open** noon-2.30pm, 6-10pm
daily. **Main courses** lunch B250; dinner B450.
Credit V. **Map** p250 F7.
This traditional slate-walled tavern a few blocks
south of Thaniya's Little Tokyo is the area's best
Japanese restaurants. Prices are slightly higher, but
reflect the quality, service and Kyoto-esque interior.

Splash out on a dinner cruise. *See p56*.

Other locations: 4th floor, Emporium, Sukhumvit Soi 24, Sukhumvit (0 2664 8590-2).

China House

Oriental Hotel, Charoen Krung Soi 38 (0 2236 0400 ext 3378/www.mandarinoriental.com). Saphan Taksin BTS. **Open** 11.30am-2.30pm, 6.30-10.30pm daily. **Main courses** lunch buffet B700; dinner B2,500. **Credit** AmEx, DC, MC, V. **Map** p250 D7.

China House, though quieter than the Oriental's other outlets, and located outside the entrance, may be its most timeless dining space. It's a Fabergé-delicate heritage house, with angular modern furniture. The long menu is firmly rooted in the haunting flavours of Cantonese tradition, but when the sense of fun kicks in this can be a forward-looking restaurant. The dim sum at lunchtime is top-shelf.

Indian Hut

311/2-5 Thanon Surawong (0 2237 8812). Saladaeng BTS/Silom subway. **Open** 11am-11pm daily. **Main courses** B200. **Credit** AmEx, DC, MC, V. **Map** p250 F6.

Don't be misled by the ill-advised Pizza Hut-style logo, this is one of the best north Indian restaurants in town. All the dishes have a deep, robust flavour, but the creamy Kashmiri options are particularly enjoyable. The second floor has the better decor.

Nam Kang

5/3-4 Soi Phiphat, Silom Soi 3 (0 2233 1480-3). Saladaeng BTS/Silom subway. **Open** 11am-2.30pm, 5.30-10pm daily. **Main courses** B170. **Credit** AmEx, MC, V. **Map** p250 F7.

Serving high-end Seoul cuisine, this is the pick of Bangkok's many Korean restaurants. Ginseng chicken is the most frequent menu order.

River City BBQ

2nd & 5th floors, River City Complex, Thanon Yotha (0 2237 0077-8). Tha Siphraya. **Open** *2nd floor* 11am-10pm daily. *5th floor* 5-11.30pm daily. **Main courses** B300. **Credit** AmEx, MC, V. **Map** p250 D6.

The Mongolian fire pot is a fun, communal style of DIY dining that's spawned Asian variants, from Japan's *sukiyaki* to Thailand's own *suki*. Grill and boil your own meat and vegetables at your rooftop table, while gawping at the stupendous riverscape.

Silom Restaurant

793 Silom Soi 15 (0 2236 4443/4268). Chong Nonsri BTS. **Open** 10am-9pm daily. **Main courses** B200. **No credit cards. Map** p250 E7.

Hainanese-style cooking was the original fusion cuisine throughout Asia. In Thailand – and at this seminal restaurant – pork chops, noodles and the like bear the imprint of palates colonial, Thai and Chinese all at once. Translation: protein enough to satisfy a big foreigner, with bold and slightly salty overtones of soy, garlic and spice that have had Thais smiling their way in and out of this warehouse-like space for years.

Smoothie Mania

22 Thanon Silom (0 2632 8785). Saladaeng BTS/Silom subway. **Open** 11am-2am Mon-Thur; 11am-3am Fri, Sat; 3pm-2am Sun. **Main courses** B100. **No credit cards. Map** p250 F6.

'Where healthiness and chic co-exist', claims this fresh-squeezed juice bar. And, sure enough, the healthiness comes from snacks like organic green salad, while the chic is in the (now slightly scuffed) brilliant white interior with a few simple canvases for colour. Located amid Silom's nightlife, Smoothie Mania is ideal for a post-club vitamin fix; alcoholic cocktails are also served.

Tamil Nadu

5/1 Silom Soi 11 (0 2235 6336/6325). Chong Nonsri BTS. **Open** 10am-10pm daily. **Main courses** B160. **Credit** AmEx. **Map** p250 E7.

The large local Indian population around the Hindu temple results in a plethora of cheap, no-frills Indian cafés. This one is clean, has air-con and offers good south Indian food, especially the masala dosa.

Eat, Drink, Shop

Thai

Competition keeps streetfood standards high around Patpong on **Thanon Silom, Thanon Surawong** and **Soi Convent**, especially at seafood stalls. For regional curries, try **Khrua Aroi Aroi** (*see p116* **One-dish wonders**).

A Day

41 Soi Yommarat, Soi Saladaeng (0 2237 6086-8). Saladaeng BTS/Silom subway. **Open** 11.30am-2pm, 6pm-midnight Mon-Fri; 6pm-midnight Sat. **Main courses** B120. **Credit** AmEx, DC, MC, V. **Map** p251 G7.

A Day has a cheeky come-one, come-all theme evidenced by playful swathes of Mondrianesque yellows, pinks and blues, and a giant teddy bear that moves places daily. Housed in a refitted 1970s house, it draws a suitably trendy crowd. The food comes fast and furious: in classic forms, such as pungent chilli dips and oily rice noodle dishes, and also with thoughtful modern touches, such as hot clams served atop eggy Portuguese bread.

Coca Suki

8 Thanon Surawong (0 2236 0107). Saladaeng BTS/Silom subway. **Open** 11am-2pm, 5-10pm daily. **Main courses** B250. **Credit** AmEx, DC, MC, V. **Map** p250 E7.

Sociability and *sanuk* converge in *suki*, a favourite Thai variant of Japanese *sukiyaki*, where you order trays of ingredients to cook in a table-top pot. **Other locations:** 416/3-8 Siam Square Soi 7, Pathumwan (0 2251 6337); 1/1-5 Sukhumvit Soi 39, Sukhumvit (0 2259 8188/9); 4th floor, Siam Centre, Pathumwan (0 2658 1105-6); Basement, Time Square, Sukhumvit (0 2 250 0052); 6th floor, Central World Plaza, Pathumwan (0 2255 6365).

Pathumwan

International

The sophisticated **Four Seasons Hotel** (*see p45*) offers free-flow alcohol at its upmarket Sunday brunch (B1,850++, including alcohol), held in various venues within the hotel.

Biscotti

1st floor, Four Seasons Hotel, 155 Thanon Ratchadamri (0 2254 9999). Ratchadamri BTS. **Open** noon-2.30pm, 6-10.30pm daily. **Set menus** lunch B490/B550 (2/3 courses); dinner B550. **Credit** AmEx, DC, MC, V. **Map** p251 G5.

Politicians, film stars captains of industry are the kind of people who dine in this Tony Chi-designed, thrillingly modern restaurant where people *need* to be seen. And they're easily spotted in the huge square room of terracotta and white, dominated by a large open kitchen. Biscotti gets absolutely jammed at lunch and dinner, with devotees of its superb Italian food.

Café Le Notre

Ground floor, Natural Ville Executive Residences, 61 Soi Lang Suan (0 2250 7050-1). Chidlom BTS. **Open** 6am-10pm daily. **Main courses** B300. **Credit** AmEx, DC, MC, V. **Map** p251 H5.

This chic outlet of a Parisian chain brings gallic savoir faire to Lang Suan. It also brings its own chefs from Paris, for a short menu of very good appetisers, salads and mains like duck confit with zucchini and tomato bayaldi, named after Imam Bayaldi, who reportedly fainted at the richness of it. Fantastic desserts; don't miss the chocolate mousse wrapped around green tea crème brûlée.

Other locations: 1st floor, Sofitel Silom, 188 Thanon Silom, Bangrak (0 2267 5292).

Calderazzo

59 Soi Lang Suan (0 2252 8108-9). Chidlom BTS. **Open** 11.30am-2pm, 6-10.30pm daily. **Main courses** set lunch B390 (4 courses); dinner B500. **Credit** AmEx, DC, MC, V. **Map** p251 H5.

This pleasing contemporary restaurant has sloping ceilings and split-level dining areas in restful creams, resulting in a warm environment in which to enjoy home-style Italian cooking. The food is good, particularly the own-made pasta, but portions are small and the desserts disappointing. There's a wide choice for vegetarians, though.

Other Asian

Thang Long

82/5 Soi Lang Suan (0 2251 3504/4491). Chidlom BTS. **Open** 11am-2pm, 5-11pm daily. **Main courses** lunch B120; dinner B230. **Credit** AmEx, MC, V. **Map** p251 H5.

There's a clean, minimalist cool to this Vietnamese eaterie – with boxy rattan chairs, loungey music and strategic placing of plants (both live and painted) – which makes it a regular of arty types. Thang Long gets busy, so book ahead.

Thai

For genuine Isaan fare at **Kai Thord Soi Polo**, *see p116* **One-dish wonders**.

Curries & More

63/3 Soi Ruam Rudee, at Soi 3 (02 253 5405-7/www.baan-khanitha.com). Ploenchit BTS. **Open** 11am-11.30pm daily. **Main courses** B200. **Credit** AmEx, DC, MC, V. **Map** p251 H5.

This place could be called Curries and Everything, so varied is the menu. Add to signature tasty Thai soups, somtams and larbs own-made Western pies, pastas, steaks, lamb chops and even trout in Louisiana sauce. Fine cakes and Brittany crêpes follow. Unusually well-trained waiters whisk around this converted house with art-laden rooms on two floors, and a water-cooled, all-weather patio.

Other locations: Baan Khanitha 36/1 Sukhumvit Soi 23, Sukhumvit (0 2258 4181); 67-69 Thanon Sathorn Tai, corner of Soi Suan Plu, South (0 2675 4200-5).

Eat, Drink, Shop

Khrua Nai Baan

94 Soi Lang Suan (0 2252 0069). Chidlom BTS.
Open 8am-midnight daily. **Main courses** B250.
Credit AmEx, MC, V. **Map** p251 H5.
This simple white wooden house on bopping Lang
Suan is a nightly dinner party of sorts, with throngs
of regulars. The cooking focuses on seafood – all
taken still breathing from the tanks out front. From
Chinese veggies to coconut-creamy *tom yum*

nam khon, Isaan-style *jim joom* (herbal soup) and
steamed squid in lemon sauce, it's hard to err.

Le Lys

75/2 Lang Suan Soi 3 (0 2652 2401). Chidlom BTS.
Open 11am-10.30pm daily. **Main courses** B200.
Credit AmEx, MC, V. **Map** p251 H5.
At Le Lys you'll find a *pétanques* court in the leafy
yard, fine salmon in the Thai *yum* and vintage

One-dish wonders

The concept of eating out is very new to
Thailand, having become common only in the
past few decades. Before that, cooking and
eating were very much confined to the home.
But some claim that the restaurant scene
has brought with it a certain homogenisation
of dishes and flavours. In an interview Thai
food scholar and Michelin-starred chef David
Thompson told the *Nation*, 'In Bangkok it is
becoming increasingly difficult to find… that
complexity of flavour'. Difficult indeed, but
not impossible. Thai food aficionados make
pilgrimages to street stalls and single-dish
shophouse specialists, whose reputation
still rings around the city. Don't let hygiene
worries daunt you – millions of people eat
this food every day. To ensure standards
look for busy vendors, whose high turnover
means fresh food and healthy patrons.
Throughout this chapter we have noted
knots of top-end stalls under area headings.

Kai Thord Soi Polo

*137/1-2 Soi Polo, Thanon Witthayu,
Pathumwan (0 2252 2252).* **Open** 7am-7pm
daily. **Main courses** B60. **No credit cards**.
Map p251 H5.
There's fried chicken and there's fried chicken
from Soi Polo. Its oily, aromatic, crispy, fleshy
balance has won devotion among Thai locals.
Owner J-Kee, though a southerner, has four
decades of experience cooking the austere
yet deeply flavoured foods of Isaan.

Khrua Aroi Aroi

*Thanon Pan, opposite Wat Khaek, Bangrak
(0 2635 2365). Surasak BTS.* **Open** 9.30am-
6.30pm daily. **Main courses** B40. **No credit
cards**. **Map** p250 E7.
Khanom jeen is a quick-fix fave of various
curries spooned over rice noodles and eaten
with cooling, crunchy herbs and vegetables.
This two-level shop – whose name means
'delicious delicious' – offers tastes from jungle
curries and chilli dips to coconut milk-rich
Muslim varieties and an archetypal green curry.

Mid Night Kai Ton

Thanon Petchaburi Tut Mai, North (no phone).
Open 7pm-4am daily. **Main courses** B40.
No credit cards. **Map** p249 & p250 F3.
This place provides late-night food in the form
of *khao man kai*, a Hainainese trader dish of
chicken-flavoured rice, steamed chicken and
broth offset by hits of ginger and chilli sauce.
The post-party customers can't get enough,
and we can see why.

Pet Tun Jao Tha

*941-7 Wanit Soi 2, Chinatown (0 2233
2541). Tha River City.* **Open** 10.30am-5pm
Mon-Sat. **Main courses** B35. **No credit cards**.
Map p249 & p250 D5.
Pet Tun Jao Tha is the place for duck and
goose, roasted or stewed, served straight up
with rice noodles and condiments.

Roti Mataba

*136 Thanon Phra Arthit, near Santichaiprakarn
Park, Banglamphu (0 2282 2119). Tha*

Eat, Drink, Shop

French wine posters hanging by Lanna textiles. The French-Thai owners have converted their home in the pursuit of taste and set themselves apart, with their European-tinged grace combined with an oh-so-Thai menu. Pickled bamboo shoot soup, red curry with duck and lychee, and squid with tamarind sauce lure young and old. As we went to press there was talk of Le Lys having to move, but no confirmation was available.

Phra Arthit. **Open** 7am-9pm Mon-Sat. **Main courses** B60. **No credit cards. Map** p248 B2.
The women who run Roti Mataba are experts at patting, flipping, filling and plaiting roti. The eponymous flatbread is available stuffed (with chicken, egg, veggies) and drizzled (with sweet milk or honey) or put to work as a dipping implement (alongside curries). *Pictured below.*

Thip Samai
313 Thanon Mahachai, behind the Golden Mount, Phra Nakorn (0 2221 6280). Tha Saphan Phan Fah. **Open** 5.30pm-3.30am daily. **Main courses** B45. **No credit cards. Map** p248 C2.
Pad Thai is the dish that all visitors know before getting their visa. Thip Samai, known by many in Bangkok as Pad Thai Pratu Pi ('Ghost's Gate Noodles'), is a legend for serving nothing but, in a neon-lit setting. Try the egg-wrapped version and the nutty-sweet coconut juice.

Other locations: 104 Narathiwat Ratchanakarin Soi 7, South (0 2677 5709).

Sukhumvit

International

The **Bull's Head** (*see p131*) serves matchless British staples. The multi-restaurant Sunday brunch at the **Sheraton** (*see p46*) is accompanied by excellent jazz (from B1,100 per person).

Baan Rai Café
Thanon Sukhumvit at Soi 63 (0 2391 9783-5/ www.banriecoffee.com). Ekamai BTS. **Open** 24hrs daily. **Main courses** B70. **No credit cards. Map** p252 M7.
This rustic 'coffee garden' on prime BTS-linked real estate can be reached via wooden boardwalks over lotus ponds. Tea and coffee come in modern and local styles (Thai tea with a jasmine tea chaser), along with cakes, internet on nine iMacs, classical Thai music piped on and on CDs for sale, and myriad books and magazines. Some books are chained to the outdoor tables where you can eat great Isaan food from the adjacent stalls. The cultural atmosphere extends to performances in the tree-shaded earthy courtyard. A 24-hour stop for Eastern Bus Station passengers.

Le Banyan
59 Sukhumvit Soi 8 (0 2253 5556/www.le-banyan. com). Nana BTS. **Open** 6.30pm-midnight (last orders 9.30pm) Mon-Sat. **Main courses** B800. **Credit** AmEx, DC, MC, V. **Map** p251 J5.
A silver salver French institution that understands the theatricality required in the field of fine dining. Many dishes are prepared at the table by the formal but amiable maître d', Bruno Bischoff, or the eccentric chef, Michel Binaux – a charming double act. The speciality is pressed duck, within a menu of superb classics. The old Thai house décor has faded at the edges, but few Bangkok restaurants are better, or better value.

Bed Supperclub
26 Sukhumvit Soi 11 (0 2651 3537/www.bedsupper club.com). Nana BTS. **Open** 7.30pm-1am daily. **Main courses** B500. **Credit** AmEx, DC, MC, V. **Map** p251 J5.
All white, space-age industrial environment in a unique tubular shell, where chef Dan Ivarie offers exquisite East-West fusion on a choice of three-course kset menus, with a surprise fixed menu on Saturdays. Diners eat off tiny tatami tables while lying on beds of white cushions either on the ground floor or the surrounding balcony. The drinking/music action then switches to Bed's other half, which is a bar (*see p130*). Ultra-strict ID checks.

Kuppa
39 Sukhumvit Soi 16 (0 2663 0450). Asoke BTS/ Sukhumvit subway. **Open** 10.30am-10.30pm Tue-Sun. **Main courses** B300. **Credit** AmEx, DC, MC, V. **Map** p252 K6.

Eat, Drink, Shop

hu'u **in bangkok**
pre-club bar I fine dining I gallery

'Best New Nightspot 2005'-BK Magazine

hu'u reservations t: (66) 2 676 6677
1 & 2/F The Ascott 187 south sathorn road
www.huuinasia.com

The best London bars & restaurants, just a click away.

Subscribe today and enjoy over 3,400 constantly updated reviews from *Time Out*'s acclaimed *London Eating & Drinking, Cheap Eats, Bars Pubs & Clubs* Guides and *Time Out London weekly.*

timeout.com/restaurants

Time Out's online bar & restaurant guide

Time Out Online

Time Out 2005/6

LONDON FOR CHILDREN

NICKELODEON

MADE FOR LONDON'S MOST DEMANDING VISITORS

Available from all good bookshops, newsagents and £2 off at www.timeout.com/shop

Time Out

This hangar of blonde wood and metal, dominated by a working coffee roaster, is Bangkok's premier modern café. It has the scale and feel of a major international restaurant, and the menu is consistently good, from duck pizza with hoi sin sauce to mighty desserts. Cultured urbanites relish the sofas, magazines and art gallery all day and all night. **Other locations**: Kuppa Restaurant & Cooking School, Playfround!, 818 Soi Thonglor, Sukhumvit (0 2714 7888).

Maha Naga
2 Sukhumvit Soi 29 (0 2662 3060). Phrom Phong BTS. **Open** 11.30am-2.30pm, 6-11.30pm daily. **Main courses** B420. **Credit** AmEx, MC, V. **Map** p252 K6.
An exquisite interior turns Maha Naga into a destination restaurant, despite the so-so food. While Thai-Western fusions like pork chop with green curry struggle for balance, the Indian glass mosaics, Moroccan ramadan lanterns and waiters' North African costumes blend seamlessly under the high Thai-style ceilings. The Andalucian fountain courtyard is framed by the new dining rooms and a bar-lounge in an art nouveau house.

Nasir Al-Masri
4/6 Sukhumvit Soi 3/1 (0 2253 5582). Nana BTS. **Open** 24hrs daily. **Main courses** B220. **No credit cards. Map** p251 H5.
The highlight of the Arabic and North African restaurants on 'Soi Arab', Nasir the Egyptian transports you to downtown Cairo, complete with the requisite sounds. On the mirror-metal terrace, men banter over Arabic music videos as they puff on shiny metal and glass *shisha* pipes. Inside, Islamic motifs and Ramadan lanterns dot yet more mirror-metal walls and ceiling. All the food is good, from kebabs to dips and the Egyptian national dish, *molokaya*. No alcohol.

New York Steakhouse
JW Marriott Hotel, 4 Sukhumvit Soi 2 (0 2656 7700). Ploenchit/Nana BTS. **Open** 6-11pm daily. **Main courses** B900. **Credit** AmEx, DC, MC, V. **Map** p251 H5.
A sensation since its 2001 debut, this restaurant led the Siamese steakhouse boom, and remains unsurpassed for its club-like sophistication. It holds superb seafood in live tanks and flies in grain-fed US Angus beef (chilled not frozen); the prime cut, served from a silver trolley, is melt-in-the-mouth. The vegetables disappoint, but then this is carnivore territory. Many wines come by the glass, and it mixes 20 Martinis. Booking is essential.

Pizzeria Bella Napoli
3/3 Sukhumvit Soi 31 (0 2259 0405). Phrom Phong BTS. **Open** 6pm-midnight Mon-Fri; 5pm-midnight Sat, Sun. **Main courses** B240. **Credit** MC, V. **Map** p252 K6.
Owner Claudio Conversi, who also makes *gelato* for many top hotels and restaurants, opened the city's first stand-alone pizza parlour in 2002. Bella Napoli was packed from day one, and copyists followed.

This small trattoria has classic Neapolitan pizzas, plus pastas and a few standard mains, and a fun, friendly atmosphere.

Other Asian

Indian/Pakistani/Persian curry houses spread from **Soi 3 (Nana)** to **Soi 11** and especially **Soi 11/1**. Meanwhile, local expats sustain a dizzying variety of Japanese restaurants throughout **Sois 23-55**.

Akbar
1/4 Sukhumvit Soi 3 (0 2253 3479/0 2255 6935). Nana BTS. **Open** 10.30am-1am daily. **Main courses** B300. **Credit** AmEx, DC, MC, V. **Map** p251 J5.
Of all the Indian restaurants around Soi 3, this mishmash of wooden ornaments, lanterns, coloured glass and Indian fabrics is the oldest. Unusually, it has a few good wines, plus Persian dishes.

Le Dalat Indochine
14 Sukhumvit Soi 23 (0 2661 7967-8). Asoke BTS/Sukhumvit subway. **Open** 11.30am-2.30pm, 6-10.30pm daily. **Set menus** lunch B500; dinner B1,000-B1,400. **Credit** AmEx, DC, MC, V. **Map** p252 K6.
Oozing class, this is one of two restaurants in this *soi* owned by the family of the 1930s Saigon socialite Madame Hoa Ly, daughter of a French governor to Indochina a century ago. Photographs of that bygone time line the lobby bar, while dining rooms upstairs and down brim with Asian antiques. Even ladies sometimes peek in the gents, to view the ribald collection of phallic objects. Specialities such as prawn on sugar cane come with a bouquet of Vietnamese fresh herb-strewn salad. Its equally impressive branch, Le Dalat, is more formal. **Other locations**: Le Dalat 47/1 Sukhumvit Soi 23, Sukhumvit (0 2260 1849).

Hazara
The Face, 29 Sukhumvit Soi 38 (0 2713 6048-9/ www.facebar.com). Thonglor BTS. **Open** 6.30pm-11.30pm daily. **Main courses** B240. **Credit** AmEx, DC, MC, V. **Map** p252 M7.
A giant Balinese *garuda* dominates the stairway to a stunning interior featuring pan-Asian religious statuary, puppet heads and carved temple doors. Hazara's high-quality menu, made up of rich North Indian curries and creamy dahls, has enticing vegetarian options, such as tandoor-roasted bell peppers stuffed with vegetables and nuts. Food aside, Hazara is in a standout venue in a purpose-built Thai-style complex of sublime proportions and it has an almost magical air.

Joke Club
155/20-25 Sukhumvit Soi 11 (0 2651 2888-9). Nana BTS. **Open** 10.30am-2am daily. **Main courses** B150. **Credit** MC, V. **Map** p251 J5.
Wok-bred sizzle and high-rise bustle à la Hong Kong are the order of the day here. Joke Club has been a

scenester since its inception, thanks to a swanky mix of thoughtful Chinese cookery and modern design – think murals, dark woods, silver detailing. While an in-house singer Bacharachs away, diners feast upon staples like rice noodles, seafood and the namesake rice porridge with all the hot-sour-salty-sweet fixings.

Kaborae

1st floor, Sukhumvit Plaza, Sukhumvit Soi 12 (0 2252 5375/5486). Asoke BTS/Sukhumvit subway. **Open** 11am-10pm daily. **Main courses** B180. **Credit** DC, MC, V. **Map** p251 J5.

Family-style Kaborae is the pick of the café-diners in the Little Seoul of Sukhumvit Plaza, where practically every shop, restaurant and bar caters to Hermit Kingdom expatriates, with more in nearby *soi*. Its diverse dishes include hot and sour soups, and the peppery noodle speciality *naingmyon*. Toast the table with the Korean rice whisky *soju*.

Rang Mahal

26th floor, Rembrandt Hotel, 19 Sukhumvit Soi 18 (0 2261 7100/www.rembrandtbkk.com). Asoke BTS/ Sukhumvit subway. **Open** 11.30am-2.30pm, 6.30-10.30pm daily. **Main courses** B375. **Credit** AmEx, DC, MC, V. **Map** p252 K6.

The superb city views and the excellent, rich, north Indian dishes make Rang Mahal worth a splurge for a romantic date, but be sure to reserve a window table. The Moghul-style decor spreads from silk sofas and ornate woodwork to the die-cut menu, while a loud and entertaining Indian band plays near the long central banquet tables. There are good

thali and a terrific value Sunday brunch buffet. Wrap up warm as the air-con is Himalayan.

Shin Daikoku

32/8 Sukhumvit Soi 19 (0 2254 9981-3/ www.shindaikoku.com). Asoke BTS/Sukhumvit subway. **Open** 11.30am-2pm, 6-10.30pm daily. **Main courses** lunch B250; dinner B500. **Credit** AmEx, DC, MC, V. **Map** p252 J5.

To get to this elegant restaurant in an old house you need to cross a Japanese-style wooden bridge. Owned by the people behind the popular Fuji chain found in malls, this flagship is a favourite for embassy entertaining. Shin Daikoku offers all the usual sushi and sashimi options, plus teppanyaki and matsuzaka beef.

Other locations: 3rd floor, InterContinental Hotel, Thanon Ploenchit, Sukhumvit (0 2656 0096-8).

Xian Dumpling Restaurant

10/3 Sukhumvit Soi 40 (0 2713 5288). Ekkamai BTS. **Open** 11am-11pm daily. **Main courses** B120. **No credit cards. Map** p252 M7.

In the sea of Chinese restaurants the world over, this pocket-sized dumpling outlet in a shadowy yet neon-strewn parking lot off Soi 40 comes across as unique. The hearty Xian food seems to owe as much to Mongolian, Muslim and Silk Road influences as it does to Sino classicism. Think shredded tripe and tofu with chilli oil, stewed aubergine, mutton soup and doughy steamed dumplings in dozens of forms. Pink cloths on the chairs and white-tile wallpaper make for a setting of good-bad taste.

Hazara. *See p119.*

Thai

Flanking Thonglor BTS, stalls at the mouths of **Soi 38 and Soi 55** are renowned for their eclectic foods, from *joke* and noodles to crispy pork and desserts such as the ginger tofu soup on Soi 55.

Ana's Garden

67 Sukhumvit Soi 55 (0 2391 1762). Thonglor BTS. **Open** 5pm-1am daily. **Main courses** B190. **Credit** DC, MC, V. **Map** p252 M6.

Thais love to eat in garden settings, but they're getting rarer in urban Krung Thep. This fine example with wooden decks in a lush green space is a refuge from bustling Thonglor beyond the (intentionally) broken front wall. Dinner here, whether steak or green curry, can turn into an all-night affair, listening to reggae and laughing the night away.

Greyhound Café

2nd floor, Emporium, Sukhumvit Soi 24 (0 2664 8663/0 2260 7149). Phrom Phong BTS. **Open** 11am-10pm daily. **Main courses** B200. **Credit** AmEx, DC, MC, V. **Map** p252 K6.

Run by, and adjacent to, the hip Thai fashion store of the same name, Greyhound retains its quirky minimalist style in the form of metal-strewn, whitewashed concrete, handwritten menus and tailor-made crockery. Thai staples, steaks and local fusion conceits, such as *spaghetti pla kem* (stir-fried pasta with Thai anchovies, chilli and garlic), are hard to fault. No surprise, then, to find assorted film, media and society types nibbling here.

Other locations: 3rd floor, Central Chidlom, Thanon Ploenchit, Pathumwan (0 2255 6965); J Avenue, Thonglor Soi 15, Sukhumvit (0 2712 6547-8); Ground floor, Empire Tower, Thanon Sathorn Tai, Bangrak (0 2670 0432); 2nd floor, Gaysorn Plaza, Thanon Ploenchit, Pathumwan (0 2656 1192).

Kalapapreuk on First

1st floor, Emporium, Sukhumvit Soi 24 (0 2664 8410-2). Phrom Phong BTS. **Open** 11am-10pm daily. **Main courses** B170. **Credit** AmEx, DC, MC, V. **Map** p252 K6.

Friendly, trendy and spacious, Kalapapruek boasts cushioned banquettes and wooden lawn benches overlooking Benjasiri Park. The menu is particularly strong on regional specialities, such as roti with curry, Chiang Mai's beloved *khao soi* and *koong foo* (crispy prawn with green mango salad). It is owned by the son of aristocrat Mom Chao Bhisadhet Rachanee, who set up the original Kalapapreuk in Bangrak. Half the menu is Western, featuring rarities (for Bangkok) like trout and blueberry cheese pie.

Other locations: Kalapapreuk 27 Thanon Pramuan, Bangrak (0 2236 4335); 5th floor, Emporium, Sukhumvit (0 2614 8149). **By Kalapapreuk** All Seasons Retail Centre, Thanon Witthayu, Pathumwan (0 2685 3860). **Extase** H1, Thonglor Soi 55, Sukhumvit (0 2381 4322).

Khrua Vientiane

8 Sukhumvit Soi 36 (0 2258 6171). Thonglor BTS. **Open** noon-midnight daily. **Main courses** B100. **Credit** AmEx, DC, MC, V. **Map** p252 L7.

A block from noisy Sukhumvit, you're practically upcountry in this *soi* that's a trove of Isaan and Lao food. This sprawling wooden compound offers seating on a balcony, in cushion-seating *salas* or around an old Banyan tree. *Pong lang* dancers and musicians (7.30-10pm daily) add to the enchanting setting. It may be popular with *farang*, but the food's authentic and the ambience rootsy.

Ruen Mallika

189 Sukhumvit Soi 22, in sub-soi to Soi 16, Sukhumvit (0 2663 3211-2/www.ruenmallika.com). **Open** 11am-11pm daily. **Main courses** B240. **Credit** AmEx, DC, MC, V. **Map** p252 K6.

Ruen Mallika is a branch of the famous ML Terb restaurant in north-east Bangkok, and is likewise based on the recipes of mid 20th-century celebrity chef ML Terb Chomsai. Servings are as huge as the wooden menu, on which there are unusual dishes such as tempura-style deep-fried flowers and the Ayutthaya-period coconut milk dessert *kanom tuay*. Opt for relaxed garden seating amid the small fountains or *maun kwan* (triangular cushions) at low tables inside this Rama I-period wooden house.

Other locations: ML Terb Royal Thai Cuisine, 13/10 Moo 9, Thanon Kaset-Nawamin, Khlong Kum, Bung Khum, North-east

Menu and etiquette

Like the culture itself, Thai cooking is a synthetic whole with influences from India, China, Myanmar, Europe and beyond. But while it can be as simple or as complex as you like, there are a few basics you need to know.

Rice is the foundation upon which most of Thai food rests. With (some) noodle preparations as an exception, rice is eaten with almost every meal or dish. Stir-fries are nestled on top of it, curries are served with it and it is sweetened with coconut milk to make *khanom* (sweets). Everywhere you go there will be *khao plao* on offer: plain white rice. It is also known as *khao suay* – 'beautiful rice'. In northern and Isaan cuisine, *khao niao* is served instead of or as well as desserts. This is sticky rice, served in small bamboo containers, and eaten with the right hand, often to wrap mouthfuls of food. Desserts (*khanom*) also often have sticky rice, sweetened with coconut milk.

Thai food often explodes in the mouth with a bewildering variety of confrontational ingredients in a single dish: incendiary chillies, tart tamarind, pungent fish sauces. Cooks balance most Thai food between hot, sour, salty and sweet, and diners sample an array of dishes with a similar mix of flavours. Two bedrocks of dining – used for balance – are *yum* (spicy complex salads, often with an acid-sweet-spicy harmony) and *nam prik* (chilli dips that can be pungent, spicy or smoky).

TABLE TIPS

All dishes, however, get re-flavoured. Diners customise their food using condiments: *khreung prung* (seasonings of dried chillis, vinegar with chillis, sugar and fish sauce with chillis) and *nam jim* (dipping sauces for specific food types). It's a hugely communal exercise that involves gossip, and giving and sharing food from the centre of the table. Diners hold the fork in the left hand to push food on to the spoon in their right. Chopsticks are used only for noodles and Chinese dishes. In all cases there is one goal to Thai cooking: maximum flavour.

Cooking terms

neung steamed; **thord** deep-fried; **phat** stir-fried; **ping** grilled (small or skewered pieces); **phao** grilled (chillis or seafood); **yaang** roasted or grilled (meats and large pieces); **op** baked; **tom** boiled; **tam** pounded; **phet** spicy; **khem** salty; **waan** sweet; **priao** sour; **jeud** bland; **sub** minced; **sod** fresh and uncooked.

Rice dishes (*khao*)

khao plao plain rice; **khao niao** sticky rice; **khao phat phak** vegetable fried rice; **khao phat kai/muu/neua/phak** fried rice with chicken/pork/beef/vegetables; **khao phat man koong** shrimp paste fried rice; **khao yum** southern-style rice salad; **khao kaeng** curry over rice; **khao mun kai** Hainanese-style chicken rice; **khao na ped** roast duck rice;

(0 2946 1180-1). **Yentafo Khreuang Song**, 7th floor, Mah Boon Krong Centre, 444 Thanon Phayathai, Pathumwan (0 2686 3509, www.yentafo. com); Srivikorn Building, 42/1 Sukhumvit Soi 21, Sukhumvit (0 2713 5599).

Vegetarian

Rasayana Retreat spa has a raw food restaurant (*see p176*).

Govinda

6/5-6 Sukhumvit Soi 22 (0 2663 4970). Phrom Phong BTS. **Open** 11.30am-3pm, 6pm-midnight Mon, Wed-Sun. **Main courses** B400. **Credit** AmEx, MC, V. **Map** p252 K6.

Owner Gianni Sotgia hails from Sardinia and, (despite the restaurant's name), his excellent food is all Italian: thin-base pizzas, pastas and risottos, all with own-made bread. The two-level interior has plenty of character, with a winding staircase and upstairs balcony. German beer too.

Tamarind Café & Gallery F-Stop

27 Sukhumvit Soi 20 (0 2663 7421/www.tamarind-cafe.com). **Open** 11am-11pm Mon-Fri; 8.30am-11pm Sat, Sun. **Main courses** B180. **Credit** AmEx, MC, V. **Map** p252 K6.

Tamarind Café offers über-tasteful dining, from the classy meat-free dishes on the Asian-European menu, through to the bright white interior, where photography is exhibited under the name Gallery F-Stop. The French-Taiwanese owners, importing the concept from their Hanoi outlet, use organic produce whenever possible in dishes like burrito with sautéed veg, paneer cheese, own-made pickles, and honey and grenadine jam.

North

International

African and Muslim cafés pack **Pratunam Market** (*see p136*) and **Sukhumvit Soi 3/1**.

Eat, Drink, Shop

khao muu daeng red-roasted pork on rice; **khao mok kai** Thai-Muslim chicken biryani.

Noodle dishes (*kuaytiao & ba mee*)

Types: ba mee egg noodles; **kuaytiao** rice noodles; **sen-lek** narrow; **sen-yai** wide; **sen-mee** fine; **haeng** dry; **nam** wet, in soup.

Noodles in a bowl: ba mee muu daeng egg noodles with red-roasted pork; **kuaytiao look chin pla** rice noodles with fish balls; **kuaytiao look chin muu** rice noodles with pork balls; **khao soi** Chiang Mai egg noodles with chicken curry broth.

Noodles on a plate: kuaytiao pad thai sen-lek stir-fry with prawns, ground peanuts, tofu, bean sprouts, spring onion and egg; **kuaytiao pad khee mao** fried rice noodles with chilli, holy basil and garlic; **pad si-ew kai sen-yai** fried in black soy sauce with vegetables and chicken; **kuaytiao rad na sen-yai** in gravy with vegetables and meat; **kuaytiao reua** (boat noodles) rice noodles with dark herbal broth.

Spicy salads (*yum*)

yum tua plu winged bean; **yum woon sen** glass noodles with pork and shellfish; **yum hua plee** banana blossom; **yum pla dook foo** fluffy fried catfish; **yum moo yang** grilled pork; **yum som-o** pomelo; **yum pla meuk** squid; **yum maa-kheua yao** grilled long aubergine with minced pork; **som tam** shredded papaya;

larb muu/ped/kai Isaan or northern-style with chilli, mint, lime, roasted rice powder, fish sauce and minced pork/duck/chicken; **muu nam tok** Isaan-style with grilled pork and roasted rice powder.

Stir-fried & fried (*phat & thord*)

Stir-fried: phat hoey lai nam phrik pao clams with roast chilli paste and holy basil; **kai phat med ma muang** chicken with cashew nuts and dried chillis; **kai phat khing** chicken with ginger; **kai phat bai kaphrao** chicken with holy basil; **kai phat priao-waan** sweet-and-sour chicken; **neua phat nam-man hoey** beef with oyster sauce; **puu phat pong karii** crab stir-fried with curry powder and egg.

Fried: kai thord deep-fried chicken; **muu thord kratiam phrik** Thai pork marinated and fried with garlic and black pepper.

Curries & soups (*kaeng & tom*)

kaeng khiao-waan sweet green; **kaeng phet** red; **kaeng luang** yellow southern-style without coconut milk; **kaeng karii** mild yellow; **kaeng Matsaman** mild Muslim-style with peanuts; **kaeng pa** jungle-style with herbs and ginger without coconut milk; **kaeng panaeng** thick red with peanuts; **kaeng tai pla** southern-style with fish stomach; **kaeng som** sour no coconut milk; **kaeng jeud tauhoo/moo sub** 'bland soup' with vegetables and tofu/minced pork; **kaeng liang** aromatic vegetable soup; **tom yum** hot-and-sour soup with kaffir lime and ▶

The Pickle Factory

55 Ratchawithi Soi 2 (0 2246 3036). Victory Monument BTS. **Open** 6pm-1am daily. **Main courses** B120. **No credit cards. Map** p249 E1.
The Pickle Factory goes to show that suburbia has its moments. Take a taxi from the BTS to this quiet *soi* for a laid-back dinner at home with long-stay American Jeff Fehr. His individually styled pizzas, ('alla vodka', 'Chiang Mai sausage') have many advocates. Visitors may also dine by the garden pool, where they can also take a dip.

Thai

For Thai specialities take a trip to **Chatuchak Weekend Market** (*see p136* **A day in JJ**) in the north of the city and especially **Or Tor Kor Market** opposite (*see p135*), which sells fruit and veg. Victory Monument's surrounds are also famed for *kwetiao reua* (boat noodles).

Hua Plee

16/74 Wiphawadi-Rangsit Soi 22 (0 2511 1397). **Open** 3pm-1am daily. **Main courses** B150. **Credit** MC, V.
This converted house jogs the memories of Bangkok residents with its old-school looks and quirks, antique fabrics and carvings, toys, bags and boxes. Greenery is everywhere, and the central Thai cooking has an authenticity that only adds to the retro trip.

Tak Sura

499/2 Ratchawithi Soi 12 (Soi Bot Xavier) (0 2354 9286). Victory Monument BTS. **Open** 5pm-1am daily. **Main courses** B100. **No credit cards**.
Tak Sura is an island of a wooden house behind a bus stop lost in a sea of concrete. There's a blurred, smoky quality to the place, which is decked out in old train benches and Chinese tea-house chairs, and hasn't changed a bit over the years. Much the same yuppie-student-artist crowd chows on chilli-laced drinking food such as *larb gai* and Thai sausages.

lemon-grass; **tom kha** coconut-milk soup
with galangal and kaffir lime; **khao tom**
boiled rice soup.

Chilli dips (*nam phrik*)

nam phrik kapi shrimp paste dip; **nam phrik
long reua** shrimp paste and spicy fried fish
dip; **nam phrik ong** roast tomato dip with
minced pork and lemongrass; **nam phrik
nuum** young green chilli dip with roast
aubergine; **nam phrik pao** sweet roasted
chilli dip with fish sauce.

Seafood dishes (*ahaan talay*)

pla meuk neung manao steamed squid in
lime sauce; **puu op woon sen** crab baked with
glass noodles; **hoey nanng rom** raw oysters
with lime, shallots, garlic and cassia; **koong
pao** grilled shrimp; **plaa jian** whole fish with
ginger, onion and soy; **pla thord kratiam phrik**
deep-fried fish with garlic and black pepper;
pla meuk phat phet squid stir-fried with chilli;
po thaek seafood hotpot.

Vegetables (*phak*)

pad phak nam phrik pao stir-fried vegetables
with roasted chilli paste; **phak boong fai
daeng** stir-fried morning glory with garlic and
chilli; **phak kha-na pla khem** Chinese kale
with Thai salted fish and garlic; **pad phak nam
man hoy** stir-fried vegetables in oyster sauce;
pad ka-na muu krob Chinese kale with crispy
pork; **pad tau-fak-yao nam phrik pao** long
beans stir-fried with roast chilli paste;

pad phak ruam-mit stir-fried mixed
vegetables; **pad hed hom** stir-fried
mushrooms; **tao hoo trong kreung** tofu
in soy gravy with vegetables; **pad phak
khee mao** stir-fried vegetables with chilli,
holy basil and garlic.

Sauces & seasoning (*nam jim & kreung prung*)

sord phrik si racha sweet chilli sauce;
nam pla fish sauce; **nam pla phrik** chilli
fish sauce; **phrik haeng** dried chilli; **nam
tan** sugar; **nam som sai chuu** clear vinegar
with chilli; **phak dong** pickled vegetables;
bai horapa sweet basil; **bai kra prao** holy
basil; **ta krai** lemongrass; **phak chee**
coriander; **si-ew dum** black soy sauce;
phrik Thai white pepper; **phrik Thai dum**
black pepper; **kratiam** garlic.

Desserts (*khanom*)

nam kang sai jellies, fruit, taro, water
chestnuts over ice with **nam choem** jasmine
sugar-syrup, and **nam krati** coconut milk
or caramel; **khanom waan** flour, sugar and
coconut cream wrapped in banana leaf with
sticky rice and banana (**khanom kluay**) or
muffin-like and deep yellow (**khanom tan**);
khanom nam kati warm reduced coconut
milk with banana (**kluay buat chii**), pumpkin
(**fak thong kaeng buat**), sago and black
beans (**saku tou tam**) or black sticky rice
(**khao niao dam**); **sangkhayaa** custard of

The new branch, set in the gardens of two old houses facing each other, feels even more casual.
Other locations: Soi Thansarot, 334/1 Thanon
Phyathai, left U-turn at north foot of canal bridge
then turn right, North (0 215 8879).

South

International

One of the great experiences of Bangkok is to
eat and drink atop a skyscraper. **Vertigo**, at
the Banyan Tree Bangkok, is a full-service,
premium-priced grill where the **Moon Bar**
(*see p132*) overlooks the city on all sides.

Café Siam

*4 Soi Si Aksorn, Thanon Chue Ploeng, South
(0 2671 0030-1).* **Open** 6pm-midnight daily.
Main courses B350. **Credit** AmEx, MC, V.
Map p251 J7.

This 1922 home of an early Thai railway boss has
antique and repro furniture all for sale (the French
management has a workshop opposite); the brass
pestle-and-mortar ashtray is particularly inspired.
The half-French, half-Thai menu does a reasonable
job and the luscious setting restrains any purist
quibbles. A *digestif* upstairs after the meal is so
beguiling you'll need to be evicted at closing time.

Cy'an

*Metropolitan Hotel, 27 Thanon Sathorn Tai (02 625
3333/http://metropolitan.como.bz/bangkok).* **Open**
6am-10.30am, noon-2pm, 6.30-10.30pm daily. **Set
menus** lunch B650 (2 courses), B750 (3 courses);
dinner B2,500 (7 courses). **Credit** AmEx, DC, MC, V.
Map p251 G7.
Talented chef Amanda Gale, who has worked with
Neil Perry in his Sydney Rockpool restaurant, runs
one of Bangkok's most creative kitchens at the stylish Metropolitan hotel (*see p48*). Her Asian-
Mediterranean menu features zesty tapas starters
and mains such as seared tiger prawns with tallegio

duck eggs, coconut cream and palm sugar, often with pandan leaves (**sangkhayaa bai toey**) or stuffed inside pumpkin (**sangkhayaa fak thong**); **khanom boeng** cigar-shaped pancake with pastes of shredded coconut, squash, taro, dried prune or sweet wax gourd; **foy thong** (golden threads) duck egg yolks spun with sugar; **man/poek/khluay ping** grilled sweet potato/taro/banana with syrup. **Seasonal desserts: khao niao ma-muang/thurian** coconut milk sticky rice with mango/durian; **khao chae** rice in cold jasmine water; **krathong loy khwae** santol fruit in sweet-sour syrup.

Drinks (*deum*)

nam plao plain water; **nam soda** soda water; **nam manao** lime juice; **nam ma phrao** coconut juice; **nam krajeab** roselle flower juice; **nam matoom** bael fruit juice; **nam ta krai** lemon grass juice; **nam ponlamai bun** iced fruit shake; **oh-liang** Chinese iced black coffee; **kafae yen** Thai iced coffee with condensed milk; **cha dum yen** Thai iced black tea; **cha Thai yen** Thai iced tea with condensed milk; **nam tao hoo** hot soya milk.

Useful vocabulary

iik neung one more; **ah-roi** delicious; **mai phet** non-spicy; **phet nit noi** a bit spicy; **chawp phet phet** very spicy; **kin jeh** vegetarian (no dairy or spices); **mung sa virat** meat-free (includes dairy); **neua** meat/beef.

Eat, Drink, Shop

tortellini, parmesan and the Moorish elements of pine nuts and raisins. The dishes show superb attention to detail, both in terms of flavour and aesthetics. Views of the pool, an icy blue bar and hand-blown Murano glass lampshades dominate an otherwise minimalist room. Amanda's innovative spa cuisine in Glow upstairs makes a breezy lunch. Highly recommended.

La Scala

Pool wing, Sukhothai Hotel, 13/3 Thanon Sathorn Tai, South (0 2344 8888). **Open** 11.30am-2.30pm, 6.30-10.30pm daily. **Main courses** B700. **Credit** AmEx, DC, MC, V. **Map** p251 G7.

An open kitchen has never been less intrusive than the island workstation of this fine restaurant. Long lamps and legless solid teak tables seating eight miraculously protrude from walls clad in terracotta and hand-cast bronze strips. The food's world class, too, with novel reinterpretations of classic components. Good music and swish waiting staff uniforms add to this minimalist, yet sociable showpiece.

Thai

For the **Blue Elephant**, *see p111* Cooking classes; for **Baan Khanitha**, *see p115* Curries & More. The streetfood in Soi Prasat Court, opposite Suan Plu Market in Soi Suan Plu, includes **Santi Asoke** vegetarian Thai café.

Celadon

1st floor, Sukhothai Hotel, 13/3 Thanon Sathorn Tai, South (0 2344 8888). **Open** 11am-2.30pm, 6.30-10.30pm daily. **Main courses** B600. **Credit** AmEx, DC, MC, V. **Map** p251 G7.

Recently revamped, Celadon is that rarity: a hotel restaurant serving the kind of fifth-gear cooking that even discerning locals will grace. Lotus ponds, bronze vases and Sakul Intakul's floral fantasies give the feeling of floating, while retaining a homely vibe. The *penang* curry, banana flower salad, lotus dumplings and betel leaf starter are must-orders. Pricing is moderate considering the pedigree of the kitchen.

Bars & Pubs

Where to drink, whether arty, chic or rough-hewn.

Bangkok is a city of extremes, and one that –
despite the zealous enforcing of a 1am closing
time and bans on alcohol sales in the afternoon
– never really stops partying. What else can be
expected from the place that invented Red Bull?
Few countries consume more alcohol per head
than Thailand, and bars cater to all tastes and
budgets, from mobile open-top *tuk-tuk* counters
to cocktail nests atop skyscrapers. You can find
bars anywhere: off dank alleys; hidden among
market stalls; tacked on to shopping centres;
teetering over canals on wooden floorboards;
even occupying '70s-style homes in suburbia.
In the cooler season, seemingly every other
forecourt becomes a beer garden.

Thai drinking habits tend to follow a
pattern (*see p130* **Drinks and etiquette**),
typically involving live bands or karaoke,
and always food. Many bars, from tiny
shophouse venues to gargantuan *rong beer*
(microbreweries), offer fine menus. Given
the culture of hosting, bars can have multiple
zones (lounge, disco, karaoke, restaurant, band,
garden) in what Thais confusingly call a 'pub'.
The Anglo-Irish definition of pub also applies
to the plentiful expat watering holes.

Though nightlife zones are muted, bar strips
tend to slip in and out of vogue. Shareholders
(often Thai celebrities) invest in emerging
locations, invite their friends, get bored and
move on to the next area. They may leave in
their wake a sustainable scene, or (as is often
the case) it may fizzle out in six months. Closing
time is now 1am and picture ID (passport, ID
card, no photocopies) is often demanded on
entry, however old you are.

Phra Nakorn & Banglamphu

Thanon Khao San is a rowdy hive of
backpacker video dens with a parallel scene
of brash Thai pubs. Lined with trees and tiny,
characterful bars displaying art and run by
ex-students, **Thanon Phra Arthit** (*see p69*)
represents a more bohemian kind of fun.

Bar Bali
*58 Thanon Phra Arthit, Banglamphu (0 2629
0318).* **Open** 6pm-1am daily. **No credit cards.**
Map p248 B2.
Like many of the arty single-room bars on riverside
Phra Athit, softly-lit Bali consists of four walls of
pictures, as well as the requisite food and cocktails.

Boh
*230 Tha Tien (Chao Phraya Expressboat Pier),
Thanon Maharaj, Phra Nakorn (0 2622 3081).* **Open**
6pm-1am daily. **No credit cards. Map** p248 B3.
Like its drinks list of local whisky and mixers,
Boh's outdoor setting (bright neon lights and floorboards on the pier) is hardly classy. But the views
are free (think sunsets behind Wat Arun reflected in
the river) and the clientele of students, artists, gays
and workers stay late.

Buddy Beer
*265 Thanon Khao San, Banglamphu (0 2629 4477-
99/www.buddylodge.com).* **Open** 24hrs daily (alcohol
served until 1am). **Credit** MC, V. **Map** p248 B3.
Part of a trendy boutique hotel, Buddy Beer represents the new face of multicultural Khao San. A service island anchors the bright roomy hall strewn
with cushioned wicker chairs, though it's the pool

The best | Bars

For an arty ambience
Any bar along **Thanon Phra Arthit**
(*see above*).

For the epitome of chic
Distil (*see p128*).

For kicking back Thai-style
Monkey Shock 3rd (*see p132*).

For breadth of drinks
Zuk and **Hu'u** (for both, *see p132*).

For good beer
Tawandaeng German Brewhouse
(*see p132*) and the **Bull's Head**
(*see p131*).

For meeting expats
The Barbican (*see p127*).

For spaced-out design
Bed Supperclub (*see p130*).

For Thai trendies
Chi (*see p131*), or any other bar
in the H1 mall.

For a decent game of pool
The Ball in Hand (*see p130*).

Diplomat Bar: a touch of class. *See p129*.

Eat, Drink, Shop

table that's the magnet for a mixed crowd of back-packers and locals. Bavarian pork knuckle and sausages complement imported and domestic beers. The owner runs several bars hereabouts, including Sidewalk Café (208 Thanon Khao San, 0 2282 5573) in an old house opposite.

Hemlock

56 Thanon Phra Athit, Banglamphu (0 2282 7507).
Open 4pm-midnight Mon-Fri; 5pm-midnight Sat.
No credit cards. **Map** p248 B2.
A pioneer of this hip strip, Hemlock is set apart by its almost Mediterranean breeziness (think white washed walls and a rock-strewn interior). The exhibitions and performances upstairs make it a happening venue, with abundant wines, teas and Thai food inspired by old royal recipes.

Phranakorn Bar

58/2 Soi Damnoen Klang Tai, Thanon Ratchadamnoen, Phra Nakorn (0 2622 0282). **Open** 6pm-1am daily. **No credit cards**. **Map** p248 B3.
Young creatives and Khao San escapees gather on Phranakorn's chilled-out trellis-and-vines roof ter-race for a view of the floodlit Golden Mount and some spicy Thai food. Others linger near the third-floor pool table listening to indie, house or '80s retro. The photographer owner displays artwork on the second floor, while the ground floor witnesses whisky drinking to live music. A supremely relaxed hangout with a holiday feel.

Suzie Pub

1085-9 Soi Rambuttri, Banglamphu (0 2282 4459). **Open** 11am-1am daily. **No credit cards**.
Map p248 B2.

Down an alley dubbed Soi Suzie, this cross between an American college bar and a dance club brought Thai nightlife to Khao San. On weekends travellers and students cram into its dark interior for the rock standards, while the laid-back weeknights leave elbow room for pool and pub dinners.

Thonburi

Dry-throated in Fang Thon? Either take a ferry to Phra Arthit (*see p77*) or head to restaurants like **Supatra River House** (*see p198*) or **River Bar Café** (*see p108*). The recent social order blitz snuffed out the bar strip near Wat Arun, but some bars remain along **Thanon Arun Amarin**, opposite Sirirat Hospital. As there's no parking, it attracts mainly young moped riders.

Bangrak

Bar-restaurants and Anglo-Irish pubs are sprinkled along **Soi Saladaeng** and **Soi Convent**. Cacophonous cul-de-sac **Silom Soi 4** has been trend central since the 1970s, while **Silom Soi 2** is purely gay. Otherwise, there's the go-go and neon of **Patpong Sois 1 and 2**, or **Soi Thaniya**'s Little Tokyo.

The Barbican

9/4-5 Soi Thaniya (0 2234 3590/www.great britishpub.com). Saladaeng BTS/Silom subway.
Open 11am-2am daily. **Credit** AmEx, DC, MC, V.
Map p250 F6.

Bangkok goes all postmodern at all-white **Bed Supperclub**. *See p130.*

From the same owners as the Bull's Head (*see p131*), this split-level pub goes against the grain of karaoke and sushi bars on Soi Thaniya. Modishly styled in wood and smooth metal, it's a magnet for trendy expats and young Westernised Thais. There are regular DJs and lucrative prize draws, plus Premiership screenings in the restaurant upstairs.

Distil

63rd floor, State Tower Bangkok, Thanon Silom (0 2624 9555/www.thedomebkk.com). Saphan Taksin BTS/Pier. **Open** 6pm-1am daily. **Credit** AmEx, DC, MC, V. **Map** p250 D7.

At Distil, inside State Tower's celebrated golden 'Dome', sophisticated Thais, expats and in-the-know tourists enjoy an outstanding array of imported wines, champagnes and spirits. Expect London prices for imported oysters, fat Cuban cigars and cocktails mixed to perfection amid a glamorous decor of stone, leather armchairs and illuminated glass; there's also an outdoor terrace. Magnificent.

Home

114/14 Silom Soi 4 (0 2238 5257). Saladaeng BTS/ Silom subway. **Open** 6pm-2am daily. **Credit** V. **Map** p250 F7.

Relatively calm for this hectic strip, Home has the de rigueur people-watching terrace, and inside there's an air of sophistication to the several floors of dark, comfy leather upholstery, bare floorboards, white walls and moody house music. The bathroom is famed for its jungle-like leafiness.

Irish X-Change

1/5-6 Sivadol Building, Soi Convent (0 2266 7160-1/
www.irishxchange.com). Saladaeng BTS/Silom
subway. **Open** 11am-2am daily. **Credit** AmEx,
DC, MC, V. **Map** p250 F7.

This brass and mahogany pub acts as a social
embassy for British Isles expats, with Irish stew and
ales aplenty on tap (Malaysian-brewed Guinness is
B181 a pint), footie on the TV and the occasional live
gig. You can easily forget you're in Thailand and
presumably that's the point.

V9

37th floor, Sofitel Silom, Thanon Silom, Bangrak
(0 2238 1991/www.sofitel.com). Surasak BTS.
Open 5pm-2am daily. **Credit** AmEx, DC, MC, V.
Map p250 F7.

In a city where wine is expensive, this slick wine
bar – overlooking Downtown through window
walls – is the best value for sampling premium vin-
tages (supplied by Wine Connection; *see p149*).
International labels by the glass or bottle are paired
to specific dishes on the menu by the sommelier.
V9's ingenious 'Wine Buffet' offers three mini-
tasting glasses (in several combinations) for the
price of a single glass. DJs (7pm-2am daily) play
sophisticated funk and chillout to facilitate that
seamless drift across to the dance area.

Pathumwan

One of Bangkok's oldest bar strips, western
Soi Sarasin is enjoying something of a
revival, thanks to bars like **70s Bar**, jazzy
Brown Sugar (*see p182*) and gay bears' bar
iChub (*see p173*). **Siam Square** falls quiet at
night (with the exception of **Hard Rock Café**;
see p187), but from November to January the
mother of all beer gardens fronts **Central
World Plaza**, with thousands of revellers
thronging round three brewers' rival stages.

Bacchus Wine Bar

20/6-7 Soi Ruam Rudi (0 2650 8986/www.bacchus.tv).
Ploenchit BTS. **Open** 5pm-midnight Mon-Thur,
Sun; 5pm-1am Fri, Sat. **Credit** AmEx, DC, MC, V.
Map p251 H5.

Ruam Rudee Village venues either stay forever or
last a wink. This four-floor, Japanese-run winebar
has enduring credentials in all departments: cellar
(sommelier-selected), cuisine (Franco-Italian), humi-
dor (Cubans) and decor. Warm rusticated sandstone,
water features, woodwork and subtle lighting make
for intimate lounging, whether at the bar, sunk in
armchairs or reclining on a 'floating' bed (both floor
and ceiling are see-through). Patrons often slip into
dance mode, especially at monthly parties with top
local DJs (Joeki, Fred, Aek).

Big Echo

1st floor, Kian Gwan Building, 140 Thanon Witthayu
(0 2627 3071-4). Phloenchit BTS. **Open** 11am-1am
daily. **Credit** AmEx, DC, MC, V. **Map** p251 H5.

Die-hard karaokeans pick from over 30,000 songs
(40% in English, the rest in Japanese, Chinese and
Thai) at this Japanese-brand parlour. The 40 rooms
(holding three to 40) offer the same nationalities'
cuisines to fuel the crooning.

Diplomat Bar

Conrad Hotel, All Seasons Place, 87 Thanon
Witthayu (0 2690 9999/www.conradbangkok.com).
Ploenchit BTS. **Open** 10am-1am Mon-Thur, Sun;
10am-2am Fri, Sat. *Bands* 6.30-8pm, 9-10.30pm
Mon-Thur; 9-11.30pm Fri, Sat. **Credit** AmEx,
DC, MC, V. **Map** p251 H5.

Bangkok's A-list joins the genteel hubbub at this live
jazz lounge off the lobby. Floral installations by
Sakul Intakul offset dark wood and backlit silk in
this lofty hub for deal-making, assignations and pre-
and post-dinner gatherings. The drinks menu is
extensive, though the cocktails don't quite match
Distil's (*see p128*). Graceful service accompanies the
smooth tones of the often Gallic chanteuses.

Fou Bar

2nd & 3rd floors, 236/3-4 Siam Square Soi 2
(0 2654 6363). Siam BTS. **Open** 11am-midnight
daily. **Credit** MC, V. **Map** p249 & p250 F4.

Big-screen sports and Thai fashion TV vye for eyes
and ears with a small stage pumping live pop and
punk at this youthful joint, Siam's main nightspot.
Student types jostle over the candy-coloured couch-
es, but most end up at simple tables and chairs sup-
ping pitchers of beer and whisky.

70s Bar

231/15 Thanon Sarasin (0 2253 4433).
Ratchadamri BTS. **Open** 6pm-1am daily.
Credit AmEx, DC, MC, V. **Map** p251 G7.

Boogie on down at this hugely popular retro bar to
the best of '70s through '90s tunes. Funkadelic
young things pack both floors at the weekend; on
other days there's more space to enjoy the food and
nostalgic ambience.

Sukhumvit

Lanes off this entertainment highway harbour
distinct scenes. Foreign lotharios follow micro-
skirted legs around **Sois 3-9**, where UV-lit pool
dens and techno-pumping 'bar-beers' share non-
stop. Designer bar-restaurants dot **Soi 11** and
the zigzagging 'Green Route' linking the back-
soi north of Sukhumvit, with a glut from **Soi
21 (Asoke)** to **Soi 31**.

   A posher swathe from **Soi 53** via **Soi 55
(Thonglor)** to **Soi 55 (Ekamai)** has several
nightlife mini-malls like **J-Avenue** (Ekamai
Soi 15), **Ekamai Shopping Mall** (corner of
Ekamai Soi 10, look for the sign 'Get Drunk
Here') and hyper-modish **H1**, where **Chi** out-
chics its neighbouring bars. Opposite H1 on
Ekamai Soi 22 (**Chamchan**), a strip of 'art
bars' (bars exhibiting art) includes **Café 50**
(*see p131*). Another kind of art bar (hostess

Eat, Drink, Shop

jazz joints dubbed Dali, Renoir, Van Gogh and Monet) clogs **Soi 33**, which rivals **Sois 22, 24** and **33/1** in tourist haunts and expat pubs. For a classier pre-or post-prandial chillout, nestle in the Chinese 'box-bed' at **Face Bar** (*see p114* **Hazara**), or sip beer while browsing through design classics at **Shades of Retro** (*see p151*).

The Ball in Hand

Rajah Hotel, 18 Sukhumvit Soi 4 (0 1917 8530). Nana BTS. **Open** 11am-1am daily. **Credit** AmEx, DC, MC, V. **Map** p251 J5.
Most pool dens around Nana seem designed for sales promotion, or to provide views of bar girls handling cues and bending over green cushions. This parlour is for another kind of player, one much more interested in the 8-ball. Games (B25 each, or B240 per hour) take place at a dozen superior tables, with table attendant and a fully stocked bar giving pool addicts a much-needed break. There are competitions on weekends (women on Sat, men on Sun), plus international contests (Apr and Oct).

Bed Supperclub

26 Sukhumvit Soi 11 (0 2651 3537/www.bedsupper club.com). Nana BTS. **Open** 7.30pm-1am daily. **Credit** AmEx, DC, MC, V. **Map** p251 J5.

One of Asia's most ambitious bars, Bed repeatedly redefines itself via performance art, exhibitions and a stream of top-notch guest DJs. Divided into restaurant and bar, Bed is an achingly hip kind of place, full of all-white futuristic flourishes: spacey oval pod architecture, mattresses, low lighting, see-through floors and look-at-me staircases leading to look-at-you balconies. Aesthetics aside, the cocktails are very good (if pricey) and star chef Dan Ivorie (who used to man the hobs at Jester's; *see p107*) conjures up culinary fusions as wickedly sharp as the DJ's playlist. As the restaurant winds down, the bar shifts up a gear. Bed is renowned for ultra-strict ID checks. For a review of the restaurant, *see p113*.

Bourbon Street

Washington Square, Sukhumvit Soi 22 (0 2259 0328-9/www.bourbonstbkk.com). Phrom Phong BTS. **Open** 7am-1am daily. **Credit** AmEx, DC, MC, V. **Map** p252 K6.
Amid several plaid-and-stetson bars located in Washington Square, this New Orleans-themed bar-restaurant stands out for its long bar and high-quality Cajun-Creole food. Along with jambalaya and pecan pie, the crawfish (fresh from the owner's farm) is a highlight.

Drinks and etiquette

When Thais go out, it's a party from the start. Groups of six or more tend to settle into one venue, their friends flitting back and forth throughout the night. Though dividing bills is creeping in, it's a face thing that the host (often the most senior person or the celebrant at birthday parties) picks up the tab, usually through buying a bottle of whisky to share. Chivas Regal and Johnny Walker Red or Black (B800-B2,000) are favoured, along with cheaper blends such as Spey Royal (B400-B600) and local rums such as fiery Mekhong (B350) or the smoother Saeng Som (B350). In villages and backstreets you may get plied with moonshine, an unregulated – but invariably strong – white liquor fermented from rice.

The deployment of whisky bottle, ice bucket, mixing sodas and lime slices has evolved into a ritual. It's very hard to monitor how much you drink, as toasts are legion and drinks are constantly topped up, often by the youngest present, out of respect touching left hand to right elbow. Whatever is left is labelled and stored behind the bar until next time, often in designated rooms.

Individual bottled beers hold less appeal as Thais like to share, so local brews such as

Singha, Chang, Kloster and licensed Heineken are often seen in huge bottles that get shared between imbibers. Hence the popularity of draught pitchers at the beer gardens that can be spotted at every mall or forecourt in the cool season. Beer is often drunk on the rocks.

Drink lists at international bars are diversifying, especially with cocktails, shots and pre-mixed bottled drinks. Lychee Martinis are also big, as are boozy iced teas and wine, although knowledge of labels and how to mix and serve them is rare.

Cocktails, too, get shared, with the staple Kamikaze coming in a jug. You may even see Saeng Som whisky and Kratingdaeng (the original Thai formula of Red Bull) mixed in a plastic ice bucket and supped through several straws on a dancefloor. Rivalling Red Bull in the energy drinks stakes are Shark, M-150 and Carabao Daeng, launched by rock singer Ad Carabao.

To absorb all this alcohol, there's a whole repertoire of *kub klaem* (drinking snacks), including cashew nuts fried and tossed with touches of chilli and kaffir lime, spicy salads, deep-fried chicken cartilage and grilled meats with chilli dips.

Eat, Drink, Shop

Bull's Head
Sukhumvit Soi 33/1 (0 2259 4444/www.great britishpub.com). Phrom Phong BTS. **Open** 11am-1am daily. **Credit** AmEx, DC, MC, V. **Map** p252 K6.
Despite a rival Robin Hood Pub setting up on the corner, this wood-and-horse-brass tavern remains the most authentic British pub in Bangkok. It draws an international (mostly UK) crowd, with hits from the past on the jukebox, pub grub, games like 'toss the boss', and the bi-monthly Punchline Comedy Club (*see p198*). And, of course, draught beer.

Café 50
24 Ekamai Soi 21 (0 2381 1773). **Open** 5pm-midnight Mon-Sat. **Credit** V. **Map** p252 M5.
This stalwart art bar pulls off the nifty trick of being a retro furniture shop (resembling the store room of a design museum) by day, then, with the flick of a dimmer switch, morphing into an edgy lounge come nightfall. Its varied music and knowingly mismatched Skandic decor appeal to the arty crowd. Oh, and there's a snooker table too.

Cheap Charlie's
1 Sukhumvit Soi 11 (0 7096 8444). Nana BTS. **Open** 5pm-1am daily. **No credit cards.** **Map** p251 J5.
This microscopic yet infinitely expandable outside bar consists of a few stools around a counter obscured by a thicket of eccentric ephemera. Post-work expats and their Thai pals down beers here on their way to elsewhere. And, yes, it's very cheap.

Chi
H1, 217 Sukhumvit Soi 55 (0 2381 7587-9). Thonglor BTS. **Open** 11am-2pm, 6pm-1am daily. **Credit** AmEx, DC, MC, V. **Map** p252 M5.
Almost every venue in the minimalist H1 enclave offers drinks amid upmarket surroundings. But, while Chi is as chi-chi as any, it also has *qi*. In this maximalist bar-cum-eaterie you can forego competitive dressing and hang as loose as the shimmering bead curtains. The taste of the owner – divine art maven Rika Dila – can be felt throughout, from the ornamental to the gustatory (Japanese-Western fusion) to the sartorial (the waiters swish by in kimono pantaloons and pleated skirts). Even the cocktails substitute staple spirits for saké.

Esco Bar
217 Sukhumvit Soi 63 (0 2711 6565). Ekkamai BTS then taxi. **Open** 6pm-1am daily. **Credit** MC, V. **Map** p252 M6.
Esco Bar is a sexy new haunt by the owners of Nung Leng next door. A bridge leads to its door of crackled glass and, within, a sophisticated crowd lounges on beige sofas to smooth house beats, or cosies up on the outdoor balcony. Reed lamps, teak and ribbed pillars of vari-coloured light soften the angles.

North

Chatuchak Weekend Market-goers later head along **Thanon Kamphaengphet** and the *soi* parallel behind, where fish and plant shops are interspersed with characterful bars like **Larb Jazz**, the ghostbusters' bar the **Shock**, filled with spooky spirit photographs, and some gay bars. Inside the market, **Viva** keeps the party going from 7am to past 9pm on weekends. For both bars and more on Chatuchak, *see p137* **A day in JJ**.

Located in one of Bangkok's three nightlife zones, **Ratchada Soi 4** is the latest clone of Royal City Avenue (RCA; *see pp188-93*), in the North-east. Beyond the flashing archway flanked by outsize blow-up dolls, a canopied path with a music-festival feel branches out into *sois* buzzing with the competitive sound systems

Fanciful fittings at **Chi.**

Eat, Drink, Shop

of theme bars. They have different names – Gig, Rad, Monkey, **China Bar** (*see below*) – but tend to be similar in character: young Thais tanked up on cheap booze nod en masse to Thai rock bands interspersed with DJ-spun hip hop.

China Bar

58 Room 1, Ratchada Soi 4 (0 2247 8832). Rama IX subway. **Open** 6pm-1am daily. **Credit** call for details.
The shared whisky bottles, football on TVs and live bands (from 9pm daily) typify the generic Ratchada style, though the theming is more sincere at China Bar than at its themed neighbours, with red lanterns, tea-house stools, latticed doors and red walls (though it does serve sushi).

Larb Jazz

807/1-2 Thanon Khamphaengphet (0 2615 7357). Kamphaengphet subway. **Open** 5pm-1am daily. **Credit** MC, V.
There's no jazz here, as the name would suggest, but *larb* is on the excellent menu of this bar, which belies its compact frontage by sweeping way back to a lofty cascade of balconies. Commercial pop gets the mostly student/first job crowd jigging on weekend nights but it can be empty midweek.

North-east

Royal City Avenue (RCA) dwindled from a long crescent of 120-plus bars to a few barns of screaming teen techno. Now an 'official' nightlife zone, it's starting to gain more edgy bars and clubs (for club reviews, *see pp188-93*).

Old Leng

29/78-81 Royal City Avenue (0 2203 0972-3). **Open** 6pm-1am daily. **Credit** AmEx, MC, V. **Map** p252 L4.
This survivor of the original RCA explosion for once merits the term 'unique' – it looks like a cowboy saloon stranded in ancient China. 'Songs for Life' (Thai blues) fans flock here for live bands; smoochers gather on the quieter front deck. Hard-drinking adults make it the most grown-up bar on the strip.

South

Thanon Narathiwat Ratchanakharin has spawned a string of bars that spreads out from residential Soi 15, where converted house-bars remain a charming, low-volume retreat. Further south, **Tawandaeng German Brewhouse** is the city's best microbrewery, and home of the avant-garde show band Fong Nam (*see p181* **Bubbling over**). Or you can try to blag your way in with the movers and shakers at the **Met Bar** at the Metropolitan hotel (*see p48*).

Hu'u

The Ascott, 187 Thanon Sathorn Tai (0 2676 6868/www.the-ascott.com). Chong Nonsi BTS. **Open** 6pm-1am daily. **Credit** AmEx, DC, MC, V. **Map** p250 F7.

Pronounced 'who', this dark, laid-back lounge bar fronting the chi-chi Ascott apartments (*see p51*) is the perfect place for suits to unwind. It's also a suave, intimate venue to deal, date, dance or dine (on holistic, organic Pacific Rim fusions). We advise you to order an obscure tipple that gets the barmen scaling ladders up Hu'u's signature feature: a two-storey-high glass matrix shelving prime wines and a breadth of speciality liquor to rival Q Bar (*see pp188-93*). The 150-plus cocktails include fruity alco-smoothies you can spoon. A glazed Hu'u Epicure eaterie on the mezzanine overlooks the bar, which in turn overlooks the busy CBD. Started in Singapore, Hu'u has another branch in Bali. DJs from 8pm on Friday and Saturday.

Monkey Shock 3rd

116 Thanon Narathiwat Ratchanakharin, South (0 2287 0957/www.monkeyislandkohmak.com). **Open** 6pm-1am daily. **Credit** AmEx, MC, V. **Map** p250 F8.
Fairy lit and rustic, this characterful spot is just about the only teak house on this long road, where bars come and go. Monkey Shock has shed its first two venues, but gained a quieter fourth in a parallel lane linking Sois 15 and 17, which has weathered boards over ponds around a lofty air-conditioned house, and a fifth in the suburbs. Plus, it has reopened a resort, this time on Ko Mak. Besides the good-value drinks and its inherent charm, the Thai menu is consistently good.
Other locations: 4th Thanon Narathiwat Ratchanakharin, between Sois 15 & 17, South (0 2286 5605); 5th, Thanon Prasertmanukit, Wangthonglang (0 2933 9165).

Moon Bar at Vertigo

61st floor, Banyan Tree Hotel, Thanon Sathorn Tai (0 2679 1200/www.banyantreebangkok.com). Lumphini subway. **Open** 6pm-1am daily. **Credit** AmEx, DC, MC, V. **Map** p251 G7.
One of the tallest open-air restaurants in the world, Vertigo boasts one of the city's best views and, as a result, booking is essential. Its Moon Bar appears to hover at one raised end of the curved roof, which has something of the feel of a Baron Munchausen flying galleon (albeit with sleeker timbers). As you sip one of the many delightful cocktails, lounge and jazz tunes waft in the considerable breeze (beware of flapping ties, hair getting stuck in lipgloss or papers fluttering skyward). If it rains, the hotel has three restaurants in which to shelter.

Zuk

Sukhothai Hotel, 13/3 Thanon Sathorn Tai (0 2287 0222/www.sukhothai.com). Lumphini subway. **Open** 4pm-1am daily. **Credit** AmEx, DC, MC, V. **Map** p251 G7.
Dark, moody and striking, this earth- and slate-toned bar lives up to its setting in Bangkok's most sophisticated hotel. The crowd is elegant and but top-line DJs ensure it's not subdued by creating an agreeably subversive vibe each night, with internationally renowned DJs spinning at special events. The Martinis are among the best in town.

Markets

Stalls and roving trolleys are the lifeblood of Bangkok, a city of the bazaar and the bizarre.

As countries modernise they tend to lose their itinerant vendors and street markets. Yet, while Thais have embraced malls with consumerist fervour and chainstores displace stallholders with alarming ease, *talad* (markets) remain the soul of Siam. They are the tap root of street-level social life and the local economy, and the best way to glimpse life as it has always been. While Bangkok's governor wants vendors gone within ten years, other officials value their charm, cultural value and tourist appeal.

Whether you're eating, shopping or sightseeing, markets are the purest expression of the sensual Thai culture, with their kaleidoscope of scents (jasmine garlands, musty puddles, durian), sounds (yelping hawkers, booming techno), sights (sleeping children, slithering eels), touch (antique silk, fake fur) and tastes (food you'll find nowhere else on earth). Specialist *talad* cater to all tastes, with **Chatuchak Weekend Market** (*see p136* **A day in JJ**) being the one essential smörgåsbord to experience. Temporary markets accompany almost every festival, often selling local foods and crafts. All the while, roving hawkers go in search of you (*see p134* **Cart blanche**).

Bargaining is normal for goods (but never for cooked food), though only tourist traps should be pared down more than ten to 20 per cent. Pre-armed with shop prices, you must remain polite and honour your bid if they accept it. Asking in Thai can lower the starting price, and walking away from an impasse may reveal the 'best price'. For street food, hotspots are noted under area headings in the Restaurants chapter, *see pp106-125*; for more on vendor food, *see p116* **One-plate pilgrims**

Clothes

Na Ram Market (between Sois 43-53, 4pm-midnight daily), in the eastern suburbs, also sells clothes.

Bo Bae
Soi Rong Muang, Thanon Krung Kasem, near Yotse Bridge, Chinatown. **Open** 9am-6pm daily. **Map** p249 & p250 E4.
This funky canalside *talad* specialises in wholesale clothes, from assembly-line rough to catwalk-worthy. Bo Bae Tower has separate floors for men,

women, children and babies. The outdoor area is also sells army surplus, camping gear and the like. **Other locations**: 1st-6th Bo Bae Tower, 488 Thanon Damrongrak, Chinatown (0 2628 1888,1999).

Saphan Phut
Thanon Triphet, Chinatown. **Open** 8pm-midnight daily. **Map** p248 C4.
Concerned that it was becoming a conduit of youth culture, officials have tried to contain this plastic-covered night market, which was evicted from a prettified Khlong Lord a decade ago. Strung like costume jewellery around Memorial Bridge, it brims with absurdly cheap vintage clothing, T-shirts, handbags, hats and fake perfume. Spot the Thai designers on the prowl. Street food is sold on the periphery.

Crafts & accessories

Amulet Alley
Trok Wat Mahathat, Thanon Maharat, Phra Nakhon. **Open** 9am-6pm daily. **Map** p248 B3.
Spilling out of a riverside lane, this speciality market is the epitome of old Bangkok, with its constant flow of human traffic browsing an array of Buddhist imagery, amulets and medals. Bargaining is a must, and there are old-school food stalls aplenty. Find more amulets at Wat Ratchanadda (*see p69*), and between Saphan Khwai Station and Chatuchak Weekend Market (*see p136* **A day in JJ**), where occult ephemera makes for a sometimes startling browse.

Amulet Alley

Eat, Drink, Shop

Cart blanche

Rot khen (vendor carts) are an integral part of Thai life. Thai hawkers tend to find themselves the most comfortable location and settle there for good. No amount of campaigns to limit their trading or restrain their encroachment of roads and pavements ever lasts long. Nor, more disquietingly, do efforts to remedy piracy, food hygiene or extortion of vendors by officials.

Hawkers relentlessly colonise any spare space. Some rove using pedal or paddle, motor or manpower. Others congregate, especially at already congested places, like *soi* mouths, shopping strips or tourist haunts. Where no stall can squeeze, groundsheet fly-pitches maximise intrusion so browsers literally stumble over 20-baht plastic fantastics they never knew they needed. *Rot khen* get piled high with brooms, ladders or even furniture; other trolleys burgeon with stickers, posters or cute ceramics. In student areas, home-made cards, notebooks, clothes or gift items catch the eye.

Food makes up about half of what is peddled. Different dishes are sold at different times of the day (doughnuts at breakfast, noodles at lunch, rolled dried squid after dark), with tell-tale bells, whistles or cries announcing what's coming round the corner. A tinkling bell heralds coconut ice-cream scooped from a drum into a bun, then slathered with peanuts. Clacks of chopstick on wood precede wheeled cauldrons of noodle soup. Hoots on a rubber-bulbed horn mean 'fruit'. Some delicacies prove more photogenic than they are palatable. Steamed bird foetuses sold from a yoke, anyone? How about insects fried and salted as a pulpy, crunchy or surprisingly zingy snack?

The preparation of fruit from iced carts resembles streetside performance art. Within seconds, the vendor can peel a pineapple into a perfect spiral, deseed a watermelon or whittle an unripe mango. As you stroll away with your 10-baht bagful, dip each cleaved segment into a sachet of *prik kap kleua* (a pink condiment of sugar, salt and chilli).

Pahurat

Thanon Chakkaphet & Thanon Pahurat, Chinatown. **Open** 9am-6pm daily. **Map** p248 C5.

The heart of Little India, Pahurat is awash with fabrics and textiles, from rainbows of saris to Thai and Chinese silks, synthetics and cottons. Winding alleys are filled with incense sellers, tea houses stocking fine *chai* tea and lassis, food markets, collectives of sewing women and a Sikh temple. Bollywood movies and sitars blare, and the onslaught of scents and colours is tuly memorable.

Sampeng

Soi Wanit 1, Chinatown. **Open** 9am-6pm daily. **Map** p248 C5.

An epic, bustling alleyway crammed with bric-a-brac and costume accoutrements, Sampeng is best tackled in sections. Out east it's hairclips, earrings, sandals and key rings. Midway you'll find ceramics, monks' bowls, Chinese lanterns, kids' shoes and wrapping paper. Across from Thanon Ratchawong are fabrics, jeans and fatigues, including denim and camouflage. Toward the Mahachai end are blankets, sarongs, buttons and laces. The honking motorbikes, smoky quarters and shouting hawkers come free.

Electronics

Baan Mor (Lang Krasuang)

Thanon Baan Mor & Thanon Atsadang, Phra Nakorn. **Open** 9am-6pm daily. **Map** p248 B4.

This spare-parts paradise clings to the peripheries of Khlong Lord and harbours just about anything for TV and audio – plus vintage LPs and army surplus (it is behind the Defence Ministry, after all).

Khlong Thom

Thanon Mahachak, between Thanon Yaowarat & Thanon Charoen Krung, Chinatown. **Open** 9am-6pm daily. **Map** p248 C4.

This sprawling area sees foreigners mingling chest-to-shoulder with Thais amid assorted engines, wheels, tractor parts and other heavy machinery. You'll also find CD/DVD player repair services and homewares, from hoses to carpentry tools.

Saphan Lek

Thanon Boriphat, around Grande Ville Hotel, Chinatown. **Open** 9am-6pm daily. **Map** p248 C4.

Named after an old iron bridge over Khlong Ong Ang, this meandering alley market dips four steps below street level. Sidewalk shelves heave with cameras, toy guns, sunglasses and shoes, while shops stock pricier appliances such as cellphones, digicams and an alphabet soup of entertainment (DVD, VCD, VDO).

Woeng Nakhon Kasem

Thanon Chakrawat, at Thanon Charoen Krung, Chinatown. **Open** 9am-6pm Mon-Sat. **Map** p248 C4.

Once dubbed 'Thieves Market', this charming, hectic area hosts all things audio – instruments, turntables, high-end stereos, you name it – as well

Floating vendor.

Function comes before aesthetics with vendors' carts, which often feature specialist equipment. Popsicles emerge from iced drums; roti pancakes get ladled with sweet fillings upon oiled griddles; eggy *khanom krok* pop from dimpled irons; liquidisers receive ladles of syrup from glass jars and condensed milk from tins to make *bun* (fruit shakes). Most amusingly, strong dark *kafae* (coffee) and brick-red *cha* (tea) get strained through blackened socks to be served hot or poured over ice-in-a-bag and drizzled with cloying evaporated milk.

When the government offered kitsch, flimsy carts to beautify the 2003 APEC (Asia-Pacific Economic Cooperation) summit, vendors preferred their trusty, time-tried *rot khen*. Cart design has been honed into a paragon of practicality, with handy slots for knives, boards, cloths, elastic bands, bags and more plastic bags to put the bags in. This ingenuity has its roots in merchant trading, when selling took place in the confines of boats, as they still do at remnant floating markets (*see pp101-104* **Further Afield**).

as culinary contraptions such as ice-cream makers, mincers, coffee grinders and coconut shredders. Home cooks, DJs, producers and the simply curious mingle at Woeng Nakhon Kasem.

Flowers & plants

Pak Khlong Talad
Thanon Chakphet, from Memorial Bridge to Khlong Lord, Phra Nakorn. **Open** 24hrs daily. **Map** p248 B5.
To really grasp the Thai love of flowers, visit this remnant of Bangkok's original fresh market – and go soon, because it slated to be redeveloped 'for tourism', which means there's a chance it could get purged of its abundant charm and authenticity. It is most spectacular from 10pm until dawn, when night owls descend after bars close. The scent of jasmine fills the air, orchids in forms unseen by most non-Asians are stacked taller than people and vendors string devotional offerings with Fabergé delicacy. Not to be missed.

Thewet
Thanon Krung Kasem, west of Thanon Samsen, Dusit. **Open** 9am-6pm daily. **Map** p248 C1.
More neighbourly and less exhaustive than Pak Khlong Talad or Chatuchak Weekend Market, Thewet is undeniably pleasant with its potted plants and canal views. It is liveliest by day and picturesque at sunset.

Fresh food

Khlong Toei
Thanon Rama IV, at Thanon Na Ranong, South. Queen Sirikit Centre subway. **Open** 6am-dusk daily. **Map** p252 K8.
This portside *talad* offers archetypal regional Thai food, with stallholders shifting vegetables, chickens and rare herbs (it's more wholesale after dusk). The big Lao Market stocks specialities from the north-east, while off-the-back-of-a-boat items at nearby Penang Market are less prevalent than before.

Or Tor Kor (OTK)
Thanon Kamphaengphet, opposite Chatuchak Weekend Market, North (0 279 2080-2). Saphan Kwai BTS/Kamphaengphet subway. **Open** 6am-6pm daily.
Across the road from Chatuchak (*see p136* **A day in JJ**), the Agricultural Market Organisation (OTK) markets some of Thailand's best fruit and veg, and prepared foods and sweets. A separate building houses products such as lychee jam and Thai arabica coffee from the Royal Projects.

Sam Yan
Thanon Phayathai, at Thanon Rama IV, Pathumwan. Sam Yan subway. **Open** *Food market* noon-midnight daily. *Market* 6am-6pm daily. **Map** p250 F6.
This night-and-day happening encompasses a multi storey building (the food is on the first floor), a wet

Eat, Drink, Shop

market and a rambling spread of street vendors. The products reflect the area's Chinese character, hence the top-grade seafood, unusual stir-fries and other more subtle (sweet and savoury) specialities, which are well worth investigating.

General markets

For **Chatuchak Weekend Market**, *see below* **A day in JJ**. For **Patpong**, *see p91*.

Banglamphu
Thanon Chakkraphong, Banglamphu. **Open** 9am-6pm daily. **Map** p248 B3.

This traditional *talad* sprawls in and out of the traffic-heavy *thanon* and quiet *sois* just north of Khao San. There are fabrics, satay, wooden crafts, fruits, clothes, uniforms – the range is enormous.

Pratunam
North & south of Phetchaburi Road, west of Thanon Ratchaprarop, North. Tha Pratunam. **Open** 9am-midnight daily.
The stalls at Pratunam ('Water Gate') burrow around Indra and Bayoke hotels. This is come-one, come-all shopping, at all times, for textiles, lingerie, ceramics, bags, T-shirts and street fashion. The seamstresses will stitch anything, judging by their Mardi Gras

A day in JJ

A quarter of a million people a week shop until they drop at **Chatuchak Weekend Market**, a sauna-like labyrinth of 8,000-plus stalls. Long famed for the sheer scope of its products from Thailand and beyond (Myanmar and Vietnam to Afghanistan and Tibet), it has now transcended its Asian knick-knack status to become a hive of young talent from Thailand, New York, London and Tokyo. In this all-in souvenir stop, you may well need its shipping agents (Sections 6 and 7, TNT 0 9202 2244, DHL 0 9924 9624, Bangkok Parcel Service 0 1457 7000).

To truly 'do' JJ (from another spelling, Jatujak) would take several weekends, but despite its apparently random nature, there's some method to the madness, so concentrating your energies is relatively easy. Numbered sections, themed and divided by *soi* (now with stall numbers too), are well sign-posted and colour-coded on maps, of which *Nancy Chandler's Map* is the best. Useful meeting points are the clock tower, the in-market subway station or tourist office/bank building (open weekends, with ATMs). Benches and trees provide in-market pitstops, the roads have been pedestrianised, and cafés and toilets dot the edges. Locals visit early to pre-empt the sweaty post-lunch throngs. A seven-storey 'JJ Mall' will be built on land next to the market by September 2006, offering similar products, but air-conditioned and open daily from 9am until 10pm. The following sections tackle the basics.

ANTIQUES, CRAFTS & FURNITURE
Thai crafts are strewn everywhere, especially in Sections 1, 24 and 26, where you also find pricey antiques. Seek out hill tribe rattanware and loom parts to hang textiles from, plus

musical instruments, bamboo boxes and *takraw* balls. In Section 1, you'll also find puppets, lacquerware, carvings, bronzes, amulets and Buddhas sourced from Chiang Mai and Myanmar. **Silpa Thai** arrays *khon* masks and puppets (Section 24, Soi 2, 0 9926 6530) from its Thonburi workshop (*see p72*). Bargain hunters might peruse the Thai silk brought by Isaan women. You may also see artisans making pottery or touching up paintings.

Wooden furniture can be bought ready to ship or crafted to spec, most cheaply from the sheds the other side of Thanon Kamphangphet 2, which are stacked with reconditioned teak furniture and panelling, and even whole Thai houses for reassembly. **JJ OTOP Centre** (Section 27, Thanon Kamphaengphet, 0 2618 2620) sells village crafts (*see p144* **High Thai designs**).

CLOTHES & ACCESSORIES
Young designers sell their threads (especially shirts and fabrics) in Sections 5-6 amid the second-hand flea market, ethnic and bohemian clobber, hats, handbags and uniforms (from Russian army to Korean boy scout). Bargain hard, as T-shirts or jeans can come as cheap as B50. New clothes fill Sections 10, 12, 14, 16, 18, and 20-26. Everything goes, including beaded handbags, batik sarongs, fishermen's trousers, leather belts, denim and Ts in wild Japanese colours or bearing 'Thainglish' phrases. **Siam Ruay** pioneered new Thai typography, which it illustrates on witty, collectable T-shirts (Section 24, Soi 33/18, 0 9815 1359, Section 4, Soi 3, 0 5907 4954). **Props Room** crowds three branches in Section 3 and there's theatrical jewellery and accessories (Soi 2, 0 1567 9025). An oasis of philosophical calm, **Common Tribe** (Section 24,

Eat, Drink, Shop

costume mannequins. Its popularity with African and Middle Eastern traders is reflected in the food available. The stalls east of Thanon Ratchaprarop have been obliterated by gaudy Pratunam Centre, a less interesting clothing mall.

Suan Lum Night Bazaar

Thanon Witthayu, at Thanon Rama IV, Pathumwan (0 2252 4776/www.thainightbazaar.com). Lumphini subway. **Open** 4pm-midnight daily. **Map** p251 H7.
Proclaimed as Bangkok's 'first official night bazaar', this neon-bright covered maze of several thousand stalls hawks mainly souvenirs and decor items. Facing Lumphini Park, it boasts a Khmer-

style fibreglass tourist police station, BEC-Tero Hall concert venue and a vast sheltered beer garden with live bands. For some time people sensed a ruse to get this vast downtown plot, a one-time cadet school, rezoned for commerce. And, sure enough, it has been declared that in 2006 it will be replaced with a 55-billion-baht complex with a mall, hotel, condo, offices and an exhibition centre. Lumphini Boxing Stadium (*see pp199-203*) has also been moved out and the Joe Louis Puppet Theater will migrate to Phuket (*see p218*). It is unclear how much of the Suan Lum Night Bazaar will remain, if anything, and we were unable to get a more precise closing date as we went to press.

Soi 2) maintains its lauded Eurasian pantaloons, jackets and casualwear in black and natural white, plus much-imitated handmade leather sandals.

DECOR & PLANTS

The boutiques in tree-shaded Sections 2-4 showcase Thai designers, who rise so quickly that their creations can often be found in Europe within months. Amid things made from zinc, *saa* (mulberry) paper, wood and lucite, look for cute creations at **Gumption** (Section 3, Soi 2, 0 1806 9568) and 1970s-inspired curtains and clocks at **70s Up** (Section 4, soi 1, 0 1438 2446). A stunning black stall lit by cloth lanterns stocks both **Cha**'s aromatic teas and **Karmakamet**'s aromatic oils and candles (Section 3, Soi 3, 0 1564 0505). **Hot April** (Section 2, Soi 3, 0 9888 4276) assembles wood, weathered just-so. This area bristles with cafés, plants, herbs, seeds and flowers, plus the pots and charms that go with them, with bushes and trees taking over the market mid week (7am-6pm Wed, Thur). More design goodies draw glances in Sections 7-8 and 24-27, including sleek contemporary room sets at **Aviv** (Section 8, Sois 16-7, 0 1906 3645) and leather innovations at **Nattha** (Section 8, Soi 17, 0 1682 5990). Art galleries line Sections 1 and 7, along with artistic decor, notably **Ego Clay**'s ceramics (Section 7, 0 2888 7546), and the filigree copper foil creations of **Subanjerd** (Section 7, 0 1439 1331).

EATING & DRINKING

As well as being a rootsy market and a major import and export centre, JJ also has a social scene. Cafés and food stalls crop up throughout, touting authentic samples of regional cuisines and snacks, with many

more at **Or Tor Kor** market (*see p135*) opposite. Isaan food fans scoff from pottery at Foon Talob (Section 26, Soi 1, 0 1838 1146). What's more, a new design awareness is sprucing up lean-to spaces, coffee houses and bars such as **Viva** (Section 26, Sois 1 & 2, 0 2272 4783, 7am-6pm Fri, 7am-9pm or later Sat, Sun). The latter starts slinging juices in the morning and continues – with roadhouse fervour, good-time tunes, beer and whisky – often until well past its 9pm closing time. Cute bars amid the fish shops line Thanon Kamphaengphet and the lane behind it, including the **Shock** (0 2619 2682, 6.30pm-1.30am daily), where followers of a ghostbusting radio show swap scare stories and post supernatural photos, and gay clubs like **Mogue** (*see p173*).

PETS, BOOKS & UTENSILS

Cages of kittens and puppies sit alongside containers of reptiles, rare birds and tanks of fish in Sections 8, 9, 11, 13, 15 and 17. In such markets there is sometimes the risk of a trade in endangered species – though a recent fad for hissing cockroaches from Madagascar has been banned. More appealing are the ceramics and kitchenware that are sold along with culinary ingredients in Sections 17 and 19; stalls selling new and well-thumbed books and magazines are here from Wednesday to Sunday, with additional discounted titles on weekends at Sections 1 and 27.

Chatuchak Weekend Market

Thanon Phahon Yothin, at Thanon Kamphaengphet, North (0 2272 4440-1). Morchit or Saphan Khwai BTS/Kamphaengphet subway. **Open** 7am-6pm Sat, Sun. *Plants only daytime Wed, Thur.*

Shops & Services

'From pestles to warships.' That's Thai retail speak to mean there's something for everyone.

Basheer Design Books. *See p140.*

Bangkok is a shopaholic's heaven. The variety of the merchandise on offer is only matched by the number of outlets in which to spend. And as the retail space available continues to expand, goods from near and far converge: modern local products, exotic crafts and global brands – all at competitive prices. Bangkok's notoriety for knock-offs is slowly waning, with crackdowns and changing trends consigning counterfeit goods to the street markets (though pirated CDs and DVDs proliferate). Attention is now more focused on the fad for East-West fusion, which has served to highlight the best in contemporary Thai designs and craftsmanship, and raised the bar on oriental style.

MALL THE MERRIER

Air-conditioned shopping centres are the norm in this hot, humid city. The major malls line a three-kilometre (two-mile) retail corridor along Thanons Rama I, Ploenchit and Sukhumvit, many linked to the BTS by elevated walkways. The place to start is around Pathumwan intersection in an area dubbed 'Siam', with the maze of faddish shoplets in **Mah Boon Krong (MBK)** centre and Siam Square. Here you'll find *dek naew* (young hipsters) browsing hundreds of micro-boutiques. The thriving vendors in these parts (many of whose sub-leases are only distantly related to the owners, Chulalongkorn University) are, however, facing a rent hike of up to 600 per cent. It is feared that this may kill the golden goose, as start-up designers can't afford rents at the level of the **Siam Centre** mall opposite. So shop while you can, or visit the luxurious **Siam Discovery** complex next to the Centre. The next big thing for label hunters is slated to be the **Siam Paragon**, a six-billion-baht behemoth by the Mall Group, due to open by 2006.

The hub of the central shopping strip is the Ratchaprasong intersection. Anchoring one corner, the colossal **Central World Plaza** (formerly World Trade Centre, renamed after a takeover by the Thai Central chain, South-east Asia's biggest retailer) encloses both the **Zen** and **Isetan** department stores. Opposite are the city's swankiest mall **Gaysorn**, crafts hangar **Narayanaphand** and discount warehouse **Big C**, with new low-end malls at the **Pratunam Centre**, across the canal near **Pratunam Market** (*see p136*).

On the south side of Ploenchit, the old Sogo has been turned into **Erawan**, a suave temple to import labels, while Amarin Plaza next door will become a design centre. South down Thanon Ratchadamri, **Peninsula Plaza** attracts high-society patrons of haute couture.

East along Ploenchit and Sukhumvit are the superior department store **Central Chidlom**, specialist shops and lesser malls like Ploenchit Centre, Landmark Plaza, Nana Square, Times Square and Robinson, a mid-range department store chain. Further down, the upmarket **Emporium** complex presides over a multi-cultural neighbourhood teeming with bookshops, pubs and restaurants.

Bangrak complements its nightlife with late-night shopping. Though **Silom Complex** and golf-oriented **Thaniya Plaza** close by 9pm, street shops and stalls continue till at least midnight, including the notorious fake vendors of **Patpong Night Market** (*see p91*).

Antiques merchants operate shops around Thanon Charoen Krung, between the Oriental Hotel (*see p42*) and River City. The area rivals Silom and Nana (lower Sukhumvit) for stalls and shophouses dealing in tasteful, if mass-produced souvenirs.

MODUS SHOPERANDI
With stores open from 10am to 8pm or 10pm (plus periodic 'midnight sales'), it's easy to shop. Fierce competition means frequent sales, often around the end of the month and its pay day, with big markdowns during each **Thailand Grand Sale** (June-July and December-January). Several stores also give instant five per cent discounts for tourists (show your passport) or for certain credit cards. However, some services, like travel agents and technical outlets, add a few per cent for credit card payments. *Baht* is the only currency needed, though some antiques and hotels are priced in US dollars.

Many retailers rely on tourists, and assistants often follow you around. Don't be offended; they're keen to serve and are on commission. They'll take your selection with cash (or card) and return from the till with bagged goods, change and a receipt. Otherwise, say *khor doo dai maii?* ('can I just look?'). If you return goods, don't expect a full cash or credit refund, but some shops may offer instore credit or a limited exchange.

Antiques & reproductions

Old Maps & Prints
4th floor, River City Complex, Thanon Yotha, Bangrak (0 2237 0077-8/www.classicmaps.com). Tha Siphraya. **Open** 11am-7pm daily. **Credit** AmEx, MC, V. **Map** p250 D6.
The best source for historical charts and hand-coloured engravings, mainly of Asia.

Oriental Place (OP)
301/1 Charoen Krung Soi 38, Bangrak (0 2266 0186-90). Saphan Taksin BTS/Tha Oriental. **Open** 10am-7.30pm daily. **Map** p250 D7.
This ritzy mall beside the Oriental Hotel is a delight for the connoisseur. The galleries include Garuda (religious artefacts and rare objects) and Objects (*lingams* and antique artists' tools).

Rare Stone Museum
1048-1054 Charoen Krung Soi 26, Bangrak (0 2236 5666/5655/www.rarestone.com). Tha Siphraya. **Open** 10am-5.30pm daily. **Credit** AmEx, MC, V. **Map** p250 D7.

Truly fantastic rock formations, from fossils to tektite from outer space (from B50). Owner/collector Banyong quotes a ballpark million-baht figure to part with a Buddha-shaped pebble.

River City
River City Complex, 23 Thanon Yotha, Bangrak (0 2237 0077-8/www.rivercity.co.th). Tha Siphraya. **Open** 10am-10pm daily. **Map** p250 D6.
A specialist mall with a fabulous range of period pieces, reproductions and antiquities (some reputedly of murky provenance) that would upgrade many a museum. Gavels clatter at auctions on the first Saturday of each month.

Silom Galleria
919/1 Thanon Silom, Bangrak (0 2630 0944-50/ www.thesilomgalleria.com). Surasak BTS. **Open** 10am-8pm daily. **Map** p250 E7.
Chinese antiques are the main commodities at this vast building. Lower floors house dealers in furniture and pottery, with art outlets higher up, including Tang Gallery (*see p170*) and Panorama Museum. Weekdays are best for browsing.

Triphum
3rd floor, Gaysorn, Thanon Ploenchit, Pathumwan (0 2656 1795-6). Chidlom BTS. **Open** 10am-8pm daily. **Credit** AmEx, DC, MC, V. **Map** p251 H5.

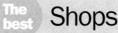

Shops
The best

For funky Thai fashion
Issue (*see p143*), **Kloset Red Carpet** (*see p146*) and **Sretsis** (*see p147*).

For gem-like jewellers
Dinakara and **Lotus Arts de Vivre** (for both, *see p149*) .

For *sanuk* gifts
Reflections Rooms in Bangkok (*see p48*) and **Geo** (*see p151*).

For Siamese style
Doi Tung by Mae Fah Luang and **Senada Theory** (for both, *see p146*).

For tastes of home
Villa Market (*see p149*).

For reproductions
Triphum (*see above*).

For Asian design
Budji, **Cocoon** and **Panta** (for all, *see p151*).

For anything and everything
Siam Paragon (*see p152*) and **Chatuchak Weekend Market** (*see p136*).

Eat, Drink, Shop

Reproduction mural paintings on tapestries and planks (plus frames and Siamese knick-knacks) – and all reasonably priced, considering they're as meticulously crafted as a temple restoration.

Books & magazines

Thanon Khao San stalls stock quality second-hand literature (*see p69*), while **Chatuchak Weekend Market** (*see p136* **A day in JJ**) is unbeatable for back issues, out-of-print finds and discounted illustrated books (Sections 1 and 27). For superior stationery, browse the eminently monogrammed, leather-bound world that is **Libreria** (0 2661 6480), a study-like shop in the Siam Society (*see p95*). The **Kinokuniya** and **Asia Books** branches in the new Siam **Paragon** (*see p152*) look set to fight it out for the title of Thailand's biggest bookshop, although the new bookshop in the Zen department store at Central World Plaza (*see p151*) might want to claim its chance for a crack at the crown. But from the bibliophile's point of view, this tri-partite race to be the biggest and best bookshop should serve to transform the quality and quantity of books available in Bangkok.

Asia Books
221 Thanon Sukhumvit, between Soi 15 & 17, Sukhumvit (0 2252 7277/www.asiabooks.com). Asoke BTS/Sukhumvit subway. **Open** 9am-9pm daily. **Credit** AmEx, DC, MC, V. **Map** p251 J5.
A large selection of English-language books published in Asia, plus UK and US bestsellers, guidebooks, lifestyle manuals and lavish tomes on Asian design, cooking and heritage.
Other locations: in malls throughout the city.

Basheer Design Books
998 Sukhumvit Soi 55 (Thonglor), Thanon Sukhumvit, Watthana (0 2391 9815-6/ www.basheergraphic.com). Thonglor BTS. **Open** 11am-10pm daily. **Credit** MC, V. **Map** p252 M6.
The focus on graphic arts, design and photography titles unavailable elsewhere in town suits the swish H1 location. Book lovers (and book sellers) take note: browsing is positively encouraged.

Bookazine
1st floor, CP Tower, Thanon Silom, Bangrak (0 2231 0019/www.bookazine.co.th). Saladaeng BTS/Silom subway. **Open** 10am-11pm daily. **Credit** AmEx, MC, V. **Map** p250 F7.
Thailand's most extensive (and freshest) selection of papers and periodicals in English, plus some popular novels, coffee-table books and a gay section.
Other locations: 2nd floor, All Seasons Retail Centre, Thanon Witthayu, Pathumwan (0 2685 3863-4); Nailert Building, Thanon Sukhumvit, at Soi 5, Sukhumvit (0 2655 2383-4); 2nd floor, Silom Complex, Thanon Silom, Bangrak (0 2231 3153); 286 Thanon Rama I, Pathumwan (0 2255 3778).

Dasa
710/4 Thanon Sukhumvit (between Soi 24 & 26), Khlong Toei (0 2661 2993/www.dasabookcafe.com). Phrom Phong BTS. **Open** 10am-9pm daily. **No credit cards**. **Map** p252 L6.
The city's newest second-hand bookshop stocks over 10,000 titles over two floors. The shelves are well organised – a real plus in this sort of bookshop where the filing plan is too often based on the whim of the proprietor – and a coffee corner urges literary types to sit down and hold forth.

Kinokuniya
3rd floor, Emporium, Sukhumvit Soi 24, Sukhumvit (0 2664 8554/www.kinokuniya.com). Phrom Phong BTS. **Open** 10am-9pm daily. **Credit** AmEx, DC, MC, V. **Map** p252 K6.
This Japanese chain has the biggest, best and best-organised stock of books in English, plus great ranges of magazines, maps, art, poetry and children's literature. Staff are courteous and informed.
Other locations: 6th floor, Isetan, Central World Plaza, Pathumwan (0 2255 9834); Siam Paragon, Pathumwan (*see p152*).

Rim Khob Fah
78/1 Thanon Ratchadamnoen Klang, at Democracy Monument, Phra Nakorn (0 2622 3510). Tha Saphan Phan Fah. **Open** 8.30am-7pm Mon-Fri; 9am-5pm Sat, Sun. **Credit** MC, V. **Map** p248 C3.
Frequent workshops on Thai culture and history attract scholars, writers and students to this specialist in publications about Thailand, though titles in English are limited.

Crafts

For the best range of crafts, ancient and modern, scour **Chatuchak Weekend Market** (*see p136*), including **JJ OTOP Centre**. For **Rasi Sayam** and **Tamnan Mingmuang**, *see p145* **High Thai designs**.

Narayanaphand
127 Thanon Ratchadamri, Pathumwan (0 2252 4670-9/www.narayanaphand.com). Chidlom BTS. **Open** 10am-8pm daily. **Credit** AmEx, DC, MC, V. **Map** p251 G5.
This dowdy hangar of Thai handicrafts stocks the largest inventory in Thailand of handmade merchandise – from lacquerware and ceramics to woodcarving and fabrics. There's also a gem section.

NV Aranyik
3rd floor, Gaysorn, Thanon Ploenchit, Pathumwan (0 2656 1081/www.aranyik.thaiexponet.com). Chidlom BTS. **Open** 10am-8pm daily. **Credit** AmEx, DC, MC, V. **Map** p251 H5.
NV Aranyik's much-imitated spoons, forks and knives – with twisted, textured or dimpled metal handles – have made it on to the tables of many top restaurants around the world during the shop's quarter century in existence. Simple, elegant cutlery that's well worth forking out for.

Eat, Drink, Shop

Department stores

For malls, see p151, including **Emporium** and **Siam Paragon**.

Central Chidlom
1027 Thanon Ploenchit, Pathumwan (0 2655 7777/ www.central.co.th). Chidlom BTS. **Open** 10am-9.30pm daily. **Credit** AmEx, DC, MC, V. **Map** p251 H5.
Central's seven-storey flagship store has the best product selection and layout in town, and legions of loyal customers. There are extensive ranges of cosmetics, international and domestic fashion labels, leatherware, children's and sporting goods, plus contemporary oriental interior design. B2S meets most book, magazine and stationery needs. Micro-shops include Jim Thompson Thai Silk, Starbucks and Tops supermarket. Central's spin-off for young professionals, Zen (0 2255 9669, www.zen.co.th), carries clothing, fads and modish decor, plus beauty tips dispensed by lab-coated consultants.
Other locations: throughout the city.

Isetan
4/1-2 Thanon Ratchadamri, Pathumwan (0 2255 9898-9). Chidlom BTS. **Open** 10am-9pm daily. **Credit** AmEx, DC, MC, V. **Map** p251 G5.
This upmarket, Japanese store is the focus for corporate *samurai* and home-makers. Expect imported, conservative attire for men, but some colour and style in womenswear, as well as superior kitchen gear. There's a first-rate Oriental Shop pâtisserie, though it's wastefully packaged (buy ten buns, get 11 bags). Greyhound and Jim Thompson Thai Silk also have outlets here.

Playground!
818 Soi Thonglor, Sukhumvit (0 2714 7888/ www.playgroundstore.co.th). Thonglor BTS. **Open** 10.30am-midnight daily. **Credit** AmEx, DC, MC, V. **Map** p252 M6.
Part of Thonglor's boutique mall boom – along with H1 and J Avenue – this swish black edifice has sections on art books, stationery, homewares, music, magazines, fashion and accessories. The products are mainly fun, funky, mid-range products from home and abroad. Many things are arranged by taste rather than genres, while events in the central atrium, and exhibitions in art or design, add creative dynamics.

Dry cleaning & repairs

Most malls host dry cleaning, mending and shoe repair services, typically near the car park access. Or risk the cobblers and sewing-machine stalls on the street for a fraction of the fee.

Electronics

PowerBuy sections in **Central** department stores (*see above*) offer personal sound systems, film and digital cameras, PDAs and all the other hi-tech gadgets you might want.

Triphum. *See p139.*

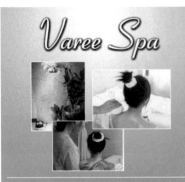

Varee Spa

Varee Spa offers a full range of Body Scrubs, Body Wraps, Body Massages, Foot Massages, Facial Treatments, Waxing and Nail Care Services.

3/6 Soi Saladang, Silom Rd., Bangrak, Bangkok 10500
Tel: +662-266-8399, +662-266-8808
Fax: +662-266-9559
e-mail: info@vareespa.com
www.vareespa.com
Open 7 days a week 11.00am-11.00pm
3 mins walk from Saladang BTS or Silom MRT stations.

To advertise in the next edition of

Time Out Bangkok

Please call us on +44 (0) 20 7813 6020
or email:
guidesadvertising@timeout.com

P พร้อมใจทันตแพทย์
PROMJAI DENTAL CLINIC

- **Endodontics**
- **Dental Implant**
- **Gum Treatment**
- **Cosmetic Dentistry**
- **Metal-Free Restoration**
- **Laser Tooth Whitening**

www.promjaidentalclinic.com
E-mail:achara @ promjaidentalclinic.com

Bangkok
Tel : (66) 0 2662 6070-2
(66) 0 2261 6229-31

Phuket
Tel : (66) 0 1893 4304
(66) 0 7634 5341 - 2

Bangkok : 18/2-3 Baan Suanpetch Condo , Sukhumvit 39 , Bangkok ,Thailand
Phuket: 5/4 Sawatdirak Rd., (2nd Fl., All 4 Diving), Patong, Phuket ,Thailand

Copperwired Apple Centre

4th floor, Siam Discovery, Thanon Rama I,
Pathumwan (0 2658 0447/www.copperwired.co.th).
Siam BTS. **Open** 10am-8pm daily. **Credit** AmEx,
DC, MC, V. **Map** p249 & p250 F4.
Adept staff demonstrate all the latest Apple models
and applications to legions of Macaholics at this
small but well-stocked showroom.

Pantip Plaza

604/3 Thanon Petchaburi, near the Indonesian
Embassy, North (0 2251 9008). **Open** 10am-9pm
daily. **Map** p251 G4.
A geek's paradise, Pantip is crammed with vendors
hawking hardware, applications, games, accessories, entertainment (CDs, DVDs, VCDs) and anything (new or used) that you can plug into your PC.
Computers can be bought turnkey, assembled to
your exact specifications or upgraded in shops that
closely resemble techno junkyards. Servicing, parts
and software for Mac or PC are all offered by knowledgeable staff. The stiff competition means that the
latest models are released at slim margins.
Warranties normally accompany big-name products, but most shops pride themselves on free post-
purchase service. Pirate and unlicensed software
keeps reappearing after raids, seemingly without
protest from licensed outlets.

Fashion

For **Chatuchak Weekend Market**, *see p136.*

Act-Cloth

205/18 Soi Thonglor Square, Sukhumvit Soi 55,
Sukhumvit (0 2381 6591). *Thonglor BTS.* **Open**
9am-6pm Mon-Sat. **Credit** AmEx, DC, MC, V.
Map p252 M5.
Prapakas Angsusingha's distinctly feminine garments neither pander to nor deviate far from trends,
striking a fine balance between sweet and sultry.

Almeta

20/3 Sukhumvit Soi 23, Sukhumvit (0 2258 4227/
www.almeta.com). *Asoke BTS/Sukhumvit subway.*
Open 10am-6pm daily. **Credit** AmEx, MC, V.
Map p252 K5.
The first store to offer Thai silk 'à la carte', as in the
lustrous cloth's design may be tailor-woven to individual requests. Top quality.

Atelier Pichita

43/27-28 Sukhumvit Soi 31, Sukhumvit (0 2261
7553-5). **Open** 9am-6pm Mon-Sat. **Credit** AmEx,
MC, V. **Map** p252 K6.
Long before the Milan Fashion Week of spring 2005
Pichita Boonyarataphan Ruksajit was the leading
lady of Thai couture. Society debs and doyennes
snap up her cosmopolitan creations by the rack and
she clad the dapper staff at the Conrad Hotel (*see
p43*) and has also designed the new Thai Airways
uniforms. Pricey, and with good reason.
Other locations: 3rd floor, Peninsula Plaza,
Pathumwan (0 2254 9098).

Fashion Society

2nd floor, Gaysorn, 999 Thanon Ploenchit,
Pathumwan (0 2656 1358/www.gaysornbkk.com).
Chidlom BTS. **Open** 10am-8pm daily. **Credit**
AmEx, MC, V. **Map** p251 H5.
This one-stop clearing house of play and work
clothes for men and women mixes leading Thai
labels and up-and-coming names, such as Muse,
Muung-doo and Sarit. Metal racks and raw decor pro-
duce a factory feel. Staff are friendly not fawning.

Fly Now

2nd floor, Gaysorn, Thanon Ploenchit, Pathumwan
(0 2656 1359). *Chidlom BTS.* **Open** 10am-8pm
daily. **Credit** AmEx, DC, MC, V. **Map** p251 H5.
Established over a decade, Fly Now entered jet-set
realms through principal designer Chamnam
Pakdisuk, whose voguish, feminine designs have
twice opened London Fashion Week.
Other locations: 2nd floor, Siam Centre,
Pathumwan (0 2658 1735).

Greyhound

2nd floor, Emporium, Sukhumvit Soi 24, Sukhumvit
(0 2664 8664). *Phrom Phong BTS.* **Open** 10am-9pm
Mon-Fri; 10am-10pm Sat, Sun. **Credit** AmEx, DC,
MC, V. **Map** p252 K6.
This legend among Thai labels offers understated
essentials that work both in and out of the office.
Designer/artist Jitsing Somboon vamps up formal
suit fabrics with bold styling and quirky details. Its
offshoot Playhound caters to more to street fads.
Other locations: in most downtown malls.

Issue

266/10 Siam Square Soi 3, Thanon Rama I,
Pathumwan (0 2658 4416). *Siam BTS.* **Open** noon-
9pm daily. **Credit** AmEx, MC, V. **Map** p250 F4.
Designer Roj Singhakul incorporates ethnic hiero-
glyphs, primitive forms and religious symbols
into his creations. Casual tops and Issue-branded
T-shirts are the mainstays among this casual clubwear for young, urban Thai individualists.

Jaspal

2nd floor, Siam Centre, Thanon Rama I,
Pathumwan (0 2251 5918/www.jaspal.com). *Siam*
BTS. **Open** 10am-9pm daily. **Credit** AmEx, DC, MC,
V. **Map** p249 & p250 F4.
Local fashion giant Jaspal takes its cue from Europe,
hiring Kate Moss and other supermodels for its ads.
The menswear can be a tad glitzy, but you can't
argue with the quality in high-tech stretch fabrics.
Other locations: in most downtown malls.

Jim Thompson Thai Silk

9 Thanon Surawong, Bangrak (0 2632 8100-4/
www.jimthompson.com). *Saladaeng BTS/Silom*
subway. **Open** 9am-9pm daily. **Credit** AmEx, DC,
MC, V. **Map** p250 F6.
The Thai silk pioneer (*see p93*) has ventured beyond
pillowcases, scarves and clubby neck ties into
the field of high fashion, such as experimental
silk art projects and lustrous upholstery for Ou
Baholydhin's trendy furniture designs.

High Thai designs

Sakul Intakul.

The language of modern design is becoming increasingly trendy in Bangkok. The new lingua permeates the glut of glossy design mags (such as *Art4D*, *room* and *daybeds*), the government's 'Thailand Design Centre' project, and everything from architecture to the home accessories sold in the city's increasingly design-oriented markets and malls.

The avant-garde of Thai product design has been honed by well-travelled global villagers and a new generation of local talents. Something of a cross between Philippe Starck and Damien Hirst, Chaiyuth Plypetch has wowed with outside-the-box ideas for **Propaganda** since 1994. His playful Match Lamp and Shark-Fin Bottle Opener have won international rave reviews and are shoo-ins as contemporary museum pieces. Bangkok-based French designer **Gilles Caffier** likewise scored a global hit with his translucent Hurricane Vase, a tubular

wooden skeleton covered with Lycra. His suave signature modernism also takes in leather pillows, vibrant glassware and subdued earthenware. Even traditional silk retailer **Jim Thompson** (*see p143*) invites Thai artists to explore the fibre's potential and he commissioned famed UK-based Thai designer **Ou Baholyodhin** to wrap his furniture in silk.

The scene is also flush with architects who turned to design after the 1997 crash left the market for new buildings flat. A true proponent of the new Asian style, Ekarit Pradistsuwana of **EGG** produces Fire+Earth ceramics and furniture employing recycled teak. Similarly, Tam Devakul's (of **T Positif**) crystal wine glasses with silver stems are finding their way to the linen-clothed tables of the world's top hotels. He also conceives distinctive rings, pendants, bracelets and cuff-links. Engineer-turned-florist **Sakul**

Intakul conjures tailor-made, architecturally impressive flower arrangements widely copied abroad and featured in his books. Inspired by Thai seeds, his flower vessels in bronze and ceramic have earnt plaudits in *Wallpaper**.

With demand high for all things aesthetic, knock-offs naturally abound: *Wallpaper*'s five-pointed asterisk gets emblazoned on mugs sold in markets; facsimiles of iconic chairs by Charles Eames and Mies van der Rohe can be custom-ordered at bargain prices; a Vernor Panton plastic seat ranges from B2,000 for a fibreglass reproduction to B20,000 for a licensed replica. But this sort of thing is not all one way: successful Thai designers such as Paragon Leather and Planet 2000 are likewise subject to copycatting, and scouts for European design houses scour **Chatuchak Weekend Market** for innovations (*see* p136 **A day in JJ**).

The thirst for ideas and materials has provided a renewed focus on Thai artisanship. The government's 'One Tambon, One Product' (OTOP) policy markets goods from the 7,000-plus *tambon* (villages). Based on a successful Japanese plan, but with echoes of Italy's regional specialisation, OTOP has flooded the market with handicraft, decor and gift items through fairs, stalls and shops, such as **JJ OTOP Centre** (*see* p136). While this has created new industries, repetition still tends to outpace innovation, and a somewhat variable quality control tends to frustrate those who envisaged the end result being high-value, high-standard exports.

Among the pioneering outlets that have ensured Thai crafts retain their associated customs are **Rasi Sayam**, a converted house stocking handiwork designs adapted for modern use in a charming domestic setting, and the shops of Pornroj Angsanakul, whose outlet **Tamnan Mingmuang** applies weaving expertise in fresh ways and exhibits astonishingly lifelike ceramics of monks. Angsanakul's unrivalled baskets, boxes and handbags also come in wild grass, water hyacinth and ultra-fine *yan lipao* vine. The Legend branch sells excellent but more mainstream souvenirs, while his other shop, Eros, is self-explanatory. At least for the time being, all these Thai designs can be made for prices western countries cannot come close to matching.

EGG
4th floor, Siam Discovery Centre, Thanon Rama I, Pathumwan (0 2658 0480/www.egg thai.com). Ploenchit BTS. **Open** 10.30am-9pm daily. **Credit** MC, V. **Map** p251 H4.
Other locations: 6th floor, Central Chidlom, Pathumwan (0 2655 7777 ext 3602); 19 Thanon New Rama IX, North-east (0 2300 5131-4).

Gilles Caffier
4th floor, Siam Discovery Centre, Pathumwan (0 2658 0487/www.gillescaffier.com). Siam BTS. **Open** 10am-8pm daily. **Credit** DC, MC, V. **Map** p249 & p250 F4.

Propaganda
4th floor, Siam Discovery Centre, Thanon Rama I, Pathumwan (0 2658 0430/ www.propagandaonline.com). Siam BTS. **Open** 10.30am-9pm daily. **Credit** AmEx, DC, MC, V. **Map** p249 & p250 F4.
Other locations: 4th floor, Emporium, Sukhumvit, Sukhumvit (0 2664 8574).

Rasi Sayam
82 Sukhumvit Soi 33, Sukhumvit (0 2262 40729/www.rasisayam.com). Phrom Phong BTS. **Open** 9am-5.30pm Mon-Sat. **Credit** AmEx, DC, MC, V. **Map** p252 K5.

Sakul Intakul
2nd floor, Promenade Decor, Thanon Witthayu, Lumphini (0 2655 4230/www.sakul flowers.com). Ploenchit BTS. **Open** 10am-6pm Mon-Sat. **Credit** MC, V. **Map** p251 H5.
Other locations: Sakul Flowers, 47 Soi Ratchavithi 2, Phayathai (0 2644 9438/9); **Playground!** (*see* p141).

Tamnan Mingmuang
3rd floor, Thaniya Plaza, Thanon Silom, Bangrak (0 2231 2120). Saladaeng BTS/Silom subway. **Open** 11am-8pm daily. **Credit** AmEx, V. **Map** p250 F6.
Other locations: (all on same floor) Eros (0 2231 2015); The Legend (0 2231 2179).

T Positif
2nd floor, Peninsula Plaza, Thanon Ratchadamri, Pathumwan (0 2652 2184/ www.tpositif.com). Ratchadamri BTS. **Open** 10.30am-7pm daily. **Credit** AmEx, MC, V. **Map** p251 G5.
Other locations: 5th floor Central Chidlom, Pathumwan (0 2655 7777 ext 3104).

Eat, Drink, Shop

Other locations: Jim Thompson's House Museum, 6 Kasemsan Soi 2, Pathumwan (0 2216 7368); 4th floor, Emporium, Sukhumvit (0 2664 8165-6); ground floor, Isetan, Central World Plaza, Pathumwan (0 2255 9805); 1st floor, Central Chidlom, Pathumwan (0 2251 9206); Siam Paragon, Pathumwan (see p152); and other outlets in many five-star hotels.

Kai Boutique

187/1 Bangkok Cable Building, Thanon Ratchadamri, Pathumwan (0 2251 0728/ www.kaiboutique.com). Ratchadamri BTS. **Open** 9am-7.30pm Mon-Fri. **Credit** AmEx, DC, MC, V. **Map** p251 G5.
Veteran designer Somchai 'Kai' Kaewtong is a pioneer of Bangkok's *dek bou* (boutique kids) and his creations have adorned local fashionistas for three decades. The Kai Boutique label is also a breeding ground for new talent. This spacious flagship focuses on wedding gowns, evening wear and accessories.

Kloset Red Carpet

2nd floor, Gaysorn, 999 Thanon Phloenchit, Pathumwan (0 2656 1144/www.klosetdesign.com). Chidlom BTS. **Open** 10am-8pm daily. **Credit** AmEx, MC, V. **Map** p251 H5.
This branch of the inventive Kloset fashion house highlights glamorous prêt-a-porter styles with bold colours and frilly accents such as lace, nets and ribbons. One of five local designers at Milan's prestigious White fashion trade fair in 2004.
Other locations: 3rd floor, Central Chidlom, Pathumwan (0 2655 7777 ext 2907); 3rd floor, Emporium, Sukhumvit (0 2664 8748); Siam Centre, Pathumwan (from Mar 2005).

Doi Tung by Mae Fah Luang

4th floor, Siam Discovery, Thanon Rama I, Pathumwan (0 2658 0424/www.doitung.org). Siam BTS. **Open** 11am-8pm daily. **Credit** MC, V. **Map** p249 & p250 F4.
This worthy crafts foundation has wowed catwalks by deviating from the conservatism that's usual in craft traditions into a stylishly cosmopolitan form, with innovative hand-loomed cottons and linens providing the key materials.
Other locations: Suan Lum Night Bazaar, Pathumwan (0 2250 0140-2).

Senada Theory

2nd floor, Gaysorn, 999 Thanon Ploenchit, Pathumwan (0 2656 1350). Chidlom BTS. **Open** 10am-8pm daily. **Credit** AmEx, DC, MC, V. **Map** p251 H5.
Ethnic influences are the main engines driving this 14-year-old fashion house. Lead designer Chanita Preechawitayakul is renowned for meticulously reconstructing Indian embroidery, Chinese silks and even grandma's tablecloths into hip streetwear.
Other locations: 3rd floor, Siam Centre, Pathumwan (0 2252 2757).

Soda

3rd floor, Siam Centre, Thanon Rama I, Pathumwan (0 2252 2124-5/Soda Men 0 2252 2123/Soda Pop (women) 0 2251 4995/Night & Day 0 2252 2123). Siam BTS. **Open** 10am-9pm daily. **Credit** AmEx, MC, V. **Map** p249 & p250 F4.
Creating bold, sexy and diverse styles for the tragically slim, Soda embellishes core items such as jeans and T-shirts with innovative sequinned and printed

Bangkok: fashion city?

Thais love to put on a show, especially if it involves beautiful people strutting their stuff. After the APEC Summit for Asia-Pacific leaders in 2003 the heads of state were treated to a catwalk of Thai silk threaded with gold when the government turned the shopping street from Siam to the Emporium shopping complex (see p151) into a five-kilometre (three-mile) fashion runway. The floats carrying 800 models strutting in 60 Thai and global labels launched 'Bangkok Fashion City', a 1.8-billion-baht project to make Bangkok a regional fashion hub by 2005 and a global fashion centre by 2012.

Detractors saw it partly as a way to win votes from the clothing industry's 1.2 million workers, but few could deny that Thai garments do need brand identity fast to prevent obliteration by Chinese rivals with their lower unit costs. Some Thai designers are already reaping dividends. With state

backing, local fashion houses **Issue**, **Greyhound** (for both, *see p143*), **Kloset**, **Seneda** (for both, *see p146*) and **Sretsis** (*see p147*) were showcased at Milan's annual White fair in 2004. Giorgio Armani has signed on as an adviser, while the Institut Français de la Mode and the French Textile Machinery Manufacturers' Association are committed to helping turn Bangkok into the Paris of Asia.

The country's readiness for such moves has come into question, though, following the outcry at Thai supermodel Methinee Kingphayom's un-Thai wardrobe 'malfunction' (her nipple sticker was briefly visible) at the pioneering *Elle* Bangkok Fashion Week. The Culture Ministry's resulting 'dress code' for modesty among models did a lot to contradict the state's commercial drive to emulate foreign influences. The success of Bangkok Fashion City may in the end depend on how socially liberal the state is willing to be.

fabrics. The several branches at the Siam Centre include one for men (ground floor) and Night & Day, which spices up sleepwear.
Other locations: 2nd floor, Emporium, Sukhumvit (0 2664 8464).

Sretsis

2nd floor, Gaysorn, Thanon Ploenchit, Pathumwan (0 2656 1125/www.sretsis.com). Chidlom BTS/Ratchadamri BTS. **Open** 10am-8pm daily.
Credit AmEx, DC, MC, V. **Map** p251 H5.
With a sensational and ultra-feminine 2003 debut collection, 'Dreamland Circus', former Marc Jacobs intern Pimdao Sukhahuta became the new darling of Thailand's fashion frontline. The quirky, retro style, with floaty chiffons and frilly laces, made this two-year-old label an instant hit for girly baby dolls. The pastel pink and powder blue refreshes after so much trendy yet tedious monochrome.
Other locations: 3rd floor, Central Chidlom, Pathumwan (0 2655 7777 ext 2907); 2nd floor, Emporium, Sukhumvit (0 2664 8000 ext 1567).

Theatre

2nd floor, Central World Plaza, Thanon Ratchadamri, Pathumwan (0 2255 9545). Chidlom BTS. **Open** 11am-8.30pm daily. **Credit** AmEx, MC, V. **Map** p251 G4.
Designer of the year in 2002, Taned Boonprasarn combines hardy fabrics with lace and chiffon. His glamorous gowns and mix-and-matches with accompanying frilly details serve to evoke an extraordinary neo-romanticism.
Other locations: 3rd floor, Siam Centre, Pathumwan (0 2251 3599).

Outsize

Browns

1st floor, U-Chu-Liang Building, Thanon Rama IV, Bangrak (0 2632 4442). Silom subway. **Open** 10am-7pm daily. **Credit** AmEx, DC, MC, V. **Map** p251 G7.
The outsized skirts, trousers and blouses here – all in light fabrics, with clean prints and patterns – are a godsend to women who find local ranges too small.
Other locations: 1st floor, Emporium, Sukhumvit (0 2664 8319); 275 Thonglor Soi 13, Sukhumvit (0 2712 7820); 2nd floor, Central Chidlom, Pathumwan (0 2655 7777 ext 3201).

Tailors

Haberdasheries crowd tourist areas, especially Sukhumvit Sois 3-11, Thanon Khao San, Thanon Charoen Krung (between Silom and River City), and downtown malls. Typically run by Thai-Indians and stitched by Thai-Chinese, these can tailor bespoke suits and dresses for bargain prices, but their aggressive touting repels many. For optimum quality and service, dismiss the gimmicky '24-hour with free kimono' packages. Most tailors are well versed in formalwear and respond professionally to customers who are thorough about cut, cloth and detailing. Give them a pattern or choose from their catalogues and magazine cuttings. Insist on at least two fittings over several days.

Nothing to wear for Mardi Gras? Prize-winning designer Tu of **Sequin Queen**

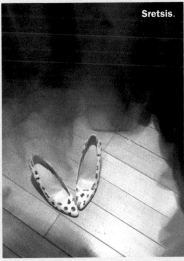

Sretsis.

Doi Tung by Mae Fah Luang. *See p146.*

(www.sequinqueen.com) can run up a spangled little number in chiffon or lycra, complete with feathered headdresses. All online orders are hand-sewn, fairly priced and custom-made (for men, women and those in between).

Art's Tailors

62/15-16 Soi Thaniya, Bangrak (0 2234 0874). Saladaeng BTS/Silom subway. **Open** 8.30am-4.30pm Mon-Sat. **No credit cards. Map** p250 F6.

Master tailors hunch over long workbenches to churn out high-quality suits at this decades-old institution – a favourite with powerful pols and corporate fat cats. Quality comes at a price; a typical two-piece suit starts from B40,000, a fortune by local standards. Allow for two fittings over two weeks.

Chang Torn

95 Thanon Tanao, Banglamphu (0 2282 9390). **Open** 9am-7.30pm Mon-Sat; 9am-3pm Sun. **Credit** MC, V. **Map** p248 C3.

In a district full of tailors, veteran Chang Torn's comes recommended by fabric sellers. His small unassuming version of Savile Row makes suits from B12,000, shirts from B1,000. Allow ten days.

River Mark

Room 238, River City Complex, 23 Thanon Yotha, Bangrak (0 2237 0077-8 ext 238). Tha Siphraya. **Open** 10am-8pm Mon-Sat. **Credit** AmEx, MC, V. **Map** p250 D6.

For those with a Milanese taste but a Mile End budget, River Mark stitches agreeable suits from B3,500. The shop also does dresses and robes. Mrs Thatcher was fitted for clothes here.

Food & drink

Tops supermarkets are found at **Central** (*see p141*), while British **Tesco Lotus** and French **Carrefour** hypermarkets face off where Thanon Rama IV meets Sukhumvit Soi 26; these supermarkets swamp so many suburbs that they have provoked protests, planning limits and even physical attacks.

La Boulange

2-2/1 Soi Convent, Thanon Silom, Bangrak (0 2631 0355). Saladaeng BTS/Silom subway. **Open** 7am-10pm daily. **Credit** AmEx, MC, V. **Map** p250 F7.

An authentic French pavement café purveying pastries, sandwiches, fresh-baked loaves and classic snack meals: croque monsieurs, salads, quiches. **Other locations**: throughout the city.

Ong's Tea

4th floor, Siam Discovery, Thanon Rama I, Pathumwan (0 2658 0445). Siam BTS. **Open** 10am-9pm daily. **Credit** AmEx, MC, V. **Map** p249 & p250 F4.

A table setting allows you to sample the leaves, mostly from China, Japan and Taiwan, amid tea ceremony calligraphy, pots, and chai-sipping music.

Thaniya Spirit

62/7 Thanon Thaniya, Bangrak (0 2234 5224). Saladaeng BTS/Silom subway. **Open** 10am-10pm Mon-Sat; 10am-6pm Sun. **No credit cards. Map** p250 F6.

Bars and clubs favour this specialist drinks merchant stocking hard-to-find international tipples. **Other locations**: VAT Spirit, Thanon Ratchadaphisek, North (0 2683 9360-4).

really out of this world, meteorites. Gold shops proliferate in **Chinatown** (*see p84* **Goldfingers**) and the **MBK** mall. To ensure you don't get ripped off by the tricksters who operate around the fringes of the industry, *see p150* **Gems without scams**.

Astral Gemstone Talismans

1875 Zone C, Joe Louis Theatre, Suan Lum Night Bazaar, Pathumwan (0 2252 1230-1/ www.agt-gems.com/rsb.html). Lumphini subway. **Open** 10am-6pm Mon-Sat. **Credit** AmEx, DC, MC, V. **Map** p251 H5.

Sidereal planetary astrology is the Vedic inspiration behind the rings and pendants custom-designed by begowned ex-rock singer Richard S Brown, lead singer of the Misunderstood, a cult rock band championed by John Peel in 1966 – how about that for an obscure pub quiz question? Your lucky gems (unflawed) are mounted in plenty of gold.

Dinakara

2nd floor, Home Place Building, Sukhumvit Soi 55, Thanon Sukhumvit, Watthana (0 2712 7174). Thonglor BTS. **Open** 10am-6pm daily. **Credit** AmEx, MC, V. **Map** p252 M6.

Creative use of precious stones and metals ensures that Yukala Iamla-or's designs enjoy a large following among artistic types.

Lotus Arts de Vivre

Four Seasons Hotel, Thanon Ratchadamri, Pathumwan (0 2250 0732/www.lotusarts devivre.com). Saphan Taksin BTS/Pier. **Open** 10am-7pm daily. **Credit** AmEx, DC, MC, V. **Map** p250 D7.

Something of an Asian Fabergé, Lotus's diverse jewellery, decorations and trinkets are as mysteriously oriental as they come. One-off pieces employ exotic materials from oyster shells and stingray leather to fine-grained roots and tyre rubber.

Other locations: 3rd floor, Oriental Place, Charoen Krung Soi 38, Bangrak (0 2235 1875); 3rd floor, Sukhothai Hotel, Thanon Sathorn Tai, South (0 2287 0222 ext 5272); Peninsula Hotel, Thanon Charoen Nakhon, Thonburi (0 2861 1168); Four Seasons Hotel, Thanon Ratchadamri, Pathumwan (0 2250 0732).

Villa Market

595 Sukhumvit 33/1, Sukhumvit (0 2662 1000/ www.villamarket.com). Phrom Phong BTS. **Open** 24hrs daily. **Credit** AmEx, DC, MC, V. **Map** p252 K6.

This expat haunt is *the* grocer for home sick ex-patriates. They come here for those comfort foods that remind them of home in the way a Thai green curry never could: from cheeses and tortillas to herrings and Marmite. There's also a good wine choice (often discounted) and a community noticeboard.

Other locations: Ploenchit Centre, Sukhumvit Soi 2, Sukhumvit (0 2656 9071-4); Sukhumvit Soi 11, Sukhumvit (0 2253 5528); Sukhumvit Soi 49, Sukhumvit (0 2662 5880-4); Trinity Building, Silom Soi 5, Bangrak (0 2636 6856); Millionaire Building, 62 Thanon Lang Suan, Pathumwan (0 2255 3066-7); 323 Thonglor Soi 15, Sukhumvit (0 2712 6000).

Wine Connection

1 Sivadon Building, Soi Convent, Thanon Silom, Bangrak (0 2234 0388/www.wineconnection.co.th). Saladaeng BTS/Silom subway. **Open** 9am-9pm daily. **Credit** AmEx, MC, V. **Map** p250 F6.

Knowledgeable and professional service adds to the fine selection of global labels at no-middleman prices. **Other locations**: 39/13-14 Sukhumvit Soi 31, Sukhumvit (0 2662 2490); V9, Sofitel Silom, 188 Thanon Silom, Bangrak (0 2238 1991).

Gems, gold & jewellery

Thaigem.com has earned trust as the leading online catalogue of precious stones, beads, crystals, jewellery and even, for something

Gifts

Reflections Shop sells wondrous kitsch items in plastic, resin, wire and fake fur at Reflections Rooms (*see p48*). Proceeds help villager empowerment projects.

Loft

3rd floor, Siam Discovery, Thanon Rama I, Pathumwan (0 2658 0328-30/www.loftbangkok. com). Siam BTS. **Open** 10am-9pm daily. **Credit** AmEx, DC, MC, V. **Map** p249 & p250 F4.

There's something for every budget at this expansive Japanese shop jumbled with gifts ranging from odd clocks and twee frames to techie gadgets and designer pens. Myriad wrappings and cards make this a one-stop present solution.

Eat, Drink, Shop

Roominteriorproducts

4th floor, Siam Discovery, Thanon Rama I,
Pathumwan (0 2658 0411/www.roominterior
products.com). Siam BTS. **Open** 11am-8pm Mon-
Thur; 11am-9pm Fri-Sun. **Credit** AmEx, DC, MC, V.
Map p249 & p250 F4.
Like inflatable plastic stuff? And we don't mean
those dodgy inflatable dolls . Roominteriorproducts,
an Australian designer duo, sells a rainbow of
kitschy props for the modern room, such as folding
chairs and beanbags in modern patterns.

Health & beauty

Chalachol

205/13-14 Sukhumvit Soi 55, Sukhumvit (0 2712
6481/www.chalachol.com). Thonglor BTS. **Open**
11am-8.30pm daily. **Credit** MC, V. **Map** p251 G6.
Somsak Chalachol revolutionised local hairdressing
with this chain of unisex designer salons. While
your hair is washed, your body gets a massage from
a vibrating chair. Cut and blow dry from B350.
Other locations: 1st floor, Siam Center,
Pathumwan (0 2658 1129); Amarin Plaza, Ploenchit
Road (0 2251 1941).

Completions

20 Thanon Silom, between Soi 2 & 4, Bangrak
(0 2234 3749). Saladaeng BTS/Silom subway.
Open 11am-6pm Mon, Tue, Thur-Sun. **Credit** MC,
V. **Map** p250 F7.
This sparse, long-standing salon's fame (and prices)
skyrocketed when the prime minister dropped in for
a trim and a chat about his holiday plans. Cut and
blow dry from B1,500 (men) or B2,500 (women).

Hanako

Siam Square Soi 11, Pathumwan (0 2255 8630-2).
Siam BTS. **Open** 9.30am-12.30am daily. **Credit**
AmEx, DC, MC, V. **Map** p250 F4.
In a city full of beauty parlours dispensing make-up,
skin whitening and elective plastic surgery, this
Japanese institute is perhaps the most reliable cen-
tre in which to get made over.
Other locations: 1st floor, PSI Tower, 29
Sukhumvit Soi 39, Sukhumvit (0 2662 5831-3).

Harn & Thann

3rd floor, Gaysorn, Thanon Ploenchit, Pathumwan
(0 6622 2014/www.thann.info). Chidlom BTS.
Open 10am-8pm daily. **Credit** MC, V. **Map** p251 H5.
Among the many efforts to turn traditional Thai
herbal remedies into modern toiletries and grooming

Gems without scams

Bangkok is a major global gems centre,
thanks to Thai cutting expertise, professional
traders and imaginatively designed settings.
It can, however, be a dizzying market for
beginners, who should wise up to the city's
equally famous gem scams. The epicentre
for loose gems and uncut stones is where
Thanons Surasak and Mahesak cross
Thanons Silom and Surwaong. The area has
some of the world's best lapidaries hidden
down dark alleys and behind undistinguished
gates (for security reasons). Upmarket malls
with jewellery retailers include **Emporium**
(*see p151*) and **Peninsula Plaza** (*see p152*),
while outlets in hotels sell tourist-oriented
pieces at frequent discounts. There are many
innovative designers around, among the best
being **Lotus Arts de Vivre** and **Dinakara** (for
both, *see p149*). To gauge prices, check the
giant online trader **Thaigem.com**.

Further afield, the east coast town of
Chanthaburi – located some 245 kilometres
(152 miles) from Bangkok – remains a global
marketplace for serious buyers, even though
the ruby and sapphire quarries around the
town have declined. Stones now come from
Myanmar, Cambodia, Sri Lanka and Africa.

Be warned that the tourist board receives
many complaints from people duped into

buying gems in the false hope of reselling
them abroad at a vast, unearned profit. The
most common ruse involves victims being
approached near tourist attractions by a
stranger telling them the site is closed for a
holiday. The prey is then enticed to tour the
city on a *tuk-tuk* that, literally and figuratively,
takes them for a ride, ending at a shop where
the 'gems to resell' offers are, quite literally,
too good to be true. Even if the conmen are
caught prosecution proves hard since the
gems are invariably real, though inferior and
near worthless. Heating, or 'cooking', to alter
a stone's appearance is another common,
but accepted, practice. While that's not
always disclosed, reputable vendors provide
honest documentation. TAT (*see p235*) is
happy to advise on reputable dealers.

You can learn to identify genuine gems
on short courses at the **Asian Institute of
Gemological Sciences** (33rd floor, Jewellery
Trade Centre, 919/1 Thanon Silom, 0 2267
4315-9, www.aigsthailand.com) or the
Gemological Institute America Thailand
(12th floor, Bisco Tower, 56/12 Thanon Sap,
0 2237 9575-7). These also teach degree-
level classes in such arcane topics as crystal
structure, geology, design and synthetics.
A full diploma takes six to nine months.

products, Harn & Thann achieves not just superior packaging and breadth of products, but high performance from eco-friendly ingredients. Think rice bran scrubs, lemon grass aromatherapy oil and strings of multi-spice soaps. Few other Thai brands match its success through 19 countries.
Other locations: stands in Ayodhya (*see p151*), Boots (*see p153*), Central (*see p141*) and most shopping malls.

Homewares

For **EGG, Gilles Caffier, Propaganda, Sakul Intakul** and **T Positif**, *see p145* **High Thai designs**.

Ayodhya

3rd floor, Gaysorn, Thanon Ploenchit, Pathumwan (0 2656 1089/www.ayodhyatrade.com). Chidlom BTS. **Open** 10am-8pm daily. **Credit** AmEx, DC, MC, V. **Map** p251 H5.
A pioneer of updating trad Thai products to today's aesthetics, Ayodhya turns out understated and useful items like seats made from tree vines and homemade soaps scented with local flowers.
Other locations: 4th floor, Emporium, Sukhumvit Soi 24, Sukhumvit (0 2664 8000 ext 1313); Panta (*see below*).

Budji

7 Soi Sangngern Thonglor 25, Sukhumvit 55, Sukhumvit (0 2712 9832/www.budji bangkok.com). Thonglor BTS. **Open** 9.30am-6pm Mon-Sat. **Credit** AmEx, MC, V. **Map** p252 M6.
Acclaimed Filipino designer Antonio 'Budji' Layug's airy showroom shows furniture and decorative items from his Movement 8 design group. Ergonomic seating made from indigenous materials is the trademark of Budji's tropical contemporary style.

Cocoon

3rd floor, Gaysorn, Thanon Ploenchit, Pathumwan (0 2656 1006-7). Chidlom BTS. **Open** 10am-8pm daily. **Credit** AmEx, MC, V. **Map** p251 H5.
Neon-hued silk pillows are the most eye-catching of the pan-Asian influences that infuse every item at this much-imitated shop. Stock runs from chopsticks and celadon bowls to incense packs and sofas.
Other locations: Peninsula Hotel, 333 Thanon Charoen Nakorn, Thonburi (0 2630 7040).

Geo

H1, 998 Sukhumvit Soi 55, Thanon Sukhumvit, Watthana (0 2381 4324-5/www.geo.co.th). Thonglor BTS. **Open** 11am-midnight daily. **Credit** AmEx, MC, V. **Map** p252 M6.
Owned by a group of elite creatives, Geo deals in high-end miscellany with an emphasis on gardening and flower arrangement. Photographs of floral designs by co-owner and *Lips* magazine editor Sakchai Guy adorn scarves and posters. Oddities include mock human skeletons, spherical stones, antique cameras and crystal chandeliers. The second floor houses designer streetwear.

Panta

4th floor, Siam Discovery, Thanon Rama I, Pathumwan (0 2658 0415). Siam BTS. **Open** 10am-9pm daily. **Credit** AmEx, DC, MC, V. **Map** p249 & p250 F4.
An artwork in itself, Panta showcases distinctly Asian experimental furniture made from natural materials such as wood, tree vines and rattan, with cushions in forest fabrics. The chic geometric designs are minimalist, yet warm and voluminous.

Retro

Shades of Retro

522/3 Thonglor Soi 16, Sukhumvit Soi 55, Sukhumvit (0 2714 9657). **Open** 11am-11pm Mon-Sat; 11am-8pm Sun. **No credit cards**. **Map** p252 M6.
This shop deals in vintage gadgets from the middle of the last century. Even if old B&O tuners, one-off turntables and rare cameras don't stoke nostalgic embers, they will reinforce an appreciation of design. And if old tuners ain't your thang, the shop doubles as a friendly and neighbourly bar.

Y50

24-26 Ekamai Soi 21 (Thonglor 20), Sukhumvit Soi 63, Sukhumvit (0 2711 5629). Ekkamai BTS. **Open** 9am-5pm daily; *cafe50* 6pm-midnight Mon-Sat. **Credit** AmEx, MC, V. **Map** p252 M7.
Resembling the storeroom of a design museum, this funky shop/bar shifts mostly Skandic chairs, lamps and table clocks from the 1950s to the 1970s. A couple of shops nearby offer similar finds.

Malls

Top-floor cinemas/bowling alleys close later than shopping zones, often past midnight.

Central World Plaza

4/1-2 Thanon Ratchadamri, Pathumwan (0 2255 9400/www.centralpattana.com). Chidlom BTS. **Open** 10am-9pm daily. **Map** p251 G4.
This dim, cavernous hulk was known as (and still gets referred to by) the World Trade Centre. It's getting revamped by new owners Central, linked to malls and the BTS by bridges, and – of course – being made even bigger. Isetan and the expanded Zen department stores (*see p141*) sandwich 300-plus shops for those seeking local labels, jade, gold, furniture and discount outlets. And when you're shopped out, head upstairs for a film at Major's Cineplex (*see p166*) or go bowling (*see p202*).

Emporium

622 Sukhumvit Soi 24, Sukhumvit (0 2664 8000/ www.emporiumthailand.com). Phrom Phong BTS. **Open** 10.30am-10pm Mon-Fri; 10am-10pm Sat, Sun. **Map** p252 K6.
Supremely successful, Emporium lures the well-off with Euro-couture (Prada, Gucci, Chanel, Hermès, Fendi) and long-established Thai jewellers. Lesser mortals come for the local and imported fashion

outlets, opticians, booksellers, hairstylists, travel agents and furnishing shops. It hosts catwalks, exhibitions, promotions and even concerts, and also boasts a fine namesake department store and a vast (yet still crowded) gourmet food hall.

Gaysorn

999 Thanon Ploenchit, Pathumwan (0 2656 1516-9/ www.gaysorn.com). Chidlom BTS. **Open** 10am-8pm daily. **Map** p251 H5.

This swanky corner landmark has posh brands (Louis Vuitton, Prada, Hermès), regional fashion houses and contemporary Thai design outlets.

Mah Boon Krong (MBK)

444 Thanon Phayathai, Pathumwan (0 2620 9000/ www.mbk-center.com). National Stadium BTS. **Open** 10am-10pm daily. **Map** p249 & p250 F4.

Don't try to make sense of the overcrowded, boisterous, chaotic frenzy in this colossal, stacked marketplace. Over 1,000 shops and stalls flog everything and anything: gold, footwear, sausages, dining tables, suitcases, youth fashion and, famously, mobile phones and portable electronics. Specialists in camping gear (*see p154*), cameras (*see p153*) and custom portraits offer great bargains and informed service – if you can find them. Above this empire's diverse food court, SF runs a cinema (*see p166*) and bowling rink (*see p202*). MBK links to the Pathumwan Princess hotel (*see p45*).

Old Siam Plaza

12 Thanon Tripetch, Phra Nakorn (0 2226 0156-8). **Open** 9am-9pm daily. **Map** p248 C4.

Styled with touches of Thai yesteryear, this three-storey indoor bazaar holds traditional jewellers and silk retailers. Stalls selling clothes, household goods and delicacies (notably desserts) fill the atrium, with a computer repair shop on the top floor.

Peninsula Plaza

153 Thanon Ratchadamri, Pathumwan (0 2253 9791). Ratchadamri BTS. **Open** 10am-8pm daily. **Map** p251 G5.

Flanked by the Hyatt and Four Seasons hotels, this quiet, faux-Parisian low-rise is a yellowing throwback to the pre-1997 boom. Still, it attracts those who own at least one two-tone, diamond-encrusted Rolex and can differentiate pre-Donnatella from post-Gianni, since the city's Versace flagship docks here, alongside Bangkok's only Loewe. Staff can be patronising to non-millionaires.

Siam Centre & Siam Discovery

989 Thanon Rama I, Pathumwan (0 2658 1000-5/ www.siamcenter.co.th). Siam BTS. **Open** 10am-9pm daily. **Map** p249 & p250 F4.

Since 1973 several Thai designers have launched careers at the Siam Centre. Although global chains muscle in, indie boutiques continue to cater to the trendiest of tastes (and slimmest of frames). CD Warehouse dominates the top floor, surrounded by sportswear and Gen-X shops for urban skate dudes and surf chicks. To differentiate from its huge new

neighbour, Siam Paragon, Siam Centre's getting a Shibuya-esque teen facelift.

Its stablemate on the other side, Siam Discovery, caters to yuppies. DKNY, Armani Exchange and Guess? provide the designer threads, while hairdressing salon Toni & Guy, Shu Uemura cosmetics and salon-spa Leonard Drake make sure that no blemishes mar the finish. But the mall's trump card is designer home furnishings by anyroom, Habitat, Panta and roominteriorproducts, among others. The fifth floor is all for children, while the cacophonous top floor houses plush EGV cinemas.

Siam Paragon

Thanon Rama I, Pathumwan (0 2658 3000/ www.siamparagon.co.th). Siam BTS. **Open** usually 10am-10pm. **Map** p251 G4.

Behind a six-storey atrium lobby and 200m (656ft) of water cascades, this truly astonishing mall will from late 2005 feature hundreds of stores including the country's largest bookshop, a digital centre, Asia's largest watch and jewellery shop, and a cavernous Paragon department store. Sitting on a 4,500-bay car park, it also holds a Gourmet Market food hall, an IMAX cinema, a 16-screen Cinepolis (*see p166*), a huge aquarium, Siam Ocean World, a 50-lane Major Bowl bowling alley, a family 'edutainment' Explorium, leading restaurants, California WOW gym, the Royal Paragon Hall exhibition centre and Siam Opera theatre (*see p196*). A lakeside terrace leads back to the five-star Kempinski Hotel and mature canalside gardens.

Music

CD Warehouse

3rd floor, Emporium, Sukhumvit Soi 24, Sukhumvit (0 2664 8520-2/www.cdwarehouse-asia.com). Phrom Phong BTS. **Open** 10am-9pm daily. **Credit** AmEx, DC, MC, V. **Map** p252 K6.

Sample the newest tunes at the listening stations of Bangkok's largest and most organised music shop. Shelves of international new releases and seasoned favourites run alongside Thai pop, classical, Canto-pop, J-pop and world music, plus blockbuster movies available on tape or DVD.

Other locations: 5th floor, Siam Discovery, Pathumwan (0 2255 2086-8); 7th floor, Central World Plaza, Pathumwan (0 2255 6552-4).

Do Re Me

274 Siam Square, Thanon Rama I, Pathumwan (0 2251 4351). Siam BTS. **Open** 1-10pm daily. **No credit cards.** **Map** p249 & p250 F4.

This treasured little shop sells new releases (on major and minor labels) at discounts. The absence of organisation tests the owner's incredible memory.

Music One

3rd floor, Major Cineplex Ekkamai, Sukhumvit Soi 61, Sukhumvit (0 2714 2891/www.musicone.co.th). **Open** 10am-9pm daily. **Credit** AmEx, DC, MC, V. **Map** p251 G7.

Who says people are ungrateful? Member discounts (plus inspired alternative tastes) have fostered loyalty to this tiny outlet with an emphasis on chillout, mood music, indie (Thai and Brit), Japanese imports, soundtracks, death metal and 12-inchers for DJs, enabling it to compete with the chains. It also has music magazines, world charts and listening stations. **Other locations**: 7th floor, Central World Plaza, Pathumwan (0 2255 6579).

Rungvadee

2nd floor, Pantip Plaza, Thanon Phetburi, North (0 2252 9933). **Open** 10am-8pm daily. **Credit** MC, V. **Map** p251 G4.
A large and diverse inventory of general release CDs from all genres of Thai music: Thai pop to *look thung*, techno to *phiphat*.

Opticians

Lauderdale

1st floor, Siam Discovery, Thanon Rama I, Pathumwan (0 2658 0102-3). Siam BTS.
Open 10am-8pm daily. **Credit** AmEx, DC, MC, V. **Map** p249 & p250 F4.
Only the most stylish frames (think Lindberg) make it to this classy, but fairly priced boutique.
Other locations: 2nd floor, All Seasons Place, Thanon Witthayu, Pathumwan (0 2685 3933).

Rajdamri Optical

2nd floor, Silom Complex, Thanon Silom, Bangrak (0 2231 3165). Saladaeng BTS/Silom subway.
Open 10am-8.30pm daily. **Credit** AmEx, DC, MC, V. **Map** p250 F7.

Run by optometrists in a mall brimming with spectacles shops, Rajdamri's emphasis is on eye care – so expect frames that are designed to enable you to see rather than ensure you are looked at.

Pharmacies

Boots

1st floor, Siam Centre, Thanon Rama I, Pathumwan (0 2658 1126/www.boots.co.uk). Siam BTS.
Open 10am-9pm daily. **Credit** AmEx, MC, V. **Map** p249 & p250 F4.
The UK chemist has dozens of branches nationwide, each with a pharmacist. Famous labels and good own-brand pharmaceuticals, cosmetics, perfume and beauty care products vie for shelf space.
Other locations: throughout the city.

Photography

Photo developers found everywhere supply snaps in free flip books at low rates, often with digital processing or scanning. Professionals choose **IQ Lab** (*see p154*) or, for artful black and white printing, Surat Suvanich's **Technilab** (0 1917 8057, 0 2636 4989).

Foto File

1st floor, MBK Centre, Thanon Phyathai, Pathumwan (0 2217 9426/www.fotofile.net). National Stadium BTS. **Open** 10.30am-8.30pm daily. **Credit** MC, V. **Map** p249 & p250 F5.
A large stock of popular SLRs and lenses, new and used, makes this a favourite among enthusiasts.

Inspired, Asian-chic decor from **Panta**. *See p151.*

Eat, Drink, Shop

And it stocks high-end and monochrome films not found at 7-Eleven. Associate shop SP Camera deals only in new photographic equipment.
Other locations: SP Camera, 4th floor, MBK, Pathumwan (0 2611 8062).

IQ Lab
ITF Building, 160/5 Thanon Silom, entrance off Thanon Narathiwat Ratchanakharin, Bangrak (0 2266 4080/www.iqlab.co.th). Chong Nonsi BTS. **Open** 8.30am-6pm Mon-Fri; 8.30am-1pm Sat.
Credit AmEx, MC, V. **Map** p250 F7.
The only Thai lab trusted by professionals for processing, retouching and outputting in all formats, colour or black and white.
Other locations: 9/32-34 Sukhumvit Soi 63, Sukhumvit (0 2714 0644).

Shipping

Though widely on sale, antique treasures (and even reproduction Buddha images) are prohibited from export without a licence from the government's Fine Arts Department, handled by the **Office of Archaeology** (81/1 Thanon Si Ayutthaya, Dusit, 0 2628 5033/5021 ext 306). Most shops and antiques dealers offer to arrange shipping.

Bangkok Shipping Agency
3rd floor, TSC Building, Ocean Tower 1, 170/7 Thanon New Rajadapisek, Sukhumvit (0 2261 3154-63). Queen Sirikit National Convention Centre subway. **Open** 8.30am-5pm Mon-Fri. **No credit cards. Map** p251 J6.
With its network of shippers and four decades of service, BSA has the resources for customs clearing and freight forwarding, covering both air and sea cargo.

Shoes

Footwork
2nd floor, Emporium, Sukhumvit Soi 24, Sukhumvit (0 2664 8375). Phrom Phong BTS. **Open** 10.30am-9pm Mon-Fri; 10am-9pm Sat, Sun. **Credit** AmEx, DC, MC, V. **Map** p252 K66.
Consistently stylish imports from Europe and South America mean Footwork's new shoe deliveries are highly anticipated by both women and men.
Other locations: 2nd floor, Central World Plaza, Pathumwan (0 2255 9547); 1st floor, Siam Centre, Pathumwan (0 2255 3926).

Ragazze
2nd floor, Silom Complex, Thanon Silom, Bangrak (0 2231 3190/www.ragazze.co.th). Saladaeng BTS/Silom subway. **Open** 11am-8pm daily.
Credit AmEx, DC, MC, V. **Map** p250 E7.
Employing both leather and lighter materials, this Italian-influenced Thai company's bags, footwear and wallets remain up-to-the-minute stylish.
Other locations: 3rd floor, Isetan, Central World Plaza, Pathumwan (0 2255 9898-9 ext 3305); 3rd floor, MBK, Pathumwan (0 2217 9364).

Tango
2nd floor, Gaysorn, Thanon Ploenchit, Pathumwan (0 2656 1047). Chidlom BTS. **Open** 10.30am-8pm daily. **Credit** AmEx, DC, MC, V. **Map** p251 H5.
Women's shoes and handbags with playful designs are Tango's signature line, but the trait is happily extending to its skirts and blouses.
Other locations: in most downtown malls.

Sport & outdoor

No-frills sport shops flank the National Stadium Pathumwan (*see p200*) and Super Sport has branches in department stores. For bling bling trainers, **MBK** and **Siam Centre** (for both, *see p152*) score highly.

Pro Cam-Fis
3rd floor, Emporium, Sukhumvit Soi 24, Sukhumvit (0 2664 8811-2/www.procam-fis.com.hk). Phrom Phong BTS. **Open** 10.30am-10pm daily. **Credit** AmEx, DC, MC, V. **Map** p252 K6.
In case you were wondering, 'Cam-Fis' stands for camping and fishing, you're supposed to provide the 'Pro' part of the title. And shopping here just might enable you to do that. The shop attracts lots of outdoors types hunting for a Maglite torch, a Swiss army knife or camouflage.
Other locations: 4th floor, Central Chidlom, Ploenchit Road, Pathumwan (0 2655 7777).

Star Soccer
3rd floor, Siam Discovery, Thanon Rama I, Pathumwan (0 2658 0375-6). Siam BTS. **Open** 10am-9pm daily. **Credit** AmEx, DC, MC, V. **Map** p249 & p250 F4.
Thai football addicts get their balls, kits and memorabilia from global and local clubs at this chain.
Other locations: 2nd floor, Pantip Plaza, Thanon Phetburi, North (0 2251 9670).

Thaniya Plaza
52 Thanon Thaniya, Bangrak (0 2231 2244/ www.thaniyagroup.com). Saladaeng BTS/Silom subway. **Open** 10am-10pm daily. **Map** p250 F7.
More than 30 golf shops make this mall a must for Tiger wannabes. They cater mainly to Japanese, hence the many Nipponese brands, often at discounts.

Travel Mart
3rd floor, MBK, Image Zone, Thanon Rama I, Pathumwan (0 2620 9734 ext 740/www.e-travel mart.com). National Stadium BTS. **Open** 11am-8pm daily. **Credit** AmEx, DC, V. **Map** p249 & p250 F4.
A well-stocked shop-cum-authority on camping and adventure gear, with obscure spare parts aplenty. Goggle strap retainer, anyone?

Toys

Most malls have activity areas and children's shops with international brands, local Learning Curve educational toys for 0-12s, or Plan Toys' imaginative wooden games.

Arts & Entertainment

Features

Festivals & Events

Thais find any reason to celebrate – any time, any season.

Chinese New Year.
See p159.

Particularly well stocked with holidays and festivals, Bangkok's calendar celebrates New Year five times, officially on the Western and Thai reckonings (*see p158* **Making a splash**), but also among Chinese, Indian and Mon communities. Thais also merrily celebrate foreign festivals such as Valentine's Day, Halloween and Christmas, as well as an increasingly cosmopolitan roster of cultural events.

Religious and royal holidays remain occasions for reverence. At the most important Buddhist anniversaries – **Makha Bucha**, **Visakha Bucha** and **Asanha Bucha** – devotees circle a temple *bot* three times clockwise at night, while bearing a lotus, incense and a lit candle, to symbolise the cycle of life. This is most impressive at Wat Benchamabophit, Wat Sakhet, Wat Suthat and Wat Bovornivet. No alcohol is sold on those days, and bars are often shut.

Regular, year-round events include monks' alms rounds, which happen daily at sunrise, and residents make morning offerings to spirit houses. Devotional rituals, including dances, happen constantly at **Erawan Shrine** (*see p95*)

and **Lak Muang** (*see p61*), as well as in periodic temple fairs (*see p160* **Wat to do?**).

It's wise to check listings through magazines, newspapers, the internet, venue staff and tourist offices (*see p235*), since information given in advance is often incomplete or changes at the last minute. For dates of public holidays and explanations of the seasons, *see p236*.

Cool season

Navaratree Hindu Festival
Maha Uma Devi (Wat Khaek), 2 Thanon Pan, Bangrak (0 2238 4007). Surasak BTS. **Date** Oct.
For the temple's annual festival, Thanon Silom, between Khlong Chong Nonsi and Soi 19, is pedestrianised for devotees in their thousands to worship Hindu shrines set up in the road. Fevered rites, blessings, spirit-channelling and parades of men pierced in acts of self-mortification culminate in massed smashing of coconuts on petal-patterned sidewalks. Wear white.

Royal Barge Procession
Chao Phraya river between Tha Wasukri & Wat Arun. **Date** Oct/Nov 2006 (call TAT to check; *see p235*).

This rare, unforgettable spectacle will likely occur next on the king's diamond jubilee in 2006, probably as a Kathin robe-giving rite. *See also p77* Royal Barge Museum.

Fat Festival

104.5 FM Fat radio station (0 2641 5234 ext 303-4/ www.thisisclick.com). **Date** 1st wkend in Nov.
Run by Fat Radio, this indie gathering has grown from a minority passion to a mass movement embracing punks and J-Pop chicks, hip hop dudes and speed metal freaks. Tens of thousands of such *dek naew* (trend kids) flock to a different venue each year to cheer 200 bands and DJs, and browse stalls of alt music, film, art and handmade books.

Bangkok Theatre Festival

Santichaiprakan Park, Thanon Phra Arthit, Banglamphu (www.lakorn.org). **Date** early-mid Nov.
Myriad kinds of performance overlap fair-like around the park and art bars along Phra Arthit. Taking place over about three weekends, it gains new audiences for both modern and traditional dance and drama. Charming and mostly accessible to non-Thais.

Elle Bangkok Fashion Week

Central Chitlom car park tent, Thanon Phloen Chit, Pathumwan (Elle magazine 0 2240 3700 ext 1703). Chitlom BTS. **Map** p251 H5. **Date** early Nov.
Since 1999 *Elle* has showcased Thai designers with such a buzz that sponsor Central holds another catwalk event here in March. Public seating is available but it's easier to obtain at runway shows on the final two public days at the Bangkok International Fashion Fair (0 2511 6020-30 ext 317, www.thaitradefair.com) in mid January.

Bangkok Pride Festival

Thanon Silom, Bangrak (www.bangkokpride.org). Saladaeng BTS/Silom subway. **Map** p250 F6. **Date** mid Nov.
Bangkok's gay days number 365 a year, but that's not stopped two charity gay festivals. Bangkok Pride is the larger, with a Siamese-style dress code to restrain Mardi Gras excesses. The Pride week of cabarets, parties, costume shows, plays and sporting contests opens with the 'Pink in the Park' fair in Lumphini Park, and concludes with a late afternoon parade in a loop from and to Silom Soi 4. Pride takes in the Utopia Awards for Asia's gay lib pioneers (www.utopia-asia.com). Pakorn Pimton, founder of the original Bangkok Gay Festival (0 1655 6920, www.bangkokgayfestival.com), still holds a small parade in late November.

Loy Krathong

Waterways nationwide (Bangkok Tourist Bureau 0 2225 7612-5). **Date** full moon of the 12th lunar month (Nov).
In this picturesque animistic rite, Thais make offerings to water spirits while cleansing sins and bad luck. The Brahman-inspired offering is a *krathong*, a delicate, candlelit float made from a banana trunk (avoid styrofoam ones), decorated with leaves, incense, flowers and other tributes. The Siamese love of finery emerges in contests for the most beautiful *krathongs* and a Miss Nopamas contest, named after the *krathong*'s ancient Sukhothai inventor. The event is most splendid in Sukhothai, but crowds flock to waterways in Bangkok, including the Chao Phraya river, Khlong Lord and ponds in the city parks and Chulalongkorn University.

Ploenchit Fair

Royal Plaza, Dusit (Carolyn Tarrant 0 2204 1587/www.bccthai.com). **Tickets** B100; B20 concessions. **No credit cards**. **Map** p249 D1. **Date** 3rd Sat in Nov.
Expat charity events don't get any bigger than this day of funfair rides, boozing and entertainment. An institution since the 1950s, Ploenchit Fair started at the British Embassy but has shifted location several times in the past few years.

Bangkok Fringe Festival

Patravadi Theatre, Thanon Arun Amarin, Thonburi (0 2412 7287-8/www.patravaditheatre. com). **Tickets** Concert B500. Open day free. **Map** p248 A3. **Date** usually Nov-Jan.
Since 1999 this centrepiece of the performing arts calendar has presented dance, drama and music of East and West, in traditional and modern forms, as well as myriad fusions. The weekend evening shows are mostly intelligible to non-Thai speakers.

Bangkok Marathon

National Jogging Association 0 2628 8361/ www.bangkokmarathon.org. **Date** last Sun in Nov, from 3.30am.
Launched in 1987, the annual full, half and mini-marathons through the old town start and finish at the Ministry of Defence, opposite the Grand Palace.

Asiatopia

Chumpon Apisuk 0 2526 8311. **Date** late Nov.
Participants from all over Asia and the West make this annual gathering for performance art, usually held in a park, the largest of its kind in the region, where it's still an emergent genre.

Trooping of the Colour

Royal Plaza, Dusit (Foundation of King Rama IX the Great 0 2356 0202-3/www.belovedking.com). **Map** p249 D1. **Date** 2 Dec.
At this grand, colourful ceremony, the Royal Guards swear loyalty to His Majesty and march past the royal family in plumed dress uniforms of brilliant hues.

King's Birthday Celebrations

Nationwide. **Date** 5 Dec.
The Thais' deep reverence for their king is displayed everywhere on what is also Father's Day (and a national holiday). Lights and decorations stretch from the Grand Palace along Ratchadamnoen Avenue via the Royal Plaza to Chitrlada Palace. In the morning His Majesty addresses massed representatives of the nation

Making a splash

Thailand's biggest holiday is the Thai lunar New Year, **Songkran**, now fixed at 13-15 April. A Sanskrit term for the sun entering Taurus (the year's hottest time), Songkran evolved from Indian powder-throwing into gentle rituals of reverence and purification, such as sprinkling monks and Buddha images with lustral water to win merit, similar gestures of respect to elders, making sand *chedi* in temples, and a big annual house-cleaning session.

Rites to honour the Phra Buddha Sihing image at Sanam Luang and to crown Miss Songkran at Wisut Kasat contrast with the aquatic warfare that also marks the event. In a mass catharsis of breakneck modernisation, youngsters grab water pistols, buckets and hoses for giddy attacks on pedestrians and each other, day and night. Revellers pack pick-up trucks with barrels of water, sometimes iced or dyed, and mixed with talc, it's plastered on to hapless faces. Officials try (and fail) to limit this to peak areas like **Patpong** (*see p91*) and **Thanon Khao San** (*see p70*), where entertainments are staged. The fun is contagious – but wear nothing precious and pack electronics and wallets in plastic.

Much of Bangkok heads upcountry for up to a week. Though city traffic becomes delightfully light, the jams in and out are horrendous, with appalling road casualties: over 500 dead and 34,000 injured in just six days. The festival's spiritual home is Chiang Mai, where rooms must be booked ahead, though there's always a second chance in Thailand: Songkran can last ten days in the north and the Mon people celebrate New Year a week later, notably in Phra Padaeng, just south of Bangkok, on 20-22 April (call 0 2463 7800 for details). Expect parades (*pictured below*), rites (including courting rituals) and the requisite dousings.

from the Ananta Samakhom Throne Hall, then countless thousands of people assemble on Sanam Luang in the early evening to light candles and sing the 'Praise the King' song, joined kingdomwide by millions of Thais pausing activity, and celebrating in community fairs and in rites at grandly illuminated buildings. After some magnificent fireworks, huge stages at Sanam Luang erupt with star performers in *luuk thuung*, *morlam* and T-Pop music, *lakhon* and *likay*. Crowds filter down fairylit Ratchadamnoen to take millions of photographs.

Miss AC/DC Pageant

0 2662 0164/www.missacdc.com. **Date** 1st or 2nd wkend of Dec.

In an uproarious, five-hour spoof of Miss Universe, drag queens 'represent' some 70 countries. They compete in 'national costumes', swimwear, evening gowns, talents (from opera to fire-juggling) and even philosophical questions (no kidding). The venue varies. Winners of the more mainstream ladyboy pageant in March, Miss Tiffany in Pattaya, enter America's Miss Queen of the Universe (and won in 1999, 2000 and 2002). The media ponders who's the prettier: Miss Tiffany or Miss Thailand, with one woman crowned a week earlier.

Hua Hin Vintage Car Parade

Sofitel Central Hua Hin Resort, 1 Thanon Damnern Kasem, Hua Hin (0 2541 1125/www.centralhotels resorts.com). **Date** mid Dec.

Emulating England's London-to-Brighton Rally, this concourse of old-time vehicles trundles from the capital to the royal seaside town of Hua Hin (*see pp208-222*).

Music in the Park

Parks throughout Bangkok (Bangkok Symphony Orchestra 0 2255 6617-8/www.bangkoksymphony. org). **Date** every Sun mid Dec-mid Feb.

Free open-air concerts in city greenswards, from nostalgic Thai melodies and folk songs to country, pop, light classics and show tunes. Picnicking listeners can forage at various stalls.

New Year Celebrations

Nationwide. **Date** 31 Dec.

Thai rites to mark the international New Year vary from the serenely sacred to the exuberantly secular. There are merit-making ceremonies at temples, gala dinners at hotels, parties in nightclubs and bars, and fireworks at Sanam Luang and the hotels along the river. Traffic is closed for a mass countdown between Siam Square, Central World Plaza and Silom, but mass transit runs all night.

National Children's Day
Across Bangkok. **Date** 8.30am-4.30pm 2nd Sat in Jan.
Doors usually closed to the public are opened today, including the inner Grand Palace, Defence Ministry and Government House. Zoos, theme parks and many other sights are free, as are tank rides as the Thai army, navy and air force allow civilian inspections. There's also a fair at Somdet Phra Srinagarindra Boromarajajonani Memorial Park.

Thanon Sai Mai Fair
Soi Prachanarumit (Pracha Rat Soi 24), North (Bang Sue District Office 0 2586 9978). **Date** last wkend in Jan.
Whittle did you know: this crafts fair has carved out its own niche in local wood products and furniture, most of it made from teak. The street dresses up in festival arches, music and munchables.

Chinese New Year Festival
Chinatown (Samphanthawong District Office 0 2234 3460). **Map** p249 & p250. **Date** late Jan/late Feb.
Thai-Chinese roots spring out during lunar New Year, when lion and dragon dances, firecrackers, Chinese opera and redoubled convoys of interesting food carts take over Chinatown's Yaowarat and Charoen Krung roads. Many businesses close for this unofficial holiday, and the traffic is super light.

Makha Bucha
Temples nationwide. **Date** full moon of 3rd lunar month (late Feb/early Mar).
On this national holiday Thais head for temples at dusk to mark the occasion when the star Makha burned at its brightest, and 1,250 disciples gathered to hear Buddha's last major sermon before Nirvana.

Hot season

Bangkok International Film Festival
Downtown cinemas (0 2250 5500 ext 1750-3/ www.bangkokfilm.org). **Date** 10 days in Feb.
The Tourist Authority of Thailand runs this massive festival, spanning the mainstream, top contributions from diverse countries and a major regional contingent. A growing film mart, seminars and appearances by major stars lend credibility. Seating is reserved via Ticketmaster, at theatres and online. For more on film festivals, *see p165*.

Tattoo Festival
Wat Bang Phra, Nakhon Chaisri-Bang Phra, Nakhon Chaisri (0 3438 9333-96). **Date** mid March.
Well over 1,000 devotees of the late abbot of this temple, located just over an hour's drive west of Downtown, gather at this annual rite. Some get more magical tattoos, others have their tattoos' spells topped up and many become entranced by the spirits depicted on their bodies (tigers, snakes, birds,

hermits, monkeys and so on) in an early morning ceremony of scary, even violent, possession.

Traditional Thai Games & Sports Festival
Sanam Luang, Phra Nakorn (Thai Sports Association 0 2448 2907). **Map** p248 B3.
Date Mar-early Apr.
There's more to Siamese sports than *Muay Thai* (kick boxing): fighting kites, *krabi-krabong* swordsmanship, Thai chess (with martial artists enacting moves on a huge board), and *takraw lod buang*, an ancestor of *sepak takraw* in which players punt a rattan ball through a suspended hoop. The Thailand International Kite Festival is now held every two years (next in March 2006), in Hua Hin.

Bangkok Fashion Week
11th floor, SM Tower, 979 Thanon Pahonyothin (0 2298 0314-9/www.bangkokfashioncity.com).
Date mid Mar.
Angel City has designs on becoming a fashion hub. The government's Bangkok Fashion City project (*see p146*) involves 11 schemes, including a mid March splurge of catwalk shows, exhibitions, designer showcases and after-parties for in-the-know fashionistas.

Bangkok International Motor Show
Grand Prix International 0 2522 1731-8/www.grand prixgroup.com. **Date** late Mar-early Apr.
Revving up Thailand's rising status as the 'Detroit of the East', this week-long show draws millions to salivate over dream cars, concept cars, motorcycles and a Miss Motor Show pageant. It's held at either the BITEC or IMPACT exhibition centre (*see p100*).

Chakri Day
Public holiday. **Date** 6 Apr.
Three royal ceremonies on this public holiday mark the 1782 founding of Thailand's current Chakri dynasty. The king and his entourage first pay respects to the Emerald Buddha in Wat Phra Kaew, followed by rites in the neighbouring royal pantheon honouring all nine Chakri kings. Finally, the king lights candles at the Rama I statue by Memorial Bridge.

Naris Day
Baan Plainoen, Thanon Rama IV, 1st soi east of the expressway, South (Naris Foundation 0 2249 4280). Khlong Toei subway. **Tickets** *Concert* B500. *Open day free.* **No credit cards. Map** p251 J7. **Date** *Concert* 4-9pm 28 Apr, 2 May. *Open day* 9am-5pm 29 Apr
Descendants of King Rama V's brother Prince Naris, a polymath revered for his arts legacy, commemorate his birth in 1863 by opening up his traditional house. Look around the exhibitions in between the classical Thai dance and music on 28 April, or all day on 29 April. Other events are held at Silpakorn University, the art school Naris helped found.

Miss Jumbo Queen
Samphran Elephant Ground, km30 Thanon Phetkasem, Nakhon Pathom (0 2429 0361-2/Jumbo Queen 02295 2938-9/www.elephantshow.com).

Wat to do?

The template for many Thai festivals is the *ngan wat,* the temple fair. Temple compounds historically held secular activities, from education and medicine to martial arts, but they also hosted village merriment, touring performers and, since their mid 20th-century boom, roving film projections. Festivals served as an important pressure valve for relaxing social strictures, and *ngan wat* unabashedly came to witness much irreverence, flirting and larking about.

With increasing modern diversions from religion, *ngan wat* have evolved into huge, elaborate occasions, partly as a way of bringing people back into the *wat.* Though festivals or rites are the pretext, and parades the showpiece event, raising funds is imperative, so many *ngan wat* have gone commercial, earning income from myriad stalls, rides and sideshows, plus singing contests and speciality foods.

Temple fairs are also the best places to experience Thai popular culture. Rival stages blare *likay* (*see p184*) or *talok* (comedy; *see p198*), *luuk thung* folk tunes (*see p184*) or the latest T-Pop diva. On the margins, punters place illegal bets on cockfights, boxing, lotteries or gaming. Drink – often moonshine – plays lubricant, not least for any spirit mediums dispensing fortunes.

Many fairs stage beauty pageants, a serious pursuit in image-conscious Thailand, where a runner-up once snatched the winner's crown live on TV. Some national contestants honed their perma-smiles and perma-hair at provincial fruit fairs, such as Miss Lychee or Miss Rambutan.

As *ngan wat* are informal and free, they're open to all. Held on each *wat*'s annual day – and at one or two temples in any given area at festive times – *ngan wat* rarely get media listings, so serendipitously look for the festive lights and signs. Alternatively, try these three famed Bangkok fairs.

Golden Mount Temple Fair
Wat Saket, 344 Thanon Chakkraphatdiphong, Phra Nakorn (0 2621 0576). Tha Saphan Phan Fah. **Date** Nov; either side of Loy Krathong (*see p157*). **Map** p248 C3.

Wat Hualumphong Temple Fair
728 Thanon Rama IV, Sri Phraya, Prathumwan (0 2222 5396). Siphraya subway. **Date** mid Jan/late Feb. **Map** p250 F6.

Wat Phlubphlachai Temple Fair
5 Thanon Mitreechitr, Chinatown (0 2222 5396). **Date** mid Jan/late Feb. **Map** p250 D4.

Tickets *Foreigners* B400; under 120cm B250. *Thais* B80; under 120cm B40. **Date** 9am-5pm 1 May. Women over 80kg (176lb) must display the grace of an elephant (a compliment) through an interview, a talent routine and a weigh-in. Fun but not condescending, the event is as serious about empowering big females as highlighting the plight of pachyderms. For more on the latter, *see p24* **Tusk force**.

Demonic
Thailand Cultural Centre amphitheatre, Thanon Thiem Ruam Mit, North (0 2247 0028/Lakfa Sarasakul 0 1750 0591). Thailand Cultural Centre subway. **Date** 1st Sat in May (biennial).

A biennial bout of death metal, hardcore and other underground music, performed by local bands. Venue may alter. The next is in 2006.

Rainy season

Royal Ploughing Ceremony
Sanam Luang, Phra Nakorn (information Department of Agricultural Extension 0 2579 0121-7 ext 130/www.moac.go.th). **Map** p249 & p250 D4. **Date** early May.

These Brahman rites to forecast the year's rainfall and harvest are the official launch of the rice-planting season. A day of Buddhist chanting and the king's blessing of rice seeds is followed on day two by a costumed procession of drummers, Brahmin priests and maidens. A ritual field is ploughed by sacred white oxen, and sown with the blessed rice. Farmers from all over Thailand then rush in to gather the lucky seeds for planting.

Visakha Bucha
Nationwide. **Date** full moon of 6th lunar month (late May/early June).
Buddhism's holiest date, when Lord Buddha was born, enlightened and died. Devotees make merit by bringing food to monks in the morning. In the evening, temples hold sermons and candlelit processions. It's also a public holiday, and most bars and businesses are closed.

Fête de la Musique
Alliance Française 0 2670 4231/www.alliance-francaise.or.th. **Map** p251 G7. **Date** 3rd Sat in June.
Run simultaneously around the globe, this Franco-backed festival spans multicultural sounds from jazz and pop to classical and ethnic, including Thai collaborations. See website for venues.

Asanha Bucha & Khao Phansa
Nationwide. **Date** full moon of 8th lunar month (late July/early Aug) & following day.
The anniversary of the Buddha's first sermon after attaining enlightenment is observed with temple rituals. Next day is Khao Phansa (the start of the rainy season), when monks begin 'Buddhist Lent': three months of meditation and prayer while confined within their temples. Some Thai youths still become a novice for this period, a step to Thai manhood that earns their parents karmic merit.

HM The Queen's Birthday
Nationwide. **Date** 12 Aug.
Heralding this royal anniversary, which is also Mother's Day, many thousand points of light decorate Thanon Ratchadamnoen and other venues. A glittering spectacle.

Short Film & Video Festival
Khun Chalida 0 1615 5137/www.thaifilm.com. **Date** mid Aug.
Indie films shine in various venues at this free festival, which is getting more international.

Chinese Mid-Autumn Festival
Nationwide. **Date** full moon of 10th lunar month (late Sept).
Tiers of tasty mooncakes in restaurants, hotels and bakeries around the country herald this ethnic Chinese festival. In 14th-century China, mooncakes conveyed messages among Han Chinese plotting to overthrow the Mongols. Traditionally eaten only after being offered on an altar to the goddess of mercy Guan Im, the cakes – some stuffed with pungent durian fruit paste – are now taken posthaste with tea. The Chinatown Food Festival, held at the same time as the Mid-Autumn Festival, takes over Thanon Yaowarat with hundreds of stalls.

World Gourmet Festival
Four Seasons Hotel, 155 Thanon Ratchadamri, Pathumwan (0 2251 6127). Ratchadamri BTS. **Map** p251 G5. **Date** mid Sept.
Since 1999 this premium event has raised Bangkok's reputation as a hub for fine dining from around the globe, which is luckily available at half the Western prices. For ten days, leading foreign chefs prepare to-die-for meals, along with cookery classes, demonstrations and wine tastings.

International Festival of Music & Dance
0 2661 6830-4/www.bangkokfestivals.com. **Date** mid Sept-early Oct.
Bangkok's biggest annual arts festival stages world-class performances at Thai middle-class prices. The focus is on opera, ballet and orchestral music, often by Eastern European companies, with leading jazz, world music and dance from elsewhere, plus some Thai acts. The festival is held at Thailand Cultural Centre (*see p97*), but Siam Opera (*see p196*) is a potential future venue.

Vertical Marathon
Banyan Tree Bangkok Hotel, Thai Wah Tower II, 21/100 Thanon Sathorn Tai, South (0 2679 1200). **Map** p251 G7. **Date** mid Sept.
There's little challenge in jogging across this super-horizontal city, so why not go up instead? Some 500 contestants pay to sprint up more than 1,000 steps to the top of this 61-storey tower for charity. Onlookers get to enjoy the food.

Vegetarian Festival
Across Bangkok. **Date** early/mid Oct.
Food stalls and restaurants go veggie (look out for yellow pennants) for this ten-day Chinese Buddhist-Taoist period of purging meat and heating foods, though self-mortification is done only by white-clad devotees down south. Chinatown explodes with colour, incense, temple offerings and the strains of Chinese opera, notably in Charoen Krung Soi 20.

World Film Festival of Bangkok
Downtown cinemas (Kriengsak Silakong 0 9026 3232/0 2325 5555 ext 3447/8/www.worldfilm bkk.com). **Date** mid Oct.
Run by the *Nation* newspaper, this cinefest of around 150 movies focuses on independent auteurship, Asian films and specific themes. For more on film festivals, *see p165*.

Ok Phansa
Nationwide. **Date** full moon of 11th lunar month (Oct).
The rainy season officially ends on this public holiday, and with it the three months of Buddhist Lent, with *wat* rituals and the shaving of monks' scalps and eyebrows.

Arts & Entertainment

Children

How to keep kids happy in the land of smiles.

Thais universally adore and coddle children – to the extent that adults will even give up seats on buses for youngsters and pet them at any opportunity (which can irritate small visitors with novelty blonde hair). Yet it's equally common to see infants perched on the tank of a mother's motorbike with a toddler clinging to her back or, indeed, a ten year old driving a motorbike with no protection at all.

This dichotomy stems from technological development having sped ahead of welfare and education, and a disregard for safety reinforced by faith in karma. So exercise caution with cheap toys or electrical appliances and when walking hazardous streets, especially with a buggy (use baby slings instead). Still, there are many fun family activities in Bangkok. Support group **BAMBI** is a useful resource.

LABOURING UNDER PRECONCEPTIONS

There's much hand-wringing about child labour in Thailand. Though exploitative or dangerous employment is far rarer than in neighbouring countries, children helping the family business are integral to farming, crafts and shophouse trades. Despite the drawbacks, many claim that life lessons in discipline, perseverance, apprenticeship, sharing and social obligation make for an unselfish respect for traditions and elders.

To ensure the continuance of traditional values the state has policies against under-age drinking and internet gaming, enforces drug testing at schools and has even proposed a 10pm teen curfew. But unconventional youth may be an unavoidable effect of efforts to steer education away from rote learning towards inquisitive thinking. Meanwhile, insufficient attention is paid to what a child needs, and not just those poor pre-teens selling garlands at traffic lights so that their family can eat. Rich kids suffer too. Overindulged by nannies, servants and short-sighted parents, numerous ten year olds haven't learned to tie their own shoelaces, while some don't know how to cross a road safely at 14, because they've been driven everywhere. Child obesity has also increased.

Attractions

Sure-fire hits with kids include boat tours (*see p56*) and **Dusit Zoo** (*see p80*), while distant attractions aimed at families may be conveniently paired to make day trips. For example, visit **Rose Garden** with **Samphran Elephant Ground** (for both, *see p102*); **Safari World** with **Siam Park** (for both, *see p100*); or **Technopolis Science Museum** with **Dream World** (*see p100*). Hotels can book these excursions.

The **Central World Plaza** (*see p151*) has a Knowledge Park with activities for children, many in Thai. This mall also has karaoke booths, as do the **MBK** shopping mall (*see p152*) and **Siam Square**, both geared to teens. Active kids may enjoy skating or trick-biking at **Red Bull X-Park** (*see p201*). Parks offer playgrounds, while most malls and department stores have play and computer game areas, rides and children's shops – notably, **Central Chidlom** (*see p141*), **Emporium** (*see p151*), **Siam Discovery Centre** (*see p152*) and **Central World Plaza** (*see p151*).

There are family events in August around the **Queen's Birthday** (Thai Mother's Day; *see p161*) and on **National Children's Day** (second Sat in Jan; *see p159*), when restricted landmarks are open.

Bangkok Dolls

85 Soi Mor Leng, Thanon Ratchaprarop, North (0 2245 3008). **Open** 8am-5pm Mon-Sat. **Admission** free. **Credit** V.
This small doll museum and cottage industry has been hidden away in its modest location since the 1950s. Its bright displays of ornate costumes and traditional scenes (the *Ramayana*, monks, ethnic groups, stilt houses) have a homespun charm, even if you're not passionate about miniatures. Most of the dolls were made here in an intriguing process you can watch, with some on sale for B400-B5,000.

Children's Discovery Museum

Thanon Kamphaengphet 4, Chatuchak, North (0 2615 7333/www.bkkchildrenmuseum.com). Morchit BTS/Chatuchak Park subway. **Open** 9am-5pm Tue-Fri; 10am-6pm Sat, Sun. **Admission** *Thais* B70, B50 under-15s. *Foreigners* B150, B120 under-15s. **No credit cards**.
A house of fun with hands-on exhibits galore, including a percussion music room and a TV/music studio where the young can star in their own movie or newsroom. Or they can visit the animal section, domain of tropical fish, parrots, snakes, reptiles and small fluffy mammals. Bring ear plugs on weekdays, when school parties beef up the decibel

levels. Up the road, pleasant Chatuchak Park has a playground, jungle gym and a railway museum.

Planetarium

928 Thanon Sukhumvit, Sukhumvit (0 2392 5951-5). Ekamai BTS. **Open** 9am-4.30pm Tue-Sun. **Admission** B20; B10 children; explanation in English B300 (by group appointment). **No credit cards. Map** p252 M7.

This stargazing centre (aimed mainly at Thais) features projections on its 13m-high (43ft) dome. The attached science museum does little to stimulate interest, with walls of text and no interactivity.

Technopolis Science Museum

Techno Thani, Thanon Rangsit-Nakhon Nayok, Klong 5, Klong Luang, Pathum Thani, North-east (0 2577 9999/www.nsm.or.th). **Open** 9.30am-5pm Tue-Sun. **Admission** B50, B60 (with Natural History Museum); free children & students. **No credit cards.**

This world-class museum is housed in astonishing steel, glass and fibreglass cubes balanced on their points. It'll take half a day to explore its six floors, the first three of which are best for kids. English-speaking assistants explain the interactive exhibitions.

Babysitting & childcare

Because expatriates and wealthy Thais with maids or extended families don't use babysitting agencies, and playgroups are for members only, childminders are scarce, so consult **BAMBI**. Most major hotels offer childminding services for B200-B300/hour, plus B100-B200 per hour per extra child, as noted in **Where to Stay** (*see pp37-51*).

BAMBI (Bangkok Mothers & Babies International)

www.bambi-bangkok.org.

A not-for-profit group offering help and information to pregnant women and parents of young children, from education to entertainment and healthcare. The website lists weekly playgroups and monthly meetings with activities (free, but donations appreciated).

Where to stay & eat

While many hotel towers focus on business or designer service, the more spacious ones score family points, such as the **Sukhothai**, **Pathumwan Princess**, group tour hotels and river hotels, especially the **Marriott Bangkok Resort** and **Shangri-la**. Many families prefer short-stay serviced apartments for their kitchenettes, mini-suites and residential informality. For all hotel reviews, *see pp37-51* **Where to Stay**).

Nearly all restaurants welcome kids and the staff are invariably doting. In addition, Thai dining can be great fun, with shared dishes and hands-on grub such as wrap-in-a-leaf *miang* or

Central World Plaza. *See p151.*

cook-at-your-table *suki* (try the **Coca** and **MK** suki chains in any mall). Chain restaurants have family facilities, but why not try eating on cushions at a dance show or aboard a boat? Vendors sell Thai popsicles from metal tubes, scoop ice-cream into bread rolls and slather crushed ice desserts with multicoloured jellies, though some distrust ice at streetstalls. Or watch Thai desserts being made at **Old Siam Plaza** (*see p87*). Many hotels' Sunday brunches offer kids' clubs with clowns, magic and playrooms, including the **Marriott Bangkok Resort** (11.30am-2pm Sun, B999, B500 4-12s) and **Shangri-la** (11.30am-2.30pm Sun; B950, B475 6-12s, free under-6s).

Film

Luxury cinemas, festivals and Cannes acclaim boost celluloid Siam.

Thailand is not only enjoying something of a filmmaking renaissance, with the results attracting increasing international interest, but there are also more and better cinemas and festivals in which to see the fruits. However, current output is only a fraction of that during the 1950s, '60s and '70s boom, with their Burton-Tayloresque romances between Mitr Chaibancha and Petchara Shaowarat, as well as Thai monsters battling in a local version of Ultraman (whose revival is being challenged by the superhero's Japanese originator). Encouragingly, this upswing is due to well-made dramas proving more popular than the teen melodramas that had by the mid '90s become marketing vehicles for their singer/model/MC stars.

The renaissance was triggered by Nonzee Nimibutr's retro 1950s hoodlum hit *Dang Bireley's and the Young Gangsters* (1997). Nonzee broke his own box office record in 1999 with a sumptuous remake of the perennial Thai ghost story *Nang Nak*. These and *Iron Ladies* – a biopic by Yongyuth Thongkongkun about ladyboys in Thailand's volleyball team – got general releases abroad.

Then, in 2002, *Suriyothai* by MR Chatri Chalerm Yukol (aka Than Mui) – the aristocrat who helmed the harrowing drug drama *Sia Dai* – surpassed all previous Thai movie budgets with its story of an Ayutthayan princess sacrificing her life in resistance to Burma. Costing B400-600 million, *Suriyothai* still turned in a profit through dutiful national film-going, though an edit by Francis Ford Coppola failed to gain foreign appreciation. A stream of Burma-bashing yarns followed, such as Thanit Jitnukul's impressive gore-fest *Bangrajan* and Than Mui's upcoming epic *Naresuan* (*see p19* **Historical flashbacks**).

Suriyothai set new local standards in ambition, logistics and marketing. But Thai films can lose impact as a result of conventions about deference, non-demonstrativeness and appearance, punctuated by mannered outbursts and slapstick humour – elements that aren't to all tastes. A new crop of indie directors, however, has started to make films with a more global appeal (*see p165* **Topical malady**).

Diverse scenery and technical expertise have made Thailand a popular Hollywood location since *The Man with the Golden Gun* was filmed here in 1974. Thailand often stands in for other countries, like Vietnam, Cambodia and Hong Kong, but, most famously, it staged that dissection of Thai tourism myths, *The Beach*.

SCREENS AND VASELINE

The main obstacle to expression, though, remains censorship. Vaseline may no longer be applied to explicit images but entire scenes still get excised by the Film Board, which also banned the 1999 movie *Anna and the King* due to cultural sensitivities. But it looks likely that the 1931 Film Act will be replaced by age ratings.

Since 1994 the number of Thai screens has quintupled, with new ones mostly in luxurious multiplexes, boasting plush upholstery, memorabilia displays and even velvet recliners, tables and waitress service. These venues are a big contrast to Thai film's origins in open-air touring projections, which still feature at community fairs, even in Bangkok.

Screen times are too unreliable for papers to print. So call the cinema chains' recorded messages or surf **www.movieseer.com**. Critic Anchalee Chaiworaporn reviews Thai

Luxurious **EGV** Gold Class. *See p166.*

Topical malady

Before 2000 few Thai movies had English subtitles, simply because Bangkok distributors couldn't imagine a foreign market for Thai films. Then a local flop – Wisit Sasontieng's hand-tinted Siamese cowboy fantasy *Tears of the Black Tiger* (2001) – became an art-house hit in the West. Ever since, the better Thai movies started making more money abroad than at home, from Tony Jaa's actioner *Ong Bak* to *Beautiful Boxer*, Ekachai Uekrongtham's biopic of transsexual pugilist Nong Toom. Wisit's latest – the pop culture homage *Mah Nakorn (Citizen Dog)* looks set to follow.

Domestic box office success eludes many of Thailand's more progressive filmmakers such as Pen-ek Rattanruang (*Fun Bar Karaoke*, *6ixtynin9*, *Mon Rak Transistor*), yet the brilliant maverick now has sufficient leverage to work with Asian stars and lauded cinematographer Christopher Doyle on both 2003's meditative *Life at the End of the Universe* and his forthcoming offbeat thriller *Invisible Waves*.

A role model to indie Thais, the young director Apichartpong Weerasethakul embodies the gulf between official Thai culture and what the postmodern world wants. In 2002 he earned Thailand's first success at Cannes, getting the 'Un Certain Regard' award for *Blissfully Yours*, an experimental love story involving an illegal Burmese immigrant. Then, in 2004, he won the 'Special Jury Prize' for *Sud Pralad* (*Tropical Malady*), a gay romance-cum-tiger-spirit-possession parable. Both controversially featured male nudity. Apichartpong's unprecedented honours were

given minimal recognition by Thai officialdom, distributors and festivals, which also ignored his co-direction of artist Michael Shaowanasai's *The Adventures of Iron Pussy*, a spoof about a transsexual ex-barboy secret agent.

Though the Culture Ministry awarded Pen-ek the inaugural Silpathorn Award for mid-career achievement in 2004, it seems that a paradigm shift would be required before Apichartpong receives such recognition.

Citizen Dog.

releases in English at www.thaicinema.org. After 20 minutes of trailers, films start with the King's Anthem (for which all must stand).

FILM FESTIVALS

Within one decade, Thai festivals have gone from barely one a year to more than one a month. Bangkok's major festivals have a passionate local following, but still lag behind those in Singapore or Korea, partly because of schisms between organisers. The founder of the **Bangkok Film Festival**, American Brian Bennett, lacked the funds to sustain it after splitting with the original sponsor, the *Nation* newspaper. The *Nation* then founded its own **World Film Festival of Bangkok** (mid Oct), featuring over 100 movies. The TAT went from sponsor to organiser, using state muscle and money to promote its

own massive **Bangkok International Film Festival** (Feb). Curated by foreign programmers, it incorporates a film mart and the Golden Kinaree Awards, with international judges.

Foreign cultural bodies pioneered the film festival boom by putting on small film festivals. Germany's **Goethe Institut** has changed from weekly films to an **Open-air Film Festival** (Dec-Feb) in its quiet compound, plus a **Science Film Festival** (mid Nov) consisting of documentaries. Though French films are now seen at the BKIFF, the **Alliance Française** often holds experimental film festivals. The **Short Film and Video Festival** (mid Aug, Chalida, 0 1615 5137, www.thaifilm.com) is a free showcase of up-and-coming talents.

First-run & IMAX cinemas

Cineopolis & IMAX
*Level 5, Siam Paragon, Thanon Rama I,
Pathumwan (0 2658 3000/www.siamparagon.co.th).
Siam BTS.* **Open** approx 11am-midnight. **Tickets**
B120-B500. **Screens** 16. **Credit** AmEx, DC, MC, V.
Map p249 & p250 F4.
A 600-seat IMAX theatre and 1,200-seat Grand
Theatre (complete with boxes and double balcony)
headline at the country's most advanced and luxu-
rious movie centre (and that's saying something).
With impressive lobby and facilities, it is often the
location for festivals, premières and galas.

EGV
*6th floor, Siam Discovery Centre, Thanon Rama I,
Pathumwan (all branches 0 2812 9999/www.egv.
com). Siam BTS.* **Tickets** B120-B500.
Credit AmEx, DC, MC, V. **Map** p249 & p250 F4.
Great seating and sightlines at all screens but
particular highlights are the red velvet recliners with
side-tables and waitress service in the opulent Gold
Class theatres (also found in many of its branches).
EGV runs D-Cine – on-demand digital mini-theatres
– here and at Metropolis.
Other locations: Seacon Square, Thanon
Srinakharin, East; Central Pinklao, Thonburi. **EGV
Metropolis** Big C, Thanon Ratchadamri, Pathumwan.

Krung Thai IMAX Theatre
*Major Cineplex Ratchayothin, Thanon Phahon
Yothin, North (0 2511 5595/www.imaxthai.com).
Phahon Yothin subway.* **Open** 11am-11pm daily.
Tickets B150. **Screens** 1 IMAX; 14 others.
Credit AmEx, DC, MC, V.
Effects films and blockbusters wow audiences
(wearing cordless headsets) at the world's largest
IMAX. It also has good first-run cinemas.

Major Cineplex
*7th floor, Central World Plaza, Thanon
Ratchadamri, Pathumwan (all branches 0 2515
5555/www.majorcineplex.com). Chidlom BTS.*
Tickets B120-B300. **Screens** 6. **Credit** AmEx,
DC, MC, V. **Map** p251 G4.
An impressive multiplex with florid decor, clear
views and superb seats, some for couples.
Other locations: Thanon Phra Pinklao, Thonburi;
Ekamai, Sukhumvit Soi 61, Sukhumvit.

Scala
*Siam Square Soi 1, Pathumwan (0 2251 2861/
www.apexsiam-square.com). Siam BTS.* **Tickets**
B100-B120. **Screens** 1. **No credit cards.**
Map p249 & p250 F4.
No longer hand-painting its posters, Bangkok's last
old-style movie hall screens blockbusters and hosts
events in its stunning art deco foyer. Nearby are the
large but tatty Siam (mainstream) and the poorly
soundproofed Lido (edgier films).
Other locations: Lido Multiplex Thanon Rama I,
Pathumwan (0 2252 6498). **Siam**, Thanon Rama I,
Pathumwan (0 2251 1735).

SFX
*The Emporium, Thanon Sukhumvit, corner of
Soi 24, Sukhumvit (0 2611 7111/all branches
0 2268 8888/www.sfcinemacity.com). Phrom Phong
BTS.* **Tickets** B120, B80 (after 8.30pm) Mon-Wed;
B140 Thur-Sun. **Screens** 5. **Credit** AmEx, MC, V.
Map p252 K6.
The main chain after Major and EGV offers comfy
suede seats, festival screenings and a huge choice of
food. Its branches cost less but aren't quite as plush.
Other locations: SF Cinema City 7th floor, Mah
Boon Krong Centre, Thanon Rama I, Pathumwan
(0 2611 6444). Central Ladprao, Thanon Phahon
Yothin, North (0 2927 2111).

Repertory & art-house

The underfunded **National Film Archive**
(4 Thanon Chao Fa, Phra Nakorn, 0 2282 1847)
hopes to get new premises for its repository,
which desperately needs restoration.

Alliance Française
*29 Thanon Sathorn Tai, South (0 2670 4200/
www.alliance-francaise.or.th).* **Open** 9am-5.30pm
Mon-Fri; 8.30am-5pm Sat. **Tickets** B30 members;
B60 non-members. **No credit cards. Map** p251 G7.
The auditorium shows French movies with English
subtitles (5.15pm Sat), hosts short film festivals and
sponsors many other events, often in Thai collaborations. This cultural centre includes a café, a
library, exhibition space and a language school.

Goethe Institut
*18/1 Goethe Gasse, Sathorn Soi 1 (JUSMAG),
South (0 2287 0942-4/www.goethe.de/bangkok).
Lumphini subway.* **Open** 8am-4.30pm daily.
Tickets free. **No credit cards. Map** p251 H7.
This charming villa-style cultural and language cen-
tre screens German films outdoors in the compound
(Nov-Jan, with English subtitles) and hosts the
Science Film Festival (Nov) in its auditorium. Also,
the wooden balconies host exhibitions and Bangkok
Poetry readings (schedule on www.bangkokpoetry.
com), while the Goethe sponsors art and perfor-
mances at other venues.

House
*3rd floor, UMG Cinema, Royal City Avenue, Thanon
Rama IX, North-east (0 2641 5177/www.house
rama.com).* **Open** 11am-11.30pm daily. **Tickets**
B100. **Screens** 2. **No credit cards. Map** p252 M4.
Bangkok's first art-house cinema offers first-runs of
niche-interest films (it's top grosser was a Taiwanese
gay romance), plus avant-garde festival screenings.
Comfy modern facilities.

Sala Chalermkrung
*66 Thanon Charoen Krung, Chinatown (0 2222
1854).* **Tickets** B300-B500. **No credit cards.**
Map p249 & p250 D5.
An unpredictable mix of premières, mainstream,
Bollywood and festival movies, plus live shows, in
grand art deco surroundings.

Galleries

From modern murals and conceptual installations to art in bars, Thai art is breaking new ground.

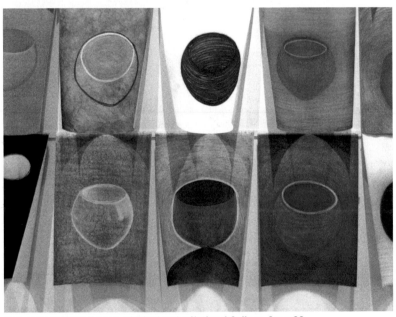

Thai artist Montien Booma exhibited at the **National Gallery**. *See p62.*

Thai contemporary art has recently made several international splashes, with the country's inaugural appearance at the Venice Bienniale in 2003; retrospectives in New York and Sydney of late installationist Montien Boonma; shows in New York by young Thai artists of Bangkok's H Gallery stable; and an exhibition in Barcelona presenting modern Bangkok through its rapidly diversifying art.

New ideas and individualism are shifting Thai art away from its previous dependence on revered templates – whether Thai tradition or Western modernism. Historically, most Thai painting and sculpture took the form of religious illustrations in temples, incrementally changing as anonymous artisans emulated earlier masters. Students still revere Silpa Bhirasri (born Corrado Ferroci) as the father of Thai modern art. An Italian sculptor commissioned to cast monumental bronzes,

Bhirasri founded the country's first art school in 1943, Silpakorn University, and enabled a generation of artists to flower before the reactionary dictatorships took hold.

Hierarchy persists in official titles like National Artist, joined in 2004 by the Culture Ministry's Silpathorn mid-career award. Oddly, the inaugural prize didn't go to a rising star, but to risen star Chalermchai Kositphiphat, whose accomplishments already deserve full National Artist recognition.

BRUSH WITH FAITH
Chalermchai Kositphiphat's sensual canvases exemplify how Thai spiritual modernism developed out of murals and later reinvigorated temple art. You can see this at his astonishing self-built Wat Rong Khun in Chiang Rai, and at Wat Buddhapadipa in Wimbledon, London, where the murals also involved the modern Buddhist painters Panya Vijinthanasarn and

Art without walls

Thailand's increasingly dynamic art world faces a paradox. Artists are breaking down the figurative walls – social, political and artistic – that until recently restrained their talents. Yet they also demand physical, tax-funded walls on which to present their works, an institutional aim that some fear may ironically limit their creativity.

In the late 1990s Bangkok Governor Bhichit Rattakul approved the construction of a contemporary art museum at a plot facing Siam Square, and the MBK and Siam Discovery malls. Its location in the heart of Bangkok's shopping and fashion nexus suited the trend of art seeking wider audiences by entering commercial, youth-oriented spaces away from the highbrow gallery scene.

The attempt by the next Bangkok governor Samak Sundavej to turn the project into another mall ignited a cause célèbre. The protests revived the 1970s *silapa puer cheewit* ('art for life') movement against dictatorship, which also embraces music (*see p185* **Songs for life**). More Lennon than Lenin, 'art for life' happenings typically involve Bangkok's cadre of performance artists, such as the Ukabat ('Fireball') agit-prop group. One of its leading lights, Vasan Sitthiket, creates thrillingly rude installation acts. An 'Art Vote' at the proposed gallery site mobilised electors in the gubernatorial

The work of **Vasan Sitthiket**.

election of 2004 and the victor, Apriak Kosayothin, revived the original project.

Meanwhile, the progressive curator Apinan Poshyananda founded a contemporary art department at the new Ministry of Culture, which plans to build its own contemporary art museum at the **Thailand Cultural Centre** (*see p197*). It would be less interactive than the artist-initiated museum and may turn into a means for the state to supervise Thai art, just as it is trying to mould Thai fashion. Thai art has developed most creatively when freed from fetters of tradition, and many fear that any kind of institutionalisation – especially given a culture minister who advocates 'patriotic art' – might make art a tool for control, rather than liberation.

Sompop Budtarad. National Artist Chakraphan Posyakrit has likewise returned from painterly vignettes to murals; *see p71* **Wat Tri Thosathep**. Spiritual modern art also takes on other forms: Pratuang Emjaroen merges Buddhist cosmology into surrealist abstractions; Tawatchai Somkong's brushwork has a raw energy; and the flamboyant Thawan Dutchanee evokes a shamanistic oriental Bosch. Others like Montien have used materials like clay, seeds, handmade paper and gold leaf to convey an earthy, everyday integration of faith and farming. Many prominent names act as a social conscience, portraying ordinary life, such as Chalood Ninsamer, Damrong Wong-uparaj and Maitree Parahom.

MOVING TOWARDS INDIVIDUALISM

Buddhism often remains a presence, even in the conceptual art for which Thais are increasingly known abroad. Pop culture is another major theme. Artist Nawin Rawanchaikul has created

installations in taxis and *tuk-tuks*; Rirkrit Tiravanija has wowed New York and published *Ver*, a picture-only magazine with interviews on CD; and Surasi Kosolwong makes installations about mundane activities, such as shopping.

Increasingly, Thai artists have traded anonymity for individualism, breaching conventions by cultivating bohemian appearances and voicing protests (such as the 'art for life' movement). Photographer **Manit Sriwanichpoom** stages 'Pink Man' compositions of fellow artist Sompong Tawee in fuchsia-hued outfits pushing a shopping trolley through temples, forests and hill tribe villages to critique consumerism, while **Chumphon Apisuk** of Concrete House (57/60 Thanon Tivanond, Nonthaburi, North, 0 2526 8311) brings together radical minds for the Asian performance art festival **Asiatopia** in late November. More subtly, **Chatchai Puipia** subverts clichés about the Siamese smile through his conflicted self-portraits.

In general, individual Thai artists have progressed further than the lacklustre commercial gallery scene has (*see p168* **Art without walls**). In a culture that fosters compliments, it takes daring to be a professional critic like Thanom Chaphakdee, a lecturer and member of performance art collective Ukabat. Yet, experimental art does flourish. A crucial seedbed, the **Goethe Institute** (*see p166*) has supported nearly every major Thai artist of the past four decades (many of whom reunite at its Christmas Art Fair on the weekend closest to Advent). Its role is now shared with the **Alliance Française** (*see p166*), a new generation of curators and the world-respected Apinan Poshyananda, who is now setting up a Contemporary Art Department within the Culture Ministry.

Key curators include Gritthiya Gaweewong of **Project 304** (www.project304.org), Luckana Kunawichianont of **Tadu** (*see p97*); Singaporean ex-performing artist Josef Ng; and Maew Yipintosoi of **About Café**. The latter has paused activity until 2007, while bolstering **Misiem's Sculpture Garden** (*see p99*). Ark Fongsmut invariably picks young future stars for the Brand New show (Jan-Apr) at **Bangkok University Art Gallery** (BUG; *see p97*).

Gallery 55. *See p170.*

Exhibition spaces

The best places to see Thai contemporary art, as with Thai antiques, are mostly private. There is a lack of arts endowments and little public art, though two art museum projects offer hope (*see p168* **Art without walls**) and private collections dot the suburbs, at **UCOM**, the **Jean-Michel Beurdeley Collection**, **Misiem's Sculpture Garden** and the new **Bangkok Sculpture Centre** (for all, *see p99* **Star cast**). Modern masterworks also fill the **Peninsula Hotel** (*see p40*), and **Benjasiri Park** (*see p97*) has some sculpture. The results of the recent artistic flourishing is largely absent from the **National Gallery**'s (*see p62*) small collection, though Bangkok Bank's annual competition canvases (by many now-big names) hangs at the **Queen's Gallery** (*see p68*), a large new exhibition space.

Otherwise, follow listings in *Metro*, *BK*, the papers or the free monthly culture map *Art Connection* for lively public openings. Alternatively, Chiang Mai is a focus of the Thai art 'new wave'. For discerning exposure of young Thai talent, see **H Gallery** (*see p170*) and the Bangkok University Gallery (BUG; *see p97*).

Commercial galleries

The idea of showing art in social spaces has taken hold since the late 1990s, pioneered by art bars along Thanon Phra Arthit (*see p69*) and **H Gallery**, which has hung art in hairdressers, car showrooms and restaurants like **Eat Me!** (*see p109*), resulting in new celebrity for some young Thai artists. Many bars, hotels and eateries now host exhibitions, like **Kuppa** (*see p113*) and the gay-oriented **Dick's Café** (*see p174*). Similarly, photography gets exposure at **Hu'u** (*see p132*), **Phranakorn Bar** (*see p127*), **Gallery F-Stop** (*see p116* Tamarind Café) and the **Foreign Correspondents Club of Thailand** (Penthouse, Maneeya Building, Thanon Ploenchit, 0 2254 8165, www.fccthai. com) in Pathumwan, which showcases photojournalism monthly. Admission is free to the following galleries.

100 Tonson

100 Soi Tonson, Thanon Ploenchit, Pathumwan (0 2684 1527/www.100tonsongallery.com). Chidlom BTS. **Open** 11am-7pm Thur-Sun. **Credit** MC, V. **Map** p251 H5.

Effective all-white spaces and knowing curatorship make this converted modernist house a prime showcase for leading locals such as Thaiwijit and top-flight

Arts & Entertainment

expatriate Thais like New York-based Richard Tsao. Dynamic openings buzz with eminent art folk who spill out to the quiet canalside at the front.

Akko Collection House

919/1 Thanon Sukhumvit, between Sois 49 & 51, Sukhumvit (0 2259 1436/www.akkoartgallery. tripod.com). Thonglor BTS. **Open** 10am-7pm Mon-Sat. **Credit** AmEx, MC, V. **Map** p252 L7.
Japanese dealer Atsuko Susuki Davies sells mostly paintings and prints by Japanese and Thai artists. Names to note include feminist woodcutter Jarrasri Roopkamdee, radical watercolourist Somboon Phuangdokmai and Sawai Wongsaprom.

Carpediem Galleries

Ruam Rudi Building, 1-1B Soi Ruam Rudi, Pathumwan (0 2250 0408/www.carpediem gallery.com). Ploenchit BTS. **Open** 11am-5pm Mon-Sat. **Credit** AmEx, DC, MC, V. **Map** p251 H5.
Singaporean Delia Oakins presents South-east Asian artists, including Symon and Krijono of Indonesia, Martin Loh of Singapore and Thai Thawun Pramarn, plus Italian master Luigi Rincicotti.

Gallery 55

Unit 212, 2nd floor, All Seasons Place Retail Centre, 87/2 Thanon Witthayu, Pathumwan (0 2685 3877). Ploenchit BTS. **Open** 11am-7pm daily. **Credit** AmEx, V. **Map** p251 H5.
Experienced dealer Ferdie H Ju schedules mostly abstract and semi-abstract shows by new Thai names and reputable South-east Asians and Europeans. Also sells Chinese antiques.

H Gallery

201 Sathorn Soi 12, South (0 1310 4428). **Open** noon-6pm Thur-Sat; by appointment Mon-Wed, Sun. **No credit cards**. **Map** p250 E7.
This wooden house contrasts with the arresting canvases of emergent Thai painters championed by US dealer H Earnest Lee. Hip opening parties here and at art bars like Eat Me! (*see p109*) have helped foster a young, middle-class market. Look out for Thaweesak 'Lolay' Srithongdee (perverse pop characters), Atjima Jaroenchit (stirring seascapes), Top Changtrakul (cartoonesque mindscapes), Jakkai Siributr (dynamic fabric art), Jaruwat Boonwaedlom (fragmented photorealism), Wuttikorn Kongka (disturbed figuration) and Jitsing Somboon (fashion portraits).

Numthong Gallery

Room 109, Bangkok Co-op Housing Building, opposite Samsen Station, Thanon Toeddamri, Dusit (0 2243 4326). **Open** 11am-6pm Mon-Sat. **No credit cards**.
Numthong Tang champions artistic individuality with a magnificent roster of works by talents like Natee Utarit, Niti Wuttuya, Chatchai Puipia, Kamin Lertchaiprasert and Montien Boonma.

Sombatpermpoon Gallery

12 Sukhumvit Soi 1, Sukhumvit (0 2254 6040-5). Ploenchit BTS. **Open** 9am-8pm daily. **Credit** AmEx, DC, MC, V. **Map** p251 H5.

A one-stop art shop, stocking mostly expressionist, figurative and abstract paintings, as well as rare early works by masters such as Thawan Dachanee, Pratuang Emcharoen and Angkarn Kalayanapongsa.

Surapon Gallery

1st floor, Tisco Tower, Thanon Sathorn North, Bangrak (0 2638 0033-4). **Open** 11am-6pm Mon-Sat. **Credit** AmEx, MC, V. **Map** p251 G7.
Selecting exquisite works for this fine two-floor space (with prices to match), Surapon focuses on prominent painters of Thai subjects (notably dance and Buddhism), such as Prasong Luemuang, Itthipol Thangchalok and Surasit Saokhong.

Tang Gallery

Unit B-28, Silom Galleria, 919/1 Thanon Silom, Bangrak (0 2630 1114 ext 0/www.tanggallery. com). Surasak BTS. **Open** 11am-7pm Mon-Sat. **Credit** AmEx, DC, MC, V. **Map** p250 E7.
Tang is a large space in a mall of arts and antiques, sometimes showing non-mainstream exhibitions by Thai, Chinese, and other Asian artists and photographers. Check website for details.

Thavibu Gallery

Suite 308, 3rd floor, Silom Galleria, Thanon Silom, Bangrak (0 2266 5454/www.thavibu.com). Surasak BTS. **Open** 11am-7pm Tue-Sat; noon-6pm Sun. **Credit** AmEx, MC, V. **Map** p250 E7.
Thailand's first online gallery also hangs exhibitions by both established and aspiring artists from the lands in its name (THAiland, VIetnam, BUrma – and Laos). It also published *Flavours: Contemporary Thai Art* by Steven Pettifor.

Timothy Yarger Fine Art

Ground floor, The Promenade Decor, Thanon Witthayu, Pathumwan (0 2655 0882/ www.yargerfineart.com). **Open** 10.30am-6pm Mon-Sat. **No credit cards**. **Map** p251 H4.
A branch of an LA dealership, this tiny showroom unveils mainstream works with LA price tags by the biggest pop names (Warhol, Leichtenstien), with celebrity-oriented openings.

Auctions

Art auctioneering came to Thailand with the sell-offs of corporate collections by **Christie's** (0 2652 1097, www.christies.com) after the 1997 crash, when Thais bid over the odds to show face. The London auction house intermittently gets out the gavel for master paintings, prints and jewellery. **Sotheby's** (0 2286 0788-9, www.sothebys.com) sources Thai art and jewellery for trading abroad, occasionally auctioning jewellery in Bangkok. The **Riverside Auction House** of River City mall (*see p139*) holds week-long viewings of East Asian antique lots before the monthly auctions (1.30pm-4pm 1st Sat).

Arts & Entertainment

Gay & Lesbian

Boys and girls come out to play in typically tolerant Thai technicolour.

Farang-Thai couple at the **Bangkok Pride** parade.

Thailand remains one of the world's most gay-friendly countries, though clichés like 'gay paradise' coined by at-ease foreign visitors hardly describe the closeted lifestyle most Thai homosexuals experience. Parades, protests and suggestive clothing ruffle a society that, while tolerant, views sexuality as an innately private matter. Homophobic violence is unheard of and anyone outing a gay would themselves lose face – and instead gain sympathy for the person exposed. Instances of prejudice often betray a Westernised education.

SIAM WHAT I AM

Thai gays are as *kaeng jai* (reticent) as any compatriot. Their families 'know but don't talk about it' and never shun gay offspring, though Sino-Thai gays hide it more and can be compelled to marry. The 'third sex' has traditionally been accepted for feminine *kathoey* (ladyboys), but it wasn't until the early 1990s that men who liked sex with men started identifying with Western-style gay liberation. Previously, they got married and paid 'money boys' or even kept *kathoey*, remaining 'real men' as long as they weren't passive.

Now largely middle-class *khon gay* (gay people) are highly visible, from the lycra-topped disco contingent to confident guppies fresh from the gym or coffee house. The majority of male prostitutes are straights earning a living. While demonstrative as *tom-dee* (tomboy-lady) couples, lesbians socialise more discreetly (*see p172* **Dee light**).

Some gays aren't shy to join the gay parades in Bangkok (Nov; *see p157*), Phuket (www.gaypatong.com; Feb, *see p221*) or Pattaya (www.pattayagayfestival. com; Nov/Dec, *see p209*). Nor is the public shy about cheering them, since *kathoey* have always been fixtures in village fairs and their modern extension, TV. Politicians have even opened some parades, which were started in 1999 by Pakorn Pimton, a brave protestor against raids on bars and saunas, and a short-lived ban on gays on TV. He maintains his truncated **Bangkok Gay Festival** (www.bangkokgayfestival.com), while a wider coalition of gay volunteer groups, academics and businessmen founded the bigger **Bangkok Pride** festival (www.bangkok pride.org; *see p157*). Bystanders roll their eyes at the self-defeating factionalism. Meanwhile, gay and lesbian organisations (*see p230*) get recognised by the Utopia Awards, presented in Bangkok Pride Week.

GAY SCENES

Gay venues have exploded since the 1980s and cruising permeates malls, streets, virtually everywhere. The trendy gay focus is Thanon Silom, where Soi 2 is all-gay and Soi 4 mixed, and the east end of Thanon Kamphaengphet's bar strip (North). Meanwhile, Trok Sake (Phra Nakorn) attacts a downmarket set, and distant Thanon Ramkhamhaeng around Soi 89/2 (East) hosts studenty bars, saunas and discos with cabarets and beauty contests. Opulent saunas, discreet massage parlours and upmarket male spas proliferate. Some venues hold ladyboy cabarets, with **Freeman**'s being the best. Venues listed are free unless otherwise stated.

Host, go-go and massage venues gather around Thanon Surawong (in Bangrak), at Soi Tawan and Soi Duangthawee Plaza, while the Thai-style 'boy bars' of Saphan Kwai (North) have declined. Freelance prostitutes hang out around Saranrom Park, western Lumphini Park and Robinson's at Thanon Silom. Another kind of 'money boy', dubbed 'professional boyfriends', receive support from multiple lovers abroad. Others simply seek a Western partner and the freedoms that may bring.

INSIGHTS

The leading gay gateway **www.utopia-asia.com** excels at events, insights, listings, links and trips for gays and lesbians, though **www.dreadedned.com** has useful listings and forums. Among the free monthly bilingual publications, *Gay Max* has good listings and the *Gay Max Guide Line* map, but the clearest map is *Gay Guide Bangkok* (**www.gayguidebkk.com**) produced by the free mag *Bangkok Variety*. **Bookazine** (*see p140*) stocks international gay books and magazines, notably the culturally astute *The Men of Thailand* and the language book/tape *Thai for Gay Tourists*.

The cross-cultural **Long Yang Club** (*see p230*) is the Thai chapter of the international group for gay Asian men and their admirers. For partywear, Silom night market stocks disco gear; for camp costuming, trawl **Pratunam Market** (*see p135*) and **www.sequinqueen.com**.

Most hotels are gay-friendly, especially the **Tarntawan Place** (*see p43*), **Babylon Barracks** (*see p174*), **Malaysia** (*see p51*) and the **Beach Residence** at the Beach Resort Sauna (*see p174*).

Utopia Tours

Tarntawan Place Hotel, 119/5-10, Thanon Surawong, Bangrak (0 2238 3227/www.utopia-tours.com). Saladaeng BTS/Silom subway. **Open** 10am-6pm daily. **Credit** AmEx, MC, V. **Map** p250 F7.
Tour company with a famous web portal (www.utopia-asia.com), which has pioneered gay travel in South-east Asia. Utopia Tours offers TAT-licensed guides for tailored tours that are resolutely non-sex trade.

Dee light

Arts & Entertainment

Strolling around Bangkok – through malls, markets or the SkyTrain in particular – you can't miss the masculine attire of the short-haired *tom* (butch) demonstratively clutching her glamorous *dee* (from 'la-dy'). As documented by sociologists like Megan Sinott (in *Toms and Dees*), Thai lesbians tend to have well-defined roles that they don't just admit to, but that form their identity. Echoing the bygone *kathoey*/real man contrast, many a *tom* drinks, dresses and joshes laddishly and protectively, sometimes out of largely unfounded concern that their *dee* would defect to a man.

The biggest lesbian organisation, **Lesla** (0 9218 9119, www.lesla.com), runs a bilingual website, a centre and library (opening in mid 2005), and Saturday parties at hired venue **Labien Leua** (Chokchai See

Soi 85, North-east) that attract 500 women. The more intellectual, Thai-language **Sapaan.org** holds discussion groups. Otherwise, *tom-dee* socialise at lesbian-owned pubs, such as the cute shophouse bar **Lamphu** and veteran pub **Vega**, which has live music, karaoke and a trendy clientele.

Lamphu

18 Thanon Phra Sumen, Phra Nakorn (0 2280 4529). **Open** 10am-midnight daily. **No credit cards. Map** p248 B2.

Vega

Sukhumvit Soi 39, 50m beyond Soi Phrom-mit, Sukhumvit (0 2258 8273/0 2662 6471). Phrom Phong BTS. **Open** 11am-2am Mon-Sat. **Credit** AmEx, DC, MC, V. **Map** p252 L6.

Bars

Balcony

86-88 Silom Soi 4, Bangrak (0 2235 5891/www.balcony pub.com). Saladaeng BTS/Silom subway. **Open** 6pm-1am daily. **Credit** AmEx, MC, V. **Map** p250 F7.
People-watching terraces spread out from this popular rendezvous. It's cheap and cheerful, with happy hour prize draws and super-friendly staff, plus chalkboards in the loos for scrawling profundities.

The Expresso

8/6-8 Silom Soi 2, Bangrak (0 2632 7223). Saladaeng BTS/Silom subway. **Open** 9pm-1am daily. **Credit** AmEx, MC, V. **Map** p250 F7.
A pre-club lounge with a soothing water-wall turns into a flamboyantly glam club as a relief from the close-pressed crowd outside the picture windows.

Happen

8/14 Silom Soi 2, Bangrak (0 2235 2552). Saladaeng BTS/Silom subway. **Open** 10pm-1am daily. **No credit cards. Map** p250 F7.
Attracting butcher men than its more camp Soi 2 neighbours, this dimly lit bar has illuminated water tanks and spins a more purist mix of house, techno and trance.

iChub

2nd floor, Zarazine, Thanon Sarasin, Pathumwan (0 2650 5598). Ratchadamri BTS/Silom subway. **Open** 6pm-1am daily. **Main course** B120. **Admission** B150. **No credit cards. Map** p251 G6.
A karaoke-oriented bar catering to chubby bears and their fans, often making a point of introducing customers to one another. Free bottles of whisky for four people exceeding 300kg (660lb). Brief Thai menu.

JJ Park & Club Café

8/3 Silom Soi 2, Bangrak (0 2235 1227). Saladaeng BTS/Silom subway. **Open** 9pm-1am daily. **Main course** B80. **Credit** AmEx, MC, V. **Map** p250 F7.
A show with loyal, long-time customers, JJ is warm and chatty, with nightly singers (real and lip-sync) and comics. Upstairs it connects via harem-esque nooks to Club Café next door, a Moroccan-themed chill-out bar with illuminated water beneath the floor.

Telephone Pub

114/11-13 Silom Soi 4, Bangrak (0 2234 3279/ www.telephonepub.com). Saladaeng BTS/Silom subway. **Open** 6pm-1am daily. **Credit** AmEx, DC, MC, V. **Map** p250 F7.
Fun and flirty, this was (in 1987) Bangkok's first Western-style gay bar. These days, it fills with pretty young things, expats and tourists. Phones enable cruisers to dial across the dimly lit bar.

Clubs

Bed Supperclub (*see p129*) runs the **Think Pink** gay night party on Sundays (show 11.45pm-midnight), while the glam-camp roving

Freeman's comic hostess Khun Day.

party night **Rehab** (www.rehabisfab.com) is run by Thai-UK-Japanese electroclash band **Futon**, who released the song *I want to be a Gay Boy*.

Disco Disco (DD)

Silom Soi 2, Thanon Silom, Bangrak (0 2266 4029/ www.dj-station.com). Saladaeng BTS/Silom subway. **Open** 10pm-1am daily. **Credit** AmEx, MC, V. **Map** p250 F7.
A miniature but more Thai-Thai version of DJ Station (*see below*) opposite, DD favours spiced-up chart hits. The crowd's very tightly packed at weekends.

DJ Station

Silom Soi 2, Thanon Silom, Bangrak (0 2266 4029/ www.dj-station.com). Saladaeng BTS/Silom subway. **Open** 10pm-2am daily. **Admission** B100 incl 1 drink Mon-Thur, Sun; B200 incl 2 drinks Fri, Sat. **Credit** AmEx, MC, V. **Map** p250 F7.
The hub on all-gay Soi 2, this three-floor nightclub has dominated for a decade and its Puppet String cabaret has barely changed. There's little room to dance as it's packed with an up-for-it throng of Thai disco bunnies and holidaying *farang*. There are wild costume parties, usually for Valentine's, Halloween, Christmas and the Gay Festival.

Freeman

60/18-21 Silom Soi 2/1, opposite Silom Complex, Bangrak (0 2632 8032-3/www.freeman club.com). Saladaeng BTS/Silom subway. **Open** 10pm-2am daily. *Shows* 11.30pm-midnight daily. **Admission** B100 incl 1 drink Mon-Thur, Sun; B200 incl 2 drinks Fri, Sat. **Credit** MC, V. **Map** p250 E7.
More Thai-oriented than DJ Station (*see above*), this disco with a sheltered chill-out forecourt has Bangkok's best *kathoey* cabaret, headlined by outrageous comic Khun Day. Some stay for the dancing and third-floor dark room, where explorers should hang on to their valuables.

Mogue

362-363 Thanon Kamphaengphet, North (0 2618 6681). Kamphaengphet subway. **Open** 8pm-1am daily. **Admission** free before 10pm, then B100 (incl 1 drink). **No credit cards.**
Chakran sauna runs the most throbbing joint on Kamphaengphet. Like nearby ICY, it's a double

Arts & Entertainment

shophouse, but camply decorated with chandeliers and steps leading from the balcony on to the bartop, where cabaret artistes sashay and local lads dance above the jiggling throng. Very Thai, few *farang*.

Saké Coffee Pub

Soi Damnoen Klang Tai, Thanon Ratchadamnoen, Phra Nakorn (0 2225 6000). **Open** 8pm-1am daily. **Credit** AmEx, DC, MC, V. **Map** p248 C3.

Local youths fuelled by Thai whisky and hormones bop to a bewildering segue of Thai and Western hits and giggle to the saucy cabaret.

See-Men

3581/14 Ramkhamhaeng Soi 89/2, East (0 2730 8399). **Open** 8pm-1am daily. **No credit cards.**

One of many gay bars, saunas and discos in this *soi* and the studenty Ramkhamhaeng area around the Mall Bangkapi, this large pub hosts cabaret and dance shows and Mr See-Men contests for a young local crowd bopping to pop-dance.

Galleries

For gay art, *see also below* **Dick's Café**.

Art At Play

114/5 Silom Soi 4, Bangrak (0 1812 0133/ www.artatplay.com). Saladaeng BTS/Silom subway. **Open** 7pm-1am daily. **Credit** AmEx, MC, V. **Map** p250 F7.

Artist/bodypainter Neung's gallery of abstract and homoerotic paintings acts as a quiet retreat amid a strip of gay bars.

Restaurants

Venues citywide are gay-friendly, but especially so at **Café Siam** (*see p120*), **Eat Me!** (*see p111*), **Thang Long** (*see p114*), plus any outlet in the **Metropolitan** (*see p48*) or **Sukhothai** hotels (*see p49*).

Coffee Society

12/3 Thanon Silom (0 2235 9784/www.coffee society.co.th). Saladaeng BTS/Silom subway. **Open** 24hrs daily. **Credit** AmEx, MC, V. **Map** p250 F6.

With elegant wooden decor, internet access, art, a people-watching terrace and a range of snacks and cakes, this relocated coffee house acts as a pre- and post-club rendezvous-cum-retreat, and hosts meetings by Long Yang Club, Bangkok Rainbow and Mac Users Group. It featured in the film *Love 101*.

Dick's Café

894/7-8 Soi Pratuchai, Thanon Silom, Bangrak (0 2637 0078/www.dickscafe.com). Saladaeng BTS/ Silom subway. **Open** 11am-1am daily. **Credit** MC, V. **Map** p250 F7.

Surrounded by the neon glare and touts of go-go-boy bars in a traffic-free enclave, this restaurant takes accents from the movie *Casablanca*. Monthly exhibits include male-related art by the likes of Neung, Symon and Lee Ming Shun.

Sphinx & Pharoah's

Silom Soi 4, Thanon Silom, Bangrak (0 2234 7249/ www.sphinxpub.com). Saladaeng BTS/Silom subway. **Open** 6pm-1am daily. **Credit** AmEx, DC, MC, V. **Map** p250 F7.

This comfy, intimate bar-restaurant serves the scene's best food (Thai and international); Pharoah's upstairs is a cosy karaoke lounge.

Saunas & fitness

Babylon & Babylon Barracks

34 Soi Nantha, Sathorn Soi 1, South (0 2679 7984-5/ www.babylonbangkok.com). Lumphini subway. **Open** noon-midnight daily. **Admission** B220 Mon-Fri; B250 Sat, Sun. **Credit** MC, V. **Map** p251 G7.

Perhaps the world's best gay sauna, opulent Babylon has it all: gym, pool, garden bars, restaurants (with jazz on Sundays), mazes and even a hotel (Babylon Barracks; rooms B1,400-B2,500).

Hotel services: *Internet (high-speed). Gym. Bar. Parking (fee). Pool. Room service. TV.*

The Beach Resort Sauna

306 Soi Panit Anant, Sukhumvit Soi 71, Sukhumvit (0 2392 4783/www.thebeach-g-thailand.com). **Open** 3pm-2am Mon-Fri; 2pm-2am Sat, Sun. **Admission** B99. **No credit cards.**

A popular, no-frills suburban sauna that's diversified with Beach Residence, comprising the lively G-host Pub disco, rooms by the night (B599-B799) or month (B7,000-B16,000) and Smart Beach Spa & Massage offering facials, slimming and 'pumper enlarge special part'.

Other locations: **Beach Residence** 159 Thanon Ratchadaphisek, North (0 2691 5769-79/Smart Beach 0 2691 5957-8).

Chakran

Soi Aree 4 Tai, Phahon Yothin Soi 7, North (0 2279 1359/5310/www.utopia-asia.com/chakran). Aree BTS. **Open** 3pm-midnight Mon-Thur; 2pm-midnight Fri-Sun. **Admission** B230 Mon-Thur; B250 Fri-Sun. **No credit cards.**

Meaning 'unquenched warrior-like desire', Chakran luxuriates in Moroccan-accented decor, with discreet seating perches around the pool and in the rooms and restaurant. Favoured by 'sticky rice' (Asians who like Asians), it's owned by the V Club massage parlour nearby.

Sauna Mania

35/2 Soi Pipat 2, Thanon Convent, Silom (0 1817 4073). **Open** 5pm-midnight Mon-Fri; 3pm-midnight Sat-Sun. **Admission** B120. **No credit cards.** **Map** p250 F7.

Stylish, minimalist new sauna on several floors.

Time Health & Spa

12/25 Thanon Thessaban Songkroh, North (0 2953 9706/www.timehealthandspa.com). **Open** 10am-11pm daily. **Credit** MC, V.

Pampering for poofs with petal-strewn baths, contemporary Balinese decor and quality treatments.

Mind & Body

Drawing on Thailand's long healing heritage, Bangkok has become a regional spa hub.

The sea of tranquillity that is the **Oriental Spa**. *See p177.*

Thailand is the holistic capital of South-east Asia, and a leader in the global spa boom. It hosts an unrivalled number of high-quality spas, massage houses and healing centres, from budget to luxury, urban to resort. Siam's escape from colonisation prevented the dilution of such indigenous medical practices as acupressure, massage, herbal steam, herbal baths, tonics, infusions and meditation that have re-emerged in spas. Early Siamese medicine (*ya samoon prai*) integrated Indian Ayurvedic and Chinese systems, adding local folk remedies and a dose of animism and shamanism. However, its core stems from Ayurvedic teachings brought over by Buddhist missionary monks during the second and third centuries BC. Hence the spiritual element that spas often revive (or exploit) in their design, therapies and marketing.

Though Siam avoided colonialism, state imposition of modern allopathic medicine and pharmaceutical monopolies marginalised *ya samoon prai*. But the crash of 1997 prompted

renewed interest in all things indigenous. To manage and promote this burgeoning industry, the state founded the Institute of Thai Traditional Medicine (0 2965 9683, www.ttmdf. or.th). Individuals and collectives tout herbal beauty and body treatments at markets and urban fairs, while firms supply health stores and mainstream shops, both in Thailand and abroad. Degree courses in Thai techniques were introduced in 2001.

With standards now an issue, some labels and catalogues carry details in English of their ingredients and supposed efficacy – although this can be daunting when you're faced with walls of tablets, potions, powders, pastes and essential oils at apothecaries in Phra Chan or Chinatown. Differentiating dosages, allergies, side effects and even signs of progress all require expert advice. State efforts to standardise prescriptions and patent active ingredients tend to favour pharmaceutical firms. Expensive branded drugs are likely to push out the old apothecaries' existing remedies and folk knowledge before they can be fully studied and applied.

Long before the advent of spas, tourists had been offered massage (*see p178*), though this often disguised a naughtier business. Though upmarket spas stress propriety, even at many 'respectable' parlours hands have been known to wander into unexpected areas.

Devotees of yoga and Pilates have increasing options and Chinese influences are highly visible in the old town herbalists and acupuncturists, and in Bangkok parks, where practitioners of *qi gong* and t'ai chi exercise.

Spas are listed and explained in the *Thai Spa Book* by Chamsai Jotisalikorn, and *Thailand Tatler*'s *The Spas of Thailand*, edited by Thai spa pioneer Naphalai Areesorn.

Holistic healing

Bahlavi Natural Health Centre

191-193 Soi Ranong 1, Thanon Rama VI, North (0 2279 5658/www.balavi.com). **Open** *Clinic* 8.30am-8pm Mon-Fri; 8.30am-7pm Sat, Sun. *Fitness* 8.30am-8pm daily. **Credit** MC, V.
English-speaking Dr Banchob offers colonic irrigation and five-day fasts, supervised by medical doctors, alongside less clinical treatments, such as Thai massage, aqua therapy, body treatments and yoga (2.30-3.30pm, 4.30-5.30pm Sat only).

Buteyko Breathing Asia

0 2253 2614/www.buteykoasia.com.
Respiratory Health Institute practitioners Jac Vidgen and Chris Drake teach these five-day workshops in the Buteyko breathing technique that was originally developed in Russia. Buteyko aims at self-management in reducing dependency on medication, improving sports performance and radically improving many conditions, from asthma, allergies and sleep apnoea to stress, obesity and migraines.

Mor Parinya Ya Thai

9 Thanon Maharat, Phra Nakorn (0 2222 1555). Tha Phra Chan. **Open** 8am-7pm daily. **No credit cards. Map** p248 B4.
Housed in a typical old apothecary, this outlet offers Thai and Chinese herb preparations, plus various massage treatments (Thai, herbal, acupressure and reflexology). Parinya's recipes for aphrodisiac, herb and alcohol *ya dong* are genuine knee-tremblers.
Other locations: 4 Thanon Maharat, Phra Nakorn (0 2221 8756); 655/13 Thanon Bangkok-Nonthaburi, North (0 2585 4312).

Rasayana Retreat & Raw Food Restaurant

57 Soi Prommitr, Sukhumvit Soi 39, Sukhumvit (0 2662 4803-5/www.rasayanaretreat.com). Thonglor BTS then taxi. **Open** 9am-9pm daily. **Main course** B120. **Credit** AmEx, DC, MC, V. **Map** p252 L6.

This modern detox centre with Chinese decor is located in a quiet compound. Having alkalised your diet, you'd typically start on the low-stress, high-modesty colonic irrigation machine, with organic replenishments. After a lymph-draining massage most finish at the garden café with juices, almond milk or wheatgrass cocktails, and raw food cuisine; the versions of pasta, sushi and pizza are a delicious revelation. Dining-only is fine, plus it has a delivery service. Cleansing/fasting programmes include full information and emotional support, with hypnotherapy counselling advised for those purging addictions. Rasayana also runs Pilates classes.

Spas

Banyan Tree Spa

Banyan Tree Hotel, Thai Wah Tower II, 21/100 Thanon Sathorn Tai, South (0 2679 1054/www.banyantree.com). **Open** 10am-10pm daily. **Credit** AmEx, DC, MC, V. **Map** p251 G7.
Bangkok's biggest spa affords amazing views from every room, though your eyes mostly remain closed. A long, luxurious menu combines Thai, Swedish and Balinese massages, petal-strewn baths and painstakingly developed in-house fusion treatments. Among the pampering packages, the three-hour Royal Banyan leaves you sleeping like a baby.

Being Spa

88 Sukhumvit Soi 51, Sukhumvit (0 2662 6171/ www.beingspa.com). Thonglor BTS then taxi. **Open** 10am-10pm daily. **Credit** AmEx, MC, V. **Map** p252 L7.
Bangkok's first non-hotel day spa pampers a regular clientele (half of them men) in an elegant house. The menu offers seven facials, 16 body scrubs and wraps, eight massages and 12 combinations of these.

Chi Spa

Shangri-la Hotel, Soi Wat Suan Plu, Thanon Charoen Krung, Bangrak (0 2236 7777/www.shangri-la.com/bangkok/). Thaksin Bridge BTS. **Open** 10am-10pm daily. **Credit** AmEx, DC, MC, V. **Map** p250 D7.
The hotel name of Shangri-la, part of a Singaporean chain, inspired a Himalayan concept in its spa, which has been brilliantly realised. It is a cavernous site, where candles cast moving shadows through wooden screens in multi-zone suites with a tea ceremony corner, luxury dressing room, pulsating infinity-edge jacuzzi, herbal sauna and unending hot towels. Balancing up the five Chinese elements, the multi-therapy 'journeys' stimulate all senses with incense, colour and sound therapy, hot stone massages and rituals with Tibetan singing bowls, whose impact resonates for days. For a review of the hotel, *see p42*.

Divana Spa

7 Sukhumvit Soi 25, Sukhumvit (0 2661 6784-5/ www.divanaspa.com). Asoke BTS/Sukhumvit subway. **Open** 11am-11pm Mon-Fri; 10am-11pm Sat, Sun. **Credit** AmEx, DC, MC, V. **Map** p252 M5.

Arts & Entertainment

A homely domain with rustic detailing in a lush garden, Divana features ceramic jar showers and properly made beds complete with pillows rather than the all-but-ubiquitous face-holes of Bangkok spas. Geared as it is towards couples and families, the emphasis here is on pampering, with scrubs, mud wraps, massages, steams, facials and milky baths all very much to the fore. While the ultra-modesty (think unisex underwear) is a comfort to many, it can just miss out on the deep thoroughness wanted by some spa aficionados. Divana aims to market its spa and Dhin organic products into a pan-Asian brand name. The Lang Suan branch has a 'Royal Thai' theme, with ultra-fine attention to detail.

Other locations: Divana Spa, 8th floor, Natural Ville, 61 Lang Suan Soi 2, Pathumwan (0 2250 7058-9).

Oriental Spa

597 Thanon Charoen Nakhon, Thonburi (0 2439 7613-4). Tha Oriental. **Open** 7am-10pm daily. **Credit** AmEx, DC, MC, V. **Map** p250 D7.

This pioneering spa remains the grande dame among Bangkok's health establishments, with top-notch service, ambience and decor. Conceived as a traditional teak house, it faces the Oriental Hotel (*see p42*) from Thonburi; it can be reached via the hotel's ferry. Prices are expensive and bookings are required – hotel guests get priority in high season.

Palm Herbal Retreat

522/2 Thonglor Soi 16, Sukhumvit Soi 55, Sukhumvit (0 2391 3254/www.palmherbalspa.com). Thonglor BTS. **Open** 10am-10pm daily. **Credit** AmEx, DC, MC, V. **Map** p252 M6.

A spa too far?

It seems that every Thai hotel now offers a spa and every street a massage parlour. As abused a term as ecotourism, spas can be anything from quick-buck pseuds and bandwagon-jumping wannabes to sincere retreats and exemplary holistic havens. As a result, the government has had to license the burgeoning industry, and now supports it by offering training and expertise in turning spas into international brands, something which Thailand sorely lacks. **Divana** (*see p176*) and **Sareerarom** (*see p178*) aim to market their own products globally, as **Harn & Thann** (*see p150*) has already done. The template for all these efforts, though, is the superlative range by Singapore's **Banyan Tree** (*see p176*) and the Metropolitan's **COMO Shambhala** (*see p48*), which have magnificent premises next door to each other in Bangkok.

Pretentious Sanskrit names proliferate, but beyond the exquisite packaging and breathless prose (heritage, royal, ancient and, everywhere, exclusive), the lotions and potions invariably do have organic ingredients. Many mix Thai components like lemongrass, rice bran and *dinso phong* (white clay) with pan-Asian goodies in scrubs and body muds that can, to the untrained nose, smell rather like curry paste.

A spa visit should be transformational, either to wind down or rejuvenate. Design can have an effect too. Whether located in the de rigueur converted house, a sublimely meditative space like **Deverana** at the Dusit Thani Hotel (*see p42*) or a spectacular environment like **Chi Spa** (*see p176*), architecture, landscaping, interiors, music, lighting can be so enveloping that they do genuinely transport you.

Raw cuisine at **Rasayana Retreat**.

Detox spas like **Chiva Som** (*see p212*) and **Rasayana Retreat** (*see p176*) offer support for people to kick cravings, whether to drugs, chocolate or attention. And, considering the growing global spa industry, we wonder whether one day the hypnotherapist might diagnose a new addiction: to spas.

Arts & Entertainment

You may be greeted by the thumping of mortar and pestle grinding fresh herbs for the natural therapy preparations applied at this pleasant spa, now relocated to a contemporary Asian building. Aside from traditional body treatments, there are also Thai, Swedish and aromatherapy massages available.

Sareerarom Tropical Spa & Prana Yoga

117 Soi Thonglor 10, Sukhumvit 55, Sukhumvit (0 2391 9919/www.sareerarom.com). Thonglor BTS. **Open** 10am-8pm daily. **Credit** AmEx, DC, MC, V. **Map** p252 M6.

Tucked away far from the mayhem that is the Bangkok traffic system, and based around a calming water garden, Sareerarom's lounging pavilions, villa-like rooms and suites all exude an authentic, pared-down Asian chic. The experienced masseuses employ a combination of Balinese, Swedish and Thai strokes, with imported essential oils. A tea house with ceremonial sets and leaves from across Asia completes the experience. Prana Yoga runs athletic classes in Baron Baptise-style Vinyasa yoga in heated rooms here and in All Seasons Place. **Other locations: Prana Yoga** 801, 8th floor, CRC Tower, All Seasons Place, 87 Thanon Witthayu, Pathumwan (0 2685 3775).

Thai massage

The best-known Thai therapy is *nuad paen boran*, an ancient massage that relieves backaches, headaches, nervous tension and fevers. Unlike Swedish, shiatsu or Balinese styles, it doesn't use oils (although many spas combine techniques using aromatherapy). The Central and gentler Northern Thai styles both use stretches and acupressure applied through thumbs, arms, elbows, knees or feet.

Lying face up in pyjamas, you initially receive a foot scrub and lengthy leg work. A

The art of doing nothing

A considerable number of visitors come to Thailand to do nothing. And we're not talking beach-bumming but learning, as the Thais say, to 'stop thinking too much'. The meditation centres listed below have courses catering to the needs of English-speaking foreigners, often without Buddhist teachings. Attempting to achieve mental calm in the chaos of Bangkok can instill discipline, but a rural retreat helps forge initial change.

The influential monk Buddhadasa Bhikku founded International Dhamma Hermitage at **Wat Suan Mokkh** (Highway 41, Chaiya, Surat Thani, 0 7743 1596, www.suanmokkh.org), some 600 kilometres (375 miles) south of Bangkok, near Surat Thani. Non-religious silent retreats are on the first ten days of each month, and there is equal space for men and women. From its hilltop *chedi* you can see Ko Pha-ngan, where regular Vipassana retreats at **Wat Kow Tahm Meditation Centre** (www.watkowtahm.org) can be booked in writing via PO Box 18, Ko Pha-ngan, Surat Thani 84280. North in Chiang Mai, **Wat Ram Poeng**'s course (0 5381 0197) requires an austere month-long immersion for 20 hours a day.

House of Dhamma Insight Meditation Centre

26/9 Lad Phrao Soi 15, North-east (0 2511 0439/www.angelfire.com/moon2/meditation /home.html). Lad Prao subway. **Open** by appointment 10am-5pm Wed-Sun.

Vipassana classes every month (second and fourth Sunday), plus group sessions and retreats of one, four or seven days.

International Buddhist Meditation Centre (IBMC)

Room 106, Vipassana Section, Mahachulalongkornrajvidyalaya University, 3 Thanon Maharat, Phra Nakorn (0 2623 6326/www.mcu.ac.th/IBMC). **Open** 1-8.30pm Mon-Sat. **Map** p248 A4.

Hosted by a Buddhist university, IBMC's English-language classes include meditation (7-10am, 1-4pm, 6-8pm daily), Dhamma talks (every 2nd and 4th Sat, 3-5pm) and upcountry retreats over weekends or five to seven days.

Wat Mahathat

3/5 Thanon Maharaj, Phra Nakorn (0 2222 6011). **Open** 7am-8pm daily. **Map** p248 A3. Instruction (in English) can be arranged for meditators staying in or outside the wat's crowded dorms. The routine (6.30am-9pm daily) includes meals and meditation (7-10am, 1-4pm, 6-9pm daily). Group walking, sitting practice and retreats are also offered.

World Fellowship of Buddhists

616 Benjasiri Park, Sukhumvit Soi 24, Sukhumvit (0 2661 1284-7/www.wfb-hq.org). Phrom Phong BTS. **Open** 8.30am-4.30pm Mon-Fri. **Map** p252 K6.

English-speaking monks from Wat Pah Nanachart give monthly talks on meditation (2-6pm, 1st Sun of the month).

Arts & Entertainment

well-trained masseur should first ask about strength of pressure and any back, joint or other pains. Those with heart problems should ask not to have their blood paused at the armpits and groin (in case you're wondering, the idea is to flush out stagnant veins). For diagnostic expertise, ask for an *ajahn* (teacher). Feedback helps, even if it's just *jeb* ('it hurts') or *jakkajee* ('it tickles').

A session should last 90 to 120 minutes and, despite occasional pain, by the end the recipient relaxes into a snooze. Aches may temporarily appear later where tension has been released. Like other therapies, it detoxifies tissues, a purge helped by the herbal tea served at the end.

Look for signs saying 'massage for health' or 'traditional massage', often depicting the body's meridian lines or foot reflexology points. At parlours signed simply *nuad* (massage), nubile numbered masseuses do their job naked, save for oil and make-up. The same goes for signs saying 'massage by men for men'.

Aside from in spas, traditional parlours proliferate in tourist areas, especially at **Surawong Plaza** on Thanon Surawong, where prices are twice those in the many good but low-privacy *nuad* houses in **Banglamphu**. Tip generously as most masseurs earn meagre piece rates. Learning the skill is an investment and you can take classes at Wat Pho, *see below*.

Arima Onsen

37/10-14 Soi Surawong Plaza, Thanon Surawong, Bangrak (0 2235 2142-3). Saladaeng BTS/Silom subway. **Open** 9am-midnight daily. **No credit cards. Map** p250 F6.
This Japanese centre offers Thai massage, reflexology, *akasuri* body rub and Nipponese-style communal showers, steam room and multi-temperature baths, plus VIP rooms and hair/nail care.

Body Tune

2nd floor, Yada Building, 56 Thanon Silom, Bangrak (0 2238 4377-8/www.bodytune.co.th). Saladaeng BTS/Silom subway. **Open** 10am-midnight daily. **Credit** AmEx, DC, MC, V. **Map** p250 F7.
Swish and modern, this centre dispenses full-body massage, reflexology and hand massage. Busiest at lunch time and as offices empty in the evening.
Other locations: Sahai Place Building, 49 Sukhumvit Soi 24, Sukhumvit (0 2661 0076-7).

Foundation for Employment of the Blind

2218/86 Thanon Chan, South (0 2678 0763-8/www.fepblind.ksc.net.th). Tha Sathorn (Saphan Taksin). **Open** 9am-8pm daily. **No credit cards.**
Furthers careers in body work for the sightless, whose touch skills are revered, and offers massage (traditional and herbal) and reflexology.
Other locations: 597/152 Yudee Soi 4, Thanon Chan, South (0 2689 9699).

Pian

108/15-16 Thanon Khao San, Banglamphu (0 2629 0924). **Open** 8am-10am daily.
No credit cards. Map p248 B3.
Intense competition keeps prices low and quality high in Banglamphu's cramped open parlours, of which Pian is the best. Men and women give reflexology, traditional and herbal massage, as well as (rather public) Swedish oil massage.
Other locations: Nancy 98 Soi Chanasongkram, Thanon Phra Arthit, Banglamphu (0 2280 7594).

Ruen Nuad

2nd floor, 42 Thanon Convent, Bangrak (0 2632 2663). Saladaeng BTS/Silom subway. **Open** 10am-9pm daily. **Credit** AmEx, DC, MC, V. **Map** p250 F7.
This picturesque wooden house (at the rear of a restaurant complex) offers Thai, aromatherapy and herbal massages with classy attention to detail.

Wat Pho

2 Thanon Sanamchai, Phra Nakorn (0 2221 2974/ www.watpomassage.com). Tha Tian. **Open** 8.30am-5pm daily. **No credit cards. Map** p248 B4.
Thailand's most famous massage and reflexology school. You can have a massage at a *sala*, near the temple's Sanamchai gate, though it's in open-air public view (9am-6pm daily). The classes, where a majority of Thai and foreign students learn massage, are given in buildings south of the temple. Murals illustrating the southern massage technique line a pavilion near the statues of various athletic yogis in self-healing postures. There are also traditional medicine pavilions beside the *chedi* (relic towers) of kings Rama II and Rama III.
Other locations: Course registration 392/25-28 Soi Penphat 1, Thanon Maharat, Phra Nakorn (0 2221 3686); **Chetawan Thai Traditional Massage School** 3rd floor, Sailom Building, Chaengwattana Soi 15, Outer North (0 2962 7338-40).

Yoga

Iyengar Yoga Studio

3rd floor, Fifty-fifth Plaza, 90 Sukhumvit Soi 55, Sukhumvit (0 2714 9924/www.iyengar-yoga-bangkok.com). Thonglor BTS. **Open** 9am-6pm Mon; 9am-8pm Tue-Thur; 9.30am-5.30pm Sat; 8.30am-1pm Sun. **No credit cards. Map** p252 M7.
German instructor Justin Herrold commands a loyal following for his Hatha yoga classes in English.

Yoga Elements Studio

23rd floor, Vanissa Building, 29 Soi Chidlom, Pathumwan (0 2655 5671-2/www.yogaelements. com). Chidlom BTS. **Open** 9am-9pm daily. **Credit** MC, V. **Map** p250 F6.
Thailand's first studio to teach Vinyasa (as well as Ashtanga and Tibetan styles), Yoga Elements is directed by US yogi Adrian Cox, who studied at India's Bihar Yoga University. Hourly classes take place daily in Thai and English; monthly workshops on topics such as meditation, Sanskrit, *pranayama* and *kirtan* are given by visiting lamas and swamis.

Arts & Entertainment

Music

From T-Pop to *phiphat*, *morlam* to indie, protest rock to Thai rap,
Bangkok has a wild soundscape.

There's a common misconception among
tourists that there's no music scene in Bangkok
– as they might have concluded in the Seattle
of 1990, the London of 1966 or the Soweto of
1980. In actuality, Thailand lives for *pleng*
(songs), which come in many alluring forms.
But it is all in the native tongue and, for
the uninitiated, can be hard to figure out.
So you can settle for 'Hotel California' on
a loop in tourist bars, wait for *morlam* to
be appropriated by Messrs Sting, Simon,
Byrne and Albarn, or hail a cab: the radio
is usually tuned to Luuk Thuung 90 FM.
Marvel at the sideways logic of *luuk thung*
and *morlam* folk (see *p184*), with its techno
beats, brass blasts and worldlywise female
raps. Or there is the blind busker's plaintive
khaen (mouth organ), the hip hop b-boys
busting out the breaks to rap act Thaitanium
or T-Pop gigs at Centrepoint (see *p180*), or join
the masses blowing their end-of-month salary
on the first Saturday night of each month – and
get ready to, as the Thais say, rock.

Newspapers and magazines give minimal
notice for gigs, so check online listings and
venue reviews at **www.bangkokpoppers.
com** or **www.bangkokgigguide.com**. While
Fat Festival (see *p157*) sates indie tastes, and
Demonic convenes metal-headz in worship (see
p160), **Pattaya Music Festival** every March
has mushroomed with state consent (contact
the TAT for info; see *p235*) into the country's
greatest music jamboree. Gigs by big-name
international acts are, however, generally sparse.

Admission to listed venues is free unless
otherwise stated, and most provide food.

Classical

Thai *phiphat*

Hearing a *phiphat wong* (Thai classical
orchestra) is a fascinating experience but
hard to find other than as tourist dance
accompaniment (see *p181* **New overtures**).
Recitals of varying quality typically occur
at the **Thailand Cultural Centre** (see
p197), **National Theatre** (see *p196*) or
Phyathai Palace (see *p96*), often presided
over, or participated in, by royalty. *Phiphat*
also features at events like **Bangkok
Theatre Festival** (see *p157*) and **Naris
Day** (see *p159*). You may be better off seeking
out practice sessions on Sunday afternoons
at **Santichaiprakarn Park** (see *p69*)
or on weekends (9am-5pm) at the **Luang
Pradit Phairoh Foundation** *phiphat*
school (47 Thanon Setsiri, Dusit, 0 2279
1509, www.thaikids.com), which both let
beginners join in.

Western-style orchestral

Paradoxically, there is an abundance of well-
publicised Western classical performances –
by the **Bangkok Symphony Orchestra**
(BSO; 0 2255 6617-8, www.bangkoksymphony.
org), multiple chamber groups and visiting
ensembles. The BSO often plays free open-air
concerts in the cool season. Most interestingly,
the **Bangkok Opera** (see *p197*) performs
European classics and new operas by
founder SP Somtow. He also assembled
the **Bangkok Sinfonietta** and organises

Arts & Entertainment

recitals at which the BSO, Meefa Orchestra and Rangsit Philharmonic regularly take the pit at the **Thailand Cultural Centre** (*see p197*). Look out for Somtow's protégé composer/musician Trisdee na Phattalung.

Dek naew (indie)

Siam Square is Bangkok's crossroads of hip individualism, of the alternative scene, known as *indie* (or *glaung sayree*, meaning 'independent drum'). Packs of spikey-haired *dek naew* (indie kids) rush into the Japanese CD store at Soi 5, or weave between the coin-op karaoke booths, art spaces and coffee shops to **New DJ Siam** (292/16 Siam Square Soi 4, 0 2251 2513), a hole in the wall that stocks the best CDs of the Thai and international underground. **Centrepoint Plaza** (Siam Sois 3-4, 0 2252 1754-6) even mixes indie into its T-pop gigs.

New overtures

Movies are often claimed to be one of the modern distractions behind the decline in *phiphat* (Thai classical music). Yet, in 2004, the hit film *Hom Rong* (*The Overture*) sparked renewed interest. Set in the early 20th century, it centres on rival *ranat* (gong-rimba) players. Though it lambasts the Phibunsongkram leadership for suppressing Thai music, the government used the film as a vehicle to encourage people to learn to play traditional musical instruments like *ranat*, as well as *cha-ke* (three-string banjo), *khlue* (flute), *khim* (dulcimer), *ree chava* (woodwind), *saw sam sei* and *saeng* (string section), cymbals, gongs and cymbal-phones.

However, beyond the hotel ensembles' standardised, competent medley of snippets to accompany dancers, there's still no equivalent to the New York Philharmonic, or even regular *phiphat* concerts. However, *ranat* players who starred in *Hom Rong* draw keen audiences. One way to hear the real thing (and to try it yourself) is to visit practice sessions at **Luang Pradit Phairoh Foundation** (*see p180*) or **Santichaiprakarn Park** (*see p69; pictured*).

Phiphat may seem dense to the uninitiated, but it has an accessible pulse, and it can truly fascinate. The simple motifs don't move melodically or harmonically, but simultaneously forward and backward, building into layers of contrast. If you break those hotel medleys apart, you'll find symphony-sized structures.

Though *Phiphat* is hard to meld with other musics, some see fusion as a saviour, given the success of bands like Boy Thai, Kangsadan and, with northern instruments, Changsothorn. The most accomplished fusion act is Fong Nam (*see p181* **Bubbling over**), whose five-volume *Siamese Classical Music* is the only complete recorded catalogue of Thai *phiphat* heritage.

From 1994 the Bakery label was almost alone in discovering and developing alternative talent, from **Modern Dog** (a proto rap-rock quartet) to **Orn Aree** (Thailand's cross between PJ Harvey and Sinead O'Connor), **Rik** (a black mass enchantress) to **Joey Boy** (the pioneer of *rap Thai*). Exposed to the New York scene as a student, Kamol 'Suki' Sukosol and his Bakery co-founders overcame limited airtime and distribution to deliver extravagant shows, videos and packaging never before seen here. Then, in 2000, while he and brother Noi formed **Pru** (a moody quartet à la Roxy Music), the dam burst. Now dozens of little labels – Hua Lampong Riddim (with its genius act Photo Sticker Machine), Small Room, Junkfood, Free/Airport, NYU Club, Genie, Lucky Café and Panda – record and press their artists' CDs. And foreign producers have got involved: David Coker (part of Futon), Sean Dinsmore, Dum Dum Project, Yuka Honda (Cibo Matto) and Tony Doogan (Belle & Sebastian) for Modern Dog, Tata and the AbbaTeens Swedish team, and Owen Morris for Sek Loso's English-language debut.

Artists to watch include **Goose** (Radiohead-alike experiments), **Apartment Khunpa** (think Black Crowes), **Space Bucha** (free improv with laptop FX), and **From the Makers of Casablanca** (pop metal punks). The breakout band is Thai/UK/Japanese foursome **Futon** (electroclash meets bastard pop), whose saucily avant-garde **Rehab** parties and album 'Never Mind the Botox' have got them some serious gigs abroad and a fifth recruit from the Britpop group Suede.

Hear them all on **104.5 Fat Radio** (7.30am-10.30pm Sun, www.thisisclick.com), which runs November's **Fat Festival** (*see p157*), featuring some 200 indie bands. Now Bakery's been sold to a major, Suki and co have launched Love Is, an indie label where artists retain many rights to their creativity (that's an insurrection in Grammyland). Another trailblazer, **House of Indies** (0 2664 0399, www.houseofindies.com) still trains DJs, but now focuses on new dance and theatre.

Rap Thai has benefitted from hip hop going mainstream, but indie rock still lacks a solid home. One-night live band parties hop venues like **Code** (*see p190*), **Bed Supperclub** (*see p129*) or even **Noriega's** (*see p183*). The best are held by **Futon/Rehab** (www.rehabisfab.com) and **DudeSweet** (www.dudesweet.org), self-proclaimed 'heroes fighting against catalogue music'. The rock band **Eastbound Downers** (www.eastbound-downers.com) hold occasional **Noise Pop** parties. Also scan **www.thaipoppers. com** for gigs.

Indie groups **Futon** and...

Arise
Soi Rambutree, Phra Nakorn, Banglamphu (0 1750 0591). **Open** 7pm-1am daily. *Bands* 7pm-10pm daily. **No credit cards**. **Map** p248 B3.
Immortal Bar – a totemic space as dilapidated and charming as New York's CBGBs or the Garage in London – has moved over to hip hop. So the owner opened Arise nearby for rock/punk/speed-metal bands, followed by hip hop or (on Tue and Thur) or drum 'n' bass.
Other locations: Immortal Bar 1st floor, Bayon Building, 249 Thanon Khaosan, Banglamphu (0 1750 0591).

Beat House
1 Soi Phromsri, Sukhumvit Soi 39, Sukhumvit (0 2662 5638). *Phrom Phong BTS*. **Open** 7pm-1am daily. *Bands* 9pm-1am daily. **Credit** AmEx, DC, MC, V. **Map** p252 L5.
A hot new pub with multicoloured square padding, Beat pledges to support all stripes of indie music, including hip hop and rock.

Jazz & blues

Jazz holds a special place in Thailand due to King Bhumibol being both an accomplished composer and saxophonist. He has played with legends such as Benny Goodman and Duke Ellington, and still jams with jazz luminaries visiting for concerts. Jazz festivals happen ad hoc in Bangkok, and every June in nearby **Hua Hin** (*see pp208-222*).

... **Modern Dog**
play the Fat Festival.
See p182.

Aside from stalwart venues, jazz features in hotel lobby lounges, such as the **Diplomat Bar** (*see p129*), and in more plentiful blues clubs like **Saxophone Pub**. The latter is one of few places featuring *dontree nanachat* (global roots music) through **T-Bone**, whose leader Gop also plays percussion to house at **Tapas** (*see p192*).

Ad Here The 13th

13 Thanon Samsen, Banglumphu (0 9769 4613).
Open 6pm-midnight daily. *Acoustic* 8.30pm-9.30pm Mon, Fri-Sun. *Bands* 9.45pm-midnight daily.
No credit cards. Map p248 C2.
Cosy pub where regulars welcome newcomers to jam the blues nightly (except jazz on Monday, which is preceded by acoustic sets).

Bamboo Bar

Oriental Hotel, 48 Charoen Krung Soi 38, Bangrak (0 2236 0400). Saphan Taksin BTS. **Open** 11am-1am Mon-Thur, Sun; 11am-2am Fri, Sat. *Band* 6-9pm. *Singer* 10pm-1am Mon-Thur; 10am-2am Fri, Sat.
Main courses B280. **Credit** AmEx, DC, MC, V.
Map p250 D7.
This snug, low-ceilinged institution is a cool cocktail lounge straight out of the 1940s, with a long jazz pedigree. Expect sultry black American singers, backed by a good house band.

Brown Sugar

231/20 Thanon Sarasin, Pathumwan (0 2250 1826). Ratchadamri BTS. **Open** noon-2pm, 5pm-1am daily. *Bands* 10pm-1am daily.
Credit AmEx, MC, V. **Map** p251 G6.

Brown Sugar is a long-time favourite that retains an earthy, clubby ambiance. Thai and expat musicians and singers reel out less commercial jazz with often inspired playing.

Living Room

1st floor, Sheraton Grande Hotel, 205 Thanon Sukhumvit, Sukhumvit (0 2653 0333). Asoke BTS/Sukhumvit subway. **Open** 9am-midnight Mon-Thur, Sun; 9am-12.30am Fri, Sat. *Bands* 9-9.45pm Mon-Thur, Sun; 9pm-12.30am Fri, Sat. **Credit** AmEx, DC, MC, V. **Map** p251 J6.
Though not that intimate, this lounge bar attracts the best jazzmen, notably ongoing residencies by genial ex-Ramsey Lewis bassist Eldee Young.

Noriega's

106-108 Silom Soi 4, Bangrak (0 2233 2813). Saladaeng BTS/Silom subway. **Open** 6pm-1am daily.
Credit AmEx, DC, MC, V. **Map** p250 F7.
The only live venue on Soi 4, this joint run by veteran publican Frank Allam offers mainly blues, but also rock, Latin, jazz, soul and indie.

Saxophone Pub & Restaurant

3/8 Thanon Phayathai, south-east side of Victory Monument, North (0 2246 5472). Victory Monument BTS. **Open** 6pm-1am daily.
Shows 9pm-1am daily. **Credit** AmEx, DC, MC, V.
Any night can be fun at this knocked-through, two-storey log and beam sculpture, a kind of trompe l'oeil hunting lodge. The regulars lay down roots, rock, reggae, jazz and blues, and are all competent-to-great. And the sound system excels – a rarity. But

Arts & Entertainment

From the Makers of
Casablanca.
See p182

Sunday belongs to T-Bone. All husky rasp and flapping dreads, Gop leads the band seamlessly from ska to samba over to reggae up to *tropicalista* and around to Senegal stomp.

Tokyo Joe's

9-11 Siwaporn Plaza, Sukhumvit Soi 24, Sukhumvit (0 2661 0359). Phrom Phong BTS. **Open** 5pm-1am daily. *Bands* 9.30pm-1am daily. **Credit** MC, V. **Map** p252 K6.

Jeff Thompson of Soi Dogs runs this small, beery den of Bangkok's blues brethren, often joining the nightly bill of regulars, and a Sunday blues jam from 8.30pm.

Luuk grung (T-Pop)

Thai multimedia giants Grammy and RS Promotions have built a virtual T-Pop duopoly of songwriters, musicians, producers, manufacturers, retailers and radio/TV/movie outlets. Many of their *luuk grung* ('city kids') popstars are exotically pale *luuk khrung* (half-*farang*). Grammy reluctantly accepted that, amid the cookie-cutter pop-fluff, wonderful aberrations could emerge. For every Nicole, Kathariya, Nat or Mai, there's now a **Palmy**, the Australian-raised Belgian-Thai hippie chick; or a **Panadda**, who's all poetry and pathos; or a **Bua Chompoo**, akin to Japan's Hikaru Utada. **Amita 'Tata' Young** also wrested the liberty to shift from puppy-love

Barbie doll to hip hop vamp. Attracting Culture Ministry censure for her pan-Asian hit 'Sexy, Naughty, Bitchy', Tata polarises Thais; some reject her for recording abroad, posing in a monk's robe for a fashion spread and dating UK footballers and tennis ace Paradorn. Yet millions evidently love her funky hits and mission to be the Thai Kylie.

Led by part-Cliff, part-Elton, part-Bowie perennial **Thongchai 'Bird' McIntyre**, the boys of T-Pop aren't as important or as liberated as the girls, but acts do break out. A blend of Bon Jovi and U2, **Sek** of **Loso** (as opposed to jet-setting *hi-so*) flips from edgy ballads to rocking protests.

T-Pop penetrates everywhere, but for live renditions join the teenyboppers in **Hollywood** (*see p192*), its near-identical next-door neighbour **Dance Fever**. Each can hold 2,000 crisply dressed fans indulging in full force *sanuk*: laughing, drinking, flirting, dancing and singing in unison.

Luuk thung & morlam

You may choose to miss reggae in Bangkok, but would anyone ignore reggae in Kingston? Samba in Rio? Blues in Chicago? *Luuk thung* or *morlam* in Bangkok? A plaintive country music, *luuk thung* ('child of the rice field') conquered the capital in the late 1980s, mostly through its own Patsy Kline, **Phomphuang Duangjian** (who died, aged 31, in 1992). She blew the style wide open with her perfect pitch (emotional and musical), encyclopaedic memory of every song she'd ever heard (she was illiterate) and her showmanship. *Luuk thung* gigs took on the spectacle of Superbowl shows, with dancing girls, orchestras and a cavalcade of stars leading up to her entrance.

Attention grew after the crash of 1997, with a heady flow of one-hit-wonder waiters and 'real people'. At temple fairs and hard-to-find venues (like late weekend nights at **Rama IX Café**; *see p198*), hit-makers Lam Yai, Joy Apaporn, Pamela or the blond Jonas (Swedish) or Kristy (English) may appear. If you're really lucky, you'll get to see Jintara or Siriporn. A Thai Dolly Parton, **Jintara Poonlap** is the sassy, sultry singer with a tiger's purr, a kitten's growl and a heartbreaker's shattered heart just looking for some relief. Like Aretha's soul or Loretta Lynn's country, **Siriporn Amphaipong** has a sandpaper sob so sorrowful, so desperate, so eloquent, resistance is futile. Siriporn sings *morlam* (literally, 'doctor dance'), an ancient folk music of Isaan that began as devotional music, the way soul began as gospel.

For the weirdest, wildest ride, sample the *likay*-style *morlam* at **Isaan Therd Terng** most nights of the week. It starts with a long, chanted overture – the original rap – over church-organ chords on *khaen* (bamboo mouth organ). A flurry of guitar arpeggios announces the *phra ek* (lead actor/singer), in a costume that blends the court of Siam with the Jackson 5, and plastered with more make-up than a Kiss/Poison double-bill. As he croons sweet plaintive hits of the day, yours will be the only dry eye – unless you speak Lao. All *morlam* is sung in that North-east dialect, but singers flip easily into Central Thai, since the genre has somewhat merged with *luuk thuung*.

Countering each *phra ek* with witty, catchy half-rap, half-torch tunes come the ladyboys (*kathoey*) and female leads (*nang ek*), dressed as if for the Miss Khorat Pageant. Mannered as Bollywood heroines, they flirt and taunt with clipped little-girl coos swirling over mandolin strums, circular-breathing saxophonics and chase-scene brass blasts. It seems she loves the guy until she unleashes the best, most accusatory use of the universal syllables of disgust 'eee-uuu'.

Khrua Yaa Jai

15/8 Lad Phrao Soi 71, North-east (0 2542 4147). **Open** 5pm-1am daily. *Shows* 8pm-1am daily. **Credit** MC, V.

Folk star Mike Piromporn owns this *luuk thuung* and *pleng puer cheewit* ('songs for life'), named 'Kitchen of Medicine for the Heart' after his hit album.

Isaan Tawandaeng

484 Thanon Pattanakarn, east of Khlong Tan intersection, East (0 2717 2321-3). **Open** 6pm-1am daily. *Shows* 8pm-1am daily. **Credit** AmEx, MC, V.

There's a diverse roster of *morlam/luuk thung* (Mon, Thur-Mon), from dancing girl revues to formation crooners in Day-Glo tuxedoes, at this comfortable venue. It has branches that (from 8pm nightly) offer *pleng puer cheewit* bands instead.
Other locations: Baan Mai Daeng Saad Saengdeuan 24 Yasoob Soi 2, Thanon Wiphawadi Rangsit, North (0 2691 5347). **Tawandaeng Saad Saengdeuan** 50/261 Thanon Kaset-Naowamin, North-east (0 2510 5027-28).

Isaan Therd Terng

104 Thanon Somdet Phra Pinklao, near Pata Pinklao, Thonburi (0 2883 44347). **Open** 8pm-1am daily. *Shows* 9.30pm-1am daily. **Credit** V. **Map** p248 A2.

This broad, dark room provides a taste of home (both musical and culinary) to migrant Isaan workers, taxi drivers, bar girls and off-duty men in uniform. Techno plays overture to a *morlam* showcase from 9pm with wild costumes most nights, and full-scale *morlam likay* productions on the first and 15th of each month. Not geared to tourists, all signs are in Thai.

Saphaa Din

888/2 Soi Sukhalumjiak, Thanon Sukhaphiban 1, North-east (0 2943 8993). **Open** 6pm-1am daily. *Acoustic* 8-9.30pm daily. *Shows* 10pm-1am daily. **Credit** MC, V.

This folk venue (translated as 'Earth Parliament') serves mixed bills of acoustic strumming preceding 'songs for life' and *luuk thung*.

Much more to Ad

Ad Carabao is the most prolific, prodigious and, possibly, profligate musician/artist/personality in Thailand. Period. Slight, humble and fiftyish, he resembles Carlos Santana or Willie Nelson: wispy moustache, stringy hair wrapped in a bandana. Like their forebears and folkier rivals, Caravan, his *pleng puer cheewit* band, formed in solidarity with 1970s anti-dictatorship protests. Exiled to the Philippines, and naming the band Carabao after Tagalog slang for 'water buffalo', they learned to rock with a new vengeance. Channelling influences like Nelson and Santana, but also Dylan, Springsteen and not least some 1,000 years of Thai folk, Carabao has cut a dozen classic albums (increasingly in solo projects) – notably *Made in Thailand*, *Welcome to Thailand* and the *Bangrajan* movie score.

But music isn't the half of it. A cultural conscience, he berates materialists, sex tourists and even generals involved in teak smuggling, who he named in a live televised concert. Lest you suspect him to be sanctimonious, check out his odes to toking, rocking, loving and cock fighting.

He's everywhere: acting as a taxi driver on TV; advertising Beer Chang; protesting the nightlife crackdown's damage in song lyrics; launching an energy drink, Carabao Daeng (Red Buffalo); championing Shan independence from Myanmar ; and appearing at an anti-piracy rally with the prime minister. What Fela Kuti was to Nigeria, Bob Marley to Jamaica, Caetano Veloso to Brazil, Bono to the MTV nation, Ad Carabao was, and is, to Thailand. But for the language problem, he'd be an international superstar.

Arts & Entertainment

Pleng puer cheewit

Meaning 'songs for life', *pleng puer cheewit* is the bluesy, socially conscious folk rock of the 1970s 'October generation'. It retains a loyal following and boasts a mega-star in the form of Ad Carabao (*see p185* **Much more to Ad**). With a loyal following, the city's hundreds of *pleng puer cheewit* clubs often resemble the set for *Rawhide*. Many are full-on stateside country and western venues, complete with log walls, wagon wheels, apache headdresses and buffalo skulls with fairylights in the eye sockets. Starting around 8pm with acoustic balladeers, the music starts to rock later on. Food is fiery Isaan, beer is cheap and whisky is sold by the bottle. A night out for four should cost less than B1,000. The leading chain of venues has divided; for Tawandaeng Khlong Tan, *see below* **Tawandaeng German Brewery**; for Baan Mai Daeng Saad Saengdeuan, *see p184* **Isaan Tawandaeng**.

Baan Sato

2578/9 Sukhumvit Soi 70, East (0 2744 8908). **Open** 6pm-1am daily. *Bands* 9.30pm-1am daily. **No credit cards**.
This is the place for southern-style *pleng puer chee-wit*. Imagine the bar where the Blues Brothers had to play behind chicken wire and you won't be far off. Three bands jam wildly for an audience of locals, bikers and aficionados.

Raintree Pub & Restaurant

116/64 Soi Rang Nam, Thanon Phayathai, North (0 2245 7230). Victory Monument BTS. **Open** 6pm-1am daily. *Shows* 8pm-1am daily. **Credit** MC, V.
Despite the C&W motifs, this stalwart feels more like a little blues bar with 'songs for life' sets nightly.

Cover music

Many hotels proffer shiny disco lounges with usually multi-racial North American bands spreading funk/hip hop/pop around the Asia hotel circuit. These clubs open with a splash, luring the yuppies, *farang* and the freelance artists of the demi-monde, and become – presto! – throbbing pick-up joints.

Most local Thai venues reprise rock, pop and country faves, now with excellent home-grown bands replacing the Filipino pioneers. They can get rather repetitive, with constant requests for the likes of 'Hotel California'. Tribute acts include several Elvii, Fab Four clones the Better, a Siamese Rod Stewart and a Thai Tom Jones. The latter plays **Radio City** (*see p187*), while **Dicken's Pub** in the Ambassador Hotel (Sukhumvit Soi 11, 0 2254 0444) stages wannabe Bee-Gees (Fri, Sat) and Elvis sightings (Tue, Thur-Sat), with a Presley birthday convention every 8 August.

Arabian Night

Ground floor, Grace Hotel, 12 Sukhumvit Soi 3, Sukhumvit (0 2253 0651-75/www.gracehotel.th.com).

Bubbling over

And now, the culmination. In one band. The melting pop of all Thai musics – *pleng puer cheewit, luuk thuung, morlam, phiphat* and cheesy covers – can be caught in the mind spasm of one man: **Bruce Gaston**. A 1970s New York avant-gardist, this US composer found himself in Thailand 'on a mission' with the premier *phiphat* ensemble, **Fong Nam** ('bubbles'). Over the following two decades, he transcribed five centuries' worth of ancient texts and whispers into both Thai and Western notation for Fong Nam to record.

On becoming Fong Nam's leader, Gaston created compositions so good he's an honoured household name. In 1999, he took to gigging nightly at **Tawandaeng German Brewhouse**, a 1,600-diner *rong beer* (microbrewery) under a barrel-shaped dome serving Thai and German fare with yard-tall tabletop kegs. Most nights Gaston's mercurial multimedia extravaganza explodes:

films, fireworks, dancing waters, dancing girls, shadow puppets, ladyboys, a repertoire from Herbie Hancock to Led Zeppelin by way of Carabao. He may croon an old Thai chestnut in drag, followed by an Elvis medley, sax pieces by the king, and a double-orchestra finale incorporating the T-Pop that comes on next. It's Sgt Hanuman's Lonely Hearts Club *phiphat wong* and he wants you all to sing along.

Tawandaeng German Brewhouse

462/61 Thanon Narathiwat Ratchanakharin, at Thanon Rama III, South (0 2678 1114-5). **Open** 4pm-1am daily. *Shows* Fong Nam 7pm-1am Mon-Sat. *Bands* 6.30-8.30pm, 9-11pm, 11pm-1am Sun. **Credit** AmEx, MC, V.
Other locations: **Tawandaeng Khlong Tan** 855/5 Thanon Pattanakarn, Khlong Tan intersection, East (0 2717 2108-9).

Nana BTS. **Open** (except Ramadan) 10pm-2am daily. *Shows* midnight-2am daily. **Credit** AmEx, DC, MC, V. **Map** p251 J5.

An awesome Arabic band blasts souk rhythms to back mesmeric singers in a vast, ornate interior. From midnight, bellydancers shimmy on tables under a shower of notes peeled off by men who dance like dervishes.

Hard Rock Café

424/3-6 Siam Square Soi 11, Pathumwan (0 2254 0830/www.hardrockcafe.co.th). Siam BTS. **Open** 11am-1am daily. *Bands* 9.30pm-12.50am daily. **Main courses** B300. **Credit** AmEx, DC, MC, V. **Map** p249 & p250 F4.

Part of the global formula, with George Harrison dominating its memorabilia and a *tuk-tuk* on the façade. Good, solid pop-rock and American fuel food. **Other locations**: Hard Rock Café & Hard Rock Hotel 429 Thanon Pattaya Beach, Pattaya (0 3842 8755-9).

Metal Zone

82/3 Soi Lang Suan, Pathumwan (0 2255 1913). *Ratchadamri BTS.* **Open** 9.30pm-1am daily. *Bands* 11.30pm-1am daily. **Admission** B300 (incl 1 drink). **No credit cards**. **Map** p251 G5.

A dragon rears off the frontage, beyond which tables of solidified chainlink cluster on a metal grate floor. The bands reanimate Priest, Scorpions and Deep Purple, by way of Tornado, Angel and HeadBanger.

Radio City

76/1-3 Patpong Soi 1, Bangrak (0 2266 4567). *Saladaeng BTS/Silom subway.* **Open** 6pm-1.30am daily. *Band* 9.30pm-1am, 1am-1.30am Mon-Sat; 9.30pm-1am Sun. *Shows* 11pm-1am Mon-Sat. **Credit** MC, V. **Map** p250 E7.

A change from Patpong's gynaecological shows, Thais impersonate Elvis (11pm Mon-Sat) and Tom Jones (midnight) to a T. Knicker-throwing is optional. Upstairs you'll find Lucifer disco (*see p193*).

Rock Pub

93/26 Hollywood Street Centre, Thanon Phyathai, Pathumwan (0 2208 9664). *Ratchatewi BTS.* **Open** 7pm-1am daily. *Bands* 7-11pm Tue-Thur, Sun; 7.30pm-12.30am Fri, Sat. **No credit cards**. **Map** p249 & p250 F3.

Entering via the mouth of an Angkor version of the talking tree from *The Wizard of Oz*, Bangkok's heavy metal devotees shake their heads to local bands expertly riffing on standards, from Scorpions to Judas Priest.

Señor Pico

1st floor, Rembrandt Hotel, 19 Sukhumvit Soi 18, Sukhumvit (0 2261 7100/www.rembrandtbkk.com). *Asoke BTS/Sukhumvit subway.* **Open** 5pm-1am daily. *Shows* 7-11pm Tue-Thur, Sun; 7.30pm-12.30am Fri, Sat. **Main courses** B340. **Credit** AmEx, DC, MC, V. **Map** p252 K6.

The Latin boom has faded, but this Cal-Mex restaurant continues to host good bands from Cuba. A favourite venue for party groups.

A *luuk thung* show in action.

Spasso

1st floor, Grand Hyatt Erawan Hotel, 494 Thanon Ratchadamri, Pathumwan (0 2254 1234). *Ratchadamri or Chidlom BTS.* **Open** noon-2.30pm, 6pm-2am daily. *Band* 10pm-2am daily. **Credit** AmEx, DC, MC, V. **Map** p251 G5.

If you've ever wondered how to get middlebrow diners (eating generic Italian meals and good pizzas) to bop to black/white US pop-soul show-bands with names like Shades, Spasso provides the Bangkok template.

Nightlife

'One Night in Bangkok' may now finish earlier than it used to, but Thais are still experts in having fun.

Thai nightlife has long been world renowned. For decades, the media sensationalised the ribald shows. Tomorrow's news may celebrate the nascent DJ scene (see p191 **Home spun**), but today's headlines are focusing on the suppression of the city's nightlife. Though the all-night partying city of legend now gets forced to bed at 1am, Thais never stop having a good time.

In terms of style, decor, music, drinks and DJs, clubs have improved hugely. DJs first surfaced in Bangkok in the 1970s, but were soon displaced by a pub scene of seated chit chat, *kup klaem* (drinking snacks) and covers from Filipino bands – or karaoke. The economic boom saw outlandish mega-discos, with some unofficial rave venues. When the crash of 1997 came, nightclubbing shifted from hangars holding 2,000 to shophouse dance bars squeezing in 200, with a few chic, mid-sized clubs in between.

Most non-international-style clubs cover their dancefloors with tall tables around which revellers jiggle, snack and top up their whisky-cokes. This is partly due to the small number of dancing licences being available and to Thais prefering to party in big groups rather than step out on to an empty dancefloor.

WHERE TO PARTY
The 'Social Order Campaign' to combat drugs and underaged drinking was initiated in 2001, though police raids and urine tests have eased off. A million incomes suffered, and venues have struggled to survive closure at 2am, then a further restriction to 1am. Promises that new nightlife 'zones' would get 4am closing weren't honoured and zoned clubs must shut by 2am (zoned music venues and bars by 1am). The authorities have hinted at a one-hour extension, yet threaten midnight closure for venues caught open after 1am or serving anyone underage.

People have compensated slightly by going out earlier, but the mood is so paranoid that everyone, even the middle-aged, must carry picture ID to prove they're over 20, and nightlife has gone increasingly underground. Streetwalkers, too, are more visible and predatory, instead of being managed by bars. Youthful drinking, flirting and whatever else continues at house parties, only without the restraining context of licensed public venues.

Mystique. See p193.

The best Nightspots

For house grooves
Tapas (see p192).

For New York chic
Q Bar (see p191).

For sweaty hip hop
Ashley's Rumour (see p190) and **Speed** (see p191).

For a Thai-style partyhouse
Hollywood (see p192).

For Thai DJs
Café Democ (see p190).

Arts & Entertainment

Discos and theme bars
dominate **Thanon Ratchadaphisek**.

Moreover, this city of ten-plus million got only three nightlife zones, which aren't fairly spread and coincidentally embrace the main strips where businessmen buy sex. The **Patpong** zone includes the original cosmopolitan bar strip **Silom Soi 4**, which also caters to gays, who have **Silom Soi 2** to themselves (*see p172*). The **Thanon Ratchadaphisek** zone harbours the theme bars of **Ratchada Soi 4**, as well as raucous discos like **Hollywood** (*see p192*). The Thanon Phetchaburi zone embraces more teenybopper theme bars on **Royal City Avenue** (RCA).

Outside the official zones, many districts host bar strips, and large discos stud the suburbs, especially along **Thanons Kaset-Nawamin**, **Ramindra** (both in North-east) and **Narathiwat Ratchanakharin** (South). Sophisticates favour the world-class clubs of **Sukhumvit**, especially around Sois Thonglor and Ekamai, yet this most responsible of nightlife areas isn't an official zone. Adults who don't want teen scenes or prostitution have nowhere to go beyond 1am. In sum, the social order policy seems a calamitous way not to solve the problem.

Tourist resorts plead for exemptions; meanwhile, all-night Full Moon Parties continue at **Ko Pha-ngan**, and minor beach scenes rock **Ko Samet**, **Ko Samui** and **Krabi**. For all, *see pp208-239* **Beach Escapes**.

In venues listed admission is free, unless otherwise stated, and most serve food. *See also pp126-132* **Bars** *and pp180-187* **Music**.

Adult nightlife

For decades visitors have been ushered – by concierges, guides, sensationalist reportage and tourist publications (including official ones) – to Bangkok's sex-oriented nightlife (*see p192* **Is go-go a-going?**). Anecdotes, boasts and jokes pump up its 'sexotic' reputation – though the rather unerotic reality suffers from premature expectation.

Go-go bars aimed at Westerners are now being marginalised by more discerning locals and visitors, as well as real estate pressures on Patpong and Sukhumvit's partly expat-oriented scenes like **Soi Zero** (under the expressway), **Nana Entertainment Plaza** (Soi 4), **Soi Cowboy** (Sois 21-23) and numerous 'bar-beers' (open-air hostess bars).

The Thai- and Asian-oriented sex industry is far larger, but less visible. They tend to favour karaoke bars (Soi Thaniya's are for Japanese only), jazzy cocktail lounges (Sukhumvit Sois 33, 55 and 63), 'no-hands' restaurants (where you are fed, and so forth, by hosts/hostesses) and massage parlours, notably along Thanons Phetchaburi and Ratchadaphisek. Some members' clubs bask in gratuitous opulence.

The moralistic crackdown initially tamed the sex shows, though many have resumed. Inflated bar bills and doped drinks are rarer now, and many bars post fixed prices. But those exploring the scene should be alert to touts, scams, their valuables and dubious scenarios.

Arts & Entertainment

Soi Cowboy. *See p189.*

Dance bars

For the innovative, futuristic **Bed Supperclub**, *see p130*. The **87** nightclub at the Conrad hotel (*see p43*) has been split into the Italianate restaurant and a dance bar **87-plus**, which now mixes DJs with the international live cover band format led by **Spasso** (*see p187*). The slick branch of London's **Met Bar** opens only to members and guests of the Metropolitan hotel (*see p48*).

Ashley's Rumour

2nd floor, Liberty Plaza, Sukhumvit Soi 55, Sukhumvit (0 2714 7861-4). Thonglor BTS. **Open** 7pm-1am daily. *Bands* 8-9.30pm; 10-11.30pm daily. **Credit** MC, V. **Map** p252 M6.

Loud, dark and packed, this isn't the ideal place to hear rumours, though it may well start some. Ear-splitting but addictive, the live music (Thai and global hits) is supported by DJ-spun pop and hip hop. The heaving, sweaty mass of young Thais lurches between low tables and red/black stools behind glass walls.

Bangkok Bar

149 Thanon Rambuttri, Banglamphu (0 2629 4443). **Open** 6pm-1am daily. **Credit** MC, V. **Map** p248 B3.

This tiny shophouse bar exudes Thainess with its cramped, dance-anywhere vibe. Dark wood and giant candles dominate the two levels, and pop, dance and house shape the mood. Frequented mainly by indie types and intrepid *farang*, it's not to be confused with Bangkok Bar in Ekkamai Soi 21, although that's a great venue too.

Café Democ

78 Thanon Ratchadamnoen, Phra Nakorn (0 2622 2571). **Open** 11.30am-1am Tue-Sun. **No credit cards. Map** p248 D3.

Named after the Democracy Monument it faces, this is more of a jazzy, chillout café during the day until 10pm when it turns into a clubbers' club, catering to harder music tastes, such as tech house, breakbeats and drum 'n' bass, with DJs the Specialist (UK) and Stewart (US) ensuring tunes are fresh and dancefloor dirty. Now-famous DJs that Democ nurtured play monthly: DJ Spydamonkee on the last Friday of the month and DJ Dragon on the second Saturday.

Code

12/135-6 Block D, Royal City Avenue, North-east (0 2203 0504). **Open** 5.30pm-2am Tue-Sat. **Credit** AmEx, MC, V. **Map** p252 L4.

Each of the five floors in this funky club has its own rhythmic code, becoming progressively harder the higher you go, from hip hop on the first three floors, to break beats, drum 'n' bass and trance above, hailing from Ko Phan-ngan's Full Moon parties. Intermittent indie gigs.

Prop

23/51 Zone F, Royal City Avenue, North-east (0 2203 0669). **Open** 6pm-1am daily. **Credit** MC, V. **Map** p252 M4.

Home spun

In the 1990s only Bangkok's pioneering rave clubs managed to keep up with the hottest imported vinyl. Elsewhere, the same old tapes ruled or else DJs talked over pop-dance to read requests. Now nearly every bar, boutique or coffee house has a DJ, and their playlists often rival anything spun abroad. DJs no longer need to lug 12-inches back from abroad; many shops now stock cutting-edge dance releases, including acts such as Armchair. For music shops, see p152.

Key factors in this transformation were the growing popularity of hip hop and a liberal new generation of rich kids who had experienced DJs while studying in London, Sydney or America's east coast. Home-grown DJ schools have also arisen, as at House of Indies (see p182). Thai turntablists to seek out include DJ Spin champions Oatawa and Kolor One, plus Café Democ graduates Spydamonkee and Dragon, Q Bar alumnus Joeki, Arsit and veteran Seed, a pioneer of Thai indie rock who features on a recent Hed Kandi album.

Expat DJs have been present since the house raves first took off in ad hoc spaces in the early 1990s. Most prominent are all-rounder **Billy V**, Futon bandmember **Bee** (who spins electronica at Rehab pary nights) and **Emmanuel** (house). Other *farang* of note inclue **Tony Sandstrom** (funky disco house), NGL (hip hop), **Ronny**, **Stewart** (breakbeat), the **Specialist** (drum 'n' bass), **Tony Hughes** (club house to progressive tech house) and Thai-American **Jay Monton** (deep house).

Paul Oakenfold has supported the Bangkok scene for over a decade and other top-flight global names play Bangok regularly, originally at **Narcissus** (see p193), but now mainly at **Bed Supperclub** (see p129), the **Met Bar** at the Metropolitan hotel (see p48), **Zuk** (see p132) and especially at **Q Bar** (see p191), which pioneered differentiated nights of the week for various musics. Now that the indie lifestyle finds common cause with hip hop, the venues and club playlists are diversifying at an inspiring rate.

Now in its fourth incarnation (previously called Absolute), this large club remains the best dance bar outside Downtown. Retro wallpaper, 'thrift shop' props and furniture of patchwork, plastic or cracked leather (all for sale or rent) spices up this otherwise white space. A staircase spiralling around myriad kooky light fixtures leads to the upper two floors. Play pool in the back to chillout lounge music on Sundays; otherwise it's rock, hip hop and Britpop.

Q Bar

34 Sukhumvit Soi 11, on sub-soi to Soi 3, Sukhumvit (0 2252 3274/www.qbarbangkok.com). Nana BTS. **Open** 8pm-1am daily. **Admission** B400 (incl 2 drinks) Mon-Thur; B600 (incl 2 drinks) Fri-Sun. **Credit** AmEx, MC, V. **Map** p251 J4.
You can't go wrong at Q Bar. Birthed at the start of the new millennium and inheriting the global repute of David Jacobson's original Saigon Q Bar (and co-owner Andrew Clark's trend awareness), this slick, New York-style conversion of a house takes off nightly from 10.30pm. This is partly due to its astonishing range of imported spirits mixed by superbly trained bartenders. There are the themed music nights (hip hop on Sundays, electric beat on Mondays) that launched many local DJs, plus frequent parties with world-famous DJs manning the decks. Attracting a mixture of visitors and trendy Thais, Q counts Matt Dillon, Michelle Yeoh and Oliver Stone among its regulars. Bangkok's first user

of vari-colour lighting, padded walls and organic furnishings lend panache, plus there's a chillout space and a balcony upstairs. One mark of its quality is that its branded merchandise actually exudes cool.

Slim & Flix

29/22-32 Block S, Royal City Avenue, North-east (0 2203 0226-8/0 6393 5273). **Open** 6pm-1.30am daily. **Credit** MC, V. **Map** p252 L4.
Book a table as the chances of getting one upon arrival are, ahem, slim. Still, it's more fun to roam the three interconnected zones catering to live Thai rock, hip hop and, in a white area branded Flix, local and imported pop-dance. Black leather sofas and low tables dot the inside, while the outside area has red and brown seating and is cordoned off by doormen pouncing on kids with fake ID. Chandeliers grace the section where live bands play.

Speed

80 Silom Soi 4, Bangrak (0 9890 8441). Saladaeng BTS/Silom subway. **Open** 9.30pm-1am daily. **Admission** B100 (incl 1 drink) Fri, Sat. **No credit cards. Map** p250 F7.
Newly enlarged, this long-standing, three-floor venue in the still-relevant original nightlife *soi* attracts a young crowd. It's gone from grafitti-covered walls to grafitti-on-canvas on the walls, but remains an authentic place for hip hop and R&B. Upstairs, a huge, round bar serves the sweaty punters a standard bill of drinks.

Is go-go a-going?

Bangkok boasts an entire genre of novels by foreigners that revel in its – we quote – 'seething underbelly', in which prostitution looms large. Prurient-cum-prudish tabloids and politically correct crusaders paint a rather shrill, West-exploits-East narrative that takes this ribald reputation beyond cliché into caricature. The famously sleazy Patpong has become a parody of itself. Amid the souvenir stalls, touts brandish menus ('Ping-pong show? Throw dart show?') to coach parties of families who come to peek – and perhaps to make themselves feel more righteous.

Spectators fuel sex tourism as much as the libidinous, or the simply lonely buying drinks for 'companions' (who are numbered, as pointing is considered rude). Some pay the 'bar fine' (B200-B500) to take the bargirl/barboy (for a tip) to a short-time hotel, a weekend in Pattaya, or maybe – many hookers hope – a new life here or abroad. The fantasy – like all forms of exploitation – can go both ways.

While the flesh trade is too lucrative for today's authorities to stop, many Thais bristle at the national loss of face and point to bigger red light industries abroad. The government now cracks down on sexual expression generally, and to some extent trafficking, in which some girls get sold or deceived into bonded brothels. Official statistics tend to be a tenth of NGO estimates, quoting 200,000 and two million sex workers respectively, of which many thousands are underaged. Illegal Asian immigrants elude the counts, as did the untold bar girls lost to the tsunami in Patong, Phuket.

Some 60 per cent of Thailand's 11.65 million tourists are male. That surplus of males evidently includes substantial numbers of sex tourists, particularly apparent in Patpong, Patong, Pattaya and the Malaysians' naughty getaway, Had Yai. Yet only about five per cent of prostitutes service Westerners.

For bar-girls in tourist areas prostitution presents a route to financial and social freedom, and the mild public reproach can be mitigated by helping family and community.

Tapas

114/17 Silom Soi 4, Bangrak (0 2234 4737/ www.tapasroom.com). Saladaeng BTS/Silom subway. **Open** 7pm-1am daily. **Admission** B100 (incl 1 drink). **Credit** AmEx, DC, MC, V. **Map** p250 F7.
A veteran from the original house boom, Tapas has yet to find a worthy adversary. The Spanish influence and intimate house party terrain keep the punters happy. DJs Neng, Wut and Oat spin Latin, deep, funk and house, often with percussionist/MCs Noom from T-Bone (11pm-1am Wed, Fri, Sat). Integral to the lives of many media types and beautiful people (both Thai and long-stay *farang*), Tapas is a place to be seen – whether out front, inside or upstairs in the members' bar.

Nightclubs

Concept CM²

Basement, Novotel Bangkok, Siam Square Soi 6, Pathumwan (0 2255 6888). Siam BTS. **Open** 9pm-2am daily. *Bands* 10.30-11.30pm, 12.30-1.30am Mon-Wed, Fri-Sun. *Boom Room* 10pm-1am daily. **Admission** B220 (incl 1 drink) Mon-Thur, Sun; B500 (incl 2 drinks) Fri, Sat. **Credit** AmEx, DC, MC, V. **Map** p249 & p250 F4.
For a decade the leading hotel disco, this low-ceilinged basement complex (CM² in Siam Square, geddit?) has themed zones around the stage and dancefloor, plus an Italian restaurant and a mega-

karaoke (over 100,000 songs in six languages). Funky cover bands on the Asia hotel circuit induce hesitant dance steps from foreign suits and less hesitant female regulars. The Boom Room spins hip hop from 10.30pm nightly.

Hollywood

72/1 Thanon Ratchadaphisek, between Sois 6 & 8, North-east (0 2246 4311-3). Thailand Cultural Centre subway. **Open** 8pm-2am daily. *Bands* 9pm-midnight daily. **Credit** MC, V.
A disco-cum-show bar, this huge hall of tiny tables piled with whisky mixer sets and fried chicken presents live *luuk grung* pop.

Lava

Basement, Bayon Building, 249 Thanon Khao San, Banglamphu (0 2281 6565). **Open** 8pm-1am daily. No credit cards. **Map** p248 B3.
This basement club has changed hands many times, but the decor remains much the same: concrete, metallic stools and glass tables. Currently red and true to its name, Lava gets pretty hot, especially when the fug of young locals bobs and paws the air to nightly hip hop. Surprisingly light on backpackers.

Lucifer

3rd floor, Radio City, 76/1-3 Patpong Soi 1, Bangrak (0 2266 4567). Saladaeng BTS/Silom subway. **Open** 9.30pm-2am daily. **Admission** B150 Fri, Sat. **Credit** MC, V. **Map** p250 F6.

The same goes for the several thousand, mostly straight bar-boys who are 'gay for pay'. Poverty and mafia influence explain much of the situation, but so do cultural differences. Newspapers fret about already affluent students selling themselves to buy luxuries. A procurer-turned-activist in Chiang Mai claims that half the male students he knows do this. Why, he posits, should they prefer turning tricks to flipping burgers? Also, studies posit that behind surface modesty, Thais tend to view sex as a private recreational urge that's less tied to love or morality than Western culture asserts.

One in four Thai males admits to buying sex regularly (60 per cent in some surveys), usually via discreet restaurants, escorts or karaoke bars. Beliefs that deflowering virgins boosts longevity and libido – and assumptions that young girls are clean of STDs or HIV – are common among Asian men, whether resident or tourists. For many, group massage parlour visits are as conventional in business as golf meetings.

Research reveals that some Thai wives find this preferable to husbands taking *mia noi* (minor wives), though historic Thai polygamy is illegal.

But Bangkok's novelists may need a new plot. Having gone some way to overcoming taboos through family planning and AIDS awareness campaigns, Thailand is gingerly questioning male sexual impunity. Harassment, wife-beating and paternity duties have started to be taken more seriously. In 2002 a Thai senator was prosecuted for sex with three girls below the 'statutory rape' age of 15 (the age of consent is 18), under a 1995 law that decriminalised prostitution while penalising procurers and brothels.

Society still won't extend male liberties to females, however. Hurrumphing greeted reports of women hiring gigolos, and tales of the teen trend for *gig* (minor boyfriends). Ironically, the rite of passage for males to pay to lose their virginity has declined because of something still deemed immoral: pre-marital sex between sweethearts.

Devil-uniformed attendants welcome you to this satanically decorated disco with diabolically loud trance that draws in young tourists and expats. Well laid-out and utterly different to the surrounding go-go bars, it occupies floors above Radio City and is part of the group also running Muzzik Café opposite, and sister trance club Lucille on RCA, which has a teenybopper bar wing called Krazy Kat. **Other locations**: Lucille 29/53-64 Zone C, Royal City Avenue, North-east (0 2203 0240-2).

Mystique
71/8 Sukhumvit Soi 31, Sukhumvit (0 2662 2374/ www.mystiquebangkok.com). **Open** 8pm-1am daily. **Admission** free Tue, Sun; B450 (incl 2 drinks) Wed; B550 for men (incl 2 drinks) Thur; B650 (incl 2 drinks) Fri, Sat. **Main courses** B250. **Credit** AmEx, MC, V. **Map** p252 K5.
Like a shard of concrete kryptonite, Mystique's exterior only hints at the world of swank behind the black-curtained door. Popular with the local international crowd, its three floors each have their own DJ, decor and vibe. The main dancefloor pumps out funky house and hip hop, while floor tiles light up, Travolta style. The upstairs room offers groovier beats and Gothic, metal-tipped armchairs and gargoyle lamps. There's also a roof terrace that opens on non-rainy weekends. The VIP sections welcome celebs or alternatively those who order a bottle; otherwise pose with the plebs on

sofas a tier down or gawp at the tank of small restless sharks (it is reported six died from vibrations in the first year).

Narcissus
112 Sukhumvit Soi 23, Sukhumvit (0 2258 4805/ www.narcissusbangkok.com). Asoke BTS/Sukhumvit subway then taxi. **Open** 9.30pm-2am daily. **Admission** B300 (incl 2 drinks) Mon, Tue, Thur, Sun; B500 (incl 3 drinks) Wed, Fri, Sat. **Credit** AmEx, DC, MC, V. **Map** p252 K5.
Fronted by the neo-classical Pegasus hostel club, this temple to kitsch attracts fewer beautiful people than it used to but remains busy thanks to a decade-plus of consistent quality. The ostentatious relaxation area in front of the ladies' offers fantastic opportunities for people-watching. The sound system offers house and trance, and tourists won't feel intimidated.

Zantika
235/11 Sukhumvit Soi 63 (between Ekamai Soi 9 & Soi 11), Sukhumvit (0 2711 5887). **Open** 8pm-1am daily. **Credit** AmEx, MC, V. **Map** p252 M6.
Spelled with a 'Z' or an 'S', this humungous partyhouse teems with young Thais and a sprinkling of expats, all resolutely marking territory in groups. Spiral staircases link tiers of terraces dotted with high tables, offering diverse vantage points on the action. Intermittent live bands cover the hits and the standard drinks are reasonably priced.

Performing Arts

With dance and drama a part of daily life, all Thailand's a stage.

In Thailand, where wedding processions dance, sacred ceremonies unfold in dramatic rites and boxing matches begin with a balletic ritual, where aesthetic presentation is imperative and grace a virtue, performance is a philosophy of life. Theatre arts exist in ceremony, the royal tradition and daily life – belonging to both a sacred sphere and common conventions.

In the most classical form, *khon*, performers must undergo years of codified training, whereas pure wit may suffice for a *talok* (comedy) star. To this day Thai thespians believe they must succumb to their characters' spirit. Before every show, from grand *lakhon* to fairground *likay*, cast and crew convene for a *wai khru* rite to honour their masters. Performance can itself be a sacred offering, as seen at the **Erawan Shrine** (*see p95* **Gods of today**), **Lak Muang** (*see p61*) and major funerals that stage *khon*.

The government's Department of Fine Arts remains a fortress of traditional forms and home to virtuoso masters with the highest title, National Artist. Since Thai theatre's modernisation during King Rama VI's reign, however, it has inclined towards Westernised styles. As with folk music, seeing a great performance is down to chance. Most temple fairs stage dance-drama, and many forms appear at the **Bangkok Theatre Festival** (*see p157*).

Dance-drama forms

Khon

This intricate and venerated genre, historically performed only before royalty, remains rare. Highly trained masked performers dance the *Ramakien*, the Thai interpretation of the Indian *Ramayana*. In this colour-coded epic, the hero, Rama of Ayodhya (green), wins back his wife Sita, who was abducted by Totsakan, the ten-faced ogre of Lanka (red; gold when romantic). Rama is helped by his brother Laksana (yellow), his adopted son Ongkot (blue), the monkey king Sangkhip (orange), and Hanuman (white), the prankish monkey general. Told in hundreds of episodes, a complete rendition would take weeks, so today what you'll see are two-hour abridgements or favourite pivotal episodes.

From an early age, dancers are trained in character styles based mostly on body type. Their traits include warlike 'lifts', Totsakan's jolting jumps and Hanuman's gymnastics and monkey twitch. Choreographic symbolism, elaborate costumes and live music eliminate the need for stage design. There's a **Khon Museum** at Suan Pakkard Palace (*see p96*).

Lakhon

Lakhon (drama) has two main threads. *Lakhon nok* typically features *Jataka* tales (Buddha's past lives), with rousing action and melodramatic plots. The more refined court recital, *lakhon nai*, belongs to the inner royal sanctum. In meticulously tuned choreography that emphasises emotion, dancers convey the romance and tragedy of such masterpieces as *Inao*, *Unarut* and *Ramakien*. Today *lakhon TV* signifies soaps, whose plots and exaggerated acting recall *lakhon nok*'s successor, *likay*.

Likay

This once ubiquitous musical theatre blends action, fantasy, tragedy and romance in diverse storylines, from folk fables to literary vignettes. High-pitched resonant singing, extravagant costumes and expressive choreography characterise this popular folk derivative of *lakhon nok* and Malay traditions. It starts with the *ohk khaek,* a solo burlesque of an Indian. From famous companies to struggling temple fair players, *likay* has steadily declined, with many talents adapting to *luuk thuung* or *morlam* music (*see p184*).

Manohra & lakhon chatri

Representing a mythical bird, the rare southern art form *manohra* (aka *Norah*) has Malay associations. Shimmying in a beaded costume, with a buffalo horn tail, the dancer twirls brass nail extensions with speed and complexity. After duelling with a masked hunter to rhythmic percussion, the bird survives to dance another day. Its distant derivative *lakhon chatri* is performed at **Lak Muang** (*see p61*) with performers dressed in *likay*-style costumes and sets.

Likay performers at a temple fair. *See p195.*

Puppetry

Rooted in Southern Thai/Malay folk tradition, shadow puppetry employs elaborately stencilled and dyed *nang* (animal hide) characters and a backlit screen (hence today *nang* means cinema). Since the Ayutthaya era, *nang yai* has showcased two-metre-tall (six-foot) puppets with no moving parts manoeuvred on sticks by visible dancers. The less formal, more popular *nang talung*, which uses puppets with hinged, moving parts, has more movement, percussive music and satirical song-like commentary from the *talung* (narrator/puppeteer).

Hun (3-D puppets) are having a revival. Several troupes perform the smallest and simplest – *hun krabok* glove puppets with stick-manipulated hands. **Joe Louis Theater** (*see p196*) is the last example of *hun lakorn lek* (small dance puppets), with three visible dancers moving limbs by hand and stick. The *hun lakorn* (large dance puppets) of **Siam Puppet Theatre** (anuchathira@hotmail.com) combine sticks with internal strings operated on a pole from below (not like suspended marionettes). Inspired by *hun*

luang (large royal puppets), these dance freely and can curl each finger into delicate gestures.

Contemporary

Modern Thai plays and musicals usually follow commercial formulas. Lack of funding hampers a rather apathetic arts scene, though interdisciplinary dialogue and unconventional venues are helping fresh talents rival shows **Patravadi** and **Dance Centre**. Thai contemporary dance often follows fads, from Martha Graham histrionics to butoh or physical theatre. Often the most original work arises from modernising Thai dance-drama.

Companies & venues

Lack of publicity and poor scheduling, especially by national institutions, deprives Thai performance of potential audiences. The few masters are kept busy with foreign tours and VIP shows. To visitors' dismay, you must rely on luck or insider knowledge to see an authentic performance at elite gatherings or festivals. Or make do with lacklustre dinner shows at touristy restaurants. Exemplary independent companies like **Patravadi**

Theatre or **Joe Louis Theater** also get insufficient support. However, the **Siam Niramit** (*see p96*) cultural show promises something out of the ordinary with its vast stage and high-tech effects on a vast stage.

Thai theatre is increasingly Western, with companies like Crescent Moon, Moradok Mai and Theatre Box staging plays (original or revivals) on socially challenging topics. **Bangkok Community Theatre** (www.bct-th.org) meets the first Thursday of every month at the British Club. This mix of Thai and expat amateurs stages plays and musicals rather well, but lost its regular venue when the Bangkok Playhouse closed (though it might reopen).

To compensate, a fully fitted Broadway theatre, **Siam Opera**, will open in March 2006 at Siam Paragon (*see p152*), with a musical by Cameron Mackintosh. As well as touring international productions, it will likely also host the new genre of Thai musicals that made do with the cavernous **Thailand Cultural Centre**, the default stage for ballet, opera and the annual **International Festival of Music and Dance** (*see p161*). The mainly *farang* **Bangkok Poetry** (www.bangkokpoetry.com) draws a hip crowd to open-mic poetry slams every six weeks at the Goethe Institut (*see p166*), with the atmosphere of a house party.

Bangkok Opera

(0 2661 4688-9/www.bangkokopera.com). **Tickets** B300-B2,000 (depending on venue).

Thailand's first Western opera company was founded by Somtow Sucharitkul, an Eton-schooled bon vivant avant-gardist who spent 15 years in LA as the screenwriter and science fiction novelist SP Somtow. On his return he penned the *Mahajanaka Symphony*, based on the king's translation of this Buddhist scripture, then the first Thai opera, *Madana* (2000), adapting a Hindu folk legend; he followed it with the ghost story *Mae Nak*; and a new ending for Puccini's *Turandot*. Compositions by Thais pepper the programme of European operas (including some foreign singers) and recitals, usually at the Thailand Cultural Centre (*see p197*). Aiming to institute South-east Asia's first genuine opera season by 2006, BO holds a Mozart Festival each March, with a new production of *Figaro* and a revival of BO's *Magic Flute* on Mozart's 250th anniversary in 2006.

Company of Performing Artists

Dance Centre, Soi Klang Racquet Club, Sukhumvit Soi 49/9, Sukhumvit (0 2259 8861 Mon-Fri/0 2712 8323/www.dance-centre.com). Thonglor BTS. **Open** 10am-6pm Mon-Fri; 10am-5pm Sat. **Tickets** B500-B1,200. **Credit** AmEx, DC, MC V. **Map** p252 L5.

Run by Vararom Pachimsawat, CPA stages fusions of classical ballet, Thai and contemporary dance at malls, parks and theatres, and hosts the Dance Day festival each May in Benjasiri Park (*see p95*).

Joe Louis Theater

Suan Lum Night Bazaar, 1875 Thanon Rama IV, Pathumwan (0 2252 9683-4/www.joelouis-theater.com). Lumphini subway. **Open** 9.30am-9.30pm Mon-Fri; 1-9pm Sat, Sun. *Shows* 7.30-8.45pm daily. **Tickets** B200 Thais; B600 foreigners; B300 concessions. **Credit** DC, MC, V. **Map** p251 H7.

The beautiful 70cm-high (28in) *hun lakhon lek* puppets come uncannily (and wittily) to life through manipulation with sticks by three dancing handlers. Despite the loss of his puppets in a fire, Joe Louis (aka Sakorn Yangkeawsot, National Artist) rebuilt this last remaining troupe with his children. They stage several, mostly classical, productions per year at this charming theatre. High costs and the closing of Suan Lum Night Bazaar herald a likely move to the new Phuket Night Bazaar in 2006, but increased support augurs well for this art's survival.

Monta Art & Performance

16/225 Wiphawadee Rangsit Soi 58, Outer North (0 2956 4180/0 1657 0241). **Open** 3 shows Sat & Sun afternoon. **Tickets** B200 adults; B100 children. **No credit cards**. **Map** p308 B3.

At his small domestic theatre, the ex-leader of the iconoclastic modern theatre company Crescent Moon, Nimit Pipitkul, presents marionnettes of traditional and modern characters in original dramas. English synopsis available.

National Theatre

Thanon Rachinee, beside National Museum, Phra Nakorn (0 2221 4885/0171). Tha Chang. **Open** *Shows* 2-5.30pm 1st & 2nd Sat, Sun of the mth; 5-7pm last Fri of mth. *Phiphat* 7-9pm 2nd Fri of the mth. **Tickets** B40-B100 adults; B20-B50 concessions. **No credit cards**. **Map** p248 B3.

Unlike most national theatres worldwide, this once prestigious venue has no permanent company, no publicity, no café, no shop, almost no productions and seemingly no energy to utilise the huge potential of this well-located, Thai-style landmark (planners want to demolish it; *see p65* **Theming heritage**). The few shows are mostly traditional dance, drama and music (with minimal explanation, rarely in English), plus some diplomat-initiated showpieces from abroad.

Patravadi Theatre

69/1 Soi Wat Rakang, Thanon Arun Amarin, Thonburi (0 2412 7287-8/www.patravadi theatre.com). Ferry from Tha Chang to Tha Wat Rakhang. **Open** 8.30am-6pm daily. **Shows** usually 7.30-9pm Sat, Sun. **Tickets** B400-B1,000. **No credit cards**. **Map** p248 A3.

Thailand's former Broadway diva Patravadi Meechudhon – actor, teacher, dancer, producer, director and writer – turned her riverside family compound into the open-air Patravadi Theatre in 1992. Now with a tent-like roof, studio annex, café and gallery, this celebrated space for independent theatre arts and dance offers diverse programmes every weekend and champions innovation. It's a cross between a 1970s artists' commune, a Thai academy

Young masters

As young Thais seek modern careers, lifestyles and entertainments, artistic traditions are in danger of disintegrating as the last few masters die before teaching or recording their largely oral skills. Paradoxically, it now requires non-conformity to practise authentic Thai culture. Happily, though, some avant-garde traditionalists do exist. They appear rarely, but do play the **Bangkok Theatre Festival** (*see p157*) and **Patravadi Theatre** (*see p196*).

The official 'preservation' of traditional Thai performing arts tends to be very rigid, often alienating the public. Historically, Thai performance arts developed over centuries as a symbiosis of indigenous, imported and innovative styles. By the same token, a wave of fresh input and experimentation is doing a better job at keeping these arts a living tradition.

Many of the young masters to look out for have spent formative time at the Patravadi creative crucible, and some return for its annual **Bangkok Fringe Festival** (*see p157*).

Choreographed by Manop Meejamras, Patravadi's original productions tour internationally, and many combine Thai with Western or Asian forms, often in collaborations (with artists-in-residence, for example, or a puppet troupe).

Perhaps Bangkok's leading contemporary dancer, **Pichet Klunchun** (*pictured left*) has an internationally reputed troupe, LifeWork, which blends physical theatre and ancient Thai dramaturgy with a tangible devotion to the deities. Another top dancer-choreographer, **Peeramon Chomthavat**, has branched out from modern ballet to hand-embroider costumes for *lakhon*. His quixotic devotion to a disappearing craft is resulting in a stitched legacy of museum quality – and sublime *lakhon* productions.

Much of this mini-revival of traditional performing arts features puppets. At **Joe Louis Theater** (*see p196*), offspring of the last master of *hun lakorn lek* (small puppets using sticks) present shows with broad appeal. Two other puppet troupes perform less often. Young dance master Surat Jongda has recreated new *hun luang* – royal puppets found in the National Museum that move fluidly via internal strings operated from below. Cultural expert and *khon* performer Anucha Thirakanont founded **Siam Puppet Theatre** (anuchathira@hotmail.com), whose performances combine both sticks and internal strings in *hun lakorn* (large dance puppets) that 'dance' with astonishing grace.

In 2004 the Culture Ministry awarded Bangkok Theatre Festival co-founder Pradit Prasartthong with the inaugural mid-career Silpathorn Prize. He contemporises neglected theatrical forms like *likay*, but his main legacy is theatre-in-education through **Makham Pom Theatre Group** (0 2616 8473-4), cultivating a new generation to find wonder in Thai drama.

and a contemporary art gallery, all mixing industrial, ethnic and rustic decor. Its annual Bangkok Fringe Festival (*see p157*) invites acts from abroad.

Thailand Cultural Centre

Thanon Ratchadaphisek, North-east (0 2247 0028/ www.thaiculturalcenter.com). Thien Ruammit subway. **Admission** varies. **No credit cards.**
Built by the Japanese, this state-run concert hall also has a small hall, an idealised Thai lifestyle exhibition and versatile outdoor spaces, with a modern art gallery planned. It's home to the Bangkok Symphony

Orchestra and most visiting dance and music performances (including September's International Festival of Dance and Music; *see p161*), though its uncomfortable seating, below par cafeteria, inadequate publicity, ageing facilities and muddy, ankle-twisting trek from the subway will all be trumped by Siam Opera.

Theatre@Metropolis

7th floor, Big C, Thanon Ratchadamri, Pathumwan (0 2250 5353/www.egv.com). Chit Lom BTS. **Open** for performances only. **Admission** B600. **Credit** AmEx, DC, MC, V. **Map** p251 G5.

Arts & Entertainment

Traditional *likay* musical theatre. *See p194.*

One cinema in the EGV Metropolis multiplex is being converted into a theatre for plays, musicals and other performances that were previously staged at the Bangkok Playhouse.

Comedy clubs

Punchline Comedy Club

The Comedy Store, The Bull's Head, Sukhumvit Soi 33/1, Sukhumvit (0 2233 4141-2/www.greatbritish pub.com). Phrom Phong BTS. **Open** *Shows* 9-11.30pm Thur-Sat 1wk in Mar, Apr, June, Sept & Nov. **Tickets** B1,500. **Credit** AmEx, MC, V. **Map** p252 K6.

On tours run by its Hong Kong namesake club, big-name international stand-ups headline every two months at this terribly English pub.

Rama IX Plaza

Soi Soonvichai, Thanon Rama IX, near Yaek Ramkhamhaeng, North-east (0 2717 2300-2). Rama IX subway. **Open** 6pm-1am daily. *Shows* 8.30pm-1am daily. **Admission** free. **Credit** AmEx, MC, V.

A bastion of irreverent variety, whether you fancy slapstick *talok* (comedy), concerts by *luuk thuung* chart-toppers, showcases of dressed-to-the-nines back-up dancers, or outrageous drag burlesques.

Dinner theatres

This genre tends towards poor food, service and value, with lacklustre shows favouring regional

dances over *khon* or *lakhon.* Among the better ones are **Yok Yor** (*see p56*) and the following.

Sala Rim Nam

Opposite Oriental Hotel, 48 Charoen Krung Soi 38, Bangrak (0 2236 0400). Saphan Taksin BTS then Oriental shuttle boat. **Open** 7-10pm daily. *Shows* 8.30-9.30pm daily. **Set menu** (excl drink) B1,850; B1,400 under 12s. **Credit** AmEx, DC, MC, V. **Map** p250 D7.

Excerpts of *khon* are performed in the round at this opulent, *vihaan*-style restaurant, run by the Oriental, with a reasonable Thai menu.

Silom Village

286 Thanon Silom, between Sois 22 & 24, Bangrak (0 2234 4581). Surasak subway. **Open** 11.30am-11.30pm daily. *Shows* indoor 8.30-9.20pm daily, outdoor 8pm, 9pm (for 15mins) daily. **Set menu** (excl drink) B500. **Credit** AmEx, DC, MC, V. **Map** p250 E7.

Regional dances and martial arts draw the camera-happy to this restaurant-cum-arcade, where you can consume lobster and *lakhon* simultaneously.

Supatra River House

266 Soi Wat Rakhang, Thanon Arunamarin, Thonburi (0 2411 0305/0874/www.supatrariver house.com). Own ferry from Tha Maharat/ferry from Tha Chang to Tha Wat Rakhang. **Open** 11am-2pm, 6-11pm daily. *Shows* 8.30-9pm Fri, Sat. **Credit** AmEx, DC, MC, V. **Map** p248 A4.

River views of the Grand Palace and Wat Arun ensure plentiful custom at this Thai restaurant in an old teak house. Patravadi Theatre opposite supplies inventive shows to Supatra's stage.

Kathoey cabarets

Perhaps Thailand's most globally famous performers are its lip-synching ladyboys (*kathoey*), most famously from Pattaya. These spectacular, slightly saucy cabarets are resolutely commercial, with umpteen Sino-ballads pleasing the Chinese coach party audience. Grittier, wittier and more inventive are the drag shows in gay clubs. For more reviews, *see pp171-174* **Gay & Lesbian**.

Mambo

Washington Theatre, 496 Thanon Sukhumvit, beside Soi 22, Sukhumvit (0 2259 5715/5128). Phrom Phong BTS. **Open** *Office* 10am-6pm daily. *Shows* 8.30-9.30pm, 10-11pm daily. **Tickets** B600-B800. **Credit** AmEx, MC, V. **Map** p252 K6.

Based at this large theatre, Mambo has toured London and the Edinburgh Festival.

New Calypso Cabaret

1st floor, Asia Hotel, 296 Thanon Phayathai, North (0 2216 8937-8/www.calypsocabaret.com). Ratchathewi BTS. **Open** *Office* 9am-5pm daily. *Shows* 8.30-9.30pm, 10-11pm daily. **Tickets** B1,000. **Credit** AmEx, DC, MC, V. **Map** p249 & p250 F4.

Bangkok's original ladyboy cabaret has intimate, plush table seating.

Arts & Entertainment

Sport & Fitness

Where to work out, play games or spectate.

Rarely seen running, Thais are understandably languid in the heat, but at dawn and dusk young and old tap shuttlecocks or rattan *takraw* balls around open ground, or conduct mass aerobics in parks.

Thailand draws world headlines for its football obsession; not for native teams, but leading foreign clubs, especially whichever English Premier League club happens to be doing well. A gilded statue of David Beckham supports the altar of Wat Pariwat, Thanon Rama III. After an aborted attempt by the Thai government to buy Liverpool FC, Beer Chang sponsored Merseyside rivals Everton, though young Thai players like Teerathep 'Leesaw' Winothai struggled while training there. But, playing to their strengths, Thailand beat Spain to finish fourth at the Beach Soccer World Cup in 2002.

Thai golf, always strong through businessmen and Japanese expats, went mainstream on discovering that Tiger Woods was half Thai. Locals now accept that Tiger cares little for his mother's homeland, and consider him aloof, so Thais now cheer home-grown successes like Thongchai Jaidee and twins Aree and Naree Song Wongluekiet (although the latter have taken their father's Korean nationality).

Tennis is the new pet sport thanks to Paradorn Srichaphan and Tammy Tanasugarn. Meanwhile, Chanya 'Cherry' Srifuengfung is making her name in equestrianism, and pop star Jetrin 'Jay' Wattanasin has been a world champion jet-skier. But the kingdom's sporting pride hinges on boxing. And not just in *muay thai* (kick boxing); its two Olympic gold medallists in conventional boxing – Somluck Khamsing in 1996 and Wicharn Ponrid in 2000 – were rightly fêted. For other Thai sports, *see p202* **Fight clubs**.

Active sports/fitness

Lumphini Park (*see p93*) is a casual sports venue. People jog and powerwalk the paths, dunk basketballs, tap rattan *takraw* balls or pump (and pose) in open-air gyms, most at dawn and dusk, when thousands practise martial arts or play Thai chess. Similar scenes fill other parks, notably **Saranrom** (*see p65*), **Benjasiri** (*see p95*) and **Benjakitti Parks**

(*see p94*). Outdoor aerobics classes in late afternoon happen in parks and also the forecourt of City Hall and on the plaza over Khlong Chong Nonsi on Thanon Surawong.

Runners can enjoy scenic routes with **Jog & Joy** (0 2741 1900, www.jogandjoy.com), or there's the expatriate social club of mad dogs and Englishmen, **Hash House Harriers** (www.bangkokhhh.com) where the focal event is getting pissed (at **Noriega's**, the bar they also assemble at; *see p183*). If you need to work up a thirst, they run between 5 and 6.30pm Monday, Wednesday, Saturday (mixed) and Sunday (men only). Silly names are compulsory.

Diving

Planet Scuba

2/17-19 Terminal Showroom, Sukhumvit Soi 24, Sukhumvi (0 2261 4412-3/www.thewildplanet.com). Phrom Phong BTS. **Open** *Training* 10am-6pm daily. **Rates** B9,500-B12,500. **Credit** AmEx, MC, V. **Map** p252 L5.
Start your PADI certification in town and complete it at sea during one of the regular diving trips. You can learn to dive at any resort, notably Phuket, Ko Tao and Pattaya (*see pp208-239* **Beach escapes**).

Football

If you want to join in a casual game, call the **British Club** (0 2234 0247) or pay B2,200 to hire the five-a-side indoor pitch at **New International School of Thailand** (NIST, Sukhumvit Soi 15, Sukhumvit, 0 2651 2065).

Golf

Well-appointed golf courses surround Bangkok, Khao Yai, Pattaya and Phuket. Many are designed by star names, and the bargain green fees have Japanese visitors flying in to play and still saving money. Cooler times of day cost more and fill up fast.

Bangkok Golf Club

99 Thanon Tiwanon, Pathum Thani province (0 2501 2828/www.golf.th.com). **Open** 5.30am-midnight daily. **Rates** *18 holes* B1,600 Mon-Fri; B2,400 Sat, Sun. *Caddy* B210. **Credit** AmEx, DC, MC, V.
Nine interesting par-threes, each designed after a world-famous hole.

Traditional Thai ball sport **takraw**. *See p202.*

Bangsai Country Club

77/3 Moo 3, Thanon Thangluang (Route 3111), Ayutthaya province (0 3537 1494-7). **Open** 7am-8pm Mon-Fri; 6am-8pm Sat, Sun. **Rates** *18 holes* B420 Mon-Fri; B930 6.30am-8.30am, B830 11.50am-3pm Sat, Sun. *Caddy* B200. **Credit** MC, V.
Bangsai Country Club is a popular, challenging course with well-tended greens.

No 1 Driving Range

19/7 Thanon Pracha Utitht, North-east (0 2935 6270). **Open** 10am-1am Mon-Fri; 10am-midnight Sat, Sun. **Rates** *Mon-Fri* 10am-1.30pm B100 per 5 trays, 1.30-4.30pm B100 per 4 trays, 4.30-10.30pm B35 per tray (coupon B350), 10.30pm-1am B100 per 4 trays. *Sat, Sun* 10am-1.30pm B100 per 4 trays, 1.30-10pm B35 per tray (coupon B350), 10pm-midnight B100 per 4 trays. **No credit cards.**
This driving range offers top-class nets, with landscaped holes, bunkers and water hazards, plus a bar, Japanese restaurant and coaching.

Royal Thai Army Golf Club

459 Thanon Ramindra, North-east (0 2521 1530/ www.rta.mi.th/armygolf). **Open** 5am-6pm daily. **Rates** *18 holes* B700 Thais; B900 foreigners Mon-Fri; B900 Thais; B1,200 foreigners Sat, Sun. *Caddy* B200. **No credit cards.**
There are two fine, good-value courses here.

Gyms & sports centres

Some hotel health clubs also have day rates.

California WOW Experience

Liberty Square, Thanon Silom, at Soi Convent, Bangrak (0 2631 1122/www.californiawowx.com). Saladaeng BTS/Silom subway. **Open** 6am-1am Mon-Sat; 8am-10pm Sun. **Rates** B1,000 per day. **Credit** AmEx, DC, MC, V. **Map** p250 F7.
A multi-floor, all-hours gym chain with immodest window walls, high-tech machines, loud music, huge classes and a hard-sell attitude – but no pool.
Other locations: 1st floor, Jasmine Tower, Sukhumvit Soi 23, Sukhumvit (0 2665 2999); Siam Paragon end of 2005.

Fitness First

4th floor, Landmark Plaza, Landmark Hotel, Thanon Sukhumvit, Sukhumvit (0 2653 2424). Nana BTS. **Open** 6am-10pm daily. **Rates** B800 per day; B2,000 per mth (min 3mths). **Credit** AmEx, DC, MC, V. **Map** p251 J5.
A well-equipped UK chain, but lacks a pool. Less hyper than California WOW.
Other locations: Bio House Building, Sukhumvit Soi 39, Sukhumvit (0 2262 0520-2).

National Stadium Hua Mark

Thanon Ramkhamhaeng, Hua Mark, East (0 2318 0940-1). **Open** *Gym* 10am-7pm Tue-Sun. *Pool* 6am-8.30pm Tue-Sun. **Rates** *Gym* B20; B375 per yr (gym plus any 2 sports). *Pool* B30 6am-6pm Tue-Sun; B50 6-8pm Tue-Sun. **No credit cards.**

The indoor stadium, velodrome and Ratchamangala Stadium were used for the 2002 Asian Games. It has a gym and pool.

National Stadium Pathumwan

Thanon Rama I, Pathumwan (0 2214 0120/ www.krompala2.com). National Stadium BTS. **Open** *Gym* 8.30am-7pm Mon-Fri. *Tennis* 6am-9pm daily. **Admission** *Gym* B10. *Tennis* B50 per hr 6am-6pm; B100 per hr 6pm-9pm. **Membership** B200 per yr adults; B100 per yr under-20s. **No credit cards**. **Map** p249 & p250 F4.

Hosts soccer matches, and has two gyms and ten tennis courts, but the 50m pool is shut until 2007.

Soi Klang Racquet Club

Sukhumvit Soi 49/9, Sukhumvit (0 2712 8010-4/www.rqclub.com). Thonglor BTS. **Open** 6am-11pm daily. **Rates** B450 per day Mon-Fri; B550 per day Sat, Sun; B12,000 per yr. **Credit** AmEx, DC, MC, V. **Map** p252 L5.

A smart sports centre with tennis, squash, badminton and basketball courts, plus snooker, swimming, gym and a branch of Dance Centre (0 2712 8323, www.dance-centre.com).

Horse riding

There are also riding options in **Hua Hin** and **Pattaya** (*see pp208-222*).

Garden City Polo Club

37 Moo 5, Thanon Bangna-Trad km 29, Samut Prakarn province (0 2707 1534-8). **Open** *riding* 9-11am, 2.30-4.30pm Tue-Sun. **Rates** B800 per hr, B700 per hr concessions Tue-Fri; B1,200 per hr, B800 per hr concessions Sat, Sun. **No credit cards**.

This residential country club an hour-plus from town has excellent facilities, with jumping, dressage and coaching.

Martial arts & *Muay Thai*

You can join in group t'ai chi every day between 4.30 and 8am at central **Lumphini Park** (*see p93*), as well as Thai martial arts such as sword-and-stick *krabi-krabong*.

Baan Chang Thai

38 Sukhumvit Soi 63, Ekamai Soi 10, Sukhumvit (0 2391 3807). Ekamai BTS. **Open** 9am-5pm daily. **Map** p252 M6.

Dedicated to preserving and teaching traditional local crafts, this house holds courses on an ancient southern form of *Muay Thai*, as well as puppet making and painting. Limited English is spoken, but course prices are a bargain.

SMAC

9th floor, Panjit Tower, Sukhumvit Soi 55 (between Thonglor Soi 5 & 7), Sukhumvit (0 2712 8810/ www.smacboxingclub.com). Thonglor BTS. **Open** 7am-9pm Mon-Fri; 1-6pm Sat. **Rates** B200 per day; B1,500 per mth. **Credit** MC, V. **Map** p252 K5.

A modern, Western-run facility offering martial arts like *Muay Thai*, kick boxing, karate and self-defence for women.

Skating

Extreme sports have caught on with *dek naew* (indie kids), though tailor-made spaces are few. Phuket often hosts an X-Games contest. The ice skating rink at **Central World Plaza** (*see p151*) will reopen in 2007.

Red Bull X-Park

Thanon Sathorn Tai, opposite Soi Convent, South (0 2670 8008/www.extrabean.com/www.redbullextra. com). **Open** 10am-9pm Mon, Wed-Sun. **Admission** B50. **No credit cards**. **Map** p251 G7.

No prizes for guessing the sponsor, this zone of ramps, half-pipes and rails lets skateboarders, trick bikers and inline skaters let off steam, according to the spiel, as an alternative to drugs. It has a café, but no gear for hire.

Snooker

Many of Bangkok's numerous snooker dens are noted for iniquity, gambling and dodgy deals, though they generally have decent tables, straight cues and cheap, late-night beers. Pool bars proliferate around Nana (for reviews, *see pp126-132*) as a way for working girls to demonstrate their skills.

Pro Q Snooker

5th floor, Charn Issara Tower I, Thanon Rama IV, Bangrak (0 2234 0011). Saladaeng BTS/Silom subway. **Open** 9am-1am daily. **Rates** B120 per hr. **No credit cards**. **Map** p251 G6.

One of the respectable parlours, with 13 tables.

Swimming

The best hotel lap pools are at **Pathumwan Princess**'s Olympic Health club (*see p45*), the **Sukhothai** (*see p48*) and the **Metropolitan** (*see p48*). **Siam Park** (*see p100*) offers every kind of water environment, even with waves.

Thai-Japan Centre

Thanon Wiphawadiragsit, North-east (0 2245 3360). **Open** 10.30am-8.30pm Mon-Sat; 1-8.30pm Sun. **Rates** B15 adults; B5 concessions. **Membership** B40 per yr adults; B20 per yr concessions. **No credit cards**.

Multi-lane Nirvana that even has starting blocks for wannabe Thorpedos.

Tennis

You'll mostly find hard courts with ball boys, racquet hire and coaching; contact the **Lawn Tennis Association of Thailand**

Fight clubs

Indigenous Thai sports are facing divergent fortunes. Some are withering away, while **Muay Thai** kick boxing has earned its own division of the World Boxing Council (WBC). The WBC will codify and sanction matches and rankings for what is now a global sport. Many foreigners train in *Muay Thai*, some going on to win titles. All fighters must wear the sacred *mongkhon* headband during the *wai khru rum muay* ritual dance to honour their teachers before every bout. They must also don the *prajiad* armlet throughout the fight, which a live band accompanies at an ever-faster fast pace. Thai boxers often wear extra amulets.

The commercialisation of this ancient hand-combat has spurred interest in older versions, such as the southern *Muay Chaiya* style taught at **Baan Chang Thai** (*see p201*). Performed with more grace and complexity, while wearing a loincloth and rope-bound wrists, ancient *muay* is often seen at festivals, including the **Traditional Thai Games & Sports Festival** (*see p159*), alongside *krabi-krabong* stick combat and Thai chess. Using slightly different pieces and rules, this variant can involve costumed martial artists enacting each move on a human-scale board. The event incorporates the **International Kite Festival** every other year, though each windy season you can see string-cutting *chula* kites in aerial fights.

Most graceful of the traditional Thai sports is **takraw**, an acrobatic game in which players knock a woven rattan ball over a net, volleyball style, or in a non-team game tap the ball through a high hoop. Thailand dominates *takraw*, which is played in parks and open grounds in late afternoon, yet it's losing popularity to football.

Some perennial pastimes have been pushed semi-undergound because they involve betting on animal contests. Famously, iridescent-finned male *pla kad* – **Siamese fighting fish** – contest in tall jars. You may hear of matches around the *pla kad* shops in Section 9 of **Chatuchak Weekend Market** (*see p136* **A day in JJ**).

Around the market's north end, bamboo coops hold prize **fighting cocks** (*kai chon*). Battling birds is legal only at two pits per province, though it takes place everywhere, even in backstreet Bangkok. Breeding is a serious business – witness Kamnan Vichien's **Fighting Cock Farm** (3 Moo 9, Thanon Suan Samphan, Nong Chok, East, 0 2543 1425). Fish and cock fans pursue these shadowy sports through magazines available everywhere, regardless of the letter of the law.

(0 2668 7624-5, www.ltat.org) for facilities. There are also courts at the **National Stadium Pathumwan** and **Soi Klang Racquet Club** (for both, *see p201*).

Central Tennis Court

Thanon Sathorn Soi 1, Bangrak (0 2213 1909). **Open** 6am-10pm daily. **Rates** 7-10am, 3-6pm B120 per hr; 10am-3pm B100 per hr; 6-10pm B200 per hr. *Instructor* B250 per hr. *Knocker* B200 per hr. *Ballkeeper* B40. **No credit cards. Map** p250 F7. Five good hard courts, with coaching, racquet hire and Thai cafeteria. Book ahead for the cooler hours.

Ten-pin bowling

Most malls have top-floor bowling alleys costing B60-B100 a game, usually with luminous light effects and dance music playing. Chains are often linked to cinema groups such as **SF Bowl** in **Mah Boon Krong** (0 2611 7171-4, www.sfcinemacity.com, 10am-1am Mon-Fri, Sun, 10am-2am Sat) and **Major Bowl** in **Central World Plaza** (0 2255 6950, www.majorcineplex.com, 11am-midnight Mon-Thur, 10.30am-midnight Fri-Sun). It is advisable to book ahead for weekends.

Football

The Football **Association of Thailand** (0 2216 4579, www.thaifootball.com) has information on league and international games. Big European teams often tour here in summer.

Horse racing

One of few sports where gambling is legal. Wise punters delay betting until they see a horse's odds moving just after the due start times; the 'off' can be ten minutes late. Illegal gambling is rife, but there's always a great atmosphere – it's a rare forum where rich and poor fraternise.

Royal Bangkok Sports Club (RBSC)

1 Thanon Henri Dunant, Pathumwan (0 2255 1420-9/www.rbsc.org). Siam BTS.

Races noon-6pm every fortnight. **Admission**
B100-B500. **No credit cards. Map** p251 G5.
A century-old club with wide-ranging facilities,
whose members either own or run the country.
Members only, except during races.

Royal Turf Club

183 Thanon Phitsanulok, Dusit (0 2628 1810-5).
Races 11am-6pm every fortnight. **Admission** B50-
B300. **No credit cards. Map** p249 E2.
The Royal Turf Club has a tight track visible from
the Dusit traffic jams.

Motor sports

North of Pattaya, **Bira International
Speedway** (Highway 36, km14, office 0 2971
6450, www.grandprixgroup.com) is Thailand's
main motor sports circuit. It is open 9am-5pm
daily, and also has a museum on royal racer
Prince Bira.

Bangkok Drag Avenue

*6/1 Moo 11 Klong Ha, Klong Luang, Pathum Thani
(0 1348 1727).* **Open** *Races* 2pm-2am Sat. *Motorcycles*
8am-6pm Sun. *Practice* noon-1am Fri. **Admission**
races B60; practice B40. **No credit cards.**
Seeking to turn Bangkok's notorious street racing
scene legal, the B90-million new BDA strip holds
mainly half-kilometre (quarter-mile) car races (plus
some gymkhana events and motorcycle drag racing)
every weekend, with practice rounds on Fridays.
Massive parking available.

Muay Thai

Bills at the two major stadia progress from
juniors to amateurs, pros and prize fights,
with novelty shows and animated gambling
adding to the colour; ringside seats are much
better. Note that ticket prices are inflated
for foreigners. The sport is governed by the
World Muay Thai Council (0 2369 2213-5,
www.wmtc.nu). For details on where to study
Muay Thai, see p234.

Lumphini Stadium

*Thanon Nang Linchee, South (reservations 0 9764
8203/Old Lumphini 0 2251 4303).* **Open** 6.30-
10.30pm Tue, Fri; 5-8pm, 8.30pm-midnight Sat.
Tickets B500 3rd class; B800 2nd class; B1,500
ringside. **No credit cards. Map** p251 H7.
Newly relocated, this legendary venue has upgraded
facilities and equipment shops.

Ratchadamnoen Stadium

*1 Thanon Ratchadamnoen Nok, Phra Nakhon
(reservations 0 1445 4150/0 2281 4205).* **Open**
6-10.30pm Mon, Wed, Sun; 5-10.30pm Sat. **Tickets**
B500 3rd class; B800 2nd class; B1,500 ringside.
No credit cards. Map p248 B3.
This stadium has basic facilities and equipment
shops with art deco details.

Ancient boxing at **Baan
Chang Thai**. *See p201.*

If you lived here, you'd read *BK Magazine.*

Pick it up free at more than 275 cool restaurants, bars, shops, and arts and entertainment spots.

www.asia-city.com

Beach Escapes

Thailand

0   200 km
0   100 miles
© Copyright Time Out Group 2005

Chiang Khong
Luang Prabang
Chiang Rai
Xieng Khoang
Mae Hong Son
Phayao
LAOS
Chiang Mai
Nan
Lamphun
Pakxan
Lampang
VIETNAM
Phrae
Vientiane
Nong Khai
Uttaradit
Loei
Udon Thani
Khammouan
Sri Satchanalai
Nong Bua
Lamphu
Nakhon Phanom
Phitsanulok
BURMA (MYANMAR)
Myawadi
Tak
Sukhothai
Kalasin
Savannakhet
Kamphaeng
Phet
Phichit
Phetchabun
Khon Kaen
Mukdahan
Moulmein
Sakon Nakhon
Amherst
Maha Sarakham
Roi Et
Amnat Charoen
Nakhon Sawan
Chaiyaphum
Yasothon
Sangkhlaburi
Uthai Thani
Ubon Ratchathani
Chai Nat
Buri Ram
Pakse
See p209
Singburi
Lopburi
Surin
Si Sa Ket
Khao Laem
Dam
Ang Thong
Nakhon
Ratchasima
Cham Pasak
Nam Tok
Suphanburi
Saraburi
Tavoy
Ayutthaya
Nakhon Nayok
Samrong
Kanchanaburi
Pathum Thani
Prachinburi
Chean Ksant
Ratchaburi
See p246-7
BANGKOK
Nonthaburi
Sa Kaeo
Sisophon
CAMBODIA
Samut Songkram
Chachoengsao
Samut
Sakhon
Samut Prakan
Phetchaburi
Chonburi
Batambang
Siem Reap
Cha-am
Pattaya
Pailin
Pothisat
Kompong Thom
Hua Hin
Rayong
Chanthaburi
Ko Samet
Pranburi
Ko Chang
Trat
Kompong Chanang
Prachuap Khiri Khan
Ko Mak
Ko Kood
Khemmarat
Phnom Penh
VIETNAM
Tad Mao
Gulf
Takeo
Svay Rieng
Ho Chi Minh
Kraburi
Chumphon
Ka Pong
Khao Lak
Plai Phraya
Victoria
Ko Tao
of
Phang-nga
Thap Put
See p214
Ranong
Lang Suan
Chaiburi
Ko Pha-ngan
Thailand
Thai Muang
Ao Luk
Ang Thong
Archipelago
Ko Samui
Khao Lam Pi
Takua Thung
Tham Phet
Ko Surin
National Park
Surat Thani
Khao Phanom
Ko Similan
Takua Pa
Tham Lot
Ao
Phang-
Nga
Tham Sadet
Phang-nga
See Inset
Ko Yao
Nakhon Si Thammarat
Krabi
Thalang
Nua Khlong
Thung Song
Krabi
Andaman
Sea
Phuket
Laguna
Ao Nang
Chao Fah
Pier
Phatthalung
Surin
Kathu
Laem Phra
Nang
Trang
Patong
Phuket City
Kata
Ko Yao Yai
Songkhla
Andaman
Sea
Cape
Phromthep
Ao
Chalong
Ko Phi Phi
Satun
Pattani
Ko Rawi
Ko
Tarutao
Sadao
Yala
Ko Racha Yai
Ko Lanta
Ko A-Dang
Langkawi
Island
Alor Setar
Narathiwat
206 Time Out Bangkok
MALAYSIA
Penang
George Town
Sungai Patani

Getting Started

Planning your sandy sojourn.

Thai beaches hold a special place in the world's holiday memories – and fantasies. And it's not mere hype or residual glamour from the book and film *The Beach*. Still, having Leo claim the world's best beach is hidden here enticed many newbies to Thailand's genuinely superb strands and mouthwash-green waters.

Many southern Thai resorts were deluged by the tsunami of December 2004. Thankfully, wave damage was initially overstated for some Andaman Sea resorts around 600-800km (400-500 miles) south of Bangkok, such as mass tourism hub **Phuket**, achingly picturesque **Krabi**, and rising beachnik retreat **Ko Lanta**. Other areas will take longer to recover (*see p211* **Tsunami: 26 December 2004**). But most of Thailand's pristine beaches weren't touched. Across the Kra Isthmus lie the Thai Gulf islands of unhurried **Ko Samui**, dive-mad **Ko Tao** and rugged, full-moon partying **Ko Pha-ngan**. Up the Gulf, the regal coastal town of **Hua Hin** has trendy hideaways. Equally close to the capital, the Eastern Seaboard harbours hyper **Pattaya**, quirky **Ko Samet** and up-and-coming **Ko Chang**.

On all coasts, the trend is upmarket. Designer chic and spa preciousness are eclipsing the gap-year backpacker ethic that pioneered the Thai beach lifestyle. Yet budget huts still proliferate and luxury pool villas are a bargain by world standards.

With planning negligible, national park regulations ineffective and 'influential people' riding roughshod over sustainable limits, inappropriate development often blights beauty spots with traffic, trash, touts and techno. The flipside is the ample amenities, from email and ticketing, to sports gear and book exchanges.

ROOMS AND RESTAURANTS

Rooms can get booked out in high season, especially around weekends. However, during the monsoons it's possible to find some sizeable discounts, although some Andaman coast resorts may close. For each coast's seasons, *see p236* **When to go**. The accommodation on offer often determines the character of a beach, so reading the relevant **Where to stay** section will tell you a great deal about any destination you're planning to visit.

Resort food varies from designer cuisine to bland tourist fodder, but you're best bet is usually to sample what locals eat. Food quality plunges and prices inflate on remote beaches, so island-hoppers should take practical supplies.

Getting there

Fly-drive holidays

Thanks to new budget airlines (*see p224*), flights south to airports at **Phuket** (0 7632 7230-7) and **Krabi** (0 7563 6543) have multiplied and prices tumbled. However, Bangkok Airways (www.bangkokair.com) owns the airports at **Ko Samui** (0 7742 2234) and **Trat** (0 3952 5767-8; for Ko Chang), charging hefty fares and airport fees. Booking airport pickups avoids taxi touts and rip-offs.

Road & rail

Beaches near Bangkok can be reached by hired car (*see p226*), airport pick-up or bus (from Bangkok terminals, *see p224*). Add an hour to drive times for buses to: Hua Hin (3hrs), frequent buses (B128); Pattaya (2hrs), half-hourly buses (B90); Ko Samet (3hrs plus 40min ferry), hourly buses to Ban Phe pier (B124); and Ko Chang (5hrs plus 1hr ferry), frequent buses to Trad (around B200), then *songtaew* to Laem Ngop pier.

You'd lose 24 hours heading to southern resorts via reckless night buses or sleeper trains from Bangkok's Hualumphong Station (*see p226*), enduring messy local bus/*songtaew*/ferry connections. It's no less exhausting on resorts' and agents' mini-bus/ferry packages. However, rail is a nice way to reach Hua Hin (11 daily, 3-5hrs, B44-B280). A taxi to Hua Hin/Pattaya/Ban Phe costs B2,200-plus. Motorcycles (from B200) and jeeps/cars (from B850) are easy to hire in resorts. Most hotels will arrange airport transfers.

Resources

ATMs, banks and exchange booths are plentiful in main resorts, but scarce, with inflated rates, on Samet and remote beaches. **Phone** and **internet** access is plentiful and cheap, except on Samet and remote beaches. TAT offices for **tourist information** open 8.30am-4.30pm daily. The national hotline (1155) for the **tourist police** alerts your nearest station.

Beach Escapes

Beach Escapes

Do the strand on Thailand's island idylls.

Eastern Seaboard

Pattaya

Pattaya has hosted raunchy mass tourism since US troops came for R&R during the Vietnam War. Uneven clean-ups of both pollution and the sex trade result in crude contrasts: eyesores scar a potentially fine corniche; few swim in waters no longer dirtied by sewage; watersports and attractions draw families, go-go bars remain top of many visitors' must-see lists.

As if in a counterfeit Elmore Leonard novel, guys in singlets pose with bikes, babes and Ray-Bans. Menus come in English, German, Arabic and Russian – nationalities that recur in lurid reports on underground activities in the *Pattaya Mail*. Yet mainstream tourists face little risk and some stay to open businesses, hence pubs called Rosie O'Grady's, Scot's Bar and Pat's Pies. Morphing into a town, Pattaya now boasts malls, 15 golf courses and a largely artificial culture. The centre is walkable, or you can flag down a *songthaew* anywhere (B10, outskirts up to B30).

The next bay south, longer, cleaner Jomtien Beach, has sparser boutique resorts, delectable seafood and fewer Pattaya-esque mistakes.

Activities

Watersports and fishing trips proliferate. **Blue Lagoon Watersports Club** (23/4 Na Jomtien Soi 14, 0 3825 5115-6) offers a private beach, kayaks, windsurfing and kite surfing. Island reefs, wrecks and instruction are the diving draws for **Aquanauts** (437/17 Thanon Beach Soi 6, 0 3836 1724) and **Mermaids** (75/122-5 Thanon Jomtien Beach, 0 3823 2219-20). **Gulf Charters** (Ocean Marina Yacht Club, Jomtien, 0 3823 7752) rents yachts, while coastal **Bungee Jump & Paintball Park** (248/10 Thanon Thepprasit, 0 3830 0608, www.paintballpark-pattaya.com), **Pattaya Kart Speedway** (248/2 Thanon Thepprasit, 0 3842 2044) and **Phoenix Golf Club** (Thanon Sukhumvit km158, 0 3823 9391-8, rates B1,000 Mon-Fri, B1,800 Sat, Sun, caddy B250) are self-explanatory.

Novelty attractions include **Ripley's Believe It or Not** (Royal Garden Plaza, 0 3871 0294-8, www.ripleysthailand.com, admission B380, B280 under-12s), showcasing freakish things, and **Sanctuary of Truth** (206/2 Naklua Soi 12, 0 3822 5407, admission B500, B250 under-15s), a fantastical, pantheistic wooden temple with a dolphin show, horse riding and speed boat trips. **Tiffany's** (464 Thanon Pattaya 2, 0 3842 1700-5, B500-B800) is the best of the three ladyboy cabarets.

Where to stay, eat & drink

The upmarket **Dusit Resort** (240/2 Thanon Pattaya Beach, 0 3842 5611-7/http://pattaya.dusit.com, double B5,800-B38,000) has a near-private beachfront, lush gardens and sporty facilities. **Sugar Hut** (391/18 Thanon Thappaya, www.sugarhutpattaya.com, double B8,430-B14,1200, main courses B200) offers gorgeous stilt bungalows and fine Thai food with optional floor seating. Music memorabilia and a climbing wall adorn the funkily designed **Hard Rock Hotel & Café** (429 Thanon Beach, 0 3842 8755-9, www.hardrockhotels.net, double $125-$990, main courses B350). Horse riding and an oriental teahouse are draws at spacious **Horseshoe Point** (Thanon Siam Country Club, 0 3873 5050, www.thehorseshoepoint.com, double B4,300-B7,500). Set in gardens on a near-private beach, **Cabbages & Condoms Resort & Restaurant** (366/11 Phra Tamnak Soi 4, 0 3825 0035, www.cabbagesandcondoms.co.th, double B2,119-B11,064, main courses B230) puts a condom under your pillow. Among rare budget digs, **J House** (595/2-3 Thanon Beach, 0 3842 0852, double B800) overlooks the sea.

Bruno's maintains fine European cuisine and service (Chateau Dale Plaza, Thanon Thappraya, 0 3836 4600-1, main courses B400). South Pattaya is full of Middle Eastern cafés, while **Shenanigans** (Marriott Pattaya Resort, 0 3871 0641-3, main courses B250) offers Irish food, Guinness and bands. **Hopf Brew House** (219 Thanon Beach, 0 3871 0650, main courses B350) mixes homebrew beer, German food and, on Saturdays, live opera!

Hell-themed, trance temple **Lucifer's Disco** (Walking Street, 7pm-2am daily) attracts young *farang*, while others frequent the open-air beer bars, brimming with 'hostesses'. Pattayaland Sois 1, 2 and 3 have the most massage parlours and go-go bars, with short-stay rooms upstairs.

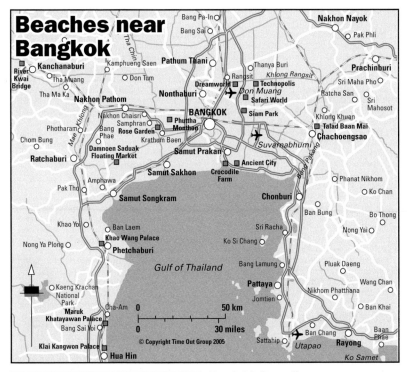

Beaches near Bangkok

Gulf of Thailand

0   50 km

0   30 miles

© Copyright Time Out Group 2005

Gay & lesbian

Pattayaland Soi 3 is 'Boys' Town'. Amid the
go-go and massage outlets are classier bars in
gay hotels, such as **Café Royale** (0 3842 3515,
www.caferoyale-pattaya.com, double B1,000-
B2,800, main courses B220-B340), **Ambiance
Hotel** (0 3842 4099, www.ambiance-pattaya.
com, double B1,100-B3,400, main courses B250)
and the swish **ICON** (146/8-9 Thappraya
Soi 1, 0 3825 0300, double B1,700-B3,000, main
courses B200). **Dick's Café** (413/129 Thanon
Tappraya, 0 3825 2417, www.dickscafe.com)
is the local branch of the dapper Bangkok
bar-restaurant. The gay beach is situated just
north of Royal Jomtien Resort, while another
crowd-puller is the **Pattaya Gay Festival**
(www.pattayagayfestival.com), which is held
in late November.

Resources

Hospital

*Bangkok Pattaya Hospital, 301 Thanon
Sukhumvit, Naklua (0 3842 7751-3/
www.pattayahospital.com).*

Tourist information

*TAT, 609 Thanon Phra Tamnak (0 3842 8750).
Also try www.pattaya.com.*

Ko Samet

Close to Bangkok and frequented by
young weekenders, this dagger-shaped isle
immortalised by poet Sunthorn Phu is actually
a national park (0 3865 3034, B200, B100 under-
16s). Smarter developments are now upgrading
its shambolic fringe of resorts with minimal
amenities and aesthetics. Boats from Baan Phe
dock at **Na Dan**, near which the squeaky white
sand of **Had Sai Kaew** is the first of a string
of pretty bays down the east side. Aside from
the jet skis, tours and inflatable banana rides,
the calm is disturbed only by beach massages,
snorkelling and a mellow party scene.

Where to stay, eat & drink

From densely packed Had Sai Kaew, resorts
get sparser as the coccyx-bruising road judders
to **Ao Phai**, **Silver Sand** (0 3864 4074, double
B1,000-B1,600), which hosts the grooviest

Beach Escapes

beachside disco with fire jugglers, and the lodges of **Samet Villa** (0 3864 4094, double B2,100-B2,300). Just beyond, gay-friendly **Tubtim Resort** (Ao Tubtim, 0 3864 4025-7, double B500-B1,500, main courses B40-B300) serves great seafood.

The busy half moon of **Ao Wong Deuan** is easier to reach via its pier. Guided groups pack the seafood restaurants. Trendies kick back to DJs at **Taleburé Bed & Bar** (0 1762 3548, 1862 9402, double B1,600-B2,400, main courses B60-B300), where retro-chic bungalows survey the bay. A short hike further, **Ao Thian** has eccentric shoreline huts at **Lung Dum** (0 1458 8430, double B500-B800).

The best food is up north at sleekly minimalist **Moo Ban Talay** (Ao Noi Na, 0 3864 4251 ,01838 8682, www.moobantalay.com, double B5,000-B8,000, main courses B250-B375), with a spa but poor sand and sea. Remote, upmarket resorts with their own ferries dot the southern tip and the humid west, nest of the snazzily romantic **Ao Phrao Resort** (0 384 4100-3, www.aopraoresort.com, double B5,200-B12,900, main courses B100-B400).

Note that during peak periods Ko Samet's rooms can get scarce after noon.

Getting there & around

By road
Open *songtaew* ply appalling tracks, so many visitors prefer to walk.

By boat
Ferries to Na Dan (B100 return; 40mins) depart Baan Phe bus station pier and Saphan Nuan Thip pier 500m into town (hourly 8am-5pm Nov-Feb, otherwise 2-hourly, plus waiting). A few serve Wong Deuan (45mins). Pricey speedboats (0 3865 1999) go direct to beaches. Boats rarely run after dark.

Resources

Hospital
Rayong Hospital, Rayong (0 3861 1104/http:// hospital.moph.go.th/rayong); Phe Health Centre (0 3865 2613).

Tourist information
Minimal leaflets at piers. Try www.kohsamet.com.

Ko Chang

Thailand's second largest island is one of 46 national park isles bordering Cambodia (0 3953 8100, admission B200, B100 concessions). Since Prime Minister Thaksin Shinawatra proclaimed it the 'next Phuket' in 2002, a land-grab has outpaced supposedly sensitive planning. Trucks rumble the road around forested mountains, which contain three waterfalls. Ko Chang's named for an elephant-shaped southern headland. Though pachyderms aren't indigenous, there's a refuge at **Ko Chang Elephant Camp** (22/4 Had Khlong Son, 0 1919 3995) and **Chang Chutiman** (0 9939 6676) runs elephant treks.

Boats dock at Tha Dan Kao, while shops, bars and restaurants centre on north-western **Had Sai Khao** beach. Dive shops access the so-so reefs (Aug-May) and offer watersports, including dinghy sailing on Klong Prao. Some head south to islands (open in dry season only) like Ko Mak, boasting white sand and internet, and the larger, more exclusive Ko Kood.

Where to stay & eat

Had Sai Khao veers from backpacker huts to smarter air-con bungalows like **Top Resort** (0 3955 1364-5, www.topresort.info, rates B800-B1,440) and **Cookie Bungalow** (0 1861 4227, rates B2,000-B5,000), known for its seafood. **Baan Nuna Bungalows** (0 1821 4202, rates B350) serves decent pizzas and Thai fare.

Heading south, resorts get sparser. On Ao Klong Prao, **Klong Prao Resort** (0 3959 7216, 01830 0126, www.klongpraoresort.com, double B1,500-B3,500), set on a lagoon with a private beach. Across the *klong*, **Panviman Resort** (0 3955 1290-6, www.panviman.com, double B5,000-B6,000) has chic bungalows and a pool, while **Boutique Resort & Health Spa** (0 9938 6403, www.boutiqueresortandhealthspa. com, double B2,000) offers treatments in wooden *salas*. The only five-star property, **Amari Emerald Cove** (0 3955 2000, rates B6,500-B14,268), boasts a 50-metre pool, Sivara Spa and the Italian restaurant Sassi.

On Ao Kai Bae, **Koh Chang Cliff Beach** (0 3955 7037, www.kohchangcliffbeach.com, double B4,000-B7,000) has villas and a pool overlooking its hideaway beach; in the resort-pocked south-east, **Bang Bao**, a fishing village on stilts, offers homestays and fresh seafood.

On Ko Mak, the best bungalows are at **Ko Mak Resort** (0 3950 1013, 03952 2134, www.kohmakresort.com, rates B600-B3,200). Ko Kood's finest is the expansive **Beach** (0 1959 5858, www.thebeachkohkood.com, double B3,800-B5,200), boasting 24-hour electricity.

Getting there & around

By road
Songtaew link bus station, pier and island bays.

By boat
Hourly ferries to Tha Dan Kao leave Laem Ngop (8am-5pm daily in high season, 1hr, B60). Car ferries

leave east of Laem Ngop (B150 per car) by three firms: Ko Chang Ferries (0 3952 8286-8), Ferries Ko Chang (0 3959 7143) or Centre Point Pier Ferry (0 3953 8196). Ferries depart Laem Ngop for Ko Maak (3pm daily Nov-Apr, returning 8am; 3hrs); and Ko Kood (noon on even dates, via Ko Chang, total 4hrs).

Resources

Hospital
Ko Chang International Clinic (9/14 White Sand Beach, 0 3955 1151/www.kohchang interclinic.com).

Tourist information
TAT, Laem Ngop (0 3959 7259-60). Also try www.kohchang.com.

Gulf of Thailand

Hua Hin & Cha-am

Founded as a royal spa, Hua Hin retains palaces, a quaint railway station and traces of fishing village charm, having restrained pollution, prostitution and development. The king still lives at the art nouveau **Phra Ratchawang Klai Kangwon** ('Far from Worries Palace') in Hua Hin, but it's tourable when he's away. Its miles-long beaches stretch north past condos, resorts and the stunning teak **Phra Ratchaniwet Marukhathayawan**

Tsunami: 26 December 2004

When the tsunami of 26 December 2004 deluged Thailand's Andaman Sea coast people around the world sorrowed for a place where many had spent their holidays. Though the area's recovery has been swift, the waves left over 5,000 people in Thailand dead, plus 3,000 missing, out of nearly a quarter-million casualties across the Indian Ocean. But the uncounted toll of prostitutes and labourers, many of them illegal immigrants, makes that estimate a low one.

Worst hit were the karstic islets of Ko Phi Phi and the beach-meets-rainforest resort of Khao Lak, south and north of Phuket respectively. Everything got washed off Phi Phi's densely built sandbar, while along Khao Lak's long, shallow seafront waves of up to six metres (20 feet) reached two kilometres (1.2 miles) inland. Around 2,000 of the victims were Scandinavians, whose patronage had helped turn Khao Lak into a major resort. On Phuket, the similarly shallow Kamala beach was also badly damaged, while the much deeper seafront at neighbouring Surin escaped unscathed. Dunes and mangroves, where not cleared by developers, proved their natural defensive merits.

Immediate efforts to rebuild left little trace of the waves at Phuket, Krabi and Ko Lanta. Reefs were less damaged than initially feared. Though salt contaminated soil and fresh water, the seas and sands – as at Phi Phi's Maya Bay, where *The Beach* was controversially filmed – had received a natural cleansing. Normality returned perhaps too soon for those who hoped the catastrophe would spur the enforcement of environmental

laws regarding the height, density and location of eyesore developments.

Despite admirable plans, like restoring dunes and turning Phi Phi's sandbar into a park, rebuilding work by well-connected people – while fisherfolk, villagers and small-time bungalow operators were illegally muscled out – was met with little or no protest by the authorities. Rumours of land-grabs by crony businessmen had hordes of backpackers helping the residents of Phi Phi and Khao Lak rebuild. However, the government quickly insisted that all volunteers apply for work permits, just as it had declined international aid. Despite pre-election promises, state aid has been limited, and NGO funds are often hard to distribute, while ordinary folk languish in planning limbo without a livelihood. Khao Lak may take two years to rise again.

Some economic harm was also done by major news reports sensationalising the scale of the damage to Phuket. Safety drills, lookout towers, warning system plans and heavy hotel discounts countered that message, and by March occupancy levels were back up to 50 per cent. The hotel industry announced its greatest obstacle – particularly among the vital Asian vacationers – is fear of ghosts. Local resort staff fearful of spirits seem to have been coaxed back by a well-publicised series of exorcism rites.

By the first anniversary, parts of an impressively designed tsunami memorial-cum-education centre are expected to have opened, probably at Khao Lak. For updates, check at www.phi-phi.com, www.railay.com, www.inet.co.th/tsunami and www.tsunamisouls.org.

Beach Escapes

Veranda Resort & Spa.

palace to **Cha-am**, a ho-hum resort catering to raucous Thai *sanuk*. South is Pranburi, a yachtie haven with designer hotels. Sand and water quality are middling, and weekends can get crowded. Hua Hin's beaches are quieter south of the Sofitel towards **Had Khao Takiap**. Hua Hin has a walkable centre, but limited transport.

Diversions include golf, and **Khao Sam Roi Yot National Park** (0 3261 9078, B200, B100 under-16s), where you can kayak in wetlands amid karsts that inspired its '300 peaks' name.

Where to eat & drink

Aside from Hua Hin's no-frills seafood jetty restaurants, for Thai try the garden at homely **Baan Youyen** (29 Hua Hin Soi 51, 0 3253 1191-2, www.youyen.com, main courses B65-B300); the chic beach property **Let's Sea** (83/155 Talay Soi 12, 0 3253 6022, main courses B250); or the dinner-theatre **Sasi** (83/159 Thanon Nhongkae, 0 3251 2488, main courses B750; and out of town, **Supatra by the Sea** (122/63 Thanon Takiab, Nong Gae, 0 3253 6561-2, www. supatrabythesea.com, main courses B120-B500), with fine hill/ocean vistas. The waterfront **Brasserie de Paris** (3 Thanon Naresdamri, 0 3253 0637, main courses B250-B995) excels. The mammoth **Hua Hin Brewing Company** (Hilton Hotel, 0 3251 2888, makes a change beer bars, as does the folk music venue **Takeang Pub** (Soi Bintaban).

Where to stay

Hua Hin has some world-class spa resorts. **Chiva Som Health Resort** (73/4 Thanon Phet Kasem, 0 3253 6536, www.chivasom.com, double B18,600-B44,000) attracts superstars to its villas and holistic treatments, while guru therapists also visit **Evason Hua Hin** (Pranburi, 0 3263 2111-40, www.evasonhuahin. com, double B5,750-B16,000), where minimalism permeates the pool, villas and spa. Mr and Mrs Beckham and hip hotel mavens gush about the remote, all-white **Aleenta** (Pranburi, 0 3257 0220, www.aleenta.com, double B5,500-B15,500), though cheery, zestful **Veranda Resort & Spa** (737/12 Thanon Mung Talay, 0 3270 9099, www.verandaresortand spa.com, double B5,800-B6,900) is a fuller designer experience.

Anantara Resort & Spa (43/1 Thanon Phet Kasem, 0 3252 0250-6, www.anantara.com, double $195-$780) feels villagey, while **Sofitel Central Hua Hin** (1 Thanon Damnoen Kasem, 0 3251 2021-38, www.sofitel.com, double B6,400-B32,000) maintains its 1920s 'grand hotel' nobility. Aristocrats have opened their old wooden beach mansions of **Baan Bayan** (119 Thanon Petchkasem, 0 3253 3544, 0 2636 6588, www.baanbayan.com, double B4,500-B26,675); a cheaper, antiquey option is **Ban Somboon** (13/4 Soi Kasemsamphan, 0 3251 1538, double B700-B900).

Resources

Hospital
San Paolo Hua Hin Hospital (222 Thanon Petchkasem, 0 3253 2576).

Tourist information
TAT, 500/51 Thanon Phetkasem, Cha-am (0 3247 1005-6).

Ko Samui

With smart hotels, gourmet restaurants, luxury spas, private villas and New Age pilgrims, Ko Samui is more cosmopolitan than Phuket, yet keeps its laid-back roots, with fishing, coconuts and backpacker huts. Accelerating development stretches that charm (and the water supply), but remains sensitive to the landscape of sweeping beaches, rugged capes and forested hills.

The commercial/official hub around the port **Nathon** boasts Hainan-influenced teak shophouses, a market and great hawker food. Just south at Lipa Noi beach, **Samui Dharma Healing Centre** (Sawai Home Bungalows, Lipa Noi, 0 7723 4170, www.dharmahealing. com, rates B500-B700) runs strict Buddhist fasts, with simple wooden beach huts. The North Coast water is less clear than in the east, but calm year-round. It spans **Bophut**, Samui's most charming village, and Had Bangrak – called **Big Buddha beach** for the 12-metre (39-foot) statue in **Wat Phra Yai** – is a tranquil spot despite the cutely rustic airport nearby.

On the east, **Chaweng**'s crescent of fine sand, swimmable waters and arching palms, is both party central and a vaguely sleazy lesson in overdevelopment, housing the best of Samui's limited shops. Over a ridge with giddying views, beautiful **Lamai** bay has crystal waters, fine sands and boulders at the southern end. Two of these, **Hinta Hinyai**, resemble genitals and have become a tourist trap. Lamai town is a mess, with its poor restaurants and bars full of prostitutes. Roads then fork inland to **Nam Tok Ta Nim** waterfall, with mountain views en route, or round the less disturbed southern beaches at Laem Set and Taling Ngam.

Activities

Samui lacks reefs, but umpteen firms serve nearby sites (best May-Oct). **Easy Divers** (0 7741 3373, www.easydivers-thailand.com) is the best chain, while boutique scuba outfit **100 Degrees East** (Big Buddha beach, 0 6282 2983, www.onehundreddegreeseast.com) also offers watersports including kiteboarding and speedboats.

Yachties have UK charter giant **Sunsail** (0 7623 9057, www.sunsail.com) and the independents **Coco Sailing** (0 9726 5728, www.cocosailing.com), **Kia Ora** (0 7742 5264, www.kiaorathailand.com) and **Siam Commercial Boat Charter** (0 1895 1183). Even better, explore the wildlife-rich karst islets of **Ang Thong Marine National Park** by kayak via **Sea Canoe** (Lamai, 0 7621 2172,

www.seacanoe.net) or **Blue Stars Kayaking** (Chaweng, 0 7741 3231, www.bluestars.info).

Eco-award-winning cyclist Michael Yantis rents top-end mountain bikes at **Red Bicycle** (just south of Hinta Hinyai, Lamai, 0 7723 2136, www.redbicycle.org) for half-day tours and longer. The vertigo immune can slide by cable between treetops above Maenam with **Canopy Jungle Tours** (Chaweng office 0 7741 4150, canopyadventures@hotmail.com).

Foodies can learn Thai cooking at the prize-winning **SITCA** (Chaweng, 0 7741 3172, www.sitca.net, B1,200-B1,600). Buffalo fighting takes place four times a year (advertised on trucks) at **Ban Bang Makham** north of Nathon.

Where to stay & eat

Just north of Nathon, purists treasure **Bang Makham**'s southern cuisine (Ao Bang Makham, 0 7742 6181, main courses B250). In Maenam, **Napasai** (0 7742 9200, www. pansea.com, double $290-$990) stands out, with tasteful, French-influenced villas you'd expect from Pansea-Orient Express.

Quaint old shophouses overlook Bophut beach, many converted into guesthouses, restaurants and shops. The **Lodge** (Fisherman's Village, 0 7742 5337, double B1,500-B1,800) is an immaculate beachside boutique hotel with sea views from its hardwood rooms. The **Shack** (Fisherman's Village, closed Sun, main courses B200-B550) barbeques marinated meat and seafood, while fans of salad and herbal tea go to **Healthy & Fun Yoga Café** (Fisherman's Village, 0 7724 5046, main courses B120-B200). Palatial villas at the pioneering resort **Tongsai Bay** (Bophut, 0 7724 5480, www.tongsaibay.co.th, double B11,000-B52,000) have balcony baths and views of its near-private beach.

Among Bangrak's decent budget digs, **Shambala** (0 7742 5330, www.samui-shambala. com, double B600-B1,000, main courses B80-B200) has simple bungalows in a mature shoreside garden, plus the area's best Thai food. On Chaweng, **Poppies** (South Chaweng, 0 7742 2419, www.poppies-samui.com, double B6,900 B11,000, main courses B300-B500) offers luxurious cottages in a seaside garden, plus Thai/Pacific Rim fine dining. **Olivio** at **Baan Haad Ngam Boutique Resort** (North Chaweng, 0 7723 1500, www.baanhaadngam. com, double B4,775-B13,000, main courses B400) draws plaudits for its Italian feasts, served beachside. The comfy, Bali-esque bungalows and hotel rooms have sweeping views. Commanding Samui's best panorama, **Jungle Club** (South Chaweng, 0 1894 2327, www.sawadee.com/samui/jungleclub, double

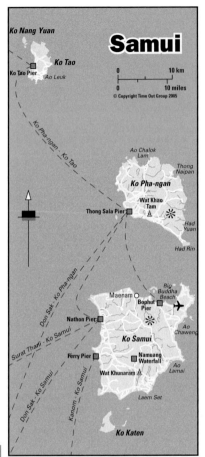

Ko Nang Yuan

Samui

Ko Tao
Ko Tao Pier
Ao Leuk

0   10 km
0   10 miles
© Copyright Time Out Group 2005

Ao Chalok Lam
Thong Naipan
Ko Pha-ngan
Wat Khao Tam
Thong Sala Pier
Had Yuan
Had Rin

Maenam
Big Buddha Beach
Bophut Pier
Nathon Pier
Ao Chaweng
Ko Samui
Ferry Pier
Namuang Waterfall
Wat Khunaram
Ao Lamai
Laem Set

Ko Katen

Nightlife

Samui's weekly Glastonbury, the family-friendly **Secret Garden Festival** (Big Buddha beach, 5.30-11pm Sun) mixes Thai and Western rock, plus the odd big name, as does **Fisherman's Village Festival** (Bophut, Aug). Banging house and trance at **Gecko Village** (Bophut, 0 7724 5553-4) are a high-decibel warm-up for the big beach parties announced on fliers.

The mellower **Two Tiger's** (sic) beer garden (Fisherman's Village, 0 7743 0439) also sells intriguing clothes and prints, while families and fans of TV sport flock to Irish-themed **Tropical Murphy's** (Central Chaweng, 0 7741 3614-5). Chaweng's big clubs (both free) – **Green Mango** (Beach Road, 0 7742 2148) and **Reggae Pub** (Chaweng Lagoon, 0 7742 2331) – draw large laddish crowds nightly. The style-conscious escape to Soi Colibiri's stark white **POD Bar** (0 1891 4042), the modern wine bar **Bellini's** (0 7741 3831, main courses B200-B400) with imaginative northern Italian cuisine, **Guapa** bar for Mediterranean tapas and **Molotov** sports bar for vodka variants.

Mind & body

Day spas and nearly every resort proffer myriad healing options. The quality massages and treatments at **Baan Sabai** (Big Buddha beach, 0 7724 5175, www.ban-sabai.com) take place in teak *salas* by the sea. Hot stone massage is one of many therapies amid the silk, carved stone and bubbling baths of **Four Seasons Tropical Spa** (Central Chaweng, 0 7741 4141-3). At **Koh Somatics** (Chaweng, 0 7743 0011, www.hannasomatics.com), Cynthia Lindway teaches the pain-relieving Hanna Somatic exercises. The sauna and plunge pool built into boulders draw regulars to **Tamarind Springs** (Lamai beach, 0 7742 4221, www.tamarind springs.com), also known for its distinctive rental villas.

Getting around

By road

Thailand's third largest island, 21x25km (13x15.5 miles), Samui takes 50mins by car to circle, 90mins by motorbike, which are lethal on the narrow, hilly, often sandy roads. *Songthaews* can be hailed anywhere as a day bus (B20-B70) or night taxi (up to B300; less if part-loaded). Motorcycle taxis are quick and negotiable. Yellow 'metered' taxis are a rip-off.

By boat

Ferries link Nathon with Surat Thani (2hrs) via **Seatran Ferry** (0 7727 5060, hourly 5.30am-5.30pm daily, B150); or with Don Sai by car ferries (6am-7pm

B450-B3,500, main courses B150-B550) is a basic, chillout bungalow set-up minus fan or air-con (not needed at this altitude), with an excellent French/Thai restaurant and a nice pool. A slog uphill, it has a free airport pick-up.

On Lamai's shallow, coral-strewn north, the renovated **Spa Samui** (0 7723 0855, www.spasamui.com, double B500-B5,500) gained fame for its colonic irrigation treatment. Devotees break fasts at its award-winning vegetarian café where free thinkers connect. It has a hillside branch. The 'Lanna minimalist' **Pavilion** boutique resort and spa (124/24 Lamai Beach, 0 2223 3083-7, www.pavilion samui.com, double B6,000-B12,000) now presides graciously over Lamai's swimmable middle stretch.

Beach Escapes

daily; to avoid 2-3hr waits, arrive by 8am) via **Racha Ferry** (0 7747 1151/2/3, hourly, B84) or **Seatran Ferry** (0 7725 1555, hourly, B80).

Resources

Hospital
Bangkok Samui Hospital, Thanon Thaweeratphakdee, Chaweng (0 7742 9500, www.samui hospital.com).

Immigration office
0 7742 1069.

Tourist information
Thanon Thaweeratphakdee, Nathon (0 7742 0504/tatsamui@tat.or.th).
Publishes *Samui Guide, Samui Dining Guide, Samui Spa Guide* and *Samui Directory.* Also try www.kosamui.com and www.samuiguide.com.

Ko Pha-ngan

An hour by ferry from Samui, Pha-ngan is ten years behind, slightly less beautiful but friendlier. It attracts a blend of backpackers, entrepreneurs, dreamers and wasters to its smaller, craggier, often reef-laden bays, despite erratic electricity and tortuous transportation. Coconuts and fishing remain village mainstays.

East of the commercial centre of Thong Sala port is **Wat Khao Tham Meditation Centre** (*see p178* **The art of doing nothing**). The other ferry dock, **Had Rin West**, is rocky and shallow, and backs on to the headland's better beach, **Had Rin East**. Home of the **Full Moon Parties**, it would be good for swimming and snorkelling if it weren't for the longtail traffic.

Where to stay & eat

Amid Had Rin's backpacker huts, the best of the few decent rooms are at **Drop In Club Resort & Spa** (0 7737 5444, www.dropinclubresortand spa.com, double B2,600-B17,500), which has a pool. Had Rin dining is quite cosmopolitan, with high-quality Italian, the **Shell** (Had Rin Lake, 0 7737 5149, main courses B150-B200), and Indian, **Om Ganesh** (Main Road, 0 7737 5123, main courses B60-B130). For burgers and beers, try the quieter **Outback Bar** (Main Road, 0 7737 5126, main courses B120-B250). On Had Yuan beach, there are stilt bungalows at **Big Blue Bungalows** (0 7742 2781, www.bigbluediving samui.com, double B500-B800), some sleeping six, plus a good restaurant.

Inspiration for *The Beach*, Had Tien's **Sanctuary Spa & Wellness Centre** is a B60 boat or 90-minute hike from Had Rin (0 1271 3614, www.thesanctuary-kpg.com,

treatments B70-B3,500), with sea-view suites, fine seafood/veggie cuisine and separate centres for fasters and spa treatments (B300-B1,000). B70 dorm beds with chores.

Flanked by Thaan Prawet and Wung Thong falls, the snorkelsome double bay of **Thong Naipan** in the north-east is better accessed by boat than the potholed track. The brick cottages with huge balconies at **Panviman Resort** (0 7723 8543, www.panviman.com, double B1,750-B11,000) have sea views and a good international menu. Down the family-oriented beach, **Dolphin** (no phone, B300-B400) has decent bungalows and a great bar serving wholefood.

On sleepy Had Salad, the chilled **Salad Hut** (salad_hut@hotmail.com, double B300-B600) has simple wooden fan bungalows. Overlooking Had Yao to the west, **Tantawan Bungalows** (0 7734 9108/0 1956 0700, www.tantawanbungalow.com, double B350-B1,200) has passable fan bungalows with shared bathrooms, great vistas, superb cuisine and a good pool.

Nightlife

Many visitors still come for one thing only: Full Moon Inc. Every month up to 10,000 partyheads rave to the hard trance on **Had Rin East** at the world's biggest beach party. Most stay on Ko Pha-ngan, but many speedboat in from northern Samui, filling rooms on both isles. Since Samui's party beach succumbed to villas, most months Had Rin also holds smaller Half Moon and Black Moon parties (consult www.kohphangan.com); dates shift on Buddhist lunar festivals.

Otherwise on Had Rin's bar strip, **Harmony** (behind Bamboozle restaurant, 9pm-2am Mon, Wed, Fri), and **Backyard** (road to Had Leela, 9pm-2am Tue, Thur, Sun) play uplifting trance and hard trance respectively.

Getting around

By road
Beach-hopping is tiresomely time-consuming. *Songthaews* run regularly to all accessible beaches from Had Rin and Thong Sala (B50-B80) when a ferry docks, otherwise once or twice a day, and at bar closing in Had Rin. Even the paved roads can be terrifying slaloms; unpaved rutted tracks are dirt-biker heaven but otherwise dodgy. Many simply hike.

By boat
Several east and north coast beaches have no land access. Ferries run from Don Sak or Surat Thani to Thong Sala (5-6 times a day, 4-6hrs), and Nathon (Samui) to Thong Sala (3 per day, 70mins). A catamaran runs between Maenam/Big Buddha and Thong Sala (2 per day, 45mins), a ferry plies Big Buddha to Had Rin (10.30am, 1pm, 4pm; return 9.30am, 11.40am, 2.30pm; 50mins) and a daily longtail from Maenam stops at all beaches between

Had Rin and Thong Naipan (noon, return 8am).
Samui-Had Rin speedboats cost B250. You can also
charter a boat (B200-B800). Longtail taxis run from
Had Rin East (B60 by day to Had Tien, B300 at
night), extorting up to B1,000 for longer rides.

Resources

Banks Had Rin ATM is often empty.

Hospitals
*Koh Phangan Hospital, north of Thong Sala
(0 7737 7034).*

Ko Tao

'Turtle Island' resembles a turtle diving south
to Ko Pha-ngan (40km/25miles) and Ko Samui
(60km/37miles). Rocky and jungly, it has a long
western strand facing **Ko Nang Yuan**, three
islets linked by a tri-star beach. Non-divers
can feel out of place, but have 11 quiet beaches,
notably **Leuk**, **Jansom** and **June Juea**. Tao's
walkable, but has bike taxis and a few *songtaews*.

Boasting good coral, swim-throughs and large
fish, the 24 dive sites have good visibility
(late May-early Oct; off limits in the Nov-Dec
monsoon). Snorkelling gear can be rented all
over; **Black Tip Diving & Water Sports** (Ao
Tanote, 0 7745 6488-9, www.blacktipdiving.com)
also has kayaks, wakeboards and waterskis.

Where to stay & eat

Over 20 resorts cater to and teach every level of
diver, notably **Koh Tao Coral Grand Resort**
(Had Sairee, 0 7745 6431-3, www.kohtaocoral.
com, double B2,100-B7,900), **Buddha View
Dive Resort** (Chalok Baan Kao, 0 7745 6074-5,
www.buddhaview-diving.com, double B300-
B1,500) and **Planet Scuba** (Mae Had pier,
0 7745 6110, www.planet-scuba.net, double
B9,300-B9,700, incl diving). A pioneer, **Ao
Leuk Resort** (Ao Leuk beach, no phone,
double B300-B400) retains a real island feel.
Sensi Paradise Resort (0 7745 6244, double
B900-B9,200) is a good upmarket option close to
Mae Had. **Baan Charm Churee** (Jansom Bay,
0 7745 6393-4, www.charmchureevilla.com,
double B2,700-B8,200) offers wood-and-wicker
rooms on a beautiful private beach. **Nang
Yuan Island Dive Resort** (0 7745 6088-93,
www.nangyuan.com, double B1,200-B4,800)
is the islet's sole, beautiful venue.

The charming **New Heaven Bakery**
(Sairee Village & Thian Og, 0 7745 6554, main
courses B50) has the best coffee. Italians swear
by the home-made fare at **La Matta** (Mae
Had, 0 9001 4046. Scoff Bailey's cheesecake
at **Farango Pizzeria** (Mae Had, 0 7745 6205,
main courses B150-B320).

Nightlife

Diving buddies often become drinking buddies,
notably at **Safety Stop** (Mae Had, 0 7745 6209,
main courses B20-B320). Beach parties vary by
day: on Had Sairee at the **AC Bar** meat market
(0 7745 6197, Tue, Thur, Sun), amid the tiki
torches and sand sculptures of **In Touch**
(0 7745 6514, Wed, Sat), and **Dry Bar** (Fri),
which occupies a gnarled live tree; and on Mae
Had at the **Whitening Bar** (0 7745 6199, Fri).

Resources

For tourist info try www.kohtaoonline.com.

Hospital
On Ko Samui or mainland at Chumphon.

Getting around

By boat
To Mae Had twice daily from Samui (1.5-3hrs, B150-
B450), Pha-ngan (1-3hrs, B250-B500), Chumphon
(2-5hrs, B400-B600) and Surat Thani (6-9hrs, B550-
B600). Contact Songserm Travel (Tao, 0 7745 6274,
Bangkok 0 2280 7897). Boats may not run in poor
weather. Longtails can always be chartered.

Andaman Sea

Ko Phuket

Thailand's largest island (49x27km/30x17
miles) has been a tourist magnet since the
1970s and a trading post for millennia. A tin
rush in the 19th century turned Phuket Town
(now City) into the island-province's capital,
brought thousands of Chinese settlers and left
the rainforested hills scarred. Phuket now
mines an even richer seam: tourism. Fishing
villages have been turned into smart resorts
or ramshackle shanties with operators offering
diving, yachting and 'eco-adventures'.

From the mainland over **Sarasin Bridge**,
or from nearby Phuket International Airport,
Route 402 threads south to Phuket City past
rubber plantations, the **Heroines' Monument**
(to two women who helped repel the Burmese
in 1785) and **Kathu**, where **Ban Kathu
Heritage Centre** (Ban Kathu School, 0 7632
1246, open by appointment) hosts a dusty
Mining Museum. Like Singapore, Melaka and
Penang, **Phuket City** retains Sino-Portuguese
shophouses and mansions, gaily decorated in
Greco-Roman and 'lucky' Chinese motifs. Some
tin baron homes along **Thanons Yaowarat**,
Krabi, **Thalang** and **Deebuk** have become
bars, boutiques or galleries. Named from *bukit*

Phuket Vegetarian Festival. *See p221*.

(Malay for 'hill'), Phuket City nestles round **Khao Rang** hill. The park at the summit offers views west to Phang-nga bay and the Sea Gypsy village on **Ko Siray**.

Though tourists visit Phuket City for shopping, dining and chores, they also come for the extraordinary bays that scallop the western and southern coasts. Even the long northern beach in Nai Yang National Park is being developed. Ao Bang Thao Mai fits hotels and golf courses of Phuket Laguna around lagoons in old mining pits, while many of the ritziest hotels, apartments, shops and villas snuggle in relatively quiet Kamala and Surin beaches. Hit badly by the tsunami, sleepy Kamala's fisherfolk had earlier been impacted by the Vegas-style **Phuket FantaSea** (0 7638 5000, www.phuket-fantasea.com, show B1,000-B1,500). Gaudily themed, it funnels coach parties into shops, an uninspiring 4,000-seat buffet restaurant and a 3,000-seat theatre for a pyrotechnic spectacle, including live animals.

Ringed by hills, the perfect crescent of **Ao Patong** is raw tourism, with pestering touts, gem stores, stalls selling fakes and bars full of prostitutes down the **Soi Bangla** strip. The developed lower west coast has arguably the best beaches, though monsoon rip tides can claim swimmers' lives off shadeless **Karon** and prettier, family-friendly **Kata**, where twin bays frame the snorkel-friendly **Ko Pu** islet. **Kata Yai** is the venue for September's windsurfing championships.

There are stunning views from beyond here, and particularly at the southern cape **Laem Phrom Thep**, which gets crowded at sunset. East round the cape, arcs dramatically beautiful, windswept **Nai Harn** beach.

Activities

Full-day eco tours (B1,500-B2,000 including lunch and transfers) are run by **Siam Safari** (45 Thanon Chao Fa West, Chalong, 0 7628 0116, www.siamsafari.com), **Green Travel** (Robinson's, Thanon Ong Sim Pai, Phuket Town, 07625 6315), **Phuket Union Travel** (64/23 Thanon Chao Fa West, Chalong, 0 7622 5522-33, www.phuket-union.com) or **Asian Premier Holidays** (74/90 Poonphon Night Plaza, Phuket City, 0 7624 6260, www.asian premier.com). Mountain bike specialists include **Bike Tours** (10/195 Thanon Kwang, Phuket City, 0 7626 3575, 01797 6540, www.biketours thailand.com). Several 4WD tours twist through the jungles and plantations. Elephant treks are mostly short bush rambles; some include mangrove kayaking.

Most canoe trips explore sea caves in the jungled karst islets soaring out of the vast bay of Ao Phang-nga. The eco-sensitive pioneer of this now often irresponsible mass activity, John 'Caveman' Gray, has split from **Sea Canoe** (0 7621 2172, www.seacanoe.net) to offer similarly educative tours through **John Gray's Sea Canoe** (0 7625 4505-7, www.seacanoe.com). Bring water, a T-shirt and sunscreen. Most boat tours of Ao Phang-nga National Marine Park take in 'James Bond Island' (**Ko Tapu**, where *The Man with the Golden Gun* was shot).

Phuket is Thailand's diving HQ, with a recompression chamber in Patong and 50-plus companies. Good ones include **White & Blue Dive Club** (0 7628 1007-8, www.white-bluedive.com), **Dive Master** (0 7629 2402-3, www.divemaster.net), **Scuba Cat** (0 7634 5246, www.scubacat.com) and **South-east Asia Liveaboards** (0 7634 0406, www.seal-asia.com). Aside from day trips, liveaboard tours take in dramatic reefs and pelagic fish at the Similan, Surin or Phi Phi islands. Access and visibility drop during the monsoon.

Golf is a major diversion, notably at **Blue Canyon Country Club** (165 Thanon Thepkasatri, Had Nai Yang, 0 7632 7440, www.bluecanyonclub.com), **Phuket Golf & Country Club** (80/1 Thanon Wichitsongkhram, 0 7632 1038-41, www.phuketcountryclub.com) and the **Laguna** (www.lagunaphuket.com).

Boosted by a cut in boat import duties, Phuket aims to be Asia's yachting hub. Operators at **Boat Lagoon Marina** (20/27 Thanon Thepkrasattri) include charter giants **Sunsail** (0 7623 9057, www.sunsailthailand. com), brokerages, service companies, a hotel, a spa and restaurants. Amateurs and day sailors may prefer to frequent the rather ramshackle **Ao Chalong Yacht Club** (Thanon Chaofa, www.acycphuket.com). Super-yachts berth at **Yacht Haven Marina** (141/2 Moo 2 Tumbol Maikhao, 0 7620 6704-5, www.yacht-haven-phuket.com), while the new **Royal Phuket Marina** (68 Thanon Thepkrasattri, www.royalphuketmarina.com) will boast a swanky mall, nightclubs and champagne bars to add a touch of St Tropez.

Mind & body

Unlike Samui's New Age wellness, Phuket tends towards high-class pampering, though its many tin-roofed herbal saunas (often at an alfresco massage parlour) purge the pores for as little as B50. While most good hotels boast a spa, world's-best rated **Banyan Tree Phuket** has its own treatments, and runs all-day packages, while the holistic Six Senses Spa at Evason Phuket (for both, *see p219*) is the best place for non-Thai massage. The jungly **Hideaway Spa** (Laguna Entrance, 382/33

Thanon Srisoonthorn, 0 7627 1549,
www.phuket-hideaway.com) adapts ancient
recipes for its herbal steam rooms.

Where to stay

Phuket has some 500 properties (many bookable
via www.phuket.com or www.hoteltravel.com),
with the best beds up north and budget rooms
limited to Patong, Karon and Phuket City, with
no bargain bungalows. Long, virgin Mai Khao
beach now hosts the sublime **JW Marriott
Phuket Resort & Spa** (0 7633 8000, double
$377-$2,968) and its chi-chi Mandara Spa. On
private Nai Thorn beach, the palatial residences
at **Trisara** (0 7631 0100, www.trisara.com,
double $575-$3,960) have private pools, live-in
maids and iPods. **Banyan Tree Phuket**
(Laguna Phuket, 0 7632 4374, www.laguna
phuket.com, double $550-$3,400) has tasteful
seaside villas and a gorgeous spa (*see p218*).

More elite still are the hillside bungalows
of **Chedi Phuket** (Ao Surin, 0 7632 4017-20,
double $160-$780) and Ed Tuttle's stylish
and influential pared-down pavilions and
villas at **Amanpuri** (Ao Surin, 0 7632 4333,
www.amanresorts.com, double $675-$7,350).
Twin Palms (0 7631 6500, www.twinpalms-
phuket.com, double $170-$590) earns plaudits
for its immaculate modernism and gardens,
while beside it on Surin Beach, **Surin Bay
Inn** (0 7627 1601, www.surinbayinn.com,
double B1,000-B3,000) balances impeccable
rooms with value.

Patong's choicest beds are now at the
handsome, artful **Burasari** (32/1 Thanon
Ruamjai, 0 7629 2929, www.burasari.com,
double B2,700-B7,600). Between Karon and
Kata, **Mom Tri's Boathouse** (182 Thanon
Kok Tanoad, 0 7633 0 015-7, www.theboat
housephuket.com, double B4,000-B35,000) is the
flagship of pioneer resort architect Tri Devakul.

Still a benchmark, **Le Royal Meridien
Phuket Yacht Club** (Ao Nai Harn, 0 7638
1156-63, www.phuket-yachtclub.com, double
$120-$610) appears to be part of a cliff
commanding Ao Nai Harn bay, a beach
where guests get shuttled downhill from the
vista-ful villas of fruit-hued **Mangosteen
Resort & Spa** (9/4 Soi Mangosteen, 0 7628
9399, www.mangosteen-phuket.com, double
B6,500-B11,000). Contrastingly minimalist,
Evason Phuket Resort (100 Thanon Viset,
Rawai, 0 7638 1010-7, www.six-senses.com,
double B6,500-B50,000) also lacks a direct
beach, but has exclusive use of Ko Bon's
velvety offshore sands. Similarly, **Maiton
Island** (0 7621 4954-8, www.maitonisland.
com, double from B6,500) is the preserve
of one posh villa resort.

Where to eat

Grab an *oliang* (Chinese coffee) over morning
dim sum, *pa tong goh* (Chinese doughnuts) or
tao sor (stuffed Chinese buns) in Phuket City's
holes in the wall or Patong's Soi Sainamyen
stalls. **Somchit** and **Ton Pho**, both by the
clock tower on Thanon Phuket, serve Hokkien
noodles *chek* (dry) or *sapam* (soupy) for lunch.

Overlooking town and sea, **Thungka** (0 7621
1500, main courses B250) offers authentic
southern fare. Nearby, there's **Tamachart**
(Soi Puton, 0 7622 4287, main courses B200)
with quirky jungle decor. Two good Italian
options are **La Gaetana** (352 Thanon Phuket,
0 7625 0523, main courses B460), where friendly
host Gianni might dole out free 'Vitamin C'
(limoncello), and **Salvatore's** (15 Thanon
Rassada, 0 7622 5958, main courses B400)
with both fine dining and a cheaper pizzeria.

The quality of resort restaurants varies
dramatically. One option worth trying is
Patong Night Market (Thanon Ratcha
Uthit). But for better seafood than Patong's
seafront strip, head north to **Pan Yaah** (249
Thanon Prabaramee, 0 7634 4473, main courses
B250), which overlooks Patong, or the bayside
Rockfish (Thanon Kamala Beach, 0 7627
9732, main courses B350), with tasty Asian
salads and cool DJs.

For Pacific Rim fusion, try the coolly
minimalist **Supper Club** (20/382 Thanon
Srisoonthorn, 0 7627 0936, main courses B500)
or the Mediterranean-hued **Tatonka** (382/19
Thanon Srisoonthorn, 0 7632 4349, main
courses B350), both near the Laguna gate.

Nightlife

In Phuket City trendy Thais frequent the
loud, starkly black and white bar **GorToi Mor**
(Thanon Chana Charoen). In a renovated Sino-
Portuguese house, the gay-friendly bar **Seua
Saming** (83-85 Thanon Yaowarat, 0 7625 9269)
is opulently decorated with purple drapes
and Indian rugs. Phuket's most popular expat
hangout, The **Watermark** (Boat Lagoon
Marina, Thanon Thepkasattri, Ko Kaew, 0
7623 9730, main courses B550), has Phuket's
best cocktail selection, plus top-end Thai
and Mediterranean/Asian fusion food. Irish
beer, hearty meals, quizzes and events are
legion at the **Green Man** pub (82/15 Thanon
Pratak, Rawai, 0 7628 0757/1445-52, www.
the-green-man.net).

Banana Pub & Disco (124 Thanon
Thaweewong, Patong, 0 7634 0306, www.see
2sea.com) is the pick of samey Euro-trash
discos with dodgy tunes and clientele. More
glam than those working the Soi Bangla beer

Pimalai Resort on Ko Lanta. *See p222.*

bars, ladyboys parade in **Simon Cabaret** (8 Thanon Sirirach, Patong, 0 7634 2114, www.phuket-simoncabaret.com).

Shopping

Souvenir-hunting and tailor selection are evening entertainment at resorts, especially Patong, though pushy touts can spoil the fun. Pearls are prominent in Patong and Rawai. **Mook Ko Kaew** (41/6-7 Thanon Vichitsongkram, 0 7622 2563-4) sells both natural and cultured pearls, plus pewterware.

Island shopping is transforming, thanks to global brands and multiplex screens at the Bangkok-standard **Central Festival** (Phuket City), and the refined interior goods, art and objets d'art at the **Plaza Surin** (5/50 Moo 3, Cherngthalay, 0 7627 1741, www.theplaza surin.com) and at the shop cluster by Laguna's gate and at Canal Village (Thanon Srisoonthorn, 0 7632 4453-7) inside Laguna.

In Patong, **Jungceylon** mall (74/204 Thanon Poonphon) should open in 2006 and so will **International Night Bazaar** (Royal Phuket City, 154 Thanon Phang-nga, 0 7623 3354, www.internationalnightbazaar.com), which will host the **Joe Louis Puppet Theater** (*see p196*). **Mom Tri's Boathouse** (*see p219*) holds art exhibitions, book launches and author talks at its Chao Phraya River Club Art Gallery.

Festivals

Phuket Vegetarian Festival (Oct, first nine days of ninth lunar month) sees self-mutilating devotees parade in and around Chinese temples, with lots of firecrackers and tofu-heavy food. The parades and entertainment of **Patong Carnival** (1 Nov) herald the week-long **Phuket International Seafood Festival**. Then **Phuket Laguna Triathlon** precedes the yachties blowing in for the **King's Cup Regatta** (early Dec); architectural walks in **Phuket Heritage Festival** (late Dec, 0 7621 2314); **Phuket Gay Festival** (Feb, www.gay phuket.com); and **Baan Kata Art Festival** with art and music at Mom Tri's Boathouse (Mar). After convoying down from Bangkok, Harley fans rev up in Patong for **Phuket Bike Week** around **Songkran** (mid Apr).

Gay & lesbian

Thanks to Phuket's 'pink baht' income, Phuket Gay Festival (Feb) can parade through Patong to the bars and clubs of phallic **Paradise Complex**, notably the unmissable cabaret at **Boat Bar Disco** (125/20 Thanon Rat-u-thit, 0 7634 2206, www.boatbar.com), drinks at quieter

James Dean Guest House (Rat-u-thit Soi 5, 0 7634 4215, www.jamesdeanbar.com, double B700-B1,000) and fine Thai food and macho dancers at **Sphinx Restaurant & Theatre** (120 Thanon Rat-u-thit, 0 7634 1500, www.sphinxpub.com). Patong's gay-friendly hotels include **Club Bamboo** (47 Thanon Nanai, 0 7634 5345, www.clubbamboo.com, double B800-B4,500), the Thai-style **Icon** (47/1 Thanon Nanai, 0 7629 6735, www.iconasia.com, double B2,000-B7,000) and the seafront **Thara Patong Beach Resort** (170 Thanon Thaweewong, 0 7634 0135, www.tharapatong.com, double B2,000-B2,550). **Connect Restaurant & Guesthouse** (125/8-9 Thanon Rat-u-Thit, 0 7629 4195, www.beachpatong.com/connect) runs gay day trips to Ko Khai (Sat, B1,500).

Getting around

Cross-island routes are surfaced but hazardously twisting. *Songthaews* provide lackadaisical shuttles; otherwise, it's *tuk-tuks*, motorbike taxis and a few taxis prone to rip-offs.

Resources

Hospital
Bangkok Phuket Hospital, Phuket City (0 7625 4421, www.phukethospital.com).

Tourist information
TAT, 73 Thanon Phuket, Phuket City (0 7621 2213, www.phukettourism.org). Also consult Phuket Gazette (www.phuketgazette.com) *and Phuket Post* newspapers (www.phuketpost.com), plus www.phuket-maps.com.

Krabi

Krabi Airport brought mass tourism to the backpacker hideaway of **Laem Phra Nang**, a cape of breathtaking karst scenery. Roadless and cut off from the mainland by towering cliffs, the cape has limited beds on the back-to-back bays of Had Railay East and West. A trail leads past caves (and a climbing rope to a viewpoint and a collapsed sea cave) to the paradisical Had Phra Nang beach, home of flame lit, full moon rites to a mythical princess.

Travellers can board longtail ferries at humdrum **Krabi Town**, passing **Susaan Hoi**, a 40-million-year-old fossil shell beach. Most commute by boat from nearby **Ao Nang**, a laid-back hub of resorts, restaurants, internet cafés and book swaps. Agencies hawk trips to islands, reefs, lagoons and inland eco tours, including **Sea Canoe** (0 7569 5387), the scuba outfits **Aqua Vision** (0 7563 7415, www.aqua-vision.net) and **Reef Watch** (0 7563 2650), and, in Krabi Town, **Chan Phen Travel** (145 Thanon Utarakit, 0 7561 2004).

Railay is a rock-climbing centre with hard après-climb partying. Climbing outfits offer training (half-day B800, up to 3 day B5,000), most reputably **King Climbers** (Ao Nang, 0 7563 7125; Railay, 0 7562 2581, www.railay.com), which wrote the route maps, and **Tex Rock** (Railay East, mobile 0 1891 1528, 9724 5525).

Where to stay, eat & drink

Krabi Town's limited options include **Star Guest House** (72 Thanon Khong Kha, 0 7563 0234, double B150), which has trad decor and a river view. **May & Mark** (6 Thanon Ruen Rudee) serves great food. At Ao Nang, try the **Cliff** (0 7563 8117, www.k-bi.com, double B5,300-B12,000), a hilltop getaway with handsome garden villas. Far distant **Sheraton Krabi Beach Resort** (0 7562 8000, double $200-$588) has Nong Thale beach to itself.

Dominating Railay, the sublime **Rayavadee Resort** (0 7562 0740-3, www.rayavadee.com, double B35,000-B150,000) has two-storey villas and full facilities. **Sand Sea Resort** (39 Had Railay West, 0 7562 2609, www.sandsearesort, double B1,450-B3,450), **Railay Bay Resort** (0 7562 2571/2, double B2,000-B7,000) and **Railay Village** (0 7562 2578, double B800-B2,500) all have pleasant bungalows and beach restaurants with chilled-out music, but **Coco's** (main courses B100) serves better Thai food, and Railay's grooviest scene is at Bobo's and Sunset Bar. **Freedom Bar** on gritty Tonsai beach holds trippy trance parties every two weeks.

Getting around

By road
Songtaews and hotel buses ply Ao Nang, Krabi Town and Krabi Airport. Leam Phra Nang is walking only.

By boat
Longtails run between Laem Phra Nang and Krabi Town (30mins plus waiting) or Ao Nang (10mins). PP Family (0 7561 2463, www.phiphifamily.com) runs ferries to Phuket, Phi Phi, Krabi, Railay, and from Hua Hin pier south of Krabi Town to Ko Lanta.

Resources

There are no banks or ATMs on Laem Phra Nang.

Hospital
Krabi Hospital, 325 Thanon Utrakit, Krabi Town (0 7561 1212/http://hospital.moph.go.th/krabi).

Tourist information
Krabi Tourism Centre, Thanon Utrakit, Krabi Town (0 7562 2163/4). Also try www.krabi.com and www.railay.com.

Ko Lanta

Inhabited mostly by Muslim Thais and *chao lay* (sea gypsies), fast-upgrading Ko Lanta Yai belongs to a National Marine Park blessed with dive sites and awesome karst outcrops. Down the sandy west coast from the northern pier hub, **Ban Sala Dan**, backpacker bungalows, lively bars and internet cafés crowd **Had Khlong Dao** and **Ao Phrae-Ae** (Long beach). As the roads deteriorate south through **Had Khlong Khoang**, **Had Khlong Nin** and **Ao Kantieng**, the resorts veer from designer getaways to ramshackle huts.

From Ban Sala Dan, land, boat and kayak trips explore the east coast's caves, mangroves, Muslim village life in **Sangka-u**, and **Lanta**, a town of old wooden shophouses where *chao lay* offer paper boats to sea gods (full moon June, Nov). Other tours take in a bat cave and a seasonal waterfall just north of **Ko Lanta National Park** (0 7562 9018-9) in the far south.

Where to stay & eat

Angular **Costa Lanta** (0 7561 8092, Bangkok 0 2662 3550-1, www.costalanta.com, double B2,750-B4,300) is the chic pick of Khlong Dao's resorts. The finest digs are at **Pimalai Resort** (0 7560 7999, Bangkok 0 2320 5500, www. pimalai.com, double B8,500-B88,000) on superb Ba Kan Tiang beach, with thatched villas, bikes and kayaks, spa and sunsets over Ko Ha from its bar and restaurant. Nearby Zen-chic **Sri Lanta** (Klongnin beach, 0 7569 7288, www.srilanta.com, double B3,200-B5,800) is similar, but more laid-back. Veggie fare is good at **Sanctuary** (Hat Khlong Dao, closed mid May-mid Oct, double B200-B500). **Faim de Loup** (Phrae Ae beach, main courses B50-B100) serves French baguettes and good coffee.

Getting around

By road
The hilly terrain suits hiking, motorbikes or 4WDs. Buses run from Krabi Town to Lanta (11am & 1pm, returning 7.30am, 8am & 12.30pm, 90mins).

By boat
Boats depart Ban Sala Dan for Krabi Town (10am & 1pm, returning 10.30am & 1.30pm Nov-Apr), or to Ban Hua Hin pier south of Krabi Town year-round (PP Family 0 7561 2463).

Resources

Hospital
Ko Lanta Hospital, 118 Thanon Sanga-ou, Ban Sala Dan (0 7569 7107).

Directory

Directory

Getting Around

Bangkok has many ways of getting around and almost as many for standing still. In rush hours (7am-9am, 4-8pm), the rainy season, school terms and holiday weekends you can waste hours. So it pays to travel at quieter times and to use the expressways, BTS SkyTrain and subway, which are transforming Bangkok's shape and flow.

The trains run well, but a jealous lack of co-operation has prevented integration of BTS, subway and buses, or even a centralised transit map, though BTS co-ordinated with the Expressboats to access the old town. Poor 'interchanges' between elevated BTS and subterranean subway are being patched by bridges, though plans for universal ticketing and massive rail expansion remain plagued by the fiefdom mindset. Many visitors relish the speed, breezes and character of river and canal boats. For boat rental and tours, see p56.

Bangkok traffic isn't considerate of pedestrians, cyclists or self-drivers, though hiring a car with a driver is an affordable option for day trips. Except for the new Bus Rapid Transit (BRT), the vast bus network is defiantly non-tourist-friendly. The famous tuk-tuk might look cute, but costs more than the plentiful taxi-meters, and isn't as nippy as a motorcycle taxi.

Arriving & leaving

Long distance trains from Singapore via Malaysia, and from the Lao border, terminate at **Hualumphong station**

(see p226). Buses terminate at one of the regional **Bus Stations** (see p225).

By air

Bangkok International Airport will move in March 2006 from **Don Muang** (literally, 'Highest Ground') 27km (17 miles) north of Downtown, to **Suvarnabhumi** 25km (15.5 miles) east at Nong Ngu Hao (Cobra Swamp). Either is half an hour from downtown via expressway, much longer in rush hours.

Don Muang Airport

Thanon Wiphawadi Rangsit, Outer North (0 2535 1111/www.airport thai.co.th).
International terminal 1 Arrivals 0 2535 1149. Departures 0 2535 1254/1123. **International terminal 2** Arrivals 0 2535 1301. Departures 0 2535 1386. **Domestic terminal** Arrivals 0 2535 1253. Departures 0 2535 1192/1377. **Thai Airways check-in** 0 2535 2242. **Tourist police** 0 2535 1641/1155. **Don Muang police station** 0 2535 6222/5666.
International terminals 1 and 2, domestic and cargo form a line. Each has arrivals on the ground level, departures upstairs. Linking passenger termini are covered bridges and a **shuttle bus** (every 15mins, 5am-11pm daily), which also accesses the **car parks** (0 2535 6635-7, free for first 15mins, then B20 for 1hr up to B220 for 7-24hrs).

Arrivals has tourist, hotel and tour information, phones and 24hr banks/currency exchanges. Departures has internet PCs, a hair/massage parlour, VAT refunds (3rd floor, terminal 2) and left luggage. King Power Duty Free (0 2996 8005-7, www.kingpower. com) operates 24hrs with poor choice and value (bring reading matter).

Don Muang Airport taxis

Public Taxi-Meter Outside arrivals, all terminals (0 2535 5774/5247). **Open** 24hrs daily.

To help prevent scams, taxi-meter hailing is managed from desks outside arrivals. You keep the card carrying the driver's number in case of complaints or lost property (0 2535 1616). At journey's end, you pay the meter fare (B150-B250 to Downtown), plus a B50 airport surcharge; en route you pay any toll fees.
TG Airport Limousine Inside arrivals, all terminals (0 2973 3191/www.thaiair.com/Thailand/limo usine). **Open** 24hrs daily.
Deceptively signed as 'Airport Taxi' inside arrivals, this limo service costs B1,000 per hr in either direction or on general hire.
Airport Associate International terminals 1 & 2 (0 2982 4900/ www.aaclimousine.com). **Open** 24hrs daily.
Cars with driver from B450 per hr for a Merc or B600 per hr for van to Downtown, or to Pattaya for B2,400.

Don Muang Airport Bus

All terminals (0 2535 7481-2). Running every 40mins 5.30am-1am Mon-Sat; 5.30am-12.30am Sun & public holidays, the airport bus is convenient for those with less luggage. Flat fare B100. Using expressways, it passes most hotel, shopping and business areas on four routes: **AB1** (to Oriental Hotel via Pratunam-Ratchadamri-Silom), **AB2** (Sanam Luang via Phyathai-Larn Luang-Banglamphu), **AB3** (Thonglor via Sukhumvit-New Petchaburi) and **AB4** (Hualumpong via Ploenchit-Siam). Routes will adjust to the new airport.

Suvarnabhumi Airport

Thanon Bangna-Trad km15, East (0 2723 0000/www.bangkokairport.co. th/www.suvarnabhumiairport.com).
The new airport will be the world's biggest single terminal airport, with a high-tech tubular design. Expect similar taxi and airport bus facilities to Don Muang. A rail link to Phyathai BTS (via a city check-in at Makkasan) will open in 2008.

Airlines

No-frills budget airlines have taken off in South-east Asia, with Bangkok a hub for **Air Asia**, **One-Two-Go** and **Nok Air**, an offshoot of flag-carrier Thai Airways.

Air Asia *Airport 0 2977 8237/ reservations 0 2977 8245/ www.airasia.com.*
Budget airline founded in Malaysia serving Chiang Mai, Chiang Rai, Udon Thani, Khon Kaen, Khorat, Hat Yai, Ubon Ratchathani, Phuket and some regional routes.
Bangkok Airways *Airport 0 2535 2497-8/reservations 0 2265 5555/ www.bangkokair.com.*
A well-run private airline serving Chiang Mai, Phuket, Krabi, Cambodia, Asian World Heritage Sites and its own airports in Samui, Sukhothai and Trad.
Nok Air *Airport 0 2535 7539/ reservations 1318/www.nokair.co.th.*
Thai Airways' budget offshoot, serving Pitsanulok, Chiang Mai, Udon Thani, Phuket and Hat Yai.
One-Two-Go *Airport 0 2525 6521/ reservations 1126/www.onetwo-go.com/www.orientthai.com.*
Budget airline serving Chiang Mai, Chiang Rai, Phuket, Hat Yai and some regional routes.
PB Air *Airport 0 2535 4843-4/ reservations 0 2261 0220-8/ www.pbair.com.*
A private airline serving Lampang, Nan, Trang, Sakhon Nakhon, Nakhon Phanom, Roi Et and Nakhon Sri Thammarat, plus regional routes.
Phuket Airlines *Airport 0 2535 6695-7/reservations 0 2679 9395/ www.phuketairlines.com.*
A private airline serving Ranong, Phuket, Krabi, Tak, Chiang Mai, Udon Thani, Had Yai, Buriram and cities in South Asia and Europe.
Thai Airways *Airport 0 2535 2846-7/reservations 0 2628 2000/ www.thaiairways.com.*
Flag carrier with a huge international and domestic network.

Maps & navigation

Many signs are in English, which is widely spoken, though often falteringly. Transliterations into English often vary between guides, maps and signs. As many streets look alike and building numbers can be non-contiguous, ask directions using body language and key words rather than abstract phrasing, since Thais rarely think in a cartographic way. One-way systems are common and taxi shortcuts can seem strange, but may be following traffic radio advice. Mobile phones help people locate each other and enable you to obtain translation. Venues and hotels often write directions in Thai.

Central Bangkok street maps at the back of this guide start on page 248. Free tourist maps are so-so; bookshops sell better ones, some marking bus routes. A unique,

hand-drawn chart of the city's quirkiest shops, eats and sights is *Nancy Chandler's Map of Bangkok*; it's invaluable for Chinatown and Chatuchak Market. The *Groovy Map* also covers nightlife scenes.

Public transport

BTS SkyTrain

BTS Tourist Information Centre

0 2617 7340-2/www.bts.co.th.
Open 6am-midnight daily. *New Year* 24hrs.
This privately-run elevated train has two lines that intersect at Siam: the dark green Sukhumvit line (Morchit to Onnut) and in future to Samrong; and light green Silom line (National Stadium to Saphan Taksin, extending soon to Thanon Phetkasem, and possibly also via the old town to Bangok Noi, dipping underground). Saphan Taksin links to Central Pier of the Expressboat network (*see p227*). The BTS connects (sort of) with the subway at Saladaeng/Silom, Asoke/Sukhumvit and Morchit/Chatuchak Park.
Trains operate 6am-midnight daily, every 5mins (3mins in peak: 7.30-9am, 4.30-8pm Mon-Fri). Clean, efficient and engineered by Siemens, the BTS has a 100% safety record. Food, drinks and smoking are banned, though the concourses are filling up with shops and stalls. More escalators and 'SkyBridges' to buildings are being built. Some stations have feeder bus routes (free with pass).
Machines issue **Single-journey** tickets (B10-B40) but don't take notes, so people queue for B5 and B10 coins from the counter. Passes are convenient but not discounted. The **Sky Card** (refillable, minimum B200 plus B30 refundable deposit) is valid for 2yrs and depletes according to distance. The **1-Day Pass** (B100), **30-Day Adult Pass** (10 trips B250, 15 trips B300, 30 trips B540) or **30-Day Student Pass** (10 trips B160, 15 trips B210, 30 trips B360, 40 trips B400) have no distance limit.

Subway

Bangkok Metro

0 2354 2000/www.bangkok metro.co.th.
The Chaloem Ratchamongkhon underground blue line arcs 20km (12 miles) from Hualumphong railway station via Rama IV and Ratchadaphisek to Bang Sue railway station. See BTS (*above*) for interchange stations. It will extend

through Chinatown, Pak Khlong Talad and Thonburi and loop back to Bang Sue. By 2011 it's envisaged that orange and purple lines will run above and below ground, plus an airport link and other lines running over the State Railway routes to replace the aborted Hopewell rail line project.
Trains run 5am-midnight, every 2-4mins peak, 4-6mins off-peak. Fare rates are B14-B36, available at station counters and machines. The 18 stations each have escalators, lifts, toilets, shops and disabled conveniences. Entrances open a metre above the highest recorded flood level.

Bus & Bus Rapid Transit

BMTA Buses

0 2246 0973/hotline 184/ www.bmta.co.th.
The Bangkok Mass Transit Authority, with private firms, runs over 13,400 buses on 442 routes around Bangkok and adjacent provinces. It's mindbogglingly complex, with new and old buses, air-con and fan, having the same number but different colours and prices – and often varied routes, with return legs sometimes diverted through loops and one-way systems. Route signs are all in Thai. Cramped standing is usual in rush hours since ordinary folk are priced out of mass rail transit. Licensed minibus routes serve areas that buses fail to cover.

Air-conditioned buses are blue with a white stripe or white and articulated (5am-11pm). Fares: B8-B16. Orange buses (5am-11pm) charge B10-B20. Mauve Micro-Buses have TV and a guaranteed seat for B25.
Non-air-conditioned buses are red/cream (5am-11pm, B4), or newer blue/white ones (5am-11pm, B5). Red/cream ones using expressways cost B5.50; running as nightbuses (11pm-5am) it's B5. Short, battered and furiously driven green buses cost B3.50 daytime, B5 after 10pm.
Bus passes (unlimited distance): 1-day B10 non-air-con, B30 with air-con; from conductor. Buy other passes (1-week B50 non-air-con, B150 with air-con; 1-month B200 non-air-con, B600 with air-con) from any route terminus (especially Victory Monument).

Bus Rapid Transit

0 2354 1224-7.
Brainchild of Bangkok Governor Apirak Kosayothin, the BRT will have dedicated central bus lanes with stations every 700m reached by

bridges. The first two lines feed the BTS at Chong Nonsi (16.5km, from Rama IX Bridge via Thanon Rama III-Thanon Narathiwat Ratchankharin) and Morchit (19.5km, from Thanon Ramindra via Thanon Kaset-Navamin-Thanon Phahonyothin). Free from jams, but subject to red lights, BRT lines will proliferate if successful, though some may get replaced by BTS or subway lines.

Long-distance buses

Rot tour (inter-provincial buses) are the mainstay of ordinary Thais and often sell out, so book ahead through travel agents, hotels or bus terminals. Buses without air-con can be gruelling and cramped; *rot air* (air-con buses) may be roomier, particularly the VIP buses serving food and drink, though overnighting by road is draining and drivers can be reckless. Be alert to the security of your bags and valuables. Minibuses run regular upcountry routes, often from Banglamphu or Soi Ngam Duphlee. www.transport.co.th provides information on all bus terminals.

Eastern Bus Terminal (Ekamai)
300 Thanon Sukhumvit, at Soi 42, Sukhumvit (0 2391 8097). Ekamai BTS. **Open** 4am-midnight daily. **No credit cards. Map** p252 M7/8.
Northern & North-eastern Bus Terminal (Morchit 2) *999 Thanon Kamphaengphet 2, North (0 2936 2852-66).* **Open** 24hrs daily. **Credit** MC, V.
This station also serves the central region.
Southern Bus Terminal *147 Thanon Boromratchachonnani, Thonburi (0 2435 5605).* **Open** 5am-11pm daily. **Credit** MC, V.
Sometimes nicknamed Sai Tai Mai, it also serves the west.

Songtaew

The mouths of local roads and narrow lanes often have ranks of open-sided pick-up truck buses called *songtaew* ('two rows') after the bench seating, *seelor* (four-wheelers) or *hoklor* (six-wheelers). Often painted with pastoral scenes and lucky imagery, they cost B3-B10 and have vague schedules, stopping at will. Just hail and hop on, paying the driver when you buzz (or bang loudly) to alight.

Rail services

Hualumphong Station

1 Thanon Rong Muang, Chinatown (0 2225 6964/booking 0 2220 4444/ schedule hotline 1690/www.srt.or.th). **Open** *Trains* 4.20am-11.40pm daily. *Booking (3-60 days ahead)*

8.30am-4.30pm daily. *Tour desk* 8.30am-4pm daily. **Credit** MC, V. **Map** p249 & p250 D/E5.
The State Railway of Thailand (0 2621 8701/0 2220 4567) runs all long-distance routes (to the east coast, lower Isaan, Nong Khai, Chiang Mai, Kanchanaburi and the Malaysian border). Most trains depart from this Italianate terminus, calling at Samsen, Bang Sue, Don Muang, Makkasan and Hua Mark stations, but strangely enough they aren't used for crossing Bangkok. Some trains for Nakhon Pathom, Kanchanaburi, Prachuap Khiri Khan and Chumphon depart from **Bangkok Noi station**, Thonburi (0 2411 3102), which has a tourist centre. A short line from **Wong Wian Yai station** in Thonburi runs to Mahachai in Samut Songkram via Samut Sakhon.

Taxi-meters

With radios and meters, these air-con cars (running on liquid gas) are cheap, plentiful and gather at shopping, tourist, nightlife and event locations. With ranks still a vague idea, they'll stop for you instantly. A red front light means it's available. Signal by flapping your fingers, palm *down* (up is rude).
Taxis are coloured by company, with red/blue being the best. Don't get in if the driver refuses to use the meter. Poor maintenance often indicates a dodgy driver. Front seatbelts are compulsory. It helps to give directions in Thai (especially written) rather than to show maps. Starting rate is B35, increasing at B2 increments with a 'stationary traffic' surcharge kicking in, with no night-time increase. Drivers often lack small change; tip up to ten per cent.
For safety and ease, 24hr call taxis (listed below) will pick up within 15-20mins (B20 surcharge). They also offer full-day taxi hire (from B1,500).
Radio Taxi *hotline 1681.*
Siam Taxi *hotline 1661.*
Bangkok Taxi Radio Centre *0 2880 0888.*
Nakornchai Transportation *0 2878 9000/www.taxithai.com.*

Taxi motorcycles

Urgent trips may require a daredevil pillion ride on *rot motocy* (or *rot jakrayan yon*) from mafia-run ranks at the mouths of most *soi*. Short runs cost B5-B20 (agree the rate first), while distant trips via main roads equate to taxi rates after the necessary bargaining. Helmets are compulsory, but rarely worn in *soi*. To ask for a helmet, say *ow muak garn knock.*

Tuk-tuks

Relished by tourists as 'authentic', the various kinds of funky *samlor* (three-wheelers) are customised from Japanese motorised rickshaws. *Tuk-tuk* means 'cheap-cheap' and replicates their LPG-fuelled chainsaw rasp; quieter electric *tuk-tuk* haven't caught on. The bench may fit three, reasonably slim, *farang.*
Tuk-tuks are open-air, so you get rain, fumes, soot and sweat en route, and even the compensating *sanuk* (fun) may fade if you haven't agreed the price beforehand. Less nippy than motorcycle taxis and pricier than taxis, they're getting rarer, partly due to self-defeating attempts to tout, cheat and overcharge.

Driving

Drivers need an international licence (foreign licences aren't accepted). Thais drive on the left, front seatbelts are compulsory and speed limits are 80kmh within Bangkok, 90kmh outside. With licences easily bought, Bangkok driving can be undisciplined but predictably so, though upcountry it can be reckless. Beware of lane-switching, too-close driving, high-risk overtaking and swarming motorcycles. Fines (and licence points deductions) can often seem arbitrary. Expect expressway tolls, narrow *soi* and many 'one-way'/'no right turn' detours.

Car & van hire

Rental firms (taking most major credit cards) offer cars from B850 per day (most including insurance). Along with travel agents, many also rent a car/van with driver (B1,500-B1,800 per day, overnight B2,000 per day, plus tip). All exclude petrol and tolls. For route advice, contact the **Department of Highways** (0 2354 6668-76, www.doh.go.th). For road problem assistance try the **Transportation Safety Centre** (0 2280 8000, hotline 1356, www.mot.go.th) or **Highway Police** (0 2354 672/hotline 1193).

Avis *(0 2255 5300-4/www. avis.co.th).* **Open** 7.30am-6pm Mon-Sat; 8am-6pm Sun.
Budget *(0 2203 0250/www.budget. co.th).* **Open** 7.30am-7pm daily.

Japan Rent *(0 2259 8867-70/ www.japanrenthailand.com).* **Open** 8am-5pm Mon-Sat.

Highway Car Rent *(0 2266 9393-8/www.highway.co.th).* **Open** 7am-10pm daily.

Lumphini Car Rent *(0 2255 1966-8).* **Open** 8am-6pm daily.

Krung Thai Car Rent *(0 2291 8888/www.krungthai.co.th).* **Open** 8am-5pm Mon-Sat.

Tranex Services *(0 2874 1174/ 0258-9/www.tranex.yellow pages.co.th).* **Open** 8.30am-5.30pm Mon-Sat.

Thai Prestige Rent-A-Car *(0 2941 1344-8/2231-3/www.thai prestige.yellowpages.co.th).* **Open** 8am-5pm Mon-Sat.

Parking & services

Street parking is increasingly restricted (it is banned 5am-10pm on some highways and bus lanes). Car parks in malls, hotels and offices charge from B40 per hr, often with a free initial period if you get the ticket stamped at a venue on site. Spaces are so rare that double parking is normal, even in car parks, and has a procedure: park in neutral, wheels straight, handbrake off, so the car can be shunted. Pay attendants of street parking outside busy venues a B10-B20 tip.

Petrol, now unleaded, is cheap (B14-B20 per litre) at the plentiful pumps. Open 5am-midnight daily with attendants, many have shops, toilets, ATMs, car washes, air hoses and repair services. In case of breakdowns try:

B-Quik Service

16th floor, 253 Sukhumvit Soi 21, Sukhumvit (0 2664 2111/ battery delivery 0 2664 2000/www. b-quik.com). Asoke BTS/Petchaburi subway. **Open** 8am-9pm daily. **Credit** AmEx, DC, MC, V. **Map** p252 K5/4.
Solves breakdown woes.

Carworld Club

2/1 Thanon Rama IV, Sukhumvit (0 2204 0666/emergency 0 2260 1111/www.cwc.co.th). Sirikit Centre subway. **Open** 8.30am-5.30pm Mon-Fri. *Breakdown service* 24hrs daily. **Credit** AmEx, DC, MC, V. **Map** p252 J7.
Full breakdown services.

Water transport

Canal boats

Quick, exhilarating, but cramped and awkward, covered longtail boats ply **Khlong Saen Saeb**, an east–west canal from Tha Saphan Phan Fah

(Golden Mount, for old town) taking 15-17mins to Tha Pratunam (change boats) and 40mins to Tha Bang Kapi. Useful stops are at Bobe Market; Phyathai (for Siam); Pratunam (for markets); Ratchadamri (for malls); Chidlom (for Central Dept Store); Witthayu (for hotels and embassies); Nana (for hotels); Asoke; Thonglor; Ekamai; and Ramkhamhaeng (for stadiums and malls).

Services, run by Family Transport (0 2375 2369, 0 2374 8990), operate every 2-11mins, 5.30am-7.30pm Mon-Fri, and every 5-11mins 6am-6.30pm Sat, 6am-7pm Sun. Tickets cost B5-B15, rising every four piers. Note: maps may show obsolete routes on Khlong Phadung Krung Kasem or Khlong Banglamphu.

Tour touts may try to stop foreigners using local *rua hang yao* ('longtail boat') routes down Thonburi canals from Tha Chang and Tha Tien piers, but their commuter timings make return trips difficult anyway.

Expressboats

Chao Phraya Express Boat, 78/24-9 Thanon Maharaj, Phra Nakorn (0 2623 6001-3). **Open** 8am-6pm Mon-Sat. **Map** p248 A3.
The private river bus service covers 18km (11 miles). Buy tickets from boat conductors or many of the 35 piers, which have been upgraded and signed in English, with Tha Sathorn (aka 'Central Pier') linking to Saphan Taksin BTS. Roof flags identify types of boat:

Yellow flag (rush-hour express) Few stops between Tha Nonthaburi and Tha Sathon (45-50mins). Mon-Fri every 10mins 6.10-6.30am, every 4mins 6.30-8.40am, every 15mins 4.30-6.20pm. Returns start at 3.45pm, then every 10mins 4-7.30pm. Fare. B15.

Orange flag (express) Major piers between Tha Nonthaburi and Tha Wat Rajsingkorn (1hr). Runs Mon-Fri every 5mins 5.50-9.15am, every 15mins 3-5.50pm. Returns every 12mins 6.30-8.45am, every 20mins 2-4pm, every 10mins 4-6pm, every 15mins 6-7pm. On Sat every 15mins 6.45-8.40pm, 4-6.20pm; no Sun service. Fare: B10.

No flag (local) All piers between Tha Nonthaburi and Tha Wat Ratchasingkorn. Returns Mon-Fri every 15mins 6-8am, every 20mins 8am-6.40pm. On Sat and Sun every 20-25mins 6am-6.40pm. Fare: B6-B10.

Expressboat tours Tourist Boat (every 30mins, 9.30am-3pm) from Sathorn Pier to piers at sights; day pass: B75. Also to **Koh Kret** (9am-4.30pm Sun, B300 adults,

B250 children) and **Bang Pa-In** (7.30am-6pm Sun, B300-B390 adults, B250-B300 children).

River ferries

Dumpy ferries (*kham fahk*) bob across the Chao Phraya river from many piers (every 5mins 5am-midnight, some until 9pm, daily) for just B2. River hotels have elegant guest ferries, nearly all calling at Tha Saphan Taksin, Tha Oriental and Tha Si Phraya (River City).

Cycling

Bangkok is flat and has canals, but this is no Amsterdam. Thai traffic and road surfaces are brutal to cyclists and there are few cycle lanes, but a cycle bridge links bike paths in Lumphini and Benjakitti Parks, which rents bikes out.

Probike

231/9 Thanon Ratchadamri, Pathumwan (0 2253 3384/ www.probike.co.th). Ratchadamri BTS. **Open** 10am-7pm Mon-Fri; 8.30am-7pm Sat; 8.30-5pm Sun. **Credit** AmEx, MC, V. **Map** p251 G6.
This bicycle and equipment shop also rents bikes for B350 per day.

Walking

Walking, though immensely interesting, can be a stressful, wearisome challenge. Vehicles trump pedestrians everywhere (including zebra crossings). Pavements, where they exist, tend to be a ramshackle obstacle course shared with stalls, carts, tables, stray dogs, motorcycles, café tables, beggars on skateboards, parked cars and lots of other people, not necessarily moving, and often standing in the shade. This anti-walking prejudice links to perceptions that darker skin from outdoor activity indicates lower status. The powerful and wealthy prefer air-conditioned transit, or the elevated walkways linking malls and BTS trains. Pedestrianisation has novelty appeal at 'walking street' festivals, but its benefits are permanent only at Thanon Khao San (*see p70*).

Directory

Resources A-Z

Addresses

Bangkok addresses are complicated. They typically start with the building's street number. Any digits following an oblique slash are the subdivision of a plot, ie 49/16, but plots are often numbered by order of development, not location. Next comes the room/unit/floor number (mixing UK/US systems, so you enter on either the first or ground floor), building name and, outside Downtown, any *moo* (estate) number/name. Then comes the *thanon* ('road') name, eg 346/2, Room 3B, Floor 2, Sri Bamrung Building, Moo 2, Thanon Srinakharin.

If it's on a named *trok* ('lane', which are rare) or *soi* ('sidestreet'), it may be followed by a *thanon*, eg Soi Phiphat, Thanon Silom. If it's on a numbered *soi* running off a *thanon*, it drops the word *thanon*, hence Silom Soi 4. If the numbered *soi* also has an oft-used name, we write it as Sukhumvit Soi 21 (Soi Asoke), though variations include: Sukhumvit 21, Soi Asoke, Soi Sukhumvit 21 or even Sukhumvit Road Soi 21 or Asoke Road (English terms like Road, Avenue, Tower or Centre are often used, eg Beach Road, Pattaya). Long roads may use kilometre markers, eg km5 Thanon Bangna-Trad.

That's all followed by the subdistrict name (*khwaeng* in Bangkok, *tambon* in villages and towns), then district name (*khet* in Bangkok, *amphoe* upcountry) and province name (*jangwat*). There follows a five-digit postcode, roughly one for each district, starting with 1 in Bangkok (eg Lumphini, Pathumwan, Bangkok 10330). Each province shares its name with its capital whose district is always Amphoe Muang ('town district') followed by the province name.

'Thailand' is anglicised from Prathet Thai, with Muang Thai a less formal name for the country.

Age restrictions

You must be 18 to drive, buy cigarettes and alcohol, or have sex (straight or gay), while under-20s aren't allowed in bars or clubs, which request picture ID of all customers.

Attitude & etiquette

Thailand is known as the 'Land of Smiles' – not one grin repeated, but specific smiles according to the myriad social concepts that govern Thai behaviour and language. Here are some dos and don'ts:

● Show respect for the monarchy, members of the royal family, Buddhism and the monkhood. Criticism causes universal offence and may be heavily penalised.
● Stand for the King's Anthem at the start of performances and the national anthem.
● The head is the highest part of the body spiritually and must not be touched or pointed at, particularly by the feet, the lowest part of the body. So never use feet to move, shut or point at things, nor step on a coin or banknotes (they bear the king's head). Sitting on the 'head' of a boat is also taboo.
● Treat Buddha images with respect. Don't point at them (especially with feet), hang anything on them or pose with them in photos.
● Inside temples, wear polite clothing (cover shoulders and knees). Sit with feet tucked back or cross-legged in front of monks/Buddha images.
● Monks are celibate and must not touch women, who give monks things via a male or by placing it down. *Mae chi* (nuns) are treated like secular women.
● Remove shoes before entering rooms in temples, palaces, homes and some museums. Step over, not on, door thresholds.
● Make a symbolic gesture to lower your head as you pass elderly/very senior Thais in a room.
● Avoid direct criticism of anyone or anything (including Thailand).
● Don't lose your temper. Anger is viewed (and avoided) as temporary insanity and prevents resolution of problems, often swapping culprit and victim in Thais' esteem. But jollying people along can accomplish great feats; Thais like to help.
● Presentable, clean clothing, footwear and hair gains you respect and help, particularly from officials.
● Eat and pass things with your right hand as the left is used for cleaning after defecating.

Business

Conventions & conferences

Impact Exhibition Centre
99 Thanon Popular, Thanon Chaengwattana, Nonthaburi Province, Outer North (0 2504 5050/www.impact.co.th).
Queen Sirikit National Convention Centre *60 Thanon Ratchadaphisek Tud Mai, Sukhumvit (0 2229 3000/www.qsncc.com).*
BITEC (Bangkok International Trade & Exhibition Centre) *8 km1 Thanon Bangna Trad, East (0 2749 3939-60/www.bitec.net).*

Couriers & shippers

DHL Express *7th-8th floors, Sathorn City Tower, Thanon Sathorn Tai, South (0 2345 5000/www.dhl. co.th).* **Open** 24hrs daily. **Credit** AmEx, DC, MC, V. **Map** p251 J4.
Federal Express *8th floor, Green Tower, Thanon Rama IV, Sukhumvit (1782/www.fedex.com).* **Open** 8am-9pm Mon-Fri; 8am-5pm Sat; 9am-5pm public holidays. **Credit** AmEx, V. **Map** p251 J7.

Travel advice

For up-to-date information on travelling to a specific country – including the latest news on safety and security, health issues, local laws and customs – contact your home country government's department of foreign affairs. Most have websites packed with useful advice for would-be travellers.

Australia
www.smartraveller.gov.au
Canada
www.voyage.gc.ca
New Zealand
www.mft.govt.nz/travel

Republic of Ireland
http://foreignaffairs.gov.ie
UK
www.fco.gov.uk/travel
USA
www.state.gov/travel

Directory

TNT Express Worldwide *599 Thanon Chua Phloeng, Bangrak (0 2249 0242/www.tnt.com).* **Open** 24 hrs daily. **Credit** AmEx. **Map** p250 F7.

Office hire & services

IB Your Office

14th floor, One Pacific Place, 140 Thanon Sukhumvit, Sukhumvit (0 2653 5000/www.office-bangkok. com). Nana BTS. **Open** 8am-6.30pm Mon-Fri. **Credit** AmEx, MC, V. **Map** p251 J5.

Flexible office rents, with own phone and fax numbers, conference rooms and secretarial support. Business addresses provided.

Mr Centre

43rd floor, United Centre Tower, 323 Thanon Silom, Bangrak (0 2631 0330/www.mrcentre.org). Saladaeng BTS/Silom subway. **Open** 8am-5.30pm Mon-Fri. **Credit** AmEx, DC, MC, V. **Map** p250 F7.

Offices for monthly rental, plus phone, fax, mail and secretarial services up and running instantly.

Women Secretaries' Association

6/2 Thanon Phichai, Dusit (0 2241 5555/www.secretarythai.and.org). **Open** 8.30am-4.30pm Mon-Fri.

Finds secretaries according to your specifications.

Translators & interpreters

Bangkok Translation Services

562 Thanon Ploenchit, Pathumwan (0 2251 5666) Ploenchit BTS. **Open** 8am-8pm Mon-Sat. **Map** p251 H5.

Between Thai and other languages for serious documentation needs. Price and time vary by language.

Interlanguage Translation Centre

501 Thanon Samsen, Dusit (0 2243 2018-9/www.itctrans.com). **Open** 8.30am-4pm Mon-Sat. **Map** p248 C2.

Official standard translations between all major languages. Cost depends on subject and language. **Other locations**: 554 Thanon Phloenchit, Pathumwan (0 2252 4307); 1 Sukhumvit Soi 1, Sukhumvit (0 2252 3877); 57/3 Thanon Witthayu, Pathumwan (0 2650 7831).

Useful organisations

American Chamber of Commerce *18th floor, Kian Gwan 2 Building, 140/1 Thanon Witthayu,*

Pathumwan (0 2254 8748/www. amchamthailand.com). **Open** 8.30am-5pm Mon-Fri. **Map** p251 H5.

Australian-Thai Chamber of Commerce *Unit 203, 20th floor, Thai Chamber of Commerce Tower, 889 Thanon Sathorn Tai, South (0 2210 0216-8/www.austcham thailand.com). Surasak BTS.* **Open** 9am-5pm Mon-Fri. **Map** p251 G7.

British Chamber of Commerce *7th floor, 208 Thanon Witthayu, Pathumwan (0 2651 5350-3/www. bccthai.com). Ploenchit BTS.* **Open** 8.30am-4.30pm Mon-Fri. **Map** p251 H5.

Canadian Chamber of Commerce *9th floor, Set Thi One Building, Thanon Pan, Bangrak (0 2266 6085-6/www.tccc.or.th). Chong Nonsi BTS.* **Open** 9am-5pm Mon-Fri. **Map** p250 E7.

New Zealand-Thai Chamber of Commerce *9th floor, ITF Tower, 140/11 Thanon Silom, Bangrak (0 2634 3283/www.nztcc.org). Saladaeng BTS/Silom subway.* **Open** 9.30am-5pm Mon-Fri. **Map** p250 F7.

Thai Chamber of Commerce *150 Thanon Ratchabophit, Phra Nakorn (0 2622 1860-76/www.tcc. or.th).* **Open** 8.30am-4.30pm Mon-Fri. **Map** p248 B4.

Consumer

Some shops might refund or exchange faulty goods (unlikely if you lose your temper). Refer complaints to the **Office of the Consumer Protection Board** (hotline 1166/0 2629 8262-4, www.ocpb.go.th) or the **Food & Drug Administration** (hotline 1556, www.fda.moph.go.th).

Customs

On arrival, fill in Passenger Declaration Form 211 for Customs (hotline 1164, www.customs.go.th). Duty-free import limits include 200 cigarettes or 250g of cigars/tobacco; 1 litre of spirits; 1 litre of wine; B10,000 of perfume; B10,000 of effects for personal or professional use. Prohibited imports/exports include drugs, pornography, protected wild animals or related products.

Goods requiring a permit for import/export include firearms, ammunition, explosives (**National Police Office** 0 2205 1000, 0 2354 6510); Buddha images, artefacts and antiques (**Fine Arts Department** 0 2221 7811); radio transceivers/ telecom equipment (**Post & Telegraph Department** 0 2271 0151-2); plants/agricultural materials (**Agriculture Department** 0 2579 0151-7); live animals/animal products (**Live Stock Development** 0 2653

4550-3); medicines and chemical products (**Food and Drugs Administration** 0 2590 7000).

Disabled

Despite general compassion there's mixed treatment of the disabled, who tend to be kept hidden, partly due to karmic belief, face and prejudice about appearance. The Thai deaf subculture's sophisticated signing is visible among deaf vendors. Maimed/leprous beggars are mostly Khmer amputees enslaved by mafia.

With bevelled kerbs few, and obstacles many, wheelchairs brave the road. Lifts at all subway and some BTS stations are rarely used, though the subway has disabled WCs. For advice, try the **Association of the Physically Handicapped** (0 2951 0445/0447, www.flyingwheelchairs.org).

Drugs

Punishment for possession – and particularly for dealing or trafficking – of illicit drugs is severe, with the death penalty enforced. Nightclubs and even schools get raided with urine tests on all to find ecstasy, cocaine and the amphetamine *yaa baa* ('crazy drug'). Those in possession face one to ten years' jail and fines of B10,000-B100,000.

Electricity

The standard current in Thailand is 220V, 50 cycles/sec, but plugs are unearthed two-pins (round or parallel flat), so beware of shocks.

Embassies & consulates

American Embassy *120-122 Thanon Witthayu, Pathumwan (0 2205 4000/www.usa.or.th).* **Open** 7am-4pm Mon-Fri. **Map** p251 H5.

Australian Embassy *37 Thanon Sathorn Tai, South (0 2287 2680/ www.austembassy.or.th)* **Open** 8am-5pm Mon-Fri. **Map** p251 G7.

British Embassy *1031 Thanon Witthayu, Pathumwan (0 2305 8333/www.britishembassy. gov.uk/thailand). Ploenchit BTS.* **Open** 8am-4.30pm Mon-Thur; 8am-1pm Fri. **Map** p251 H5.

Canadian Embassy *15th floor, Abdul Rahim Place, 990 Thanon Rama IV, Bangrak (0 2636 0540/ www.bangkk.gc.ca). Saladaeng BTS/Silom subway.* **Open** 7.30am-4pm Mon-Thur; 7.30am-1pm Fri. **Map** p251 G7.

EU Delegation *19th floor, Kian Gwan Building II, 140/1 Thanon Witthayu, Pathumwan (0 2305 2600/www.deltha.cec.eu.int).* **Open** 8.30am-5.30pm Mon-Thur; 8.30am-12pm Fri. **Map** p251 H5.

New Zealand Embassy *14th floor, M-Thailand Building, 87 Thanon Witthayu, Pathumwan (0 2254 2530/www.nzembassy. com/thailand). Ploenchit BTS.* **Open** 7.30am-4pm Mon-Fri. **Map** p251 H5.

Emergencies

First ring the responsive, English-speaking **Tourist Police** (24-hour hotline 1155) or **Tourist Assistance Centre** (0 2281 5051). If necessary, try the 24-hour **Police Hotline** (191) or police stations (*see p233*). For utilities crises call the **Bangkok Metropolitan Administration Call Centre** (hotline 1555). For Bangkok hospitals, *see p231*; for helplines, *see p231*. Most embassies (*above*) have duty staff outside office hours.

Gay & lesbian

Help & information

Bangkok Rainbow Organization

0 6607 1069/www.bangkok rainbow.org.
Part of the Asian Rainbow network, this group promotes understanding and provides counselling for gays.

Lesla

0 9218 9119, www.lesla.com.
Thailand's biggest lesbian organisation runs socials.

Long Yang Club

PO Box 1077, Silom, Bangkok 10504 (0 2266 5479/www.longyang club.org/thailand).
East-West gay social club.

Health

Accident & emergency

Road casualties often get picked up by Chinese charities, such as Poh Tek Tung; many end up in the **Police Hospital** or **Bangkok Hospital** (for both, *see p231*).

Erawan Centre

514 Department of Medical Services, Bangkok Metropolitan Administration, Thanon Luang, Phra Nakorn (0 2223 9401-3/

hotline 1646/1554). **Open** 24hrs daily. **Map** p248 C4.
Free emergency medical treatment and distribution of ambulances and doctors, plus health advice.

International SOS Services Thailand

11th floor, Diethelm Tower, 93/1 Thanon Witthayu, Pathumwan (0 2256 7145-6/www.international sos.com). **Open** 24hrs daily. **Map** p251 H5.
Tackles any emergency, emphasising speedy ambulances and police contact.

Before you go

It's wise to get vaccinations for hepatitis A and B, polio, rabies, typhoid and tuberculosis, but cholera shots are widely discredited. Also ensure full immunisation for tetanus, diphtheria, measles, mumps and rubella. Arrivals from Africa or Latin America must be vaccinated for yellow fever. For bird flu, seek ongoing advice. Some vaccinations require widely spaced shots up to six weeks before departure. Avoid wading in floodwater, which may be infectious from rat urine, etc.

Malaria is only an issue on the Burma, Laos or Cambodia borders and in remoter forests, visitors to which should consult specialists, like **Travel Doctor** (www.traveldoctor. com.au). Tropical medicine experts often caution against malaria prophylaxis due to resistant strains and side effects (particularly from Larium). Avoiding bites is best, so wear white and use insect repelling lotions (Jaico is reliable), sprays, coils and electric tabs. Most rooms have screens or nets.

That's also the only defence against haemorrhagic dengue fever (*kai leuad ok*), which has increased lately, notably in cities during rainy season. Passed on by the daytime, striped-legged Aedes mosquito, dengue has similar symptoms to malaria, but no prophylaxis or cure. It is most serious in children, the elderly and repeat sufferers. Seek early diagnosis (before the rash).

Contraception

Planned Parenthood Association of Thailand

8 Thanon Wiphawadi Rangsit, North-east (0 2941 2320/www.ppat. or.th). **Open** 9am-4.30pm Mon-Fri.
The clinic advises on contraceptives (also sold here), pregnancy and family planning.

Population & Community Development Association (PDA)

8 Sukhumvit Soi 12, Sukhumvit (0 2229 4611-28/www.pda.or.th). Asoke BTS/Sukhumvit subway. **Open** 8am-4.30pm Mon-Fri. **Map** p251 J5.
Founded by ex-minister and social campaigner Senator Mechai 'Mr Condom' Viravaidhya, PDA advises on family planning, AIDS and unplanned pregnancy; supplies morning-after pills and contraceptives; and promotes sustainable development.

Dentists

Asavanant Dental Clinic
58/5 Sukhumvit Soi 55, Sukhumvit (0 2391 1842/www.asavanant.com). Thonglor BTS. **Open** 9am-8pm Mon-Fri; 9am-5pm Sat, Sun. **Credit** AmEx, MC, V. **Map** p252 M5.

DC-One Clinic
31 Thanon Yen-Akart, Sathorn (0 2240 2800/www.dc-one.com). **Open** 9am-8pm Mon-Sat; 9am-4pm Sun. **Credit** AmEx, MC, V.

Dental Hospital *88/88 Sukhumvit Soi 49, Sukhumvit (0 2260 5000-15/ www.dentalhospitalbangkok.com).* **Open** 9am-8pm daily. **Credit** AmEx, DC, MC, V. **Map** p252 L6.

Glas Haus Dental Centre
Glas Haus (Baan Chiang), Sukhumvit Soi 25, Sukhumvit (0 2260 6120-1). Asoke BTS/Sukhumvit subway. **Open** 10am-6pm Mon-Sat. **Credit** AmEx, MC, V. **Map** p252 K6.

Complementary medicine

Thai and Chinese herbal apothecaries and traditional doctors are widespread everywhere, but most visible in the old town. In a bid to exploit this indigenous knowledge, many mainstream stores and fairs now sell manufactured versions of ancient remedies, plus vitamins and Western holistic supplements. Also *see pp175-179* **Mind & Body**.

Holistic Health Systems

438/13 Thanon Ekamai, Sukhumvit Soi 63, Sukhumvit (0 1627 0312/ 0 2711 5102/www.thailand chiropractor.com). Ekamai BTS then taxi. **Open** 8am-7pm Mon-Thur, Sat, Sun; appointment required. **No credit cards.**
Dr Mark Leoni's homely chiropractor clinic.

Directory

Doctors & hospitals

State hospitals range from the humble to teaching institutions. Private hospitals have English-speaking doctors in outpatient clinics, which also dispense medication. Beware of over-prescription. The efficient, luxurious, private **Bangkok, Bumrungrad, BNH** and **Samitivej Hospitals** all have multilingual clinics.

Bangkok Hospital *2 Soi Soonvijai 7, North-east (0 2310 3000/www. bangkokhospital.com).* **Map** p252 M4.

BNH (Bangkok Nursing Home) Hospital *9/1 Thanon Convent, Bangrak (0 2632 0550-60/www. BNHhospital.com). Saladaeng BTS/Silom subway.* **Map** p250 F7.

Bumrungrad Hospital *33 Sukhumvit Soi 3, Sukhumvit (0 2667 1000/www.bumrungrad. com). Nana BTS.* **Map** p251 J4.

Police Hospital (state) *492/1 Thanon Ratchadamri, Pathumwan (0 2252 8111-25/www.hospital. police.go.th). Chidlom/Ratchadamri BTS.* **Map** p251 G5.

Samitivej Hospital *133 Sukhumvit Soi 49, Sukhumvit (0 2711 8000/www.samitivej.co.th).* **Map** p252 K6.

Sirirat Hospital (state) *2 Thanon Prannok, Thonburi (0 2419 7000).* **Map** p248 A3.

Opticians

Hospitals also have eye clinics, notably **Samitivej** *(see above).*

Laser Vision Lasik Centre

49/1 Viphavadee Rangsit Soi 38, North (0 2939 5494/www.laser vision.co.th). Morchit BTS/Chatuchak Park subway. **Open** 8am-8pm Mon, Tue, Thur, Fri; 8am-6pm Wed, Sat. **Credit** AmEx, DC, MC, V. **Map** p249 & p250 F4.

Rutnin Eye Hospital

80/1 Thanon Sukhumvit Soi 21, Sukhumvit (0 2639 3399/www. rutnin.com). Asoke BTS/Sukhumvit subway. **Open** 8am-8pm Mon-Sat; 8am-7pm Sun. **Credit** AmEx, DC, MC, V. **Map** p252 K5.

Pharmacies & prescriptions

Hospitals dispense in-house at inflated prices. Medicines are also sold from any *kai yaa* (pharmacy) without prescriptions, except those with major physiological, mental or narcotic impact. This has

Health tourism

Some come to Thailand for herbal therapies, but others (including some European health services) seek high-tech medicine at up to half Western rates: surgery, gamma-scans and Caesarean sections (the desire for auspicious birth dates make Caesareans the norm in Thailand). Private Thai hospitals also offer spacious five-star surroundings and smiley care. **Bumrungrad Hospital** (*see below*) even has room service from restaurants in its opulent atrium. Dental tourism, in particular, benefits from expertise derived from the Thais' low pain threshold. Some specialists say you get what you pay for and cases of misdiagnosis do surface, partly driven by widespread over-prescription.

Thailand is also reputed for plastic surgery (slim noses and eyelid folds carry social cachet). And there's an informal global network among ladyboys to advise on coming to Thailand to change sex. Born in the wrong body? Avoid the plethora of dubious clinics and consult the **Society of Plastic & Reconstructive Surgeons** at the Sirirat Hospital (*see p231*).

prompted indiscipline with drugs like antibiotics, which reduces their effectiveness.

Community Pharmacy Laboratory

22 Thanon Phayathai, Pathumwan (0 2218 8428-9/www.pharmacy chula.ac.th/osotsala). National Stadium BTS. **Open** 8am-7pm Mon-Sat. **Map** p249 & p250 F4. Pharmacists and trainees from Chula Uni advise on symptoms and sell drugs cheaply without prescription.

Plastic surgery

Thai plastic surgery is world-famous, particularly beautification and sexual reassignment. It's regulated by the **Society of Plastic & Reconstructive Surgeons** (0 2716 6214, www.plasticsurgery.or.th).

Yanhee General Hospital

454 Thanon Charan Sanit Wong Soi 90, Thonburi (0 2879 0300/ www.yanhee.net). Renowned for plastic surgery and sex changes (sex change $5,000, Adam's apple removal $580).

STDs, HIV & AIDS

The **PDA** (*see p230*) has been pivotal in HIV/AIDS prevention, for which Thailand's pioneering role has been hailed.

Anonymous Clinic

1871 Thanon Ratchadamri, Pathumwan (0 2256 4107-9/ www.redcross.or.th). Ratchadamri BTS. **Open** noon-7pm Mon-Fri; noon-4pm Sat. **Map** p251 G5. Thai Red Cross HIV/AIDS testing, information, counselling and treatment.

Division of Venereal Disease

Bangrak Hospital, 189 Thanon Sathorn Tai, South (0 2286 0108/ 0431/www.sti-thai.org). **Open** 8.30am-4.30pm Mon, Wed, Fri. **Map** p250 F7. Information and cures for STDs. **Other locations**: Bang Kaen, North-east (0 2972 9606).

Médecins Sans Frontières

311 Lad Phrao Soi 101, North-east (0 2375 6491). **Open** 8.30am-5pm Mon Fri. Worldwide charity. Nurses offer data, advice and initial treatment for HIV/AIDS, then patient home visits.

Helplines

Alcoholics Anonymous

Holy Redeemer Church, 123/119 Ruam Rudi Soi 5, Pathumwan (0 2256 6305/6157). **Map** p251 H5. **Meetings** 7-8pm Mon, Wed, Fri, Sun; 5-6pm Tue, Thur; 4.30-5.30pm Sat.

Narcotics Control Board (ONCB)

5 Thanon Din Daeng, North-east
(0 2247 0101/0901-19/www.oncb.
go.th). **Open** 8.30am-4.30 Mon-Fri.
Info on all narcotics, plus advice on
quitting and treatment.

New Community Services

230/60 Soi Thai Chamber of
Commerce University, Thanon
Wiphawadi Rangsit, North-east
(0 1692 2981/0 2275 6762/
www.ncs-counselling.com).
Open 9am-5pm Mon-Fri.
Thai and non-Thai counselling
on any problem (family, addiction or
anxiety, cross-cultural adjustment),
group therapy, training and
seminars.

Quit Line

Hotline 1600.
Service offering help coping with
mental problems and quitting tobacco.

Samaritans of Thailand

PO Box 63, Por Nor For
Santisuk, Bangkok 10113, South
(0 2713 6793/www.geocities.com/
samaritansthai). **Open** Helpline
noon-10pm daily.
Trained volunteers provide a friendly
ear to those with emotional and
mental problems.

ID

If possible, always carry your
passport or photocopy, especially for
hotel check-ins, cashing travellers'
cheques or exchanging more than
$500. Store copies off your person.
Nightlife venues now insist you
show picture ID (passport or ID
card), even if you're obviously twice
the minimum age to drink.

Insurance

It's advisable to bring travel
insurance, including health
cover; otherwise try **American
International Assurance** (0 2634
8888, www.aia.co.th) or **Ayudhya
Allianz CP Life** (0 2305 7000,
www.aacp.co.th).

Internet

Many shops stock prepaid online
packages, including **CS Loxinfo** (0
2263 8222, www.csloxinfo.co.th), **IEC
Internet** (0 2617 3999, www.asia
access.net.th), **KSC** (0 2979 7000,
www.ksc.net), **Pacificnet** (0 2618
8888, www.pacific.net.th) and **Qnet**
(0 2377 0555, www.qnet.co.th).
Terminals are common in business
and tourist areas, most cheaply in

Banglamphu, while **CATNET** at
selected post offices costs B0.12
per minute using CATNET cards
(B100, B300, B500). The following
provide net access:
AIT Internet Center 1C16-1C17,
Warner Tower, Thanon Mahesak,
Bangrak (0 2635 9039-41/www.ait
center.com). Surasak BTS. **Open**
9am-10pm Mon-Sat. **Rate** B30 per hr.
Map p250 E7.
Amazing Cyber 925/6-8 Thanon
Rama I, Pathumwan (0 2216 6236-7/
www.bossapparels.com). National
Stadium BTS. **Open** 9am-8.30pm
daily. **Rate** B50 per hr. **Map** p249
& p250 F4.
Olavi Internet Service 53 Thanon
Chakrabongse, Phra Nakorn (0 2629
2228-9/www.olavi.com). **Rate** B40
per hr. **Open** 10am-8pm Mon-Sat.
Map p248 B3.
Time Internet Café 2nd floor,
Times Square, Sukhumvit Soi 12,
Sukhumvit (0 2653 3636-9/www.it.
co.th). Asoke BTS/Sukhumvit
subway. **Rate** B1 per min. **Open**
9am-midnight Mon-Sat; 10am-
midnight Sun. **Map** p251 J5.

Left luggage

Bangkok Airport International
Terminal 1 (arrivals/departures 0
2535 1250). International Terminal
2 (arrivals 0 2535 2102/departures
0 2535 2010). **Open** 24hrs daily.
Rates B90 per piece per day.
Hualumphong Station Thanon
Rama IV, Chinatown (0 2224 6165).
Open 4am-11pm daily. **Rates** B20
per piece per day; B100-B150 per
bicycle/motorcycle. **Map** p249 &
p250 D5.

Legal help

In legal difficulties, immediately
inform your embassy, then a
lawyer. The following firms are
English-speaking. Some may not
take criminal cases.

Baker & McKenzie 22nd-26th
floors, Abdul Rahim Place, 990
Thanon Rama IV, Bangrak (0 2636
2000/www.bakernet.com). Saladaeng
BTS/Silom subway. **Map** p251 G7.

**Legal & Commercial Services
International** Suite 1703-4, 17th
floor, Two Pacific Place, 140 Thanon
Sukhumvit Soi 4, Sukhumvit (0 2255
4941/www.legalcommercialservices.
com). Nana BTS. **Map** p251 J5.

FBLP Legal 14th floor, Silom
Complex, 191 Thanon Silom,
Bangrak (0 22665234/www.fblp
legal.com). Saladaeng BTS/Silom
subway. **Map** p250 F7.

Tilleke & Gibbins 64/1 Soi
Ton Son, Ploenchit, Pathumwan

(0 2263 7700/0 2254 2640-58/
www.tillekeandgibbins.com). Ploenchit
BTS. **Map** p251 M5.
Vovan & Associés 17th floor,
Silom Complex, 191 Thanon Silom,
Bangrak (0 2632 0180/www.vovan-
associes.com). Saladaeng BTS/Silom
subway. **Map** p250 F7.

Libraries

Most libraries are members-only, but
allow reading on site. Photocopying
is available at libraries in the
National Library (see p80), Siam
Society (see p94) and universities;
the **British Council** (see p93) also
rents UK videos.

Neilson Hays Library

195 Thanon Surawong, Bangrak
(0 2233 1731/www.neilsonhays
library.com). Saladaeng BTS. **Open**
9.30am-4pm Tue-Sun. **Map** p250 E7.
A beautiful old building with the best
range of English reading in town,
plus exhibitions in the Rotunda.
Entry for non-members is B50.

Lost property

Quickly report losses to the police
(see p233) to get a statement for
insurers.

Airport

For lost tickets, contact the airline.
For property lost at the airport, call
Bangkok Airport (0 2535 1254).

Public transport

BMTA Bus Operation Division
Hotline 184/0 2246 0973/0339/
www.bmta.moct.go.th
BTS SkyTrain 0 2617 7141/
7142/www.bts.co.th.
Hualumphong railway station
24hr hotline 1690.
Subway 0 2690 8200/www.bangkok
metro.co.th

Taxis

**Jor Sor Roi (JS100) Radio
Station** 100FM (hotline 1137).
**Ruam Duay Chuay Kun
Community Radio Station** 96FM
(hotline 1677).
Drivers often tune into these Thai-
language radio stations, which
broadcast lost items and traffic news.
Reports to police should note the
taxi's colour (ie company) and
number (printed inside and out).

Media

Freedom of expression and public
access to information are enshrined
in the Thai constitution, though
the USA and other agencies have
complained of pressure against

Directory

journalists and self-censorship. Many foreign news agencies have bases here. For the **Foreign Correspondents Club of Thailand**, *see p169*.

Newspapers & magazines

In 2005 *Thai Day* (and supplement in the *International Herald Tribune*) joined two high-quality English daily newspapers, *Bangkok Post* and the feistier *Nation*, publishing local and international news and current affairs, with event listings every Friday. The trendy, free bi-weekly *BK* carries listings, while *Art Connection* is a free monthly map of exhibitions. Thai monthlies in English include *Metro* (akin to *Time Out*), *Farang* (backpackers), *Big Chilli* (expats) and *Thailand Tatler* (high society). Free tourist monthlies vary in quality. Papers, listings mags and free booklet *Shakers & Movers* carry classified ads, as does the **Villa Market** (*see p149*) expat noticeboard.

Radio

FM and AM broadcasts in Thai and English tend to play mainstream music with news bulletins. The army tries to keep control of most frequencies and **Radio Thailand**'s official pronouncements override 95.5FM, 105FM and 918AM at 7-8am, noon-1pm, 7-7.30pm and 8-8.30pm daily. English language stations include:

Chulalongkorn University 101.5FM. 9.35pm-midnight daily. Classical.
Eazy FM 105.5FM. 6am-midnight daily. Easy listening.
Virgin Hitz 95.5FM. 5.30am-midnight daily. Pop dance and hits.
Get Radio 102.5FM. 24hrs daily. DJs' choice, from retro and pop rock to indie and dance.
Smooth 105FM. 5am-midnight daily. Easy listening.
Voices of Thailand 95.5FM & 105 FM, 8.15am-8.30pm daily. Features.

Television

Of the six stations, two are commercial: **Channels 3** and **7** show mass market soaps, game shows and so on. **Channels 5, 9** and **11** are government/army-controlled and broadcast news, documentaries and fewer entertainment shows. Independent Television (**ITV**) was set up to do investigative news; it's now owned by Thaksin's family firm. Many hotels offer satellite/cable channel **UBC** (0 2271 7171,

www.ubctv.com), offering BBC, CNN, CNBC, MTV, Channel [V] and international movie, sport and entertainment channels, mostly in English.

Money

Thailand's currency is the *baht* (B). B1 equals 100 *satang*. B1 and B5 coins are silvery; B10 coins are copper with a silver rim; 25 and 50 *satang* coins are copperish. Bank notes are B20 (green – the most used note), B50 (blue), B100 (red), B500 (purple) and B1,000 (grey). At the time of writing, £1=B71, US$1=B40.

ATMs, banks & exchange

ATMs are plentiful at banks, malls, petrol pumps and many shops. They're open 24 hours, and most accept credit cards.

Banks generally open 9.30am-3.30pm Mon-Fri, except bank holidays. Some in department stores may open 10am-8pm daily; those in Chatuchak Weekend Market open 7.30am-8pm Sat, Sun; airport branches open 24hrs. Bureaux de change are found in tourist areas, usually opening 8.30am-9pm daily.

Credit cards

Most hotels, restaurants, shops and department stores catering to foreigners or middle-class Thais accept credit cards. Visa, MasterCard and American Express are more widely accepted than Diners Club.

Lost/stolen credit cards

All are open 24 hours daily.
American Express 0 2273 5500.
Diners Club 0 2238 3660.
MasterCard 0 2260 8573.
Visa 0 2256 7324-7.

Opening hours

Banks 9.30am-3.30pm Mon-Fri.
Malls 10am-10pm daily, although many shops close at 9pm, cinemas around midnight.
Shops outside malls: usually 10am-8pm daily, some business supply shops 9am-6pm Mon-Fri, 9am-noon Sat.
Restaurants 11am-10pm daily (some close in afternoons or stay open till late).
Bars/music venues 5pm-1am daily. **Nightclubs** 9pm-1am daily, some until 2am.
Government offices 8.30am-4.30pm Mon-Fri.

Museums state 8.30am-4pm Wed-Sun; private 9am-6pm daily (some close Sun).

Police

The **Tourist Police** at Tourist Information, 4 Ratchadamnoen Nok Avenue, Dusit (0 2678 6801-9, national hotline 1155) are best for English skills, perseverance, efficiency and familiarity with non-Thai concerns. Most other police speak little English, with procedures that may add to stress. Stations come under the **Metropolitan Police Bureau**, 323 Wang Parus, Thanon Si Ayutthaya, Dusit (hotline 191/ 0 2280 5060-4, www.police.go.th).

Bangrak Police Station *50 Thanon Naret, Bangrak (0 2234 0242/0 2631 8014-7/0 237 2601).* **Map** p250 F7.
Chakkrawat Police Station *324 Thanon Chakkrawat, Chinatown (0 2225 4077-8).* **Map** p249 & p250 D3.
Chanasongkram Police Station *74 Thanon Chakrabongse, Banglamphu (0 2281 8786/8574/ 0 2282 1374).* **Map** p308 B3.
Dusit Police Station *75 Thanon Rama V, Dusit (0 2241 2361-2/ 4399).*
Huay Kwang Police Station *2000 Thanon Pracha Songkhro, North-east (0 2277 2629/0630).*
Pathumwan Police Station *1775 Thanon Rama VI, Pathumwan (0 2215 2991-3).* **Map** p251 G5.
Thonglor Police Station *800 Sukhumvit Soi 55, Sukhumvit (0 2390 2240-2).* **Map** p252 M6.

Postal services

Letters not over 20g cost B3 within Thailand; postcards and letters abroad B12-B19; aerogrammes B15. Newly revamped **Post Offices** (hotline 1545) have parcel packaging, express and registered mail, and CATNET terminals (*see p232*), usually opening 8.30am-4.30pm Mon-Fri, 9am noon Sat. The CPO holds **Poste Restante** mail for up to a month (bring ID, fee payable). Stamps are sold at convenience stores and souvenir shops.
Central Post Office (CPO) *Thanon Charoen Krung, at Sois 32-34, Bangrak (0 2233 1050-80).* **Open** *Packing* 8am-4.30pm Mon-Fri; 9am-noon Sat. *Post* 8am-8pm Mon-Fri; 8am-1pm Sat, Sun. *Postal orders & money services* 8am-5pm Mon-Fri; 8am-noon Sat. *Poste Restante* 8am-8pm Mon-Fri; 8am-1pm Sat, Sun.

Directory

Prohibitions

Smoking is now prohibited in all air-conditioned buildings and many public places. The B2,000 littering fine has greatly cleaned up Bangkok. Jaywalking on designated congested roads carries a minimum B200 fine.

Religion

For **Maha Uma Devi** (Hindu), see p90. For **Sri Gurun Singh Sabha** (Sikh), see p88.

Anglican

Christ Church 11 Thanon Convent, Bangrak (0 2234 3634/ 0 2233 8525). Saladaeng BTS/ Lumphini subway. **Open** 8.30am-4.30pm Mon-Fri. **Services** 7.30am (Eng), 10am (Eng), 3pm (Thai), 5pm (Eng) Sun. **Map** p251 G7.

Baptist

Calvary Baptist Church 88 Sukhumvit Soi 2, Sukhumvit (0 2251 8278/www.thai-info.net/ churches/calvary). Nana BTS. **Open** 8am-4pm daily. **Services** English 10am (nursery) Wed; 9.30am-noon (in Eng), 2-4pm (Bible study, in Thai) Sun; noon-6pm (in Burmese) Sun; 11am-12.30pm (in Nepalese) Sun. **Map** p251 J5.

Buddhist

Thai Theravada Buddhist temples typically open 6am-8pm daily; bot (ordination halls) may open 9am-5pm daily or require permission. Daily services, in Thai, are generally 7-9pm or longer, with prayer, dharma sermons and meditation. Wat Suthat is a model example.

Wat Suthat 146 Thanon Bamrung Muang, Phra Nakorn (0 2224 9845/ 0 2222 9632/www.watsuthat.org). **Open** 8.30am-9pm daily. **Meditation** Thai noon-1pm, 7-9pm Mon-Fri; 1-3pm, 7-9pm Sat, Sun. **Map** p248 C4.

Catholic

Holy Redeemer Catholic Church 123/19 Soi Ruam Rudi 5, Pathumwan (0 2256 6305/6422). **Open** 8.30am-8.30pm daily. **Services** 6.30am (Thai), 7am (Eng), 8am (Eng), 5.30pm (Eng) Mon-Sat; 7pm (Thai) Sat; 6.30am (Thai), 7.30am (Thai), 8.30am (Eng), 9.45am (Eng), 11am (Eng), 12.30pm (Thai), 5.30pm (Eng) Sun. **Map** p251 H6.

Jewish

Even Chen Synagogue 4th floor, Chao Phraya Tower, Shangri-La Hotel, Soi Wat Suan Plu, Bangrak (0 2236 7777). **Open** 6pm Fri; 9am-6pm Sat.

Muslim

Darul Aman Mosque Phetchaburi Soi 7, North (0 1325 1617). **Map** p250 F3.

Safety & security

Bangkok is about as safe as metropolises get. Some foreign women urbanites live here because it's so unthreatening, even at night, with minimal hassle from men. Muggings and rapes of foreigners are rare (but disproportionately publicised).

Still, it pays to be cautious and guard against pickpocketing, theft, scams, credit card fraud and planting of contraband in your bags. Ignore touts, gem scammers, predatory tuk-tuk drivers or approaches by private guides. Avoid walking in very quiet or dimly lit areas at night. Avoid involvement in narcotics, gambling, prostitution or illegal activities. Keep passport, credit cards, insurance, air tickets or ID separate, with copies elsewhere.

Smoking

Prohibited in all air-conditioned buildings and transport (fine B2,000), but allowed in some bars and clubs. Global brands are usually available.

Study

Thai universities have some courses open to foreigners, with Thai language the main subject. For **Thammasat University**, see p64. **Chulalongkorn University** (see p64) teaches Thai Studies BAs and MAs in English.

Many courses teach cooking in English (see p111), diving (see pp208-222), gemology (see p150), meditation (see p178), Muay Thai boxing (see p201), Thai massage (see p178) and crafts (in tourist areas). To learn about Thai culture contact **Origin** (see p55); for Thai or modern dance, try **Dance Centre** at Soi Klang Racquet Club (see p201) or **Patravadi Theatre** (see p196); for phiphat music, see p180; for Thai art, contact **Silpakorn University** (see p64).

Thai language classes

Jentana Personal Tutors 5/8 Sukhumvit Soi 31, Sukhumvit (0 2260 6138-9/www.thai-lessons.com). Phrom Phong BTS. **Map** p251 K6. **Nisa Thai Language School** 32/14-16, Thanon Yen Akat, South (0 2671 3343-4). **Open** 8am-7pm Mon-Fri, 9am-5pm Sat. **Map** p251 H8.

Siri-Pattana Thai Language School 15th floor, YWCA, 13 Thanon Sathorn Tai, South (0 2213 1206/0 2677 3150). Lumphini subway. **Open** 8am-9pm daily. **Map** p251 G7. **Union Language School** 11th floor, CCT Building, 109 Thanon Surawong, Bangrak (0 2233 4482/ www.geocities.com/union_lang). Saladaeng BTS/Silom subway. **Open** 8am-noon, 3-5pm (private lessons) Mon-Fri. **Map** p250 F6.

Tax

VAT of 7 per cent is included on most shop and restaurant prices, but vendors avoid paying it. Hotels and top restaurants add 10 per cent service plus VAT (known as 'plus plus' or '++'). You can fill in VAT refund forms for purchases over B2,000+VAT (and totalling over B5,000+VAT) at participating stores. You collect the rebate at **VAT Refund Tourist Office** (0 2272 9387-8/www.rd.go.th/vrt) desks in airports, including **Bangkok Airport**, 3rd floor, International terminal 2 (0 2535 6577-8), and **Phuket Airport** (0 7632 8267).

Telephones

Dialling & codes

You must dial the area codes in Thailand, even within the same area. So Bangkok's 7-digit numbers are prefixed with an 0 2 code, and provincial 6-digit numbers with 3-digit codes (Samui 0 77). Local calls cost B3 (unlimited time). Dialling upcountry (that is, not 0 2 numbers) is expensive, but cheaper if you dial 1234 first. Long-distance is also better value via mobile phones, which follow the 9-digit format, including the prefixes 0 1, 0 5, 0 6, 0 7 or 0 9 (hence area codes and mobile numbers aren't easily distinguished).

To dial Thailand, dial the country code 66, omit the 0, then dial the remaining 8 digits. To call outside Thailand, internet dialling is possible, and there are several other ways:

International Subscriber Dialling (ISD) Dial 001 or 008 then the country code, area code and destination number. Peak time is 7am-9pm; off-peak 9pm-midnight; cheapest is midnight-5am, 5am-7am. The domestic network now enables cheap calls to major countries by dialing 007 first.

eFone is an automatic international telephone service via a special network with one cheap 24hr rate. No need to register; dial direct 001 809 (home phone) or 009 (on mobile), then dial country code, area code and phone number.

Thaicard is a prepaid card for calling internationally from and to anywhere in the world, charged at the ISD or IDD rate (1 unit = 6 sec). Cards costing B100, B300, B500, B1,000 or B3,000 are available at post offices, shops with the Thaicard sign or offices of the Communications Authority of Thailand (CAT; 0 2614 1000, www.cattelecom.com).

PhoneNet (0 2252 3888, www.hatari.net) is another CAT prepaid card using Hatari technology, similarly priced and distributed.

Public phones

Call boxes require B1, B5 or B10 coins and/or a phone card. Some accept credit cards for international calls. Calling within the Greater Bangkok 0 2 area, the minimum price is B1 for 3mins, from B5 for 15mins. Dialling a mobile costs B3 for 1min. Buy phone cards at post offices or convenience stores.

Operator & directories

For operator assisted calls, dial 100 and let the operator call (includes surcharge of 3mins cost before you start speaking).

There are two phone directories. **TOT Corporation** (www.tot.co.th) has data on people, companies and organisations. **Teleinfo Media** (www.yellowpages.co.th) focuses on business and services.

Directory inquiries *Hotline 1133 Bangkok; 183 regional.* 24hrs; free.

Talking Yellow Pages *Hotline 1188.* 24hrs; B6 per min.

Mobile phones

Thailand is addicted to *meur teur* (mobile phones) and their customisation with ringtones, animated displays, multicolour re-casings, cute accessories and numbers with auspicious digits. Subscriber penetration has increased vastly, with great benefits (and new costs) for remote locations, villagers, vendors, drivers, etc. Liberalisation laws have been only partially implemented, and competition restricted. Visitors can use global roaming, buy a cheap local phone (from B3,500 including some calls), or, if sharing the Thai GSM 900 or 1800 systems, buy a local prepaid SIM card. Sold at some corner stores or any phone shop (in most malls), rechargeable SIM cards include a number and some free calls, from AIS One-2-Call, DTAC's D-Prompt,

Orange's Just Talk or Hutch's Say Prepaid. Americans using 1900 GSM should consult their service provider.

Time

Thailand is seven hours ahead of Greenwich Mean Time, 12 hours ahead of US Eastern Standard Time, and three behind Sydney. The Thai calendar is 543 years ahead of the Gregorian calendar, starting at the Buddha's enlightenment; hence 2005 AD is 2548 BE (Buddhist Era).

Tipping

In this hierarchical culture, service is not a professional calling, but a role (sometimes temporary; even a poor diner gets to summon a waiter as *nong*, 'younger sibling'). Hence tips are a small B20 (maxium B50), though *farang* often leave 10 per cent. Taxi drivers might round *down* a metered fare, such is the Thai heart, but passengers typically round *up* to the nearest B5.

Some view big tips as 'spoiling' expectations and inflating costs for all, though equally it might improve standards. Clever Thais tip beforehand, as you would a hotel bellhop on arrival. The host at a group meal may slip the head waiter B100 to ensure prime attention. Hotels and posh venues add 10 per cent service, but they don't always divvy that out, so leave more change.

Tips are expected for guides and maids, maybe drivers, but not hairdressers or food vendors. Masseurs get low piece rates and rarely any salary, so reward them well. To Thais generosity necessarily breeds good karma.

Toilets

A campaign to improve *hong nam* or *suka* has had some results. Public conveniences are rare, so use those in gas stations, department stores, hotels, temples or (asking politely) pubs, restaurants or shops where you're not a patron. You literally have to spend a penny (B2) at WCs in markets, stations and public places. Mobile toilet buses are provided at large events.

Squat pans are common, with a plastic dipper and a water trough for cleaning yourself and flushing. Flush toilets usually have a spray hose. Tissue paper is often not provided (carry some) and must go in the basket so that it doesn't block the pipes. *Hong nam* ('water rooms') are indeed often wet, yet often lack hooks for bags. Male WCs often have unfazed women cleaners. Attendants in night venues may massage men's

shoulders while they (attempt to) pee; decline with a polite *mai ow khrap* ('no thanks') or tip B10 for this woeful, non-sexual job.

Tourist information

Many firms use the 'i' logo to lure in the tourists; though they tend to be biased, they may offer more info and convenience than some tourist offices. **Tourist Line** (0 2617 7340) is a phone service on every imaginable topic, with messages in English. **BTS Tourist Information** is at Siam, Nana and Saphan Taksin stations.

Bangkok Tourist Bureau

17/1 Thanon Phra Athit, under Phra Pinklao Bridge, Phra Nakorn (0 2225 7612-5/www.bangkok touristi.com). **Open** 9am-7pm daily. **Map** p248 B2/3.

An excellent source of information on Bangkok's many attractions and tours, plus BTB's own rewarding trips around town (*see p55*). The white BTB booths are numerous and easy to spot, found at tourist, hotel and shopping areas.

Tourism Authority of Thailand (TAT)

TAT Building, 1600 Thanon Petchaburi Tud Mai, North (0 2250 5500/www.tat.or.th). **Open** 8.30am-4.30pm Mon-Fri. **Map** p251 J4. TAT's head office publishes lots of useful leaflets that are not always to be found at the various TAT offices nationwide. However, the latter can often provide local insights although they can't recommend particular companies or hotels.

Other locations: 4 Thanon Ratchadamnoen Nok, Dusit (0 2282 9773); Bangkok Airport: Terminal 1 (0 2504 2702), Terminal 2 (0 2504 2703).

Visas & work permits

US, UK, Australasian and most European nationals can get a visa on arrival for 30 days, though this is under review. As well as business visas, Royal Thai embassies and consulates abroad grant tourist visas for 60 days, extendable by 30 days, then 15 days only.

Work permits (and tax returns) are required for those seeking paid work in occupations not restricted to Thais, and require the correct business visa and paperwork. Certain workers are eligible for the faster visa.

Directory

One-Stop Service Centre (0 2693 9333-9, visas ext 225, work permits ext 301, www.doe.go.th/workpermit/onestopservice).

Immigration Department

507 Soi Suan Plu, Thanon Sathorn Tai, South (0 2287 3101-10/www. imm.police.go.th). **Open** 8.30am-4.30pm Mon-Fri. **Map** p251 G8.

Water & hygiene

Drink more water than you're used to. In fact, drink even if you're not feeling thirsty. If, however, you should get dehydrated, take a mixture of glucose and mineral salts with your water (this is why Thai fruit and juices often come with salt/sugar as dips/mixers). Sea or rock salt is best. Coconut juice is an all-round replenisher and, when drunk directly from the shell, a safe source of uncontaminated liquid. The tap water in Bangkok and other major cities is filtered and chlorinated, but that doesn't make it good for drinking. Bottled and filtered water is everywhere (clear bottles signify more filtration than white bottles). Ice cubes (or rings) are frozen filtered water, shaved ice often is not.

Peel fruit, check expiry dates and in street eateries wipe plates and cutlery (as the Thais do) with the otherwise uselessly tiny napkins.

Weights & measures

The metric system now predominates. Distance is measured in mm, cm, m and km; food in kg or g; petrol, water, milk or beer in litres. Fabric is measured in metres (or yards), but there's a Thai measurement for land: 1 *wa* = 2sq m; 1 *rai* = 4 *ngan* or 400 *talang wa* (square *wa*); 1 *rai* = 1,600sq m; 1 acre = 2.5 *rai*; 1 hectare = 6.25 *rai*. Gold comes not in ounces, but non-monetary *baht* (15.2g) and *saleung* (25 *satang* = 0.25 *baht*) weights.

What to take

Thailand is tropically humid, so pack loose-fitting, lightweight clothes. Clothes and shoes are cheap and fashion-aware here, but rarely in large sizes. Learn from the Thai jacket shirt: free-hanging tops cool by convection. The sun is also bright and burning, so bring hats, shades and sunscreen. White deflects glare (and deters mosquitoes). For the May-Oct rains an umbrella is useful

(and widely sold), but raincoats act like saunas. Winter nights are cool in Bangkok and really cold up north; wearing layers and one sweater/fleece and/or light jacket is wise, and trekkers need a sleeping bag. Boots or trainers with ankle support are wise for trekking, but lace-ups are a bore as you must shed shoes continually. Velcro strap-sandals are practical, but announce you're a tourist. Have one smart-ish ensemble for bureaucratic or social situations. The lack of neatness and cleanliness is severely judged by Thais, who recoil at unkempt *farang kee nok* ('birdshit Westerners').

On arrival, buy a sarong; not so much to wear, but as a multi-purpose cloth to change in, lie on, picnic upon, wrap or carry things, cover dirty surfaces or burnt shoulders, or fold into a cushion. Many visitors find wrap-around *gahng-gaeng talay* (fisherman's trousers) ideal at beaches or leisure, but look crass in Bangkok (where Thai ensembles look hip only if done with panache).

In urban/tourist areas, most medicines are notoriously easily obtainable without prescription (except very strong ones), so only bring specialised personal medication. Other essentials include door and luggage locks, a money belt, insect repellent, photocopies of documents, sunscreen (minimum SPF 15), spare batteries and an electrical adaptor. You might also want candles, a phrasebook, a torch, a penknife (not packed in hand-luggage or it will be confiscated and destroyed at airport check-in), a teaspoon, toiletries, sanitary towels and an umbrella.

When to go

Climate

Thailand is tropical but has various climate zones. It stretches south to a near-equatorial, rainforested peninsula with different monsoons in each ocean causing rains intermittently year round; most severe in late Oct-Dec in the Thai Gulf (Pacific Ocean) and June-Oct in the Andaman Sea (Indian Ocean), most pleasant in May-Oct and Nov-Mar respectively.

Bangkok sits in the hotter, humid, less breezy central plain, which, like the east coast, follows clear seasons. It's the world's hottest city since it doesn't vary hugely by hour or season from an average 27.8°C (81°F) and 77% humidity. The north-eastern plateau (Isaan) and the north roast in summer and get cool in winter thanks to winds from China, though the highlands (actually Himalayan foothills) are always cool at night and may hit zero in winter.

Get forecasts from the **Meteorological Department** (0 2399 4012-4, hotline 1182, www.tmd.go.th). The seasons are:
Hot mid Feb-mid May, hottest in Apr (hitting 40°C/104°F), windiest in Mar.

Rainy mid May-Oct, starting with heavy, unpredictable downpours (as early as mid Apr) and after a lull, regular rain in the late afternoon or evenings, with Sept being wettest. Flood risks are worst at the first rains and in early Oct.

Cool Nov-mid Feb, when days are sunny, clear and fresh, and nights balmy. This is the tourist high season, when it's fine across most of Thailand.

Public holidays

New Year's Day 1 Jan.
Makha Bucha Day Jan-Mar (lunar).
Chakri Day 6 Apr.
Songkran (Thai New Year) 13-15 Apr.
National Labour Day 1 May.
Coronation Day 5 May.
Royal Ploughing Day (officials only) 9 May.
Visakha Bucha Day May-June (lunar).
Khao Phansa (Buddhist Lent) July (lunar).
HM The Queen's Birthday (Mother's Day) 12 Aug.
King Chulalongkorn Day 23 Oct.
Ok Phansa (end of Buddhist Lent) Oct (lunar).
HM The King's Birthday (Father's Day) 5 Dec.
Constitution Day 10 Dec.

Women

National Council of Women of Thailand

Baan Manangkasila, 514 Thanon Lan Luang, Dusit (0 2281 0081/ www.thaiwomen.or.th). **Open** 8.30am-4.30pm Mon-Fri. **Map** p249 & p250 D3.
An organisation with members nationwide that aims to improve women's status in every field.

Office of Women's Affairs & Family Development

Government House, 1 Thanon Lan Luang, Dusit (0 2612 8764-66/www. women-family.go.th). **Open** 8.30am-4.30pm Mon-Fri. **Map** p249 D2.
Conducts policy research and data analysis, as well as co-ordinating gender equality work, protection of women's rights and furthering of female participation.

Language

Though daunting, attempting Thai is useful and delights locals. The Thai language expresses cultural contexts of hierarchy, social obligation and the culture's multiple origins. Many words and boast a lineage from Indian Sanskrit and Pali. Modern nouns such as *torasàp* ('telephone') are assembled from these Asian classical cousins to Latin and Greek, forming one tenuous link to European tongues; the other is a smattering of English, French and Portuguese words. Otherwise, Thai is utterly alien to Romance, Teutonic or Slavic speakers, using an Indianised script without word spaces. Hailing from Chinese are monosyllables, numbers, many words and the notorious five tones (low, falling, flat, rising and high) that turn the same sound into different words. Meanwhile, regional dialects demonstrate the influence of Mon, Khmer, Burmese, Lao or Malay or Sinified Tibeto-Burman tongues.

Central Thai is the standard, but – just as Londoners range from 'BBC English' to dropping their Cockney Hs – Bangkokians enunciate special languages to address royalty, nobility or monks, even though many 'drop' their Rs in a vernacular that turns Rs into Ls and Ls into Ns, especially in Bangkok's slightly Sinified accent. Be careful who you learn from: talk *pàk tàlàad* ('market speak') and you won't get far in society.

Politeness is ingrained in different layers of personal pronouns, in closing each sentence with *khâ* for females or *krúb* for males (which is like saying 'please'), in opening requests with *khŏr* ('I would like'), and in multilevel words such as the verb 'to eat'. In everyday lingo it's *kin, than*

is more polite, *rápprathan* formal, *chan* only with monks, and *sawŏey* just with royalty.

Transliteration & grammar

Many contradictory systems are used, partly because monosyllables lead to conglomerate words being separated out, partly as there are more consonants and vowels than ways to write in them in English, with several Ks, Ts, Js, Ps, As, Ss, Us, Ts, etc. An H following a T, P, K or B softens and aspirates it, those without are harder, explosive, sounding more like DT, BP, G or P; hence Phuket is not Fookhet but Pooget. Even academic spellings require phonetic letters to approximate Thai sounds, so accept the many anomalies. While wrong tones may possibly be understood through context, mistaking a long or short vowel is fatal to comprehension. Grammar has no articles or tenses; adjectives follow the noun; the name of a road, canal, hotel etc follows its generic noun (eg Thanon Silom, Tha Chang, Rong Raem Sukhothai), but numbers go before the 'generic counter' of any quantity, hence *sôm-ò sŏng lûuk* (two rounds of pomelo) or *baeb form săm bai* (three sheets of forms), with *un* (small thing) being a multi-purpose counter. Consonants often change sounds, whether at the end of a word or when put together. Thais can't pronounce most combinations of two consonants together without putting a sound in between, and some spellings reflect that: *pŏllámái* (fruit) is said *pŏnlámái*; *stàng* (cent) is pronounced *satàng*; *spaghétti* is rendered 'sapaa-gét-tîi'. Grasping such 'Thainglish' pronounciation of foreign words is a good first step.

Consonants

bh as in peace
j is like ch, often spelled ch or tch
kh as in camel
k like g in began, not George
ll in mid word becomes -nl-
ng as in sing without the 'si'
p like bp, as in explode
ph as in pine, not f
r is trilled, or slurred to l
ss in mid word becomes -ts-
t like dt, as in bottle
th as in Thai, not 'the'/'three'
v is like w

When ending a word or syllable: **-j**, **-ch** and **-s** becomes -t; **-r** often becomes -orn; **-l** becomes -n; **-tr** becomes -t; and **-se** and **-ha** are usually silent.

Vowels

a as u in upon
aa as in barn, with no r
ae as in air, with no r (also used for a as in cat)
aew as in air-uw with no r
ai as in high
ao as in how with no w
aw as in awe with no w or r
e as in hay
eu as in urban, but flatter
eua as above with a rising a
i as in hit
ii as in teeth
o as in hot
oe as in earn with no r
oh as in so
oo or **u** as in book
uu as in fool
uay as in oo-way with no w

Tones

There are five tones, signified thus: high (ó), falling (ô), neutral (no mark), rising (ŏ), low (ò).

Thai names

Thais have at least three names. Formal first names are words with auspicious meanings, followed by a family name. Every Thai person gets a nickname from birth, sometimes later; they're often descriptive like Daeng (red), Nèung (one), Lék (small), Yài (big) or amusing, such as Mŏo (pig), Ódd (tadpole), Gòp (frog) or Maew (cat), even fashionable: Bénz, Gòlf or Neòn. Monks get a special name on ordination.

Vocabulary

Basics

hello *sàwàsdee;* goodbye/see you later *la kòrn/láew jeur kun;* good luck *chók dee;* what's your name? *khun chêu arai (khã/krúb);* my name is...*chán/phõm chêu ....* I *chán (female)/phõm (male);* Mr/Mrs/Miss/you *khun;* he/she *khão;* girl/boy friend *faen;* friend *puêan;* wife *mia;* husband *samee;* minorwife *mia-nói;* monk *luang phõr;* child/boy/girl *dek/dekchai/dekying;* man *phûchai;* women *phûying;* gay *gay,* ladyboy *kàtoey;* lesbian *tom-dêe.*

yes *châi;* no *mâi châi;* can *dâi;* cannot *mâi dâi;* please *pròd, gàrúna;* thank you *khòb khun khã (female)/krúb (male);* excuse me *kõr thõd khã/krúb;* I'm sorry *chán /phõm sĩa jai (khã/krúb);* never mind *mâi pen rai.*

ask/can I have... *chán /phõm kõr...;* excuse me *kõr thõd (khã/krúb);* please help me *dâi pròd chúay chán/phõm nòi;* wait a moment *ror sàk khrù (khã/krúb).* what is this in Thai? *Nii ríak pen Thai wâh arai?* do you speak English? *khun phôod pasãa angid dâi mái (khã/krúb)?* sorry, I can't speak Thai *sĩa jai, chán/phõm phôod pasãa Thai mâi dâi (khã/krúb);* I can speak Thai a bit *chán/phõm phôod pasãa Thai dâi níd nòi;* I don't understand *chán/phõm mâi khâo jai;* speak more slowly, please *pròd phôod chã nòi (khã/krúb),* why? *tham mai?;* when? *múea rài?;* who? *krai?;* what? *arai?;* where *têe nãi?;* how? *yàng rai?,* informal *yàng ngài?*

very *mâak;* and *láe;* or *rue;* with *dûay;* without *mâi mee* open *pèrd;* closed *pìd;* what time does it open/close? *pèrd/pìd kèe mong?* I want/would like... *chán/phõm tông karn...(*I want...*);* how many would you like? *khun tông karn thâo rai?;* I like... *chán/phõm chôrp...;* I don't like... *chán/phõm mâi chôrp...;* OK/fine *OK;* that's enough *por láew.*

price *raakha;* rent, hire *châo;* free *free;* discount *lód raakha;* how much? *thâo rai (khã/krúb);* could you discount? *lód raakha dâi mái (khã/krúb);* that's expensive/cheap *paeng mâak/tòok mâak;*

the bill/check, please *chék bin (khã/krúb);* do you have any change? *khun mee torn mâi (khã/krúb).*

what's that? *nân arai?;* where is...? *...yòo têe nãi?;* I'm going to... *chán ja pai.*

good *dee;* bad *mâi dee;* big *yài;* small *lék;* little *nói;* entrance *thang khão;* exit *thang òkk;* painful *jèb;* help *chúay;* dangerous *antarai;* ; accident *ôobùtihéd;* doctor *mõr;* medicine *yaa;* on one's own *khon dêe-o;* smile *yím.*

Places

bridge *sàphan;* canal *khlong;* main road *thanõn;* side road *soi;* alley *tròk;* expressway *thang dòuan;* river *mâe nám;* pier *thá;* station *sàtaanee;* shop *ráan ká;* temple *wát;* bank *thãna karn;* post office *prai sa nee;* restaurant *ráan ar-hãrn;* ...hospital *rong phaya bâan...;* ...palace *wang...;* house *bâan;* housing estate *mòo bâan;* town *meuang;* island *kò;* beach *hàad;* bay *ào;* mountain *khão;* forest *pà;* market *talàd;* embassy *sàtãan tôot;* province *changwàt;* district *amphoe* (in Bangkok *khet);* sub district *tambon* (in Bangkok *khwãeng);* country *prathêt;* where's the toilet? *hông nám yoo nãi (khã/krúb).*

Transport

Bicycle *rót jàkràyan;* boat *ruea;* bus *rót may;* car *rót;* express boat *ruea dòuan;* ferry *ruea khâm fàk;* long-tailed boat *ruea hãang yao;* motorcycle *motersài;* taxi *táirk-sîi;* train *rót fai;* skytrain *rót fai fáh;* subway *rót fai tâi din;* pickup bus *sõngtãew;* plane *krêuang bin;* platform *charn cha la;* ticket *tua;* one way *têo dîi-o;* bus stop *pâai rót may.* do you know the way to...? *khun róo thang tee... mãii (khã/krúb)?* to the end of the street/lane *sòod thanõn/soi;* near *klâhy;* far *klaii;* right *khwã;* left *sáai;* stop *yùut;* stop here/there *yùut tíi- nii/tíi-nán;* return *pai klàb;* turn *lî-o;* u-turn *lî-o klàb;* opposite *trong khâm;* beside *khãng khâng;* the next stop *paai nâa.*

Accommodation

...hotel *rong raem...;* room *hông;* with/without bathroom *mee hông nám/mâi mee hông nám;* shower *fàk bua;* air-conditioned *hông air;* fan-cooled *hông phát lom;* double bed *tiang khòo;* breakfast included *ruam ar-hãrn cháo;* lift *lif;* swimming pool *sà wâi nám;* an inside/outside room *hông dâan nai/hông dâan nók.*

do you have a double/single room for tonight/one week? *khun mee hông khõo/hông dèow s_mrùb kheun nii/nèung aa-thít;* we have a reservation *rao jong hông láew;* where is the car park? *tii jòrd rót yòo tíi nãi.*

Time

morning *torn cháo;* midday *klang wan;* noon *thiang wan;* afternoon *torn bài;* evening *torn yen;* night *torn klang kheun;* midnight *thiang kheun;* early *cháo;* late *sài;* week *aa-thít;* weekend *wan sòod sàb da;* now *torn nii;* later *pai lãng;* today *wan nii;* yesterday *mêua wan nii;* tomorrow *wan prôong nii;* delayed *lâa cháa.*

what's the time? *kèe mong;* hour *chûamong;* in an hour *iik nèung chûamong;* last 2 hours *chái way-la sõng chúamong;* at 8am *pàed mong cháo;* at 1pm *bài mong;* at 2pm *bài sõng mong;* at 7pm *nuèng thûm;* at 8pm *sõng thûm.*

day *wan;* Monday *wan jun;* Tuesday *wan ankarn;* Wednesday *wan phúd;* Thursday *wan páréuhàssàbordii, wan páréuhàt;* Friday *wan sùk;* Saturday *wan são;* Sunday *wan athít.*

Month *deuan;* January *mókkàrakhom;* February *koomphaphan;* March *meenakhom;* April *maesãyon;* May *prúedsàphakhom;* June *míthiunayon;* July *kàràkkadakhom;* August *singhãkhom;* September *kunyayon;* October *tùlakhom;* November *prúesàjikayon;* December *thanwakhom*

summer *réudoo rórn;* rain *réudoo fõn;* winter *réudoo nãow;* year *pii.*

Slang

handsome *lõr;* cute *nâa-rák;* beautiful *suãy;* delicious *aa-ròi;* cool *jèng;* lousy *hûay tàek;* international *inter;* modern *dêrn;* going out *pai tíi-o;* ticklish *jàkkàjíi;* exclamation sound *oõ-ii.*

Numbers

0 *sŏon;* 1 *nèung;* 2 *sõng;* 3 *sãm;* 4 *sìi;* 5 *hâa;* 6 *hòk;* 7 *jèd;* 8 *pàed;* 9 *kâo;* 10 *sib;* 11 *sib-èt;* 12 *sib-sõng;* 13 *sib-sãm;* 14 *sib-sìi;* 15 *sib-hâa;* 16 *sib-hòk;* 17 *sib-jèd;* 18 *sib-pàed;* 19 *sib-kâo;* 20 *yî-sib;* 21 *yî-sib-èt;* 22 *yî-sib-sõng;* 30 *sãm-sib;* 31 *sãm-sib-èt;* 32 *sãm-sib-sõng;* 40 *sìi-sib;* 50 *hâa-sib;* 60 *hòk-sib;* 70 *jèd-sib;* 80 *pàed-sib;* 90 *kâo-sib;* 100 *nèung-rói;* 101 *nèung rói nèung;* 200 *sõng rói;* 1,000 *nèung phun;* 10,000 *nèung mèun;* 100,000 *nèung sãen;* 1,000,000 *nèung láan;* 1st *têe nèung;* 2nd *têe sõng;* 3rd *têe sãm;* last *tíi sòod.*

Further Reference

Books

Fiction

Bunnag, Tew *Fragile Days: Tales form Bangkok* Poised, poignant vignettes from every social strata, rich with cultural colour.
Burdett, John *Bangkok 8, Bangkok Tattoo* New benchmark of the 'Bangkok underworld novels' genre.
Cunningham, Philip *Peacock Hotel* Unusually thoughtful take on relationships and society in modernising Bangkok.
Lapcharoensap, Rattawut *Sightseeing* Multi-prizewinning young writer fillets Thai life in dazzling short stories.
Needham, Jake *The Big Mango* Asia Books' Elmore Leonard gives the usual suspects unusual panache.
Pramoj, Kukrit *Si Phaendin (Four Reigns)* Life under Ramas V-VIII by a noble late PM of deep wisdom.
Somtow, SP *Jasmine Nights* Bangkok coming-of-age tale, written with edge, beauty and wit.
Srinawk, Khamsing *The Politician & Other Stories* Scathing progressive prose fables of modern village life.
Sutham, Pira *Shadowed Country* Historical novel by an Isaan villager turned Sussex expat dissecting the roots and results of corruption.

Non-fiction

Some books are mentioned in the **History**, **Galleries** and **Mind & Body** chapters.
Cornwel-Smith, Philip *Very Thai: Everyday Popular Culture* Zesty insight into modern Thai life, with photos by John Goss and author.
Eckhardt, James *Bangkok People* Portraits of the prominent, from expats to eccentrics.
Ekachai, Sanitsuda *Keeping the Faith* Thai beliefs.
Fellowes, Warren *The Damage Done* Excoriating exposé of Thai prisons by a former inmate.
Jackson, Peter *Dear Uncle Go: Homosexualities in Thailand.* Letters to a Thai agony uncle analysed by trailblazing academic.
Jotisalikorn, Chami *Classic Thai* Traditional arts and design.
Klausner, William *Transforming Thai Culture* Third volume of the anthropologist's lucid view.
Odzer, Cleo *Patpong Sisters* A window on Thai prostitution.
Pannapadipo, Phra *Peter Phra Farang* Memoirs of an ordained Western monk.

Phongpaichit, Pasuk & Baker, Chris *Thaksin: The Business of Politics in Thailand and Thailand's Boom and Bust* Revelations about Thai power. *A History of Thailand* Dissects the official historical narrative.
Rajadhon, Phya Anuman *Essay on Thai Culture* Definitive wisdom on the way things were.
Redmond, Mont *Wondering into Thai Culture* Incisive ponderings on manners and behaviour.
Van Beek, Steve *Bangkok Then and Now* A century of change, through pictures and clippings. Plus any of his waterways tomes.
Warren, William *Bangkok* Informed long-time reflections on the city's changes.
Wyatt, David *Reading Thai Murals* Acclaimed historian reveals what pictures say.
Ziv, Daniel & Sharrett, Guy *Bangkok Inside Out* Quirky, realistic portrait of the Big Durian.

Music

Classical/*phiphat*

Bangkok Symphony Orchestra *Mahajanaka Symphony* (BSO Foundation) The pastiche that launched an opera house. Conducted by composer (and writer) SP Somtow.
Fong Naam *Jakajan* Bruce Gaston's compositions and/or arrangements for *phiphat*, plus rock/jazz ensemble.
Kangsadan *Golden Jubilee Overture* (Pisces) Modern *phiphat* ensemble outdoing the Latin, jazz and lounge fusion of labelmates Boy Thai.
Harvey, Richard *The Spirit of Suriyothai* (Asian Music International) Distillation/elaboration of his original film score.

Luuk thung/morlam

Amphipong, Siriporn *Greatest Hits Vols 1-5* (MGA) Vol 3 is easiest on Western ears (feels like the blues).
Duangjan, Phomphuang *Through the Years, Vol 1 & 2* (Topline) The Thai equivalent of Hank Williams versus modern C&W.
Poonlarp, Jintara *Greatest Hits Vols 1 & 2* (MGA) Over 30 CDs, so pick this collection from Grammy's Nashville/Khorat division.

Indie/dance

A Mosquito *This is Asia* (Red Beat) Peculiarly Thai dance music. Too fast and pretty loopy, but funky.

Futon *Never Mind the Botox* and *Love Bites* Outrageous Thai-Brit-Japanese group pit witty lyrics in English to infectious electrotrash.
Joey Boy *Anthology* (Bakery Records) From funkfest 'Chinese Connection' to 'Fun Fun Fun'; plus any of the Gang Core releases.
Modern Dog *That Song* (Bakery) Produced by Tony Doogan, the original indie nu-metal heroes in their best album since *Café*.
Photo Sticker Machine *Color Lab* (Hualampong Riddim) Think Stereolab, Tortoise, Cornelius... Now put this on and stop thinking.
Pru *From Hero to Zero* State of the art prog rock from indie's first family.

Pleng puer cheewit

Carabao, Ad *Best of* (Warner) Splendid gold-covered primer.
Caravan *Best of: Vol 1* (UPL) Songs that sparked a revolution; James Tayloresque ballads to rootsier folk.
Khampee, Pongsit *Best of ... 2530* (ATO) Sweet-voiced, deep-thinking rebel; Thailand's Jackson Brown.
Marijuana *Buppha Chon* (Milestone/MGA). The mellow Deadhead side of *pleng puer cheewit*.

T-Pop

LOSO *The Red Album* (Grammy) Testosterone power ballads and raunchy rock by Bangkok's Bon Jovi. Look for Sek Loso's English-language debut *For God's Sake*.
McIntyre, Thongchai 'Bird' *Faen Jaa* Perennial pop fusionist enlists rap and folk to zeitgeisty effect.
Palmy *Palmy* (Grammy) Hook laden, non-stop hip-sway grooves in a hippie-dippy trip-hop-lite mode.
Young, Tata *I Believe* (BEC Tero) Kid star turned Thai Kylie. Funky, vampy pop dance from the 'Sexy, Naughty, Bitchy' girl who went *inter*.

Websites

www.bangkokhipster.com Trendy city webzine.
www.bangkokpost.net Online newspaper.
www.bangkokrecorder.com Hip, clubby web mag.
www.eThailand.com Gateway with community emphasis.
www.nationmultimedia.com Diverse media homepage.
www.tat.or.th Official gateway. UK office runs www.thaismile.co.uk.
www.travelfish.org By and for independent travellers.

Index

Index

Z

Advertisers' Index

Place of interest and/or entertainment	
Railway & bus stations	
Parks	
Hospitals/universities	
Neighbourhood	DUSIT
Subway station	U
Subway route	
Skytrain route	
BTS/BRT route	
Skytrain station	S1
Temple	🛕

Maps

Greater Bangkok

To Bangkok Sculpture Centre

NORTH-EAST

NORTH-EAST

Royal Thai Air Force Academy

Don Muang Railway Station

RTAF Museum

Amari Airport Hotel

Bangkok International Airport

Robinson Department Store

Central Department Store

THANON PHAHON YOTHIN

THANON WIPHAVADI-RANGSIT

Army Golf Course

Sri Pathum University

THANON RAM INTHRA

THANON WAT LAD PLAKHAO

THANON KASETNAWAMIN

RAM INTHRA-AT NARONG EXPRESSWAY

THANON NUANCHAN

SOI 87

SOI CHOK CHAI 4

Kuan-Im Shrine

OUTER NORTH

Laksi Plaza

Laksi Railway Station

THANON CHAENG WATTHANA

THANON PRACHA CHUEN

THANON KAMPHAENG PHET

Rama Gardens

Ratcha Phruk Golf Course

Rajpreuk Golf Course

Dhurakit Bundit University

Kasetsat University

THANON PHAHON YOTHIN

THANON NGAM WONG WAN

Siam Jusco Supermarket

Major IMAX

SCB Park Plaza

Exhibition Hall

Civil Court

RATCHAYOTHIN JUNCTION

Central Sofitel

Central Plaza

Thai Airways International Building

NORTH

Sirikit Park

Chatuchak Park

Muang Thong Thani Sports Complex & Impact Arena

Khlong Prem Prison

Banglamphu Dept. Store

Golden Dragon

OUTER NORTH

THANON PRACHA RAT

THANON PRACHA CHUEN

WONG SAWANG

Northern Bus Terminal

North Eastern Bus Terminal

RACHA RAT 1

PRACHA RAT

DUSIT

Sukhothai Thamma Thirat University

THANON SAMAKKHI

Srithanya Hospital

THANON TIWANON

THANON RATTANA THIBET

THANON REWADI

NONTHABURI

THANON PRACHA RAT

RAMA VII BRIDGE

Pakkret District Office

Wat Poramai

Mon Village

Ko Kred

Chao Phraya River

Nonthaburi Pier

Nonthaburi Provincial Office

RAMA V BRIDGE

THONBURI

NONTHABURI

PHRA NANG KLAO BRIDGE

Wat Chaloem Prakit

THANAM NONTA

BIRI

Wat Pho Bang-O

DET PHRA KIAT

THONBURI

Khlong Om

Khlong Om

THANON RATTANA THIBET

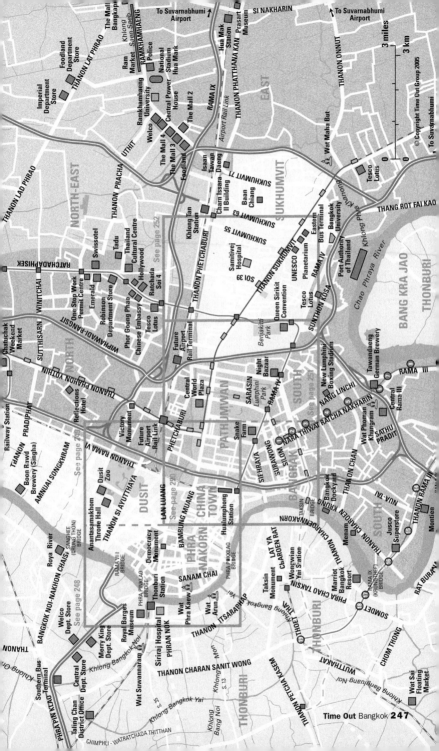

To Suvarnabhumi Airport

SI NAKHARIN

To Suvarnabhumi Airport

The Mall Bangkapi

Foodland Department Store

THANON LAT PHRAO

Imperial Department Store

THANON LAT PHRAO

Khlong Saen Saeb

RAMKHAMHAENG

Ram Market (Krung Thep)

Ramkhamhaeng University

Police

National Stadium Hua Mark

Hua Mak Station

Prasart Museum

Central Power House

THANON PHATTHANA KAN

EAST

© Copyright Time Out Group 2005

To Suvarnabhumi

THANON ONNUT

3 miles

3 km

NORTH-EAST

THANON PRACHA UTHIT

THANON LAD PHRAO

Welco

The Mall 4

The Mall 3

The Mall 2

RAMA IX

Foodland

Airport Rail Link

Isaan Tawan

Charn Issara II Building

SUKHUMVIT 71

Baan Chiang

SUKHUMVIT

THANON RATCHADAPHISEK

WINITCHAI

RATCHADAPHISEK

SUTTHISARN

Swissotel

Tadu

Thailand Cultural Centre

Hollywood

THANON PHETCHABURI

Khlong Tan Station

SUKHUMVIT 63

SUKHUMVIT 55

SUKHUMVIT

Eastern Bus Terminal

Bangkok University

Khlong Phra

Chatuchak Weekend Market

One Stop Work Permit Centre

Emerald

Robinson Department Store

Phor Goung Phao

Chinese Embassy

Tesco Lotus

Ratchada Soi 4

See page 252

RAMA IV

Samitivej Hospital

SOI 39

THANON SUKHUMVIT

UNESCO

Planetarium

SUNTHON KOSA

Port Authority of Thailand

Chao Phraya River

BANG KRA JAO

THONBURI

THANG ROT FAI KAO

SUTTHISARN

WIPHAWADI-RANGSIT

THANON PHAHON YOTHIN

NORTH

Future Airport Rail Terminal

Queen Sirikit Convention

Tesco Lotus

Benjakiti Park

Tawandaeng German Brewery

RAMA III

Railway Station

THANON PRADIPHAT

Reflections Hotel

PHETCHABURI

Victory Monument

Future Airport Rail Link

THANON RAMA VI

PHETCHABURI

Central World Plaza

PATHUMWAN

SARASIN

Lumphini Park

Night Bazaar

RAMA IV

New Lumphini Boxing Stadium

See page 25

NARA THIWAT RATCHA NAKHARIN

NANG LINCHI

Wat Phoman Khungram

SATHU PRADIT

Central Rama III

RAMA III

THANON VIPHAWADI

Boon Rawd Brewery (Singha)

AMNUAI SONGKHRAM

Dusit Zoo

THANON SI AYUTTHAYA

DUSIT

Snake Farm

SILOM

SI PHRAYA

SURAWONG

BANGRAK

SOUTH

Bangkok Dockyard

THANON ON CHAN

TAKSIN

KRUNG

NUA-YAI

THANON RAMA III

Jusco Superstore

Montien

Anantasamakhom Throne Hall

LAN LUANG

BAMRUNG MUANG

CHINA TOWN

Hualumphong Station

See page 250

PHRA NAKORN

RAMA VIII BRIDGE

SANGHEE (KRUNG THON) BRIDGE

Roya River

BANGKOK NOI-NAKHON CHAISI

See page 248

Welco Dept. Store

Merry King Dept. Store

Royal Barges Museum

Siriraj Hospital

PHRAN NOK

Democracy Monument

SANAM CHAI

PHRA PINKLAO BRIDGE

Thonburi Station

RAMA VIII (KHUNGRAF) BRIDGE

Wat Phra Kaew

Wat Arun

THANON ITSARAPHAP

LAT YA

CHAROEN RAT

Wongwian Yai S-tation

Taksin Monument

THANON CHAO TAKSIN

PHRA CHAO TAKSIN

THANON CHAROEN KRUNG

Menam

Marriot Bangkok Resort

RAMA IX (KHUNGHEF) BRIDGE

SOMDET

THONBURI

CHOM THONG

Wat Sai Floating Market

RAT BURAN

THANON

Southern Bus Terminal

PHRA PIN KLAO

Taling Chan District Office

Central Dept. Store

Wat Suwannaram

THANON CHARAN SANIT WONG

Khlong Bangkok Noi

Khlong Mon

S. 13

Khlong Bang Noi

Khlong Bangkok Yai

THANON PHETCHA KASEM

WUTTHAKAT

Khlong Bangluang Nol

CHIMPHLI - WATRATCHADA THITTHAN

Time Out Bangkok **247**

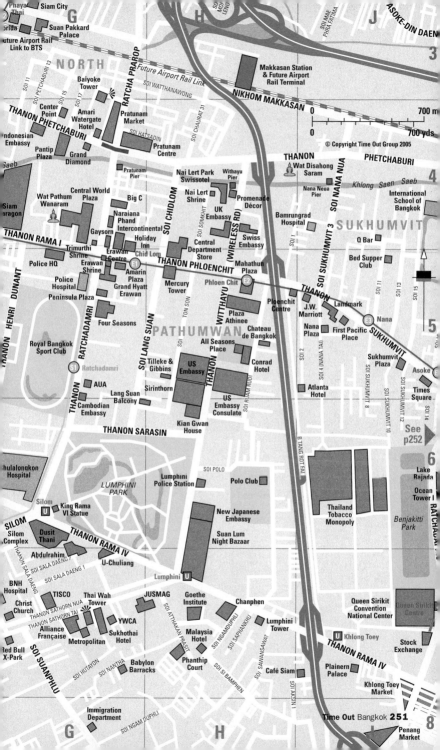

Street Index

EVERYTHING YOU NEED
FOR THE
PERFECT BREAK

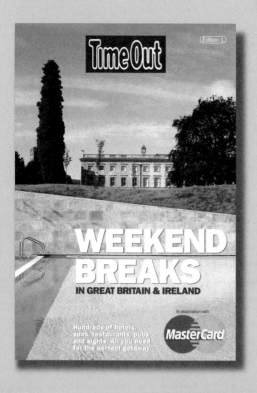

Available at all good bookshops and
£2 off at www.timeout.com/shop

Bangkok Transport

	BTS Sukhumvit Line
	BTS Silom Line
	Subway
	BRT Line (due 2006)
	River Express Boat

THANON RATTANA THIBET

Rajpreuk Golf Course

THANON NGAM WONG WAN

THANON PRACHA RAT

OUTER NORTH

RAMA V BRIDGE

Phibun Songkram 2 N29

Wat Khien N28

Wat Tuek N27

Phibun Songkram 1 N25

Nonthaburi (Phibun Songkram 3) N30

WONG SAWANG

THANON PRACHA CHUEN

Wat Khema N26

RAMA VII BRIDGE

Rama VII Bridge N24

Wat Soythong N23

Bang Pho N22

DUSIT

Bangsue

THONBURI

PRACHA RAT

THANON PRACHA CHUEN

Northern Bus Terminal

Sirikit Park

North Eastern Bus Terminal

NORTH

Phahonyothin

NORTH-EAST

Kiek Khai N21

TH PRADIPHAT

Kamphaengphet

Chatuchak Park

Morchit

Lad Phrao

THANON LAD PHRAO

Kiaw Khai Kao N20

Royal Irrigation N19

Phayab N18

AMNUAI SONGKHRAM

Wat Thephari N17

BANGKOK NOI-NAKHON CHAISI

Sang Hee Bridge N16

SANGHEE (KRUNG THON) BRIDGE

THANON PHAHON YOTHIN

Saphan Khwai

SUTTHISARN

WINITCHAI

RATCHADAPHISEK

Sutthisarn

Ratchadaphisek

NORTH-EAST

Huay Khwang

Thewet N15

RAMA VIII BRIDGE

Rama VIII Bridge N14

Banglamphu N13

TH SI AYUTTHAYA

THANON RAMA VI

Future Station

NORTH

Aree

WIPHAWADI-RANGSIT

TH PRACHA UTHIT

Phra Pinklao Bridge N12

Thonburi Station N10

DUSIT

Sanam Pao

Thailand Cultural Centre

Thonburi Station

Wang Lang N10

Tha Chang N9

BAMRUNG MUANG

LAN LUANG

PHRA NAKORN

Victory Monument

PHETCHABURI

St Ayutthaya

Pra Ram IV

Tha Tien N8

CHINA TOWN

Ratchathewi

Phetchaburi

THANON PHETCHABURI

Tha Ratchinee N7

National Stadium

Chidlom

PHRA POKKLAO BRIDGE

Ratchawongse N5

Hualumphong Station

Siam

Ploenthit

Memorial Bridge N6

Hualumphong

PATHUMWAN

Ratchadamri

Asoke

Sukhumvit

SUKHUMVIT 55

SUKHUMVIT 63

TH ITSARAPHAP

Harbour Dept N4

Siphraya

SARASIN

SIPHRAYA

Siphraya N3

Lumphini Park

Benjakitti Park

SOI 39

THANON SUKHUMVIT

Phrom Phong

Thonglor

Khlong Bangkok Yai

SURAWONG

Silom

Saladaeng

RAMA IV

Ekamai

Wat Muang Khae N2

SILOM

Chong Nonsi

Lumphini

Khlong Toey

Queen Sirikit Centre

SUKHUMVIT

Oriental N1

BANGRAK

Future Station

SOUTH

RAMA IV

Phra Khanong

Sathorn CEN

Saphan Taksin

Sathorn S1

NANG LINCHI

SUNTHON KOSA

Eastern Bus Terminal

PHRA CHAO TAKSIN

CHAROENNAKORN

Wat Sawetchat S1

THANON CHAN

Chao Phraya River

Khlong Phra Khanong

THANG ROT FAI KAO

Onn

Wat Worachanyawat S2

SATHU PRADIT

NUA-TAI

RAMA III

BANG KRA JAO

Yai

SOMDET

RAMA IX (KRUNGTHEP) BRIDGE

Wat Rajsingkorn S3

SOUTH

RAT BURANA

Rat Burana S3

THANON RAMA III

RAMA IX BRIDGE

THONBURI

0 — 3 miles

0 — 3 km

© Copyright Time Out Group 2005